The *Ethos* of Rhetoric

Studies in Rhetoric/Communication

Thomas W. Benson, Series Editor

The *Ethos* of Rhetoric

Edited by
Michael J. Hyde

Foreword by
Calvin O. Schrag

University of South Carolina Press

© 2004 University of South Carolina

Published in Columbia, South Carolina,
by the University of South Carolina Press

Manufactured in the United States of America

08 07 06 05 04   5 4 3 2 1

Library of Congress Cataloging-in-Publication Data

The ethos of rhetoric / edited by Michael J. Hyde ; foreword by Calvin O. Schrag.
      p. cm. — (Studies in rhetoric/communication)
   Includes bibliographical references and index.
   ISBN 1-57003-538-5 (hardcover : alk. paper)
   1. Rhetoric. I. Hyde, Michael J., 1950– II. Series.
   P301.E84 2004
   808—dc22

                                                          2003027600

Contents

Foreword

These contributions, arranged and edited by Professor Michael Hyde, provide testimony of sustained explorations of the originative meaning of *ethos* as the dwelling or abode from which our communicative practices of entwined discourse and action take their rise and to which they return for their validations of sense and reference. The grammar of *ethos,* we quickly learn from the different voices in the collected essays, is not a grammar of recent date. It reaches far back into the origins of Western thought, possibly even further. Homer and Hesiod, Isocrates and Aristotle are names that come to mind. In its originative range of signification, *ethos* as dwelling antedates its offsprings ethics and morality. It is older than ethical imperatives and tables of virtue defining moral character. As such, its proper locality is in a proto-disciplinary space in which the discipline of ethics as theory of human rights and duties and the discipline of rhetoric as the science of persuasion through character first stake out their disciplinary matrices. *Ethos* antedates specific ethical prescriptions and prohibitions and marks out a region of knowing and working together in advance of strategies to achieve consensus in the public forum.

Poets, philosophers, and rhetoricians alike have at various times been disposed to speak of the importance of *ethos* as dwelling. Friedrich Hölderlin set to verse our *poetical* dwelling upon the earth. Martin Heidegger appealed to the ancient notion to elucidate the *existential* dwelling of Dasein's being-in-the-world. Michael Hyde has time and again called our attention to the truth of our *rhetorical* dwelling in response to the call of conscience. That the notion also plays in the court of the natural and the social sciences comes as no surprise. Scientific knowledge is always contextualized against the background of an *ethos* of social practices and agreed-upon investigative procedures. This background comprises the milieu for the required objectification in scientific inquiry. Although the background, infused as it is with interpretation from bottom up, cannot itself become an object for scientific validation, it remains the source of all objectification and quantification. Edmund Husserl, in his classic work *The Crisis of the European Sciences,* came upon a specific name for *ethos* as the background of scientific discovery and verification. He called it the concrete "lifeworld" (*Lebenswelt*). The lifeworld, as described by Husserl, is the habitat of our doxastic perception, ordinary language, and everyday preoccupations. It marks out the region of our cultural history and our intersubjective transactions, the lived concreteness of which resists reduction to objectified relations. It was Husserl's use of this concept that enabled him to stem the tide of European rationalism with its ideal of a decontextualized *mathesis universalis* that occluded the concretely functioning intentionality of lived experience.

There are many lessons to be learned across the disciplines from their variegated perspectives on *ethos.* Chief among these is instruction on the requirement for a *proto-* and *post*-disciplinary critical discourse. The issues of human concern that stimulate the economy of one's *ethos* are not bounded by disciplinary matrices. The experienced lifeworld does not come to us in the demarcated departmental enclaves, with their often self-isolating vocabularies, that structure the modern-day university. The texture of human knowledge is not a collage of discrete units of information but a tapestry of intercalating explanations and interpretations. No body of knowledge is an island of itself, cut off from the mainland of human endeavors. The goal of multidisciplinary inquiry and critique is given timely expression in the essays Professor Hyde has assembled for the current volume. Hyde's introduction to the volume and the selected presentations illustrate profoundly the requirement for collaborative critical discourse across the standardized disciplines of academe.

Calvin O. Schrag
George Ade Distinguished Professor of
Philosophy, Emeritus, Purdue University

Series Editor's Preface

In *The Ethos of Rhetoric,* editor Michael Hyde, University Distinguished Professor of Communication Ethics at Wake Forest University, brings together a dozen outstanding scholars. In essays theoretical and critical, Hyde and his collaborators reconsider both the traditional concept of *ethos* as the role of moral character and ethics in persuasion. Hyde proposes to press *ethos* back to its "primordial" sense as referring to "the way discourse is used to transform space and time into 'dwelling spaces.'"

The book attempts to revive a theoretically important sense of the concept of *ethos* as a central feature of rhetoric, moving *ethos* beyond "credibility" to take in its role as central to place, community, identity, and moral action. This is a bold and original move—sufficiently original that it is going to require a readjustment of some of our settled teachings.

Craig R. Smith reviews the history of reading Aristotle on *ethos* and offers his own view that Aristotle's notion of *ethos* as a mode of proof presupposes earlier concepts of *ethos* as dwelling place. Smith argues that a hermeneutic reading of Aristotle's *Rhetoric* that takes into account the context of the *Rhetoric* in Aristotle's other work and in the history and culture of Athens helps to resolve earlier disputes about the status of *ethos* in the *Rhetoric.* Margaret D. Zulick proposes a marriage between ethics and aesthetics in the *ethos* of invention, a project for which she finds support in the works of theorists Kenneth Burke and Mikhail Bakhtin. Robert Wade Kenney writes of *ethos* as "the quality of personhood that calls for humanity to care for its self, its world, and its others in such a manner that . . . our Being is made possible." Kenney finds this *ethos* realized through the imaginative, which he expounds both as central to the theory of rhetoric and as illuminated in the works of William Blake, W. H. Auden, Frank Capra, and Winston Churchill. Barbara Warnick asks how rhetorical critics can satisfy their roles as both scholars and engaged citizens. A realignment of critical practice might emerge, argues Warnick, through a reconsideration of engagement versus scholarly observation, authorial intentions versus larger shaping conditions, traditional standards of judgment versus alternate standards, focus on method versus evocation.

Walter Jost takes Sidney Lumet's film *12 Angry Men* as the ground on which to examine both the way the jurors in the film deliberate about a murder trial and the way we are invited to deliberate about the jurors. Jost opens the discourse of the film through a topical analysis of "the little things" that are so obvious they go unnoted even while performing their work in our lives. John Poulakos writes of a letter sent by a young marine officer in Vietnam to his family. Poulakos finds the rhetoric of the letter in its turning away from war to a moment of beauty. Eric King Watts explores the work of Larry Neal, a spokesperson for the Black Arts movement of the 1960s, and the maturation of Neal's thought, centered on the claim that "nationalism is the central mode of black liberation."

Martin J. Medhurst finds the *ethos* of American democracy in the presidential campaign of 2000, in which both major candidates invoked religious values as the common ground motivating policy choices and a sense of shared responsibility. David Zarefsky considers the rhetoric of President George Bush in September 2001, following the terrorist attacks of September 11. Zarefsky finds that Bush at first made a series of disappointing and inadequate speeches, but that in his September 20, 2001, address to the Congress and the nation, Bush fulfilled the requirements of the situation, articulating the peculiar nature of a war against terrorism as a new kind of war, with a new kind of enemy, and a call for citizens not so much to sacrifice as to demonstrate that everyday life could proceed as usual.

Carole Blair and Neil Michel describe "the Rushmore effect," which takes us through an analysis of the precursors, production, and effects of the South Dakota monument to the conclusion that the "deplorable" and "odious" response elicited by the memorial is one "of imperialist pride, an obsession with outlandish size, and a 'aesthetic sensibility' that approves of accomplishing national commemoration by dynamiting scenic places." Carolyn R. Miller investigates the ethos of human-computer interaction, contrasting the mechanization of knowledge and authority in expert systems, which invoke an *ethos* of machine rationality. Miller notes that if in Aristotelian rhetoric "*ethos stands in for expertise,*" in the world of expert systems, "*expertise stands in for ethos.*" Miller argues that the model of expert systems has given way to the model of the cyborg, in which the machine as intelligent agent appeals for our trust. The shift from expert systems to intelligent agents swings from "an overemphasis on expertise to an overemphasis on interaction, from a logos-centric to a pathos-centric *ethos.*"

The essays in this book are deeply informed by theory, grounded in practice, and original in conceptions and claims. They richly fulfill Michael Hyde's call for studies that "define the grounds, the abodes or habitats, where a person's ethics and moral character take form and develop."

Thomas W. Benson

Acknowledgments

An Ethics and Leadership Grant from Wake Forest University enabled me to organize the conference on which this collection is based. I am indebted to the faculty, staff, and students of the Department of Communication, Wake Forest University, for providing me with a community that makes teaching and research an immense joy. In particular, I wish to thank Allan Louden, Jill McMillan, Ananda Mitra, Jarrod Atchison, Sam Gladding, Susan Faust, and Ed Wilson for their support. Special thanks are also due to Kate Hawkins and Martin Medhurst, who helped to ensure that the conference served the important goals of the Southern States Speech Communication Association. As in the past, Barry Blose was a guiding light in working with the staff of the University of South Carolina Press. Five outstanding teachers who taught me the true existential meaning of *"ethos"* when I began my graduate career also warrant heartfelt acknowledgment: Barbara Ewbank, Henry Ewbank, Ralph Webb, Don Burks, and Calvin Schrag.

Michael J. Hyde

Introduction

Rhetorically, We Dwell

MICHAEL J. HYDE

The essays in this volume are revised versions of invited presentations delivered at a two-day conference, on "The *Ethos* of Rhetoric," held in conjunction with the Annual Convention of the Southern States Speech Communication Association, hosted by Wake Forest University in April 2002. In preparing those presentations, the contributors were asked to keep in mind a specific meaning of *ethos* that pre-dates its more familiar and related translations as "moral character" and "ethics," a meaning that is too often forgotten when these translations occupy the attention of rhetoricians and other scholars and that, in its relationship with rhetoric, further reveals the fundamental status and dynamics of this art. Abiding by this more "primordial" meaning of the term, one can understand the phrase "the *ethos* of rhetoric" to refer to the way discourse is used to transform space and time into "dwelling places" (*ethos;* pl. *ethea*) where people can deliberate about and "know together" (*con-scientia*) some matter of interest. Such dwelling places define the grounds, the abodes or habitats, where a person's ethics and moral character take form and develop.

Understood in this specific way, the *ethos* of rhetoric directs one's attention to the "architectural" function of the art: how, for example, its practice grants such *living room* to our lives that we might feel more *at home* with others and our surroundings. The *ethos* of rhetoric would have one appreciate how the *premises* and other materials of arguments are not only tools of logic but also mark out the *boundaries* and *domains* of thought that, depending on how their specific discourses are *designed* and *arranged,* may be particularly inviting and moving for some audience. The *ethos* of rhetoric makes use of our inventive and symbolic capacity to construct dwelling places that are stimulating and aesthetically, psychologically, socially, and perhaps theologically instructive. We *are* creatures who are destined to be caught up in the process of providing the openings of these places wherein good (and bad) things can happen. I will have more to say about this process later on, when I discuss the ontological nature and significance of the *ethos* of rhetoric.

p/

In the final portion of his book *Communicative Praxis and the Space of Subjectivity* (1986), the philosopher Calvin Schrag initiates a phenomenological and hermeneutical inquiry into this particular topic as a way of showing how rhetoric can deal with certain issues of legitimacy and identity that have long been raised against it throughout the history of philosophy and are still found lurking in the literatures of critical theory and poststructuralism, both of which influence Schrag's thought. I have always believed that Schrag was on to something important here; his work provides the opening of a dwelling place where the scope and function of rhetoric can be thought out in terms that are respectful of the art's potential for constructive action. The conference on which this collection of essays is based was in part inspired by Schrag's groundbreaking work and what he began to build with his philosophical rhetoric.

This is not to say, however, that the goal of these essays is to further an exclusively philosophical appreciation of the *ethos* of rhetoric. Philosophy has a role to play in this collection, but all essays gathered here are first and foremost concerned with the theory and practice of rhetoric. Most of the essays, in fact, provide case studies of how the *ethos* of rhetoric actually manifests itself in our everyday existence. Students of rhetoric will recognize in these studies a host of concerns that have long been a part of the rhetorician's education. The *ethos* of rhetoric, especially as it is appreciated in this collection, is foundational to all else that can be said about the art and its use by others whose vocations also call on them to create places where people can dwell with and for others. To appreciate this foundational nature of the *ethos* of rhetoric is to discover a major source of legitimation for an art that was long ago fated in its ancient struggles with philosophy to be ever on the lookout for things that justify its activities.

In the remainder of this introduction, and as a way of further orienting readers to the essays contained in this collection, I elaborate on this last point by discussing how the meaning of *ethos* points to an essential relationship that exists among the self, communal existence, discourse, Being, and, perhaps, God. The *ethos* of rhetoric speaks to us of existential, ontological, and metaphysical matters. One perceives this specific pathway of thought unfolding in the theories of *ethos* provided by Isocrates, Aristotle, and Martin Heidegger. In bringing these theories together, one can avoid the problem that Dilip Gaonkar addresses when he cautions against leaving "key terms" in rhetorical scholarship "undertheorized," whereby the full meaning and significance of the term in question remains unclear and thus underappreciated.[1]

The Meaning and Significance of Ethos

> The man who wishes to persuade people will not be negligent as to the matter of character [*ethos*]; no, on the contrary, he will apply himself above all to establish a most honorable name among his fellow-citizens; for who does not

know that words carry greater conviction when spoken by men of good repute than when spoken by men who live under a cloud, and that the argument which is made by a man's life is more weight than that which is furnished by words?[2]

For Isocrates, *ethos* is both a legitimating source for and a praiseworthy effect of the ethical practice of the orator's art. Isocrates advances this claim as he abides by the sophistic, and thus anti-Platonic, thesis that, owing to the contingency of human existence, "truth" is at best grasped in terms of "probabilities"; uncertainty is always a given. Hence, Isocrates maintains that "since it is not in the nature of man to attain a science by the possession of which we can know positively what we should do or what we should say, in the next resort I hold that man to be wise who is able by his powers of conjecture to arrive generally at the best course" (*Antidosis,* 271).

Isocrates associates such powers with a person's rhetorical competence, that is, one's "natural" capacity to use language to deliberate skillfully and artfully with oneself and others about the importance of matters and about the goodness of actions. He sought to cultivate such competence in his students by selecting "the most illustrious and most edifying" examples of human action. By "habituating himself to contemplate" such deeds, the orator will "feel their influence . . . in all the actions of his life," learning to love wisdom and its virtues and to display these goods in his communicative and rhetorical transactions *(Antidosis,* 277–78). This process is, for Isocrates, what genuine character development is all about: the orator is necessarily both a student and a teacher of the dynamics of civic responsibility. Heeding the call of *public* service as a person of "good repute," his presence and rhetorical competence are a "showing-forth" (*epi-deixis*) of an *ethos,* a principled self, that instructs the moral consciousness and actions of others and thereby serves as a *possible* catalyst for them to do the same for the good of their community.

Isocrates anticipates the doctrine of *ethos* developed in Aristotle's *Rhetoric,* but with this doctrine comes a significant change in the technical use of the term. For Isocrates, rhetorical *paideia,* education and socialization, serves the process of character development, but it is a person's character itself, his stellar reputation, that anchors the persuasive capacity of rhetoric. "The power to speak well" is credited as being "the surest index of a sound understanding, and discourse which is true and lawful and just is the outward image of a good and faithful soul" (*Antidosis,* 255). Aristotle, on the other hand, associates *ethos* not primarily with the orator's reputation for being such a soul but rather with the actual rhetorical competence displayed in the orator's discourse:

[Persuasion occurs] through character [*ethos*] whenever the speech is spoken in such a way as to make the speaker worthy of credence; for we believe fair-minded people to a greater extent and more quickly [than we do others] on all

subjects in general and completely so in cases where there is not exact knowledge but room for doubt. And this should result from the speech, not from a
previous opinion that the speaker is a certain kind of person; for it is not the
case, as some of the technical writers propose in their treatment of the art, that
fair-mindedness on the part of the speaker makes no contribution to persua-
siveness; rather, character is almost, so to speak, the controlling factor in per-
suading.[3]

The practice of rhetoric constitutes an active construction of character; *ethos*
takes form as a result of the orator's abilities to argue and to deliberate and thereby
to inspire trust in an audience. Aristotle thus directs our attention away from an
understanding of *ethos* as a person's well-lived existence and toward an understanding of *ethos* as an artistic accomplishment. Eugene Garver's discussion of this
distinction is noteworthy: "The *ethos* which the audience trusts . . . is the artificial
[artistic or 'artful'] *ethos* identified with argument. It is not some real *ethos* the
speaker may or may not possess. It is an *ethos* not necessarily tied to past experiences of the speaker, not an *ethos* acquired through performing similar actions in
the past. It may be *likely* that the good speaker is able to deliberate intelligently
because of past experiences, but it is not *ethos* qua product of past experience that
the audience trusts, but *ethos* as exercised in some particular argument."[4]

Indeed, Aristotle treats *ethos* as a component of rhetorical argument. Garver's
way of stating this point is noteworthy because it allows for the possibility that the
speaker's reputation as a good and faithful soul can play a role in the artistic
process. Aristotle's specific appreciation of *ethos,* which he formulates by going
back to first principles to ask what rhetoric is and how it functions, provides a
more systematic and analytic response to Plato's call in the *Phaedrus* for a "science
of rhetoric" than does Isocrates' teachings about related matters.[5] These teachings,
however, remain relevant for developing a hermeneutically rich reading of Aristotle's understanding of the topic.

For example, does not Aristotle's understanding of artful *ethos* presuppose that
the character that *takes place* in the orator's specific text is itself contextualized and
thereby made possible by past social, political, and rhetorical transactions that
inform the orator's and his audience's ongoing communal existence: the "places,"
"habitats," and "haunts" (*ethea*) wherein people dwell and bond together? This
question echoes the earliest use of *ethos* that dates back to Homer and Hesiod,
influences Isocrates' theory of rhetoric and moral character, and, as Charles Chamberlain notes, "refers to the range or arena where someone is most truly at home
and which underlies all the fine appearances ['habits' and 'customs': also *ethea*] that
people adopt."[6] Aristotle, too, develops this particular usage of *ethos* when, in the
Nicomachean Ethics, he discusses how, beginning in childhood, "ethical" virtues can
be trained and made habitual.[7] He also emphasizes this habituating process in the
Eudemian Ethics when he identifies *ethos* with the "irrational part of the soul" that

is still capable of following the orders of reason.[8] Hence, according to Chamberlin, "the implications of Aristotle's definition of *ethos* pick up the strands of implication already implicit in the word. In doing so, he regards its full history which goes back to Homer."[9]

With Aristotle, then, the meaning of *ethos* is both affirmed and extended. The extension shows itself in a keenly focused assessment of *ethos* as a component of rhetorical argument and thus as a mode of artistic achievement. *Ethos* brings to mind a person's moral character, communal existence, and oratorical skill. The rhetorical tradition owes its technical use of the term to Aristotle's emphasis of this third component of *ethos,* whereby, according to James Baumlin, we learn that "the rhetorical situation renders the speaker an element of the discourse itself, no longer simply its origin (and thus a consciousness standing outside the text) but rather a signifier standing *inside* an expanded text. The rhetor's physical presence and appearance, his gestures, inflections, and accents of style, are all involved in acts of signification."[10] With the historical meaning of *ethos* in mind, however, the "expanded text" referred to here can be further expanded to include the very Being of human being. One learns how to make this ontological move with the help of Martin Heidegger's 1924 lecture course on Aristotle's *Rhetoric* and his further commentary on the text in his *Being and Time.*

Heidegger admires Aristotle's treatment of the orator's art. "Contrary to the traditional [scholastic] orientation, according to which rhetoric is conceived as the kind of thing we 'learn in school,' this work of Aristotle must be taken as the first systematic hermeneutic of the everydayness of Being with one another," he notes.[11] Indeed, as made clear throughout his lecture course, Heidegger acknowledges Aristotle to be instructing us on the importance of developing our rhetorical competence such that we might maintain and improve the sociopolitical workings and well-being of our communal existence.

Moreover, Heidegger is especially taken with Aristotle's treatment of a topic (i.e., the *pathe,* or emotions) that, as discussed in the *Rhetoric,* is necessarily related to *ethos* as a component of rhetorical argument: The establishment of a speaker's character is dependent on, among other things, his ability to put his hearers into the right frame of mind so that their emotional state during the oration and subsequent deliberations are advantageous to the speaker's persuasive intent (*Rhetoric,* 1377b2–4). Heidegger restates the point: the "feeling of the one being addressed must be taken into account, as must the particular situation at the time and the speaker's own attunement to the issue at hand." ("Es muss bei der Vorgabe anderes in Hinsicht gestellt werden, es muss Rechnung getragen werden der Stimmung derkenigen, zu denen gesprochen wird, die jeweilige Lage der Dinge und die Art und Weise, wie man zelbst zur Sachen steht.") And the orator "must understand the possibilities of moods in order to rouse them and guide them in a right and just manner." ("Er bedarf des Verständnisses der Möglichkeit der Stimmung, um sie in der rechten Weise zu wecken und zu lenken.")[12] Heidegger thereby affirms that there is something "good" about the practice of rhetoric, something that enables it to be more than a mere communicative device for the "received opinion" (*doxa*) heard in the public's "idle chatter" (*Gerede*).

This affirmation is worth noting because Heidegger can easily be read as holding the traditional philosophical bias against the "manipulative" nature of the orator's rhetorical competence and resulting character.[13] Heidegger's positive take on the workings of the entire process is further suggested when he notes how the understanding constituting the received opinion of a given public "reveals authentic being-with-one-another in the world" ("Die Doxa ist die eigentliche Entdecktheit des Miteinanderseins in der Welt"; GBAPh 19.6.24), and how the emotional workings of rhetorical speech are committed to the everyday world of practice and know-how wherein the "taking care of things" (*Besorgen*) is worked out and accomplished and where rhetorical speech functions to exhort people to an active *krisis* or decision (GBAPh 4.7.24, 5.6.24, 6.6.24). For Heidegger, the emotional fabric of a person's existence constitutes the "ground and soil of the Logos" ("den Boden des Logos selbst konkreter zu sehen"; GBAPh 23.6.24) that nourishes and is nourished by the everyday rhetorical practices of communal existence. He also recognizes how the primary function of the enthymeme— which, for Aristotle, plays a crucial role in the generation of the speaker's *ethos*— is associated with engaging others in the emotional process of "taking something to heart" ("sich etwas Zu Herzen nehmen"; GBAPh 5.6.24) so that they might be moved to thoughtful action. The enthymeme, *ethos,* and pathos work together: the moving of the passions (taking something to heart) is a prerequisite of persuasion; truth alone is not sufficient to guide the thoughtful actions of human beings. A speaker's *ethos* takes form in the light of the success of this process.[14]

Like Aristotle, Heidegger understands this process as one that transforms the spatial and temporal orientation of an audience, its way of *being situated or placed* in relationship to things and to others. The genuine enhancement of public opinion requires, among other things, that the orator "modify" the lived and attuned space of others by "making present" to them what the orator has reason to believe is true, just, and virtuous. The practice of rhetoric operates in the immediacy of the present; it seeks thought and action in the everyday world of the here and now. The orator calls upon emotion in order to facilitate this pragmatic endeavor.[15] In so doing, he not only places his own character on the line and in the text but also clears a place in time and space for people to acknowledge and "know-together" (*con-scientia*) what is arguably the truth of some matter of importance. The ethical practice of rhetoric entails the construction of a speaker's *ethos* as well as the construction of a "dwelling place" (*ethos*) for collaborative and moral deliberation.

In Aristotle's *Rhetoric,* Heidegger finds a hermeneutic assessment of a specific art that leads one to consider what Heidegger maintains is the "basic character" of our relationship to all that stands before us (Being). In the most original sense of the term, writes Heidegger, "*Ethos* means abode, dwelling place. The word names the open region in which man dwells."[16] The point was made earlier when noting Homer's and Hesiod's original use of the term. Heidegger makes the point with the help of a story that Aristotle reports in *De parte animalium* (I.5.645a17) regarding a group of strangers who visit the renowned philosopher Heraclitus as he is sitting next to a stove in his sparse "abode" or living quarters:

> In this altogether everyday place [Heraclitus] betrays the whole poverty of his life. The vision of a shivering thinker offers little of interest. At this disappointing spectacle even the curious lose their desire to come any closer. . . . Such an everyday and unexciting occurrence—somebody who is chilled warming himself at a stove—anyone can find any time at home. So why look up a thinker? The visitors are on the verge of going away again. Heraclitus reads the frustrated curiosity in their faces. He knows that for the crowd the failure of an expected sensation to materialize is enough to make those who have just arrived leave. He therefore encourages them. He invites them explicitly to come in with the words *Einai gar kai entautha theous,* "Here too the gods are present."[17]

Heidegger's understanding of the meaning of the story permeates his entire later philosophy, wherein he continues his phenomenological investigations of the *ethos* of human existence (*Dasein*) or the essential way that we exist in relationship with Being. For Heidegger, Heraclitus's "Here too" refers not merely to the "thinker's" humble living quarters but also to the primordial dwelling place that gives grounds to this habitat. Heidegger thus constantly reminds us that the spatial and temporal character of human being—the way that it is "always already" open to the objective uncertainty of the future, what is "not yet"—is the genuine place in which Being discloses and shows itself as something that can be thought about, understood, and expressed in symbolic form. Human being holds a special relationship with Being; we belong and are appropriated to it in a distinctive manner. Heidegger puts the entire matter this way: "Man obviously is a being. As such he belongs to the totality of Being—Just like the stone, the tree, or the eagle. To 'belong' here still means to be in the order of Being. But man's distinctive feature lies in this, that he, as the being who thinks, is open to Being, face to face with Being; thus man remains referred to Being and so answers to it. Man *is* essentially this relationship of responding to Being, . . . Being is present and abides only as it concerns man through the claim [or 'challenge'] it makes on him."[18]

This challenge shows itself in the way the objective uncertainty of our spatial and temporal existence is forever "calling" us to assume the ethical responsibility of affirming the burden of our freedom of choice whereby, through thought and action, we bring a sense of order and meaning to our lives. Human existence is both an evocation and a provocation: a showing-forth of something that *is* and that necessarily calls us into question. Human being is thus always first on the receiving end of existence, ever in need of being receptive and responsive to the demands of its challenging call. This is how systems of ethics and morality come into being in the first place. The language of ethics and morality is the language of responsiveness and responsibility. The primordial call of human existence defines what Heidegger thus terms the original "call of conscience."[19]

Notice that this call is always already operating before specific ethical prescriptions and prohibitions are formulated by human beings and before the operation is reduced to human measurements (e.g., seconds, minutes, hours, days, years). The call of conscience is not a human invention; we did not create the ontological (spatial/temporal) structure of existence—the way it opens us to the uncertainty of the future and thereby, within this openness, *gives us a place to be* toward all that stands before us. The call of conscience *is* human existence disclosing itself to the one who is living it and who can and must respond to its challenge, but it is also something *other* than a human accomplishment: an alterity or otherness that lies at the heart of the self, of one's own way of living everyday existence.

What exactly is this alterity that permeates our existence and that is more commonly and easily recognized in the mere presence of things and others that are not oneself? Answering this question in an authentic manner requires that we remain open to the presence (and, hence, otherness) of all that stands before us such that we might be able to *tell* something of its truth. This endeavor, for Heidegger, defines "the proper dignity" of human beings: to be receptive to the truth of things and others and to bring something of this truth into language. The human being is called to be true to its essential character (*ethos*): We *are* the openness of a dwelling place where the truth of what is—be it a stone, tree, eagle, ourselves, or whatever—can be taken to heart, appreciated, and cared for.

Although Heidegger never admits it, this way of characterizing human being plays an essential role in religious thought, especially traditional Judaism. The key term used in Judaism for this phenomenon is the *shechinah,* which literally translates as "the dwelling place of God." Such a dwelling place is most commonly associated with the tabernacle (*mishkan*) or portable synagogue that God told Moses and his people to build and to carry with them in their nomadic wanderings as a reminder of God's presence in the world. The *shechinah* also is understood to be situated in the human heart and makes itself known with the wondrous happenings of life that present themselves to us and inspire moral consciousness. The openness of human being and God's presence go hand in hand.[20] Heidegger emphasizes that with his philosophical project "nothing is decided about the 'existence of God' or his 'non-being.'" Still, he sees his project as offering an authentic and enlightening approach to the matter of the "holy" other. As he puts it, "Only from the truth of Being can the essence of the holy be thought. Only from the essence of the holy is the essence of divinity to be thought. Only in the light of the essence of divinity can it be thought or said what the world 'god' is to signify. . . . How can man at the present stage of world history ask at all seriously and rigorously whether the god nears or withdraws, when he has above all neglected to think into the dimension in which alone that question can be asked?"[21]

Heidegger tells us that such thinking, whereby a person is being true to his or her essential character, requires "perseverance," as well as the ability to express oneself and to act at "the right time" or "moment."[22] The rhetorical tradition has, of course, long recognized the importance of this observation and its relevance to the development of a speaker's *ethos.* In Greek rhetoric, the rhetor aims at finding *to prepon,* what is appropriate, right and fitting, for the situation, which in Cicero and Quintilian becomes "propriety" or "decorum," the master principle of rhetoric analogous to *phronesis* (practical wisdom). As referred to by Heidegger, then, appropriateness is a phenomenon that calls our attention to a complex dynamic of related phenomena that, as I have tried to make clear above with the help of Isocrates, Aristotle, Heidegger, and others defines the robust meaning and significance of *ethos:* It is a matter, at the very least, of character, ethics, Being, space and time, emotion, truth, rhetorical competence, and everyday situations that are contextualized within the dwelling place of human being—a place known to encourage metaphysical wonder.

To repeat: We did not create the fundamental structure and workings of this primordial place and its attending call of conscience; rather, they are "givens," they come with the Being of existence, they are part of the essential character of human nature. We are creatures who dwell on this earth and who are thereby destined to hear and answer a call that, among other things, requires a capacity for practicing the art of rhetoric. The ontological structure of existence is such that we must learn to *dwell rhetorically.* This artful way of being, as Richard McKeon reminds us, is "architectonic": "Rhetoric provides the devices by which to determine the characteristics and problems of our times and to form the art by which to guide actions for the solution of our problems and the improvement of our circumstances."[23] The call of human being, of conscience, calls on us to be rhetorical architects whose symbolic constructions both create and invite others into a place where they can dwell and feel at home while thinking about and discussing the truth of some matter that the rhetor/architect has already attempted to disclose and show-forth (*epi-deixis*) in a specific way with his or her work of art. Such a work of art thus assumes an epideictic function. With architecture in mind, one might also speak of the work as an "edifying" discourse (in Latin "to edify" is *aedificare,* from *aedes,* "dwelling," and *fiacre,* "to make" or "to build") whose communal character takes form as the artist uses materials (e.g., tropes, figures, topics, arguments, narratives, emotions) to attract attention, maintain our interest, and encourage us to judge the work as praiseworthy and persuasive.[24]

Existence calls, and for the sake of others and ourselves, we are obliged to respond in a responsible and thus rhetorically competent way. Something that is *other* than the self demands nothing less. The demand comes with acts of disclosure, with a showing-forth of all that there is. Here then, one might say, we are witnesses to the most original epideictic event that there is. At its best, the every-day practice of rhetoric sounds this same call. It would seem, then, that it is not only the case that we are called to dwell rhetorically, but the call itself shows itself to be a rhetorical happening, one that *gives ground* to all else that can be said about the art. The *ethos* of rhetoric runs deep—to the very heart (and beyond?) of human existence.

The Essays

The contributors to this book were asked to keep in mind this extensive charac-ter of rhetoric as they composed their essays. Hence, as can be seen in their indi-vidual treatments of the *ethos* of rhetoric, the authors speak of a variety of ways of understanding the topic. But their particular takes on the matter also express an appreciation of the topic's fundamental nature. The *ethos* of rhetoric, its dwelling place, extends far and wide and thereby entails a lot: author, text, audience, histori-cal context, and the ontology of human being and the metaphysics that go with it. Acknowledging the full meaning and significance of *ethos* allows one to appre-ciate what it really means, in both a broad and narrow sense, to speak of rhetoric as being a "hermeneutic" and "situated" practice, an art that informs and is in-formed by the way human beings dwell on earth.[25] Indeed, to repeat Goankar's earlier noted caution, we should not leave "key terms" in rhetorical scholarship in an "undertheorized" state.

The first four essays attend to the matter by continuing primarily to theorize about the relationship between *ethos* and rhetoric. Craig Smith does this as he offers an intricate hermeneutic reading of Aristotle on "credibility" that extends significantly what has been noted so far about this philosopher's theory of *ethos*. For example, Smith makes much of how virtue, wisdom, and goodwill inform the *ethos* of the speaker and its subsequent effect on the character of the audience. Smith thus directs readers to a process of rhetorical invention that he maintains is an ontological feature of human existence.

Margaret Zulick attends to what she terms "the *ethos* of invention" in order to counter the philosophical tendency of seeing ethics and aesthetics as being mutu-ally opposed categories. Her thinking here is directed by the related work of Ken-neth Burke and Mikhail Bakhtin—two thinkers who, she contends, construct worlds of theory in which ethics and aesthetics are coordinate acts of a "symbolic imagination" that precedes and generates both of these categories. For Zulick, the "convergence of ethics and aesthetics in the *ethos* of invention lies at the heart of rhetorical practice."

Wade Kenny provides a further consideration of imagination in order to elu-cidate the role played by this phenomenon in the rhetorical construction of humankind's dwelling places. Kenny's work is steeped in Heideggerian philosophy; the majority of his many keen insights take form, however, as he appropriates and extends a theory of imaginative vision found in the writings of Northrop Frye and then briefly illustrates the significance of his findings by relating them to such rhetorical artifacts as Frank Capra's classic film *It's a Wonderful Life* and the speeches of Winston Churchill.

In turning to Barbara Warnick's contribution, one still remains primarily in the realm of theory, but now what is being theorized about is the *ethos* of rhetorical *criticism,* the dwelling place of a specific critical and artistic practice. Warnick would have rhetorical critics enlarge their professional terrain and attending responsibilities by turning away from a preoccupation with disciplinary identity in order to ensure that they act as engaged and committed spokespersons on the major issues of the times. Warnick's specific perspective on *ethos* thus addresses an issue that is also emphasized by Goankar when he speaks of the need to clarify the "key terms" that inform the rhetorical tradition: "The task of conceptual elaboration cannot be left exclusively to theory in an art so insistently practical and public as rhetoric. The interpretive value of a key term in rhetoric becomes apparent only when it is forced to grapple with and to journey through the vicissitudes of a discursive formation. Hence, rhetorical criticism bears the double burden of simultaneously illuminating the critical object and facilitating 'concept formation.'"[26]

The next seven essays make the move from theory to practice as their authors take on this burden by providing extended case studies of how the *ethos* of rhetoric actually manifests itself in our everyday lives. The theoretical considerations raised in the first four essays are certainly applicable here and should help readers better appreciate the rhetorical criticism that unfolds throughout the remainder of the collection.

Walter Jost initiates the move with an exceptionally close reading of a film that has long been used as a pedagogical tool by communication scholars and consultants interested in conflict resolution and in group and organizational communication: Sidney Lumet's *12 Angry Men.* Jost's unique reading of the film unfolds as he shows in stunning detail how the *ethos* of rhetoric functioning in the film informs its ethical, political, and ontological appeal as a "work of art." Jost speaks to us of an artistic creation that demonstrates the convergence of ethics and aesthetics in the *ethos* of invention, in a dwelling place for critical reflection made possible by the creative and entertaining use of a host of rhetorical topics that are all too easily overlooked by viewers who are not used to "thinking like a rhetorician." To think this way about the film is to become interested in "what is not obvious, *not* because it is hidden but just *because* it is made so palpably visible and audible to us, right in front of our noses, in our ears: water to fish."

What Jost does with a film, John Poulakos does with a letter written by a soldier fighting in the Vietnam War in 1967. Poulakos reads the letter as a rhetorical artifact that "invites us to reflect on the objects of our attention and the subjects of our writing when finding ourselves in inhospitable places," places where we must dwell in suffering and pain, where we most definitely do not feel at home, and where we learn that "life without beauty is a mistake." Poulakos writes beautifully about a marine writing about beauty in order to demonstrate how "rhetoric derives its *ethos* from the principle of topical preference" and how the topic of beauty can and must constantly direct humankind's attention if we expect to know anything about the "truth" of what it means to dwell in peace.

Like Jost and Poulakos, Eric Watts is taken with the topic of aesthetics and its relationship to the *ethos* of rhetoric. He explores this relationship by way of a masterful critical assessment of how a principal public intellectual and artist of the Black Arts movement, Larry Neal, developed an "aesthetic praxis" directed toward a hermeneutic appreciation of "liberation" that was not predicated upon "the destruction of whiteness" and thus showed "how a black aesthetic can survive its own negative racial critique." For Watts, Neal's rhetorical imagination offers itself as "a way of manufacturing livable space—a dwelling place—for black folk" whose "homes" should and must be "part of the neighborhood."

Interested as they are in the relationship between the *ethos* of rhetoric and aesthetics, Jost, Poulakos, and Watts provide ample opportunities for recalling the significance of a point made at the beginning of this introduction: the *ethos* of rhetoric directs one's attention to the "architectural" function of the art, its way of using its material (language) in an appropriate and edifying manner to build a habitat, a dwelling place, where in moments of moral responsibility people can deliberate and "know-together" (*con-scientia*) what is, arguably, the "truth" of some contested matter and what actions should follow in light of the decision needed here. The *ethos* of rhetoric and aesthetics go hand in hand with our being social, political, and metaphysical beings. Recall that this last mentioned feature of human existence makes its presence known when the dwelling place that we *are* for Being becomes the dwelling place that we *are* for God. This transformation defines an effort in rhetorical imagination and invention, an effort that, certainly within the Judaic-Christian tradition, is understood as something made possible by a generous gift from God: the Word and the capacity to spread it to others.

Martin Medhurst helps to register the significance of these recollections as he identifies a "dimension" of the 2000 presidential campaign that allows him to examine "what the role of religious rhetoric suggests about the state—the *ethos*—of our American form of democracy." Medhurst inspects the rhetoric of both "the Right" and "the Left" (from late 1998 until election day 2000) as he addresses the issue and in a compelling fashion develops the suggestion that Americans are "a people, a *demos,* hungry for spiritual values and willing to support those who articulate with clarity and passion the specifically moral, ethic, and spiritual dimensions of public policy choices." With Medhurst, then, readers are offered a case study of how the *ethos* of rhetoric, among other things, informs and is informed by humankind's metaphysical propensities.

David Zarefsky also turns to presidential rhetoric to explore the workings of the *ethos* of the art, especially as it is employed in "times of crisis and uncertainty."

4

In these moments, we "call for our leaders to articulate a vision to which we can subscribe. . . . In these moments we dwell in a rhetorical culture and are glad to do so." Zarefsky's case study is the response of President George W. Bush to the terrorist attacks of September 11, 2001. Zarefsky notes that Bush "began to find the appropriate voice" as he spoke of how "the country was united" and "sought divine guidance and blessing." There is, to be sure, a metaphysical aspect to Bush's discourse. For Zarefsky, however, the president's "most significant rhetorical decision" was made when he decided "to describe the situation as war." Zarefsky's penetrating analysis of the war metaphor in Bush's rhetoric leads to an equally insightful and disturbing analysis of the "unintended consequences" that such rhetoric might encourage as the war on terror unfolds and as we find ourselves in dwelling places built on a rhetoric "not of the open hand but of the closed fist."

Carole Blair and Neil Michel share with Medhurst and Zarefsky an interest in presidential discourse; they explore the *ethos* of rhetoric by "reading" a "memorial" —Mount Rushmore—that both figuratively and literally constitutes "a dwelling place of national character" meant to inspire patriotism with its carvings of four "heroic" presidents: George Washington, Thomas Jefferson, Abraham Lincoln, and Theodore Roosevelt. For Blair and Michel, however, the "ideological" discourse that informs the "text" in question "promotes an image of the national *ethos* that is anything but virtuous."

The authors develop their position by way of an exceptionally rich hermeneutical and critical assessment of the Monument and the historical narrative that has long promoted its patriotic (surface) meaning. What they find covered up by this meaning "is an image of imperialist pride, an obsession with outlandish size, and an 'aesthetic sensibility' that approves of accomplishing national commemoration by dynamiting scenic places. [Mount Rushmore] implores us to be enthusiastic or at least acquiescent about any representation—even an odious part of our national past—as long as it is immense."

Like Blair and Michel, Carolyn Miller's study of the *ethos* of rhetoric also takes form as she examines a phenomenon of questionable character: "the *ethos* of the culture of cold war technology" that insists "that expert knowledge produces progress; that mechanization reproduces expertise; that expertise implies authority; [and] that expert authority convinces the rational." Miller's intricate and illuminating exploration of the topic details how the art of rhetoric and its function of creating dwelling places that can foster moral character is necessarily transformed and restricted as the art is made to serve the workings of computerized expert systems with their "cyborg discourse." She notes that the "technical *ethos* must be informed but impartial, authoritative but self-effacing" and reveals how such an *ethos* "denies the importance of *ethos,*" especially as the meaning of the term can be appreciated from an Aristotelian perspective. For Miller, the consequences that follow from this specific denial "warrant our vigilance." The legitimacy of this claim is especially powerful in light of Miller's contention that an "*ethos* may metonymize a community that is oppressive, restrictive, secretive, deceptive; its virtues may be ones we would not choose to emulate, even though in many situations we may find ourselves persuaded by them."

This collection of essays thus ends with a piece that, in a sense, directs readers back to the beginning of the collection as it echoes certain claims offered by Calvin Schrag in the foreword: "The texture of human knowledge is not a collage of discrete units of information but rather a tapestry of intercalating explanations and interpretations. No body of knowledge is an island of itself, cut off from the mainland of human endeavors." In the beginning, we have five chapters (including this one) that emphasize history and theory, followed by seven chapters that emphasize practice. As suggested earlier, *The Ethos of Rhetoric* was organized with this progression in mind. It is one book composed of two complementary movements, which the contributors and I hope prove instructive for understanding a key term in the rhetorical tradition.

Notes

1. Dilip P. Gaonkar, Introduction, "The Forum: Publics and Counterpublics," *Quarterly Journal of Speech* 88 (2002): 410–12.

2. Isocrates, *Antidosis,* trans. George Norlin, Loeb Classical Library (Cambridge: Harvard University Press, 1982), 278. Further references to this work will be cited in the text.

3. Aristotle, *Aristotle on Rhetoric: A Theory of Civic Discourse,* ed. and trans. George A. Kennedy (New York: Oxford University Press, 1991), 1356a4. Further references to this work will be cited in the text.

4. Eugene Garver, *Aristotle's Rhetoric: An Art of Character* (Chicago: University of Chicago Press, 1994), 196.

5. George Kennedy, *The Art of Persuasion in Greece* (Princeton, N.J.: Princeton University Press, 1963), 174–206; Brian Vickers, *In Defense of Rhetoric* (New York: Oxford University Press, 1988), 159–60; James S. Baumlin, "Ethos," in *Encyclopedia of Rhetoric,* ed. Thomas O. Sloane (New York: Oxford University Press, 2001), 263–77; and James S. Baumlin, "Introduction: Positioning Ethos in Historical and Contemporary Theory," in *Ethos: New Essays in Rhetorical and Critical Theory,* ed. James S. Baumlin and Tita French Baumlin (Dallas: Southern Methodist University Press, 1994), xi–xxxi. In his introductory essay, Baumlin makes brief reference to how the meaning of *ethos* can be associated with "haunts" or "places of belonging," although none of the sixteen essays contained in his collection follow up on the matter.

6. Charles Chamberlain, "From 'Haunts' to 'Character': The Meaning of Ethos and Its Relation to Ethics," *Helios* 11 (1984): 99. On this point, also see Eric A. Havelock, *Preface to Plato* (Cambridge: Harvard University Press, 1963), 63; and Edward S. Casey, *The Fate of Place: A Philosophical History* (Berkeley and Los Angeles: University of California Press, 1997), xiv.

7. Aristotle, *Nicomachean Ethics,* trans. W. D. Ross, revised by J. O. Urmson, in *The Complete Works of Aristotle,* vol. 2, ed. Jonathan Barnes (Princeton, N.J.: Princeton University Press, 1984), 2.1.1103a17–30.

8. Aristotle, *Eudemian Ethics,* trans. J. Solomon, in *The Complete Works of Aristotle,* vol. 2, ed. Jonathan Barnes (Princeton, N.J.: Princeton University Press, 1884), 2.2. 1220b2–6.

9. Chamberlain, "From 'Haunts' to 'Character,'" 103. Also see Arthur B. Miller, "Aristotle on Habit and Character," *Speech Monographs* 41 (1974): 309–16.

10. Baumlin, "Introduction," xvi.

11. Martin Heidegger, *Being and Time,* trans. John Macquarrie and Edward Robinson (New York: Harper & Row, 1962), 178.

12. The first quotation is from Martin Heidegger, "Grundbegriffe der Aristotelischen Philosophie," unpublished transcript of Heidegger's 1924 Summer Semester lecture course at Marburg, in the Marcuse Archiv, Stadtsbibliotek, Frankfurt, 23.6.24 (hereafter cited in the text as GBAPh). The second quotation is from Heidegger's *Sein und Zeit* (Tubingen: Niewmeyer, 1979), 138–39. Translations are mine.

13. For a detailed discussion of this point, see my article "The Call of Conscience: Heidegger and the Question of Rhetoric," *Philosophy and Rhetoric* 27 (1994): 374–96.

14. For an excellent discussion of Heidegger's reading of Aristotle's *Rhetoric* and related works, see P. Christopher Smith, *The Hermeneutics of Original Argument: Demonstration, Dialectic, Rhetoric* (Evanston, Ill.: Northwestern University Press, 1998).

15. Craig R. Smith and Michael J. Hyde, "Rethinking 'The Public': The Role of Emotion in Being-with-Others," *Quarterly Journal of Speech* 77 (1991): 446–66; Michael J. Hyde and Craig R. Smith, "Aristotle and Heidegger on Emotion and Rhetoric: Questions of Time and Space," in *The Critical Turn: Rhetoric and Philosophy in Contemporary Discourse,* ed. Ian Angus and Lenore Langsdorf (Carbondale: Southern Illinois University Press, 1993), 68–99.

16. Martin Heidegger, "Letter on Humanism," in *Basic Writings,* ed. David Farrell Krell (New York: Harper & Row, 1977), 233.

17. Ibid., 234.

18. Martin Heidegger, *Identity and Difference,* trans. Joan Stambaugh (New York: Harper & Row, 1969), 31.

19. See Michael J. Hyde, *The Call of Conscience: Heidegger and Levinas, Rhetoric and the Euthanasia Debate* (Columbia: University of South Carolina Press, 2001), 21–78.

20. See Daniel C. Matt, *Zohar: Annotated and Explained,* ed. Daniel C. Matt (Woodstock, Vt.: SkyLight Paths, 2002), esp. 73–82 ("The Gift of Dwelling"). Also see Hyde, *Call of Conscience,* 2–3.

21. Heidegger, "Letter on Humanism," 230.

22. Martin Heidegger, *An Introduction to Metaphysics,* trans. Ralph Manheim (New Haven, Conn.: Yale University Press, 1959), 206.

23. Richard McKeon, "The Uses of Rhetoric in a Technological Age: Architectonic Productive Arts," in *The Prospect of Rhetoric,* ed. Lloyd F. Bitzer and Edwin Black (Englewood Cliffs, N.J.: Prentice-Hall, 1971), 52.

24. Karsten Harries, *The Ethical Function of Architecture* (Cambridge: MIT Press, 1997), 2–13. Also see Lawrence W. Rosenfield, "Central Park and the Celebration of Civic Virtue," in *American Rhetoric: Context and Criticism,* ed. Thomas W. Benson (Carbondale: Southern Illinois University Press, 1989), 221–66.

25. See Edwin Black, *Rhetorical Criticism: A Study in Method* (New York: Macmillian, 1965) and Lloyd F. Bitzer, "The Rhetorical Situation," *Philosophy and Rhetoric* 1 (1968):

1–13. These two works are typically acknowledged as initiating present-day debates concerning rhetoric's hermeneutic and situated status. Also see Michael J. Hyde and Craig R. Smith, "Hermeneutics and Rhetoric: A Seen but Unobserved Relationship," *Quarterly Journal of Speech* 65 (1979): 347–63, for an in-depth discussion of hermeneutical theory that both commends and critiques Black's and Bitzer's groundbreaking work. In his *Communicative Praxis and the Space of Subjectivity* (Bloomington: Indiana University Press, 1986), esp. 179–214, Calvin O. Schrag provides the first extensive treatment of how the notion of *ethos* as dwelling place is necessarily involved in the relationship between rhetoric and hermeneutics. Regarding this specific matter, also see Michael J. Hyde, "Hermeneutics," in *Encyclopedia of Rhetoric,* ed. Thomas O. Sloane (New York: Oxford University Press, 2001), 329–37. I also make much of the matter throughout my *Call of Conscience* (e.g., 75, 95, 196, 201).

26. Goankar, 411.

Ethos Dwells Pervasively

A Hermeneutic Reading of Aristotle on Credibility

CRAIG R. SMITH

Hermeneutics has evolved over the centuries since the first formal hermeneutic, the *interpretatio scripti,* was used to decipher legal documents during the Hellenistic period. Later, as Eden notes, Roman rhetors such as Cicero used it extensively. St. Augustine converted this forensically oriented praxis into a means of discovering intuitive truth and objectifying the word of God. Augustine believed that context was crucial to interpretation. Much later this biblical hermeneutics grounded reformed interpretations and translations by such noted scholars as Erasmus, Luther, and Melanchthon.

The practice took on new meaning, however, when contemporary scholars argued that it is more important for hermeneutic readings to open documents than objectify them. This position is reflected in Hans-Georg Gadamer's *Truth and Method:* method is not necessarily justified by its correctness but by its fruitfulness, that is, whether it yields insights into the text.

In response, Gaonkar noted that "rhetoric has entered the orbit of general hermeneutics," a shift he attributes directly to Hyde and Smith,[1] who argue that rhetorical theory would be improved if scholars would approach it from a hermeneutic perspective. They contend that hermeneutic readings placed in a phenomenological context produce fruitful interpretations; they illustrate this claim with a reading of Aristotle on pathos.[2] Synthesizing the theories of Husserl and Heidegger, Hyde and Smith demonstrate that individuals shape existence through language while their culture provides the linguistic realm, that is, the fore-structure, through which they acquire language.

The purpose of this chapter is to employ a hermeneutic praxis to read Aristotle on *ethos.*[3] By "praxis," I mean a procedure for a reading in the tradition of the Greek *methodos,* referring to a "way of doing." The way of doing this reading is a hermeneutic, by which I mean a close textual reading guided by a healthy consideration of the context of the text and its author. My position is simply that interpretive understanding is enhanced by a knowledge of social context. In this case, we need to consider the Athenian fore-structure, that is, the linguistic realm of possibilities, born out of the pre-Socratic and sophistic tradition. We also need to consider Aristotle's debt to this tradition, to his teacher Plato, and to Isocrates, the most mentioned figure in the *Rhetoric*. Finally, we need to read Aristotle on *ethos* with his *Nicomachean Ethics* in hand since it supplies the ideal version of his system of morality while completing many of the definitions Aristotle leaves incomplete in the *Rhetoric*.

Reading Aristotle's *Rhetoric* without this hermeneutic method is difficult because its cryptic style opens it to contradictory interpretations, particularly with regard to *ethos*.[4] Inconsistent readings problemitize the development of rhetorical theory especially if *ethos,* as Aristotle claims, is the most potent means of persuasion (*Rhetoric,* 1356a4). No other Aristotelian "proof" has been subjected to more empirical examination than *ethos.* Paul Rosenthal was one of the first to ground the concept of *ethos* empirically.[5] The trend continued most significantly with James McCroskey's conversion to the position that Aristotle's notion of "goodwill" can be tested as "perceived care giving."[6] Thus, a more consistent reading of *ethos* may contribute to both rhetorical and communication theory.

Interpretations of Ethos

The *Rhetoric* is a compilation of lectures written over a twenty-six-year period during which Aristotle changed his thinking on the subject. However, at no place does Aristotle see *ethos* as a dwelling in the sense that Heraclitus used the term. In fact, Aristotle makes only one reference to Heraclitus (1407b14) and then it is to point out how obscure he is.[7] The first *place* that Aristotle acknowledges in the rhetoric is the Areopagus, the high court, where, of course, *ethos* was enormously important. As we shall see, however, a hermeneutic reading reveals that Aristotle presupposes the pre-Socratic notion of *ethos* as dwelling place in the introduction to his book. For Aristotle, it is a given: everyone has *ethos* whether it be noble or ignoble. Before one even speaks, that *ethos* has an ontological dimension because it emerges from the way one makes decisions, the way one lives on a day-to-day basis, the way one dwells. Those decisions are informed by one's values, one's practical wisdom, and one's goodwill, all of which are addressed in detail by Aristotle. Thus, Aristotle *assumes* the knowledge of the Athenian fore-structure of *ethos* as a dwelling place and then reformulates the notion of dwelling place to present a rhetorical understanding of *ethos.* As an empiricist, he examines not what is given in the culture, but the notion of *ethos* as the *public* manifestation of a person. Thus, we must ask, where for Aristotle does *ethos* dwell? The obvious answer is in the speaker's "personal character" before the *boulē* or in the courts of the agora.[8] A subtler answer emerges from a close reading. Before moving to that reading, let me acknowledge previous work on reading the *Rhetoric* and examine some of the important disagreements among these interpretations.

Scholars agree on some basic tenets that are consistent throughout Aristotle's theory. W. D. Ross demonstrates that *ethos* reflects the "character" of the speaker, patho*s* arouses the "emotion" of the audience, and logos is the "sheer force" of the argument.[9] The three divisions of *ethos* first advanced by Edward Cope remain virtually unchallenged by contemporary scholars.[10] However, I believe we can obtain a clearer and more consistent view of these divisions if we read them into Athenian culture. The first, *ethos* in the speaker, includes three components: practical wisdom, virtue, and goodwill; the second dwells in the character of the audience; and the third dwells in the speaker's style. As we shall see, a hermeneutic reading provides insight into the evolution of this tripartite division in Aristotle's theory, which will demonstrate that Aristotle's notion of *ethos* presupposes *ethos* as a dwelling place.

Disagreements over Aristotle's theory stem from differences over how one is to read the *Rhetoric*. Several scholars believe that the *Rhetoric* was written as a practical handbook that separates ethics from persuasion. Hence, they contend that Aristotle did not view rhetoric as ethically grounded. V. E. Simrell claims that the *Rhetoric* is a "cook-book" that merely satisfies the "perverted" human appetite; consequently, if Aristotle had the last say "rhetoric would have been mere rhetoric, a method justified by circumstantial necessity, not by inherent worth."[11] B. A. G. Fuller argues that rhetoric encourages speakers to persuade without regard to ethics. He contends that Aristotle's treatment of rhetoric is done "in the spirit of his discussion of current politics, medically, not morally."[12] Everett Lee Hunt claims that the *Rhetoric* is completely "detached from both morality and pedagogy; . . . it is an unmoral and scientific analysis of the means of persuasion."[13] Whitney J. Oates argues that the most "striking" characteristic of Aristotle's *Rhetoric* is its "immoralism."[14]

On the other hand, contextualists such as William Grimaldi read the *Rhetoric* in light of Aristotle's other writings and "consonant with his general thinking."[15] Grimaldi asserts that Aristotle's notion of persuasion provides people with all the means necessary for good decision making, "decisions made toward further growth in understanding."[16] Those who interpret the *Rhetoric* to advocate "persuasion at any cost" are misreading it.[17] Thomas Farrell agrees and reads the *Rhetoric* in the context of the *Nicomachean Ethics* and the *Politics*.[18] McCabe and Smith support an organic, holistic reading of the *Rhetoric*.[19]

The debate between Eckart Schutrumpf and G. F. Held synthesizes these differences. Schutrumpf contends that Aristotle's *Nicomachean Ethics* and *Rhetoric* describe *ethos* differently and should not be compared.[20] He claims the *Ethics* defines *ethos* in a "narrow" sense, limiting it to morals exclusively or the sum total of people's moral qualities. The *Rhetoric,* however, describes *ethos* in a "broad" sense, incorporating both morals and the "thinking faculty," or the sum total of the intellect.[21] Held disagrees, noting that the *Ethics* includes intellectual qualities that, according to Aristotle, are important for the pursuit of the proper "end."[22]

Schutrumpf's reply to Held indicates the lack of consensus on this issue: "It is simply not enough to state that in the *Poetics ethos* is used in the same sense as in the *Ethics* or—if one could prove this—in the *Rhetoric*. One has to take into account the character and scope of these different works and explain how this affects the meaning of *ethos* as used in each of them."[23]

Others have rallied to Schutrumpf's position. Jakob Wisse asserts that the *Ethics* and *Rhetoric* are so conceptually different in their description of *ethos* that the *Ethics* "cannot be used for elucidating the *Rhetoric*."[24] Wisse cites a passage in the *Ethics* that states a person who is truly "good" must be "possessed of good sense" (1144a36–37); "the *Rhetoric* offers a very different point of view . . . that a speaker of good sense may be wicked, and hide his thoughts."[25]

My hope is not only to adjudicate this debate but also to reveal that once we understand that the notion of *ethos* as dwelling place is assumed in Aristotle, his ontological understanding of *ethos* becomes clearer. In 1979, Hyde and I contended that rhetoric's ontological nature can be uncovered through a hermeneutic analysis. In 1991 and 1992, we uncovered the ontological structure of pathos using the same perspective. We demonstrate that the "universe" of language that history "projects" on human beings is the ontological basis for understanding meaning.[26] The past informs the present; the Athenian fore-structure informs Aristotle's theory.

The question of the ontological nature of *ethos* leads to different readings; in other words, because *ethos* informs decision making, thus moving a people to their potentiality, it is ontological.[27] Because choice is an ontological structure, Farrell writes that "apart from rhetoric, there is literally no systematic way of exploring the particular, probable issues of choice and avoidance."[28] Because character is a controlling factor of persuasion (1356a4), speakers are forced to make choices on the basis of *ethos,* underlining its ontological nature, a finding that may have motivated Aristotle's belief that *ethos* was the most potent proof.

Reading Aristotle on Ethos

Aristotle spent nearly twenty years studying with Plato as a pupil and colleague. His earliest writings are Platonic in content and form.[29] However, Aristotle's philosophy became grounded in the physical world. His political theory was more pragmatic than Plato's "ideal state" because it was empirically based on a study of existing constitutions in their historical development. The same is true for his treatment of rhetoric. In the opening paragraph of the *Rhetoric,* he notes that empirical analysis is the key to discovering effective rhetoric. "It is possible to observe the cause why some succeed [in persuasion] by habit and others accidentally," he states (1354a2). Thus, for most of the *Rhetoric,* he developed the empirical pragmatism of the Sophists rather than idealism of Plato.[30] Aristotle studied speakers and their audiences, observed what proved to be effective, and systematized it.

The idealism that does exist in Aristotle's *Rhetoric* is more likely to have been influenced by Isocrates than Plato. For Aristotle, *ethos* was about building the credibility of a speaker before an audience, not about the speaker's inherent worth.

Combining the external influences on Aristotle—pre-Socratics, Plato, Isocrates, and the Sophists—with his *Nicomachean Ethics,* his *Eudemian Ethics,*[31] and his *Politics,* one can read Aristotle on *ethos* hermeneutically. Hopefully, such a reading will bring together the disparate references to *ethos* in the *Rhetoric* and contribute to rhetorical theory by resolving the disagreements surrounding the text.

Ethos *in the Rhetoric*

Aristotle finished most of his work on ethics while he was composing a series of lecture notes that eventually became the *Rhetoric.* There he tells us, in its second chapter, "Persuasion is achieved by the speaker's personal character when the speech is so spoken as to make us think him credible. We believe good men more fully and more readily than others" (1356a4–6). A few sentences later, Aristotle reformulates his definition of this proof in an interesting way, telling us that to be effective speakers must "understand human character and goodness in their various forms" (1356a22–23). Thus it is not enough for a speaker to *be* good, a speaker must understand virtue; the virtue of the culture is one of the fonts (dwelling places) of *ethos.*

The development of character in book 1 of the *Nicomachean Ethics* sets out four types: the virtuous, the continent, the incontinent, and the vicious. The virtuous person is the one who takes the appropriate moral course, one who acts for the good and thereby achieves contentment. The continent person acts correctly but against his or her own desires. It is more difficult for continent persons to achieve happiness since they must struggle with issues of conscience and desire. Shakespeare's Hamlet is such a personality type. The incontinent person knows what should be done but chooses not to do it. Such persons give in to their desires, ignoring the call of conscience. Aristotle described the incontinent as weak willed. Shakespeare's King Claudius from *Hamlet* is such a person. On the other hand, the vicious person is not weak willed but acts in accordance with his/her desires and enjoys doing so. Shakespeare's Richard III and Iago are built from this type. Once he has established these personality types, Aristotle goes on to create his system of ethics that provides a context for the reading of *ethos* in the *Rhetoric.*

My hermeneutic reading forces me to begin with a note about prior reputation. While it is deemphasized because Aristotle wishes to focus on what can be created *in* the speech, it is more than implied as a potent part of *ethos.*[32] For example, near the end of the *Rhetoric,* Aristotle advises, "With regard to moral character: there are assertions which, if made about yourself, may excite dislike, appear tedious, or expose you to risk of contradiction. . . . Put such remarks, therefore, into the mouth of some third person" (1418b25). Is not this the advice we give to those who are to introduce us so that we do not sound like braggarts about our prior achievements? Earlier in the *Rhetoric,* Aristotle tells his readers that speakers are judged by their past decisions, that is, the grounding of their public personae. More specifically, in his discussion of happiness and virtue in book 1, chapter 5, Aristotle discusses a whole of list of prior attributes that audiences tend to admire, including "good birth," "good fortune," health, beauty, good friends, good children, fame, honor, money, and the like. All of these are part of prior reputation, which is revealed as a fourth constituent of *ethos* by this hermeneutic reading. On top of that, it is clear that prior reputation may dwell in the culture of the city-state. An oligarch will be more admired in Sparta than in Athens; a democrat will be more admired in Athens than in Sparta.

What makes us happy, claims Aristotle, we generally admire in others. Aristotle complicates his description of these admirable traits by giving them a hierarchy. For example, we admire those who love their friends more than we admire those who love their money because loving friends is more "honorable." Reflecting Socrates position in the *Gorgias,* he claims that it is more honorable to suffer injustice than to inflict it. This discussion of honor is the heart of the assumed issue of prior reputation, and Aristotle takes some time to get us to that dwelling place. The hierarchy tells speakers what they should primarily reveal to their audiences: the more honorable over the less honorable. "We shall," he writes, "be finding out how to make our hearers take the required view of our own characters" (1366a25). As we shall see, there is one more complication to the formula: what the audience believes is honorable is more persuasive than what is actually honorable. Determining the audience's beliefs is the key to successful adaptation in terms of building credibility. In this way, *ethos* dwells not only in the speaker, as Plato and Isocrates would have us believe, but also in the audience.

This analysis of prior reputation reveals that Aristotle's references to *ethos* are scattered and disjointed in his book on rhetorical theory; however, there are two passages that ground the concept. The first, in book 1 (1356a4), explains that *ethos* is a persuasive proof. The second, in book 2 (1378a5), describes the components that comprise *ethos:* "There are three reasons why speakers themselves are persuasive. . . . [P]ractical wisdom [*phronesis*] and virtue [*aretē*] and goodwill [*eunoia*]." Aristotle proceeds to deep structure his theory; as he begins, he says some important things about decision making: "But since rhetoric exists to affect the giving of decisions—the hearers decide between one political speaker and another, and a legal verdict is a decision—the orator must not only try to make the argument of his speech demonstrative and worthy of belief; he must also make his own character look right" (1377b21). He then lays out his understanding of credibility building by first analyzing the three components of *ethos*—virtue, wisdom, and goodwill. Next, he examines the persuasive nature of *ethos* in rhetorical situations. And finally, he discusses the role of *ethos* in a speech.

Virtue

Aristotle defines virtue as the ability to produce and preserve the good (1366a4). For Aristotle, the ultimate good is happiness, "at which everything aims" (1094a), he claims at the opening of the *Ethics*. It is the *"telos"* of his philosophy of moral values and, hence, a guiding light for *ethos*. Aristotle contends that virtue is a "state of character" concerned with "choice" (1106b36–40), and the proper choice contains moral and/or intellectual virtue that will lead to or reinforce happiness, which he defines as contentment. This task is not easy since humans are often distracted by "gratification . . . a life for grazing animals" (1095b20) or political activity.[33] In his elevation of soul searching over politics, Aristotle demonstrates the influence of his mentor Plato.[34] In fact, Aristotle wrote that "by human virtue we mean virtue of the soul, not of the body, since we also say that happiness is an activity of the soul" (1102a15).

Moral virtue is concerned with motivations and actions that lie on a continuum running from excess to deficiency, either end being a vice, the intermediate or mean position being a virtue (1106b14). It is important to note, as Hyde and I found with pathos, how proportional Aristotle's system is. The fact is that though the virtues in the *Ethics* are ideals in the Platonic sense, in the *Rhetoric* they are moving targets established by the audience. That is, speakers must understand that one audience's notion of courage might be another audience's notion of rashness. Effective speakers must either adapt to the audience's conception of courage or persuade the audience to move along the virtue's continuum until its notion of courage aligns with that of the speaker. Once again we find dimensions of *ethos* dwelling in the audience.

Courage is an example of moral virtue. The vices fall short of or exceed what is right concerning motivations and actions, while virtue finds and chooses the mean (1106b35). This "disposition" (*hexis*) in speakers or hearers is a character trait that moves them along the various means (continua in the soul). That is, courageous action is neither rash nor cowardly but well motivated and productive of good decisions. In the real world, however, audiences differ over what is rash, what is courageous, and what is cowardly, and thus, speakers must adapt. Spartans believed it was cowardly to show one's nervousness in battle, while Athenians tolerated such quaking as a fact of life.

Aristotle's references on moral virtue can be gathered into three categories: virtue and vice, virtue as a result of choice, and praise and blame to establish or discredit character. The discussion begins with a description of the various virtues and their corresponding vices. Virtues are incorporated into the doctrine of *to kalon,* which, reflecting the theory of Prodicus, distinguishes what is "honorable," "fine," or "noble" and their opposites: "the means by which one might appear prudent and good [in character] are to be grasped from analysis of the virtues" (1378a6). The reader is directed to the list of nine virtues in book 1: justice, courage, self-control, liberality, magnanimity, magnificence, prudence, wisdom, and gentleness.

The greatest virtues are those that are most useful to others (1366b5–13). For example, justice and courage are the most important because the latter benefits people during war and the former in times of war and peace. However, these descriptions of the virtues are incomplete since they do not include fulsome discussions of magnanimity, prudence, wisdom or gentleness (1366b16ff). One must turn to the *Nicomachean Ethics,* books 2, 3, 4, and 5, to complete the descriptions.

The entire book 5 of the *Ethics,* for example, is concerned with justice in terms of its universal and particular applications. Universal justice corresponds to the laws on the books that Aristotle hopes have been built from his system of virtues. Laws should command and forbid acts as the virtues dictate (1129b13–1130a5). For example, stealing and murder are universally condemned. In terms of universal justice, the just are the lawful and fair, the unjust, the unlawful and unfair. Universal justice is thought to be the greatest of the virtues because it enacts all the virtues toward one's neighbor (1130a6–10).

Particular justice corresponds to fairness and reciprocity in specific cases. Stealing in order to feed one's starving children, in other words, might not be severely punished if the robber took from a plentiful store of food. Thus, practical justice is reciprocity in accordance with proportion. For instance, if a shoemaker and carpenter do work for each other, there should be equal compensation for each person's work (1133a1–1133b30). People act unjustly when they take an excess of what they deserve or assign to another person more than their fair share (1136b13–32).

The rest of the virtues are developed in the same way and sometimes linked to the *pathē,* which further complicates Aristotle's theory. For example, courage is concerned with feelings of fear and confidence and is the mean between the two. Those who exceed in confidence are rash; those who fall short of confidence and are excessively fearful are cowardly (1107a26–1107b22). Temperance is characterized as the virtue that "preserves intelligence" (1140b12). Thus, the *Ethics* significantly enhances the understanding of virtue, and from this vantage point the virtues can be addressed in accordance to character. For example, the commander who faces battle must decide to act courageously; however, that may mean a prudent withdrawal, a dashing charge, or a defensive stance, each of which may be uncourageous in a given context. Because the world is contingent, speakers need to understand universal and ideal virtues, and how these virtues function in the everyday world.

Perhaps that is why Aristotle further deepens his notion of *ethos* by exploring the dimension of choice, the most ontological theme in the *Rhetoric.* In book 3, Aristotle argues that one "certain" way to convey character within a speech is to illustrate effective "deliberate choice" (1417a16ff). Character is based on what deliberate choices have been made; that is, the "end" achieved by the choice illustrates good or bad character (see also 1374a10). In the discussion of forensic arguments, Aristotle reinforces his concern for intent when he claims that even though an action may appear unjust, if not done with deliberate choice, the action is not unjust—unjust actions are done with "deliberate choice." Here apparent intent is elevated over effect.

The discussion of virtue in the *Ethics* reinforces the position that character is derived from deliberate choice. As we have seen, moral virtue is concerned with passions and actions that lie on a continuum of excess to deficit (1106b14). People of moral virtue not only discover the mean or virtue between the two vices but also "choose" to act in accordance with it (1106b36–40). Ethical individuals recognize the vices and the virtue, and have the character to choose virtue. They know how to act virtuously and such knowledge is a kind of wisdom (see below).

The connection between choice and character is further developed in book 2 of the *Ethics,* where a virtuous act reflects virtuous character only when three conditions are satisfied: there is knowledge of the act to be performed; the person chooses to perform the act; and the action proceeds from unchangeable character (1105a25–1105b5). In book 3, Aristotle bolsters the argument that choice and virtuous character are intrinsically related when he takes the existential position that because choice is a result of deliberation, it is a more reliable indication of character than is action (1111b3–6). Additionally, moral character is conveyed through the choice of speaking style, which is expressive of character because there is an appropriate style for each moral state and style conveys impressiveness (1407b26ff).[35] A moral state is an acquired moral principle that has become *a permanent habit of character*.[36] Speakers who choose a style appropriate to their moral state create a sense of character. Therefore, word selection is another way in which moral character is conveyed through choice.

Aristotle also develops the position that praise and blame serve as a means of demonstrating virtuous character. Virtue and vice serve as the foundation for praise and blame because they describe what is honorable and dishonorable (1366b14–15). Aristotle advises speakers to "seize an opportunity in the narration to mention whatever bears on your own virtue or bears on the opponent's wickedness" (1417a5). It is clear that by following this advise, speakers make themselves appear honorable and praiseworthy, and make their opponents appear wicked.

Additionally, in his discussion of enthymemes, Aristotle contends that virtue and vice serve as "relevant facts" that speakers utilize to praise or blame (1396a6–8). That is, virtue and vice serve as premises for enthymemes, thereby sometimes functioning as *topoi* for the development of arguments. Thus, the virtue and vices can be seen as dwelling places for the invention of *ethos* as well as logos. Moreover, Aristotle asserts that praise and blame are important parts of most speeches. Epideictic speeches, for example, have "much amplification" about what is good and advantageous in actions of the person being praised (1417b3). In a speech's epilogue, speakers should show themselves as truthful and their opponents false (1419b1). Thus, praise and blame are based on virtue, and they are an important aspect of *ethos*.

This reading of Aristotle on virtue is congruent with prevailing theory in the Athenian fore-structure. For example, Prodicus's "Choices of Heracles" illustrates the human conflict between choices of virtue and vice. Additionally, the notion of civic virtue and ethical behavior pervades the teachings of Protagoras. Lysias was instrumental in the development of praise and blame as a tool to enhance or devalue character.

Wisdom

Wisdom, the second of the three components of *ethos,* has been subjected to various interpretations over time: good sense, practical wisdom, sagacity, expertise, and intelligence.[37] What is clear from early on in the *Rhetoric* is that a public speaker must know a great deal to be successful. In just one category of knowledge, here is what Aristotle writes: "With regard to the Food Supply: he must know what outlay will meet the needs of his country; what kinds of food are produced at home and what imported; and what articles must be exported or imported. The last he must know in order that agreements and commercial treaties may be made with the countries concerned. There are, indeed, two sorts of state to which he must see that his countrymen give no cause of offense, states stronger than his own, and states with which it is advantageous to trade" (1360a12–18). Imagine all of the other knowledge one must possess on taxes, war, and the like, and one begins to understand what a daunting task achieving *ethos* in terms of expertise is.

Cope's commentary of 1867 on "intelligence" notes that a speaker must be "intelligent" enough to understand the facts of the case and demonstrate the ability to form a judgment.[38] Aristotle informs this assessment Platonically in the *Ethics* when he writes, "Intelligence, this eye of the soul, cannot reach its fully developed state without virtue" (1144b30).[39] As we saw above, there is a correlation between wisdom and virtue; the truly credible speaker must possess both, for wisdom guides one to virtue and is itself a virtue.

In book 6 of the *Ethics,* Aristotle describes the five "chief" intellectual virtues: scientific knowledge, art, practical wisdom, intuitive reason, and philosophic wisdom (1139b14–1141b24). They serve as guides for the prudent advocate and his/her audience. *Nous* is the sensed data that the mind perceives. *Dianoia* is the ability to make connections and associations. While *nous* and *dianoia* serve as foundational wisdom and clearly inspired John Locke's epistemology, humans are also capable of learning *episteme,* or scientific knowledge. *Sophia* is theoretical knowledge that Aristotle attributed to the study of philosophy. *Technē* is knowledge of scientific or artistic principles that allow for such creative activities as composing music or describing the movement of planets. Finally and most important for the speaker is *phronesis* or practical wisdom.

Based on Aristotle's description, practical wisdom is part of *ethos* because it is concerned with intellectual virtue. Practical wisdom is a capacity for discerning in the sphere of action the intermediate point where right conduct lies in any given situation. It is a capacity for applying a rational principle to practical situations that call for choice about action (1143a6–8, 1144a1–10). As noted above, a virtuous act reflects virtuous character only if the act reflects deliberate *choice;* practical wisdom is deliberation that results in the choice (1144a11–25). Therefore, a person must have practical wisdom to make a choice in favor of virtuous character.

In this way *phronesis* combines virtue and knowledge. It is knowledge based on the speaker's experience that guides good practice (*eupraxis*) in a contingent, diverse world. The experience conditions the human to repeat good decisions, to be in the habit of good decision making. Barbara Warnick refers to these as "means of judgment" used to make choices about truth and falsehood, right and wrong, and what action to take.[40] Persuasion results because "fair-minded" people are believed more quickly on general subjects and are believed completely on subjects "where there is not exact knowledge but room for doubt." Moreover, the display of fair-mindedness should come from the speech itself, not from audiences' previously conceived opinions of the speaker. This created sense of character becomes the most controlling factor in persuasion (1356a4).

Reading Aristotle in the context of the Athenian fore-structure and his own *Ethics* leads to the conclusion that the first meaning of wisdom is that speakers must have "knowledge" of the subject they are discussing (1396a4, 1359b7–1360b1). The second interpretation requires an understanding of practical wisdom to which a large section of the *Ethics* is dedicated. Aristotle points to that discussion in his remarks about "practical sense" and "prudence" in the *Rhetoric* (1366b13); furthermore, "the means by which one might appear prudent and good are to be grasped from analysis of the virtues" (1378a7).

Goodwill

In the *Rhetoric,* the passage that follows the listing of the three components of *ethos* states that even though speakers have wisdom and virtue, if they lack goodwill they might withhold the best advice (1378a6). Aristotle then refers the reader to his "discussion of the emotions" (1378a7) for further advice on goodwill. However, the discussions of emotion and friendship do not contain a definition of goodwill. Thus, a hermeneutic reading is required to uncover an understanding of the term that remains vague in rhetorical literature.

Aristotle compares "friendliness," which is treated as an emotion in the *Rhetoric,* with goodwill, even though friendliness is not listed as a component of *ethos*. In the context of the Athenian fore-structure, specifically in Plato's *Gorgias,* the characters Socrates and Callicles use the terms goodwill and friendship in similar ways. Callicles in passages 485E3 and 486A4, and Socrates in passages 487A3, B1, D4, and E5 use the terms *philikos* (friend), *eunoia* (goodwill), *philos* (beloved friend), *hetairotatois* (intimate friend). Thus, if Aristotle's comparison of goodwill and friendliness is conventional, then friendliness is wanting others to receive things that are good and things that produce good solely for the benefit of the other person (1380b2). This definition reenforces another passage in which he defined a friend as one who is active in providing another with the things that are of benefit (1361b16). Friendliness appears consistent with Aristotle's brief description of goodwill: the speaker should share the best advice out of goodwill (1378a6) as one would share the best advice for the sake of a friend.

This notion of goodwill is differentiated from friendship in book 8 of the *Ethics.* Aristotle begins by arguing that those who wish good for others have goodwill if they are not seeking reciprocation. Reciprocated good is done out of a more advanced kind of friendship in which each person recognizes the reciprocal nature of the relationship (1155b33–1156a5). Thus, goodwill is wishing good for others for their sake; it is the beginning of friendship (1167a)[41] but not the same thing as friendship, since friendship requires reciprocation. To put this definition into a political context, Alcibiades would demonstrate goodwill he told an audience to do something that would benefit them but not him; he would demonstrate friendship if he did something for them knowing they would do something for him in return, perhaps making him a general. Thus, for most audiences goodwill generates more credibility than friendship.

The Character of the Audience

Having completed a reading of the three components of *ethos,* I turn to the often ignored yet larger dimension of the persuasive force of *ethos* through the speech and by adapting to the character of the audience. In book 1 of the *Rhetoric,* Aristotle sees the interaction between speech construction and *ethos,* and delivery and *ethos.* Speakers are assessed on the basis of how the speech is constructed, well organized versus poorly organized. Furthermore, a speech evinces *ethos* when it is "spoken in such a way" that the speaker is made "worthy of credence."

Kennedy's translation clarifies that the phrase "spoken in such a way" refers to the *thought and content* of the speech, not the style in which the speech is delivered. Additionally, the term "credence" refers to trustworthiness.[42] Even with these points of clarification, however, the passage is ambiguous about the means to persuade through character. For example, the passage does not explain what "thought and content" lends to a speakers' credence.

Light is shed on these passages when we turn to book 2 of the *Rhetoric,* where Aristotle contends that the three components of *ethos*–wisdom, virtue, and goodwill—are attributes people "trust" outside of logical demonstration (1378a5). The *thought and content* of the speech enhance the three components of *ethos* and make speakers more worthy of trust. For example, practical wisdom (see above) demonstrates fair-mindedness (see above) in two ways: it allows people to construct correct opinions based on knowledge and it deliberates on the means to reach virtue. Thus, the speech itself conveys *ethos* when it enhances the fair-mindedness of the speaker in thought and content, is properly constructed, and well delivered.[43]

The question of adapting one's character to an audience is also part of *ethos*. Aristotle recommended at least two ways to achieve this objective: affiliating with the audiences' political constitution and relating to the "character" of the audience. Advocating actions that preserve the constitution is effective because people believe that preserving their constitution is advantageous (1365b2). The strategy is amplified in book 8 of the *Ethics* in which Aristotle observes that people form communities with a view to a common advantage. Similarly, legislation is made in the interest of the common advantage. Speakers who adapt to the audience's sense of community and legislative needs appear to be in accord with the common advantage. In other words, the speaker should adapt to the communal dwelling place, a narrower dwelling place than the realm of linguistic possibilities.

Aristotle also advises speakers to be familiar with the different characters in the audience—the young, the old, those in the prime of life, those of good birth, of wealth, and those who have power (1388b1–1391b6). To aid speakers, he describes each group. Aristotle's penchant for continua upon which the mean is the best or happiest place once again provides coherence and proportion to his theory. The young are impetuous and "inclined to do whatever they desire." The old act in the opposite manner of the young; they are cynical, cowardly, and reticent to change. Those in the prime of life are the mean between the young and old; they make realistic judgments and direct their lives by what is fine and advantageous. Good birth refers to excellence of family; those of good birth tend to be ambitious and contemptuous. People of wealth are insolent, arrogant, and pretentious; the "newly rich" carry vices to a worse degree than those of old wealth because of a lack of experience and educational tradition. Those with the character of power are similar to the wealthy but are better because they are more earnest. Speakers should have knowledge of these different characters and make choices in their speeches that identify with the particular audience (1390a16). In fact, character can be demonstrated through style because there is an appropriate style for each *genus*—boy, man, old man, and so on (1408a6). For example, a "rustic" person and an "educated" person will not say the same thing nor speak in the same way (1408a7), nor will they be appreciated the same by different audiences.

Thus, an audience has character or characters; it has an *ethos* of its own to which speakers must attend. In adapting, they enhance their own *ethos;* if they fail to adapt, their *ethos* will be diminished. Beyond that, however, speakers can move the audience to conform to the speaker's *ethos* and modify the audience's habits and values. Such identification with a leader is difficult to achieve, but when accomplished, is the most powerful kind of persuasion.

The Pervasive Nature of Ethos

This reading leads to the conclusion that *ethos* is pervasive in the speaking event. The *Rhetoric* advises speakers to establish character in the proem, epilogue, and narrative of a speech liberating it from the limits placed on it in other handbooks.

Aristotle's treatment of the narrative was a major advancement for the theory of *ethos* because he recommends that speakers utilize the narrative to "mention whatever bears on your own virtue . . . or bears on the opponent's wickedness" (1417a5). Thus, a theory of anti-*ethos* springs from his theory of *ethos* building. *Additionally,* the narration ought to be indicative of character and ought to be dispersed throughout the speech thereby dispersing *ethos* and anti-*ethos* along the way.

The pervasive nature of *ethos* is also apparent in Aristotle's discussion of the arguments within a speech. For instance, he distinguishes between maxims and enthymemes as tools for demonstrating character. Maxims make general assertions about preferences; thus maxims that are "morally good" make the speaker seem to have good character (1395b16). Maxims should be used in both narration and proof (1418a8–9). They are a "great contribution" to speeches because people are pleased when their opinions about particular instances are incorporated into the general statements by speakers (1395b15). Thus, the *topoi* for enthymemes are not only a source of rhetorical arguments but, when linked to the audience through maxims, generate *ethos.* To put it another way, logical demonstrations, though within the realm of linguistic possibilities, have neither *ethos* nor moral purpose per se and thus cannot be used to demonstrate character (1418a8). However, enthymemes may have premises based on common virtues or praise and blame that also lie within the realm of linguistic possibilities. These are more likely to evince *ethos* not only because they deal with virtuous character but also because they drawn on commonly held premises of the community (1396b16). Thus, given the choice, speakers should prefer enthymemes over demonstrations. In short, *ethos* is not some category to be filled at a set point in a speech; it permeates the speech as it is mingled with other proofs, most notably word choice, enthymemes and narration.

A more informed reading is possible if the context of a text and its creator is taken into account. In Aristotle's case, the Athenian fore-structure, its realm of linguistic possibilities, Aristotle's debt to Plato, the Sophists, especially Isocrates, the pre-Socratics, and the *Ethics* create the context for this close reading. This application enhances the understanding of *ethos* in at least three ways: it provides a contextualized understanding of Aristotle's notion of *ethos,* it reinforces the ontological nature of *ethos,* and it helps resolve conflicts in commentaries on *ethos.*

First, the reading suggests that the definitions of the virtues listed in the *Rhetoric* are enhanced in the *Nicomachean Ethics.* The *Ethics* explains how moral virtue reflects choice, moral character, and how it can be used for praise and blame. The same kind of deep structuring was found for goodwill, which was defined as unreciprocated "wishing-well" for others for their own sake. Furthermore, the *Rhetoric* posits a two-tiered definition of practical wisdom. While speakers should have the knowledge to form correct opinions and adapt to their audience, Aristotle also intended speakers to have the practical wisdom to make decisions based on sound deliberation; deliberation is sound when it proceeds according to the dictates of rational principle (*logos* of the *phronimos*), which is purely intellectual virtue. Choice, on the other hand, is moral when it originates in a settled disposition (character) that is conditioned by habit to desire in accordance with the dictates of principle (*Ethics,* book 2, 1–6; book 7, 1–2, 5, 7, 9, and 13). The two-tiered definition addresses Pross's observation that wisdom as a component of *ethos* can be translated as knowledge and practical wisdom;[44] both are correct interpretations, depending on context of the passages being read.

Furthermore, Aristotle's statement in the *Rhetoric* that speakers should convey character—an ambiguous, undefined phrase—can be linked to four, not just three, components of *ethos* to reveal that he meant to include prior reputation along with practical wisdom, virtue, and goodwill. He contends that the style of a speech should be appropriate for the situation and the subject matter, and reflect the moral state and character of the audience. Furthermore, "this aptness of language is one thing that makes people believe in the truth of your story" (1408a20). *Ethos* is also an integral part of narration, amplification, arrangement, word choice, and logo*s* inclusive of maxims and premises of enthymemes. Aristotle claims that narration, for example, can reveal character depending on how the story is told. With regard to amplification, if an audience does not believe that something is true, the speaker must expand on the causes of it to convert the audience to that belief. That is why Aristotle's notion of *ethos* is pervasive throughout the speech. Second, this reading reveals the ontological nature of *ethos* in four ways: audience adaptation, informed decision making, choice, and potentiality. "Choice" emerged as a controlling ontological factor of *ethos.* For example, choice in behavior demonstrates character; credible people choose to act in accordance with virtue instead of vice and choose to act based on deliberation rather than rashness. Aristotle writes, "Virtue, then, is a state that decides, using a mean that is relative to us, which is defined by reference to reason" (1107a).

Another way *ethos* is ontological is that speakers are persuasive through *ethos* by demonstrating character through choice. That is, *ethos* reveals the speaker's habit when it comes to making decisions; the speaker's history of decision making is a history of individual enactment.[45] In this way, *ethos* is an ontological structure that leaves a trail that reveals moral fiber and standing. Since audience adaptation is based on choice and speakers make choices within the speech, the entire speech conveys character when speakers choose a style that is either well- or ill-suited to the content and situation.

Ethos is also ontological because it is a moral enterprise; practical wisdom, virtue, and goodwill, the three components of *ethos,* aim toward a moral end (a *telos*). Practical wisdom is the capacity to base decisions on sound deliberation; virtuous action is a rejection of the vices; and goodwill wishes well for others for their own sake. The teleological dimensions of *ethos* lead the speaker toward a higher potential, one capable of advancing a cause, uplifting an audience, and guiding a society aright, one that can improve the mutual dwelling place. The *Ethics* supports this position when it contends that the end of an individual's life should aim toward a common good.

This reading can be used to resolve contradictory interpretations of the *Rhetoric* mentioned at the outset of this study. As we have seen, Schutrumpf and Wisse contend that the *Rhetoric* and *Ethics* are so dissimilar in thought that they should not be compared. Oates and Hunt believe the *Rhetoric* to be amoral. My reading, however, indicates that the two books are interconnected, which vindicates the position of Kennedy, Farrell, and Grimaldi. Furthermore, since Aristotle wrote that rhetoric is an offshoot of dialectic and ethical studies (1356a7), the ethical aspect of rhetoric stems from the speaker's intent (1355a). Thus, Johnstone's contention that "Aristotle's theory of rhetoric is grounded in and guided by the ethical principles developed in his moral theory" seems reasonable.[46]

My reading also supports the majority view on *phronesis.* In the *Ethics,* Aristotle defines *phronesis* as a guide for behavior. As John Herman Randall notes, practical wisdom is deliberation toward moral choice of action.[47] Speakers must posses ethical intelligence or practical wisdom in addition to technical skill. As Self argues, "It is only when practical wisdom is applied to rhetoric that we witness the ideal case in which the name 'rhetorician' denotes excellence both of artistry and purpose."[48] G. R. Mure puts it this way: "Practical wisdom . . . is not something added to, or fused with, virtuous character, but [is] its completion and culmination."[49]

Thus, this hermeneutic reading indicates that the *Rhetoric* and *Ethics* are inextricably bound and both are essential to understanding Aristotle's rhetorical theory. Such a reading uncovers the role Aristotle's fore-structure played in his construction of *ethos* inclusive of the magic nature of the number three in Greek thinking and that society's penchant for proportion and symmetry. It demonstrates that he assumed the ancient notion of *ethos* as dwelling place, advanced it, and took for granted that prior reputation among the demos was important to credibility. Aside from broadening the intertextual understanding of *ethos,* this reading demonstrates the importance of the concept in terms of pervasiveness in the speech text and its audience. Thus, I conclude that for Aristotle *ethos* dwells pervasively in the rhetorical situation.

Notes

1. Michael Hyde and Craig R. Smith, "Hermeneutics and Rhetoric: A Seen but Unobserved Relationship," *Quarterly Journal of Speech* 65 (1979): 347–63.

2. Craig R. Smith and Michael J. Hyde, "Rethinking 'the Public': The Role of Emotion in Being-with-Others," *Quarterly Journal of Speech* 77 (1991): 446–66. Michael Hyde and Craig R. Smith, "Heidegger and Aristotle on Emotion: Questions of Time and Space," in *The Critical Turn: Rhetoric and Philosophy in Postmodern Discourse,* ed. Ian Angus and Lenore Langsdorf (Carbondale: Southern Illinois University Press, 1992), 68–99.

3. I use *Rhetoric and Poetics of Aristotle,* trans. W. Rhys Roberts (New York: Modern Library, 1957), along with George Kennedy's *Aristotle on Rhetoric: A Theory of Civic Discourse* (Oxford: Oxford University Press, 1991) to guide my reading. Furthermore, throughout the text, when quoting from the *Rhetoric* or the *Nicomachean Ethics,* I insert the universal numbering system, generally 1300 and 1400 numbers for the *Rhetoric* and 1000 and 1100 numbers for the *Ethics.*

4. William W. Fortenbaugh, "Persuasion through Character and the Composition of Aristotle's *Rhetoric,*" *Rheinisches Museum* 134 (1991): 152–56; William W. Fortenbaugh, "Aristotle on Persuasion through Character," *Journal of History and Rhetoric* 10 (1992): 207–44; Christopher L. Johnstone, "An Aristotelian Trilogy: Ethics, Rhetoric, Politics, and the Search for Moral Truth," *Philosophy and Rhetoric* 13 (1980): 1–24; Lois S. Self, "Rhetoric and *Phronesis:* The Aristotelian Ideal," *Philosophy and Rhetoric* 12 (1979): 130–45; W. M. Sattler, "Conceptions of *Ethos* in Ancient Rhetoric," *Communication Monographs* 14 (1947): 55–65; E. L. Pross, "Practical Implications of the Aristotelian Concept of *Ethos,*" *Southern Communication Journal* 17 (1952): 257–64.

5. Paul I. Rosenthal, "The Concept of *Ethos* and the Structure of Persuasion," *Communication Monographs* 33 (1966): 114–26; "Specificity, Verifiability, and Message Credibility," *Quarterly Journal of Speech* 57 (1971): 393–401.

6. McCroskey's work is a corrective on his earlier research, which eliminated goodwill as part of *ethos.* See James C. McCroskey, symposium conducted at California State University, Long Beach, February, 1996; "Special Reports: Scales for Measurements of *Ethos,*" *Communication Monographs* 33 (1966): 65–72; James C. McCroskey and T. J. Young, "*Ethos* and Credibility: The Construct and Its Measurement after Three Decades," *Communication Studies* 32 (1981): 24–34.

7. He is referring to the pre-Socratic Heraclitus of Ephesus, who advised that we could not stick our foot in the same river twice. Heraclitus believed change was reality and that the logos brought things together in their unity. In a world of change, perhaps a dwelling place would be quite welcome.

8. Rhetoric's place in the law courts and the assembly are discussed briefly at the beginning of the *Rhetoric* at 1355a1–4. In such places, *ethos* is a necessary proof (strategy) because people are not educated enough to decide issues based on their knowledge (1355a25).

9. W. D. Ross, *Aristotle* (New York: Charles Scribner's Sons, 1924), 271.

10. Edward M. Cope, *An Introduction to Aristotle's Rhetoric: With Analysis Notes and Appendices* (London: Macmillan, 1867), 109–13.

11. V. E. Simrell, "Mere Rhetoric," *Quarterly Journal of Speech,* 14 (1928): 360.

12. B. A. G. Fuller, *History of Greek Philosophy: Aristotle* (New York: Henry Holt, 1931), 3:294.

13. Everett L. Hunt, "Plato and Aristotle on Rhetoric and Rhetoricians," in *Historical Studies of Rhetoric and Rhetoricians,* ed. R. F. Howes (Ithaca, N.Y.: Cornell University Press, 1961), 56.

14. Whitney J. Oates, *Aristotle and the Problem of Value* (Princeton, N.J.: Princeton University Press, 1963), 335.

15. William M. A. Grimaldi, *Studies in the Philosophy of Aristotle's Rhetoric* (Wiesbaden: Franz Steiner Verlag GMBH, 1972), 21.

16. Ibid., 5.

17. Ibid., 2.

18. Thomas B. Farrell, *Norms of Rhetorical Culture* (New Haven, Conn.: Yale University Press, 1993).

19. M. M. McCabe, "Arguments in Context: Aristotle's Defense of Rhetoric," in *Aristotle's Rhetoric: Philosophic Essays,* ed. D. J. Furley and A. Nehamas (Princeton, N.J.: Princeton University Press, 1994); Craig R. Smith, "Criticism as Rational: An Argument from Disciplinary Integrity," in *Argumentation and Values: Proceedings of the Argumentation Conference at Alta* (Salt Lake City: University of Utah Press, 1995): 456–60.

20. E. Schutrumpf, *Die Bedeutung des wortes ethos in der Poetic des Aristotles* (Munich: Beck, 1970); E. Schutrumpf, "The Meaning of *Ethos* in the *Poetics*—A Reply," *Hermes* 115 (1987): 175–81.

21. As cited in G. F. Held, "The Meaning of *Ethos* in the *Poetics*," *Hermes* 113 (1985): 280.

22. Held, "Meaning of *Ethos*," 280, 286–89.

23. Schutrumpf, "Meaning of *Ethos*," 180.

24. Jakob Wisse, *Ethos and Pathos from Aristotle to Cicero* (Amsterdam: Adolf M. Hakkert, 1989), 30.

25. Wisse, *Ethos and Pathos,* 31.

26. Hyde and Smith, "Hermeneutics and Rhetoric," 350.

27. Grimaldi, *Studies,* 5.

28. Farrell, *Norms of Rhetorical Culture,* 48.

29. Aristotle's first work on rhetoric, the dialogue *Gryllus,* makes arguments that directly conflict with the *Rhetoric.* Aristotle's *Gryllus* is most likely a direct reflection of Plato's arguments against rhetoric, which Aristotle later rejects.

30. This is also true of Aristotle's *Nicomachean Ethics,* trans. Terence Irwin (Indianapolis: Hackett, 1985), xiii.

31. Since the *Eudemian Ethics* is incorporated into the *Nicomachean Ethics,* scholars generally recognize the latter as Aristotle's most thorough and refined work on ethics. See, for example, Irwin, *Nicomachean Ethics,* xxi.

32. See 1356a4ff. In his commentary, Kennedy makes of much the fact that Aristotle claims in these lines that *ethos* is generated in the speech by the speaker. Rhys Roberts's translation, which is used for reference in this study, translates the lines this way: "Persuasion is achieved by the speaker's personal character when the speech is so spoken as to make us think him credible. We believe good men more fully and more readily than others."

33. Aristotle's comparing humans to the herd predates the same sentiment expressed by such existentialists as Søren Kierkegaard and Martin Heidegger.

34. Later, at 1177b27–1178a3, Aristotle argues that the "divine element" in humans allows them to rise above the material and to become proactively immortal. Again reflecting Plato, he writes "for however much this element may lack in substance, by much more it surpasses everything in power and value."

35. Aristotle is specifically referring to the way things "ought" to be said before an audience. See 1403b15.

36. Aristotle put it this way in the *Ethics:* "Virtue of character results from habit; hence its name 'ethical,' slightly varied from '*ethos*'" (1103a16).

37. Pross, "Practical Implications," 259.

38. Cope, *Introduction to Aristotle's Rhetoric,* 109.

39. Conversely, "full virtue cannot be acquired without intelligence" (1144b17). See also 1178a20, where "intelligence is yoked together with virtue or character."

40. Barbara Warnick, "Judgment, Probability, and Aristotle's *Rhetoric,*" *Quarterly Journal of Speech* 75 (1989): 299.

41. Book 9 of the *Ethics* reiterates and slightly enhances the distinction between friendship and goodwill. Aristotle notes that goodwill is a "friendly sort of relation" but is not friendship. The difference is that one may have goodwill toward another *without* the latter's knowing, a definition that does not meet the condition of friendship. In other words, we can express goodwill toward those we do not know, but we can not be friendly with them. However, goodwill can originate in friendship "in the way that pleasure coming through sight originates erotic passion" (1167a5).

42. Kennedy, *Aristotle on Rhetoric,* 38.

43. Aristotle's holistic notion of *ethos* significantly influenced Roman rhetorical theory. In *The Arts of Poetry,* Horace concurred: "[I]f a speaker's words are out of gear with his fortunes, all Rome, horse and foot, will guffaw." Allan H. Gilbert, *Literary Criticism: Plato to Dryden* (Detroit: Wayne State University Press, 1962), 131.

44. Pross, "Practical Implications," 259.

45. Jean-Paul Sartre would refer to this historic enactment as the essence of a being.

46. Johnstone, "Aristotelian Trilogy," 11.

47. John H. Randall Jr., *Aristotle* (New York: Columbia University Press, 1960), 268–69.

48. Self, "Rhetoric and *Phronesis,*" 143.

49. G. R. Mure, *Aristotle* (New York: Oxford University Press, 1964), 143.

The *Ethos* of Invention

The Dialogue of Ethics and Aesthetics in Kenneth Burke and Mikhail Bakhtin

Margaret D. Zulick

Ethos is a powerful but ambiguous term. Depending on the source, it can refer to ethics, to argument, or to personal or collective identity. Heidegger points us to the esoteric fact that it once meant "animal lair" or "haunt," from which, in his reading of a passage from Heraclitus, he derives first "abode," next "dwelling place," and thence that which "contains and preserves the advent to what belongs to man in his essence."[1] To the philologist, however, there is a rather stark contrast between the archaic meaning of "haunt" or the habitual territory of a wild animal to the late classical "character." Charles Chamberlain's etymological study reveals, however, an intermediate, metaphorical application of the term to mean "custom" or "habit."[2] One can perhaps see how the name has traveled from "lair" to "habit" (via "habitat") to "character" in the sense of the constellation of habits of thought, manners, and reputation that constitutes a rhetorical subject. For my purposes, therefore, *ethos* represents "dwelling place" as the locus of convergence of ethics and aesthetics in the subjective act of invention. In other words, this chapter is about the *ethos* of invention, understood as neither a solely linguistic phenomenon nor a solely psychological phenomenon, but as the point of intersection between language and subject where invention occurs.

There is a story from Thomas Merton's *Way of Chuang Tzu* about a master carpenter who, when asked to create a chair for the emperor, first went out into the forest and searched until he came to a tree that had the chair inside it.[3] They say about Mozart that he heard the entire score of his compositions in his head and composing was merely a process of writing it down, that he died in the act of dictating his Requiem to one of his students, and only because he could not dictate it fast enough is his Requiem incomplete. Mozart died with the Requiem complete in his mind, but unuttered.

They say the same of Beethoven. He must have imagined his music as a whole fabric, complete, since his deafness did not put cease to his utterance but only made it somewhat harder to sing; passages of the Ninth Symphony and the *Missa*

Solemnis are not meant for any mortal voice, let alone that of a poor half-gifted chorister.

In a recent interview, *Lord of the Rings* director Peter Jackson said,

> When we're first starting to write the screenplay, I've got a good ability to imagine the film in my head. . . . Even the very first page of the script, as we do it, I can start to imagine the camera angles, the music. I can start to feel how the film's coming together. And I sort of have this imaginary film starting to be put together. And that's right back at the beginning. . . . And then what happens during the course of the movie is that this—this film that's playing in my head always gets modified because as you design the sets, you know, then the sets that we've designed replace the ones that I originally sort of imagined. And then as the actors come on board, their faces put [unintelligible] to the characters I imagined.[4]

There is an often-repeated theme in stories of invention that the inventor experiences the act of invention as one of *perceiving* something new as if it already existed and craft was needed to bring it out in expressed form. Let this serve to illustrate the principle that pattern invention and pattern recognition—cognition and re-cognition—are part of the same process in the mind. This is what Kenneth Burke intimates in his discussions of the "psychology of form"—that the inventor and the audience of any formal expression share in its production at the formal level as well as at the social level. Perhaps this also underlies Bakhtin's quantum theory of language, the roots of dialogue in the indivisible structure of the utterance. One cannot recognize an utterance without at once aligning oneself with its dialogic structure. The single process of pattern perception and pattern creation must underlie both ethics and aesthetics, since both are ways of ordering chaos. That is, when an inventor is in that posture of invention, at the moment the mind is directed toward the thing made in the act of making, the various materials out of which an inventive mind constructs an artifact must be arranged in a unique but convergent whole. Rhetoricians have continuously asserted that that capacity, to take the materials of rhetorical art and produce a harmonious whole, cannot be taught and to some extent cannot be predicted. This is true not only for works of genius but also for routine creation in its moments of felicity.

Thus, the customary line between ethics and aesthetics disappears when we begin with their convergence in the *ethos* of invention. From this standpoint, ethics and aesthetics appear not as mutually opposed categories but as coordinate acts of imagination that spring from the same inventive source in the social mind. Yet philosophical aesthetics has been primarily about reception, about the passive appreciation of beauty or spectacle. As such it is divorced from ethical action as well as invention itself. Makers of the beautiful, it seems, do not possess an aesthetic in the act of creation; the works of great artists are born de novo, not invented out of preexisting material.

In this essay, I cannot trace in full the philosophical divorce of ethics and aesthetics. I wish instead to "prove" their marriage—in the sense of testing its mettle, of trying out the possibility of a reunion of ethics and aesthetics. The proving will take the form of a comparison of two theorists who are touchstones for me, Kenneth Burke and Mikhail Bakhtin. It is my thesis that in contradistinction to the general flow of philosophical tradition, they are alike recalcitrant with respect to the divorce of ethics and aesthetics. Instead, each constructs a world of theory in which ethics and aesthetics are coordinate acts of a symbolic imagination that precedes and generates both. In the process, I also hope to show that the convergence of ethics and aesthetics in the *ethos* of invention is at the heart of rhetorical practice; thus rhetorical theory is diminished by the attempt to keep them separate and restored in their reunion.

The Traditional Opposition of Ethics and Aesthetics

Even a superficial glance through the literature shows that since its inception, aesthetic theory has been founded in meditation on the appearance of beauty. Its standpoint is not with the invention of beauty, form, and variety but with its reception. The opposition of the good and the beautiful goes back at least as far as Plato. His famous discussion of painters and poets as producers of illusion turns not upon the imagination of the artist but upon the sensory appearance of the finished work to the observer or listener.[5] This is the only way in which his opposition can make sense, for it derives from the idea that artists, in merely representing the superficial appearance of goodness, its color and shape rather than its substance, miss the ethical mark and merely reproduce undisciplined emotions. The focus on representation in the finished work does not query, in this context, the sources of artistic invention.

In Plato's train, Plotinus focuses on the apperception of beauty, taking most of his examples from the natural world. In both Plato and Plotinus, when the good is juxtaposed to the beautiful it becomes aestheticized in the passive sense as a kind of transfigured desire.[6]

Hume's essay "Of the Standard of Taste" also proceeds from perception rather than invention. His opposition between sentiment and understanding oddly resembles Aristotle's epistemological distinction between rhetoric and dialectic:

> All sentiment is right; because sentiment has a reference to nothing beyond itself, and is always real, wherever one is conscious of it. But all determinations of the understanding are not right; because they have a reference to something beyond themselves, to wit, real matter of fact; and are not always conformable to that standard. Among a thousand different opinions which different men may entertain of the same subject, there is one, and but one, that is just and true: and the only difficulty is to fix and ascertain it. On the contrary, a thousand different sentiments, excited by the same object, are all right; because no sentiment represents what is really in the object.[7]

For Hume, the parallel between aesthetics and other forms of intellect lies in judgment, and by this he means primarily the judgment of the audience: "The object of eloquence is to persuade, of history to instruct, of poetry to please, by means of the passions and the imagination. These ends we must carry constantly in our view when we peruse any performance; and we must be able to judge how far the means employed are adapted to their respective purposes."[8]

The divorce, which is implicit at best in Plato, achieves complete separation in Kant. In *The Critique of Judgment,* the judgment of taste is explicitly noncognitive, and demands the absence of any interest—it must remain "a pure disinterested satisfaction." On the other hand, the good is always "bound up with interest."[9]

Because rhetorical invention, like all forms of artistic invention, is a social act, it must always encompass ethical as well as aesthetic enactments of form. Thus the characterization of the artist as genius in Nietzsche and Schopenhauer is no remedy but is instead the eventual outcome of the divorce between aesthetics and the act of invention. Because there is no rooting of genius in the ordinary production of journeyman art, the genius appears as if from behind a curtain, an unearthly and disconnected being. Only someone who has immersed himself as a listener in the sounds of music but knows nothing of its material recalcitrance in the form of the physical properties of sounds and the effort required to produce them, can say, as Schopenhauer does, that "music, since it passes over the Ideas, is also quite independent of the phenomenal world, positively ignores it, and, to a certain extent, could still exist if there were no world at all."[10]

It is curious that in many of these classic texts, ethics and aesthetics are consistently dealt with in tandem only to be explicitly opposed to one another or treated as parallel in some sense but in different orders of cognition whose common roots are left unexposed. The point to be made here is that if aesthetics were not from the outset passive, cast from the point of view of an observer rather than a creator of form, the opposition would lose its cogency. Ethical and aesthetic orders, seen from the "dwelling place" of invention, are integral to the same creative act. Any act of invention initiates a momentary ordering of chaos, generating out of the material of chaos ethical and aesthetic forms. Cicero hit on the nexus of ethics and aesthetics in the voice of Crassus: having just delivered his description of all that is required of the perfect orator, Crassus is asked what more is needed. He states, "What else do you suppose . . . but enthusiasm and something like the passion of love?" ("Quid censes, inquit, Cotta, nisi studium, et ardorem quemdam amoris?") For, he continues, assuredly endeavors to reach any goal avail nothing unless you have learned what it is that leads you to the end at which you aim.[11] Surely here we have another way entirely of looking at the marriage of ethics and aesthetics, for when we contemplate this passage it is hard to see where the one leaves off and the other begins. Is the perfect orator an aesthetic that must be set in motion by an ethical impulse? Or is the decorum of the perfect orator a communitarian ethic that must be set in motion, moved to act, by an aesthetic desire?

Just as surely, whichever way we look at it, the art of rhetoric lies directly on the fault line between ethics and aesthetics. For no rhetoric can approach the sublime except by a unique and powerful aesthetic expression of an ethical imperative. In moments of the sublime, the aesthetics of rhetoric gives voice to its ethical imperative and the ethics of rhetoric empowers its aesthetic voice.

In the remainder of this chapter we will look at two theorists who strike at this fault line in very similar ways, in the hope of constructing an alternate picture of the dialogue of ethics and aesthetics.

The Dialogue of Ethics and Aesthetics in Burke

Kenneth Burke's fistful of critical perspectives seems calculated to demonstrate that there is no such thing as a pure work of genius, de novo or ex nihilo, standing apart from all human motives. In every iteration, he chips away at the divorce of ethics and aesthetics. The word "act" itself is pregnant with this implication, since in Burke it is always used in contradistinction to motion. At some level, Burke's use of the term "motive" itself can only be construed in a double sense: as the ethical impulse or interest underlying discourse and as "motif," the thematic threads that run through discourse and generate its symbolic fabric.

Several other global terms in Burke share this dual nature, having both a formal and a social or ethical aspect: for instance, form itself, identification, and symbol. Each of these terms is structurally dialogic (to import an expression from Bakhtin). Each serves Burke's recalcitrance to two intellectual movements of his age, scientism, on the social side, and on the aesthetic side, objectivism or the New Criticism.

The rhetorical turn for Burke is tied to his move toward a psychological understanding of form.[12] When Burke asserts that form is "the psychology of the audience,"[13] he works into his definition of form the idea that it operates as a kind of ligature between the work and its audience; thus the creation of form in the work, and the recognition of form in the mind of the audience, is *the same creative act*. This insight into the full dialogics of form is exactly parallel to Bakhtin's insight into the dialogic structure of the monad of communication, the utterance.

The nexus of ethics and aesthetics in Burke is perhaps most apparent in the global term *identification*. Identification is both transitive and intransitive—in the transitive, formal sense it means to put a name to something, in the intransitive, social sense it means to identify *with*. Burke uses the term in both senses, but the two senses are not merely interchangeable; rather, the one invokes the other. Consider his intricate reading of Milton's *Samson Agonistes* in the beginning of "The Range of Rhetoric": the identification of the Puritans with the Israelites, of Milton with Samson. Yet these do not reduce to a purely psychological reading. "We do not mean to suggest that the figure of Samson in Milton's poem is to be interpreted purely as a 'rationalization,' in the psychoanalytic sense," Burke notes. "We are taking the poem at its face value. If two statements, for instance, one humorous and the other humorless, are found to contain the same animus against someone, we are not thereby justified in treating them as the same in their motivational core. For the humorless statement may *foretell* homicide, and the humorous one may be the very thing that *forestalls* homicide."[14]

In other words, the calculus of identification is not external, but is embedded in the form of the work itself. Therefore, the work not only springs from this identification but also reproduces it. So that when Burke says a bit later that "the *killing* of something is the *changing* of it, and the statement of the thing's nature before and after the change is an *identifying* of it,"[15] he is scribing a path from one kind of transformation to the other—once identification is engaged, the formal transformation elicits psycho-social transformation, and this is intrinsic to the workings of form.

Finally, the symbol itself is also composed as a ligature between the formal and the social—very simply in the notion of the symbol as the "verbal parallel to a pattern of experience."[16] But understanding this simple concept in its full depth is key to understanding Burke's thought: the notion that form and symbol (as significant form) not only carry and reproduce motivation but also sustain a pure formal motive of their own—the motive to carry a form to its completion. This is the ground of Burke's version of *entelechy,* which turns "art for art's sake" on its head.[17] For Burke, even when all prior and posterior motives to a work are bracketed, the entelechial motive that wills its own completion remains.

Burke occasionally addresses the issue of ethics and aesthetics directly. In "The Nature of Art under Capitalism," an early essay included in *Philosophy of Literary Form,* he reveals the ethical basis of his objections to both scientism and objectivism. On the one hand, "'pure' art tends to promote a state of acceptance" of whatever moral code is in the ascendant, namely, capitalism. Under a morally faulty system such as capitalism, "art cannot safely confine itself to merely *using* the values which arise out of a given social texture and integrating their conflicts. . . . It must have a definite hortatory function . . . it must be partially *forensic.*"[18] However, Burke ends the brief essay with a devastating caveat for socialist art. "It is questionable as propaganda," he says, "since it shows us so little of the qualities in mankind worth saving."[19] Those qualities are ensconced in action, not motion. A scientistic approach that considers art only for its political or social use loses not only the value but also the character of art. Burke's brand of materialism sought to preserve in dramatism some of the quality of the lost *mysterium,* by translating the Word to words. In a fanciful moment, I might call his position "magic humanism."

Burke addresses Kantian ethics explicitly in his essay "A Dramatistic View of the Origins of Language." His main purpose with Kant is to show the origins of language in the negative and the origins of the negative in language: "[*T*]*he essential distinction between the verbal and the nonverbal is in the fact that language adds the peculiar possibility of the Negative.*"[20] This purpose is somewhat tangential to any interest in ethics as such. In the process of his discussion, he notes Kant's opposition between the law and the senses in *Critique of Practical Reason.*[21] But by locating the negative in language, which seems to mediate between the physical and the metaphysical (the metaphysical being limited in Burke to the "more than verbal"),[22] Burke induces this opposition to cross back over itself, showing on the side of philosophy that "animalistic" positives like appetite can be treated "as an incipient manifestation of ideal love" and that, conversely, the poet can take an ethical idea and express it "in terms of sensory images."[23] In sum, he says, "we hope to have so treated the distinction between 'the senses' and 'the law' that the reader both sees how it looks when reduced to the distinction between linguistic and nonlinguistic motives, and sees that such reduction by no means imposes impoverishment or distortion upon the analysis of human motives."[24]

This brief discussion of the dual ethical and aesthetic aspect of Burke's analysis of form, motive, identification and symbol should show us that his dramatism is aimed directly at confusing the clean distinction between aesthetics and ethics, and that his own motive in so doing shares in the same dual nature. David Cratis Williams underscores both these points in his introduction to *Unending Conversations: New Writings by and about Kenneth Burke.* Williams argues that "Burke's trilogy on motives had an explicit . . . humanitarian motive of its own: he hoped to foster analytic, critical, and ultimately philosophical appreciation of the resources and nature of language that, in Burke's understanding, culminated too frequently in conflict, scapegoating, and war."[25] Williams also quotes Burke in a rare moment of clarity about his own work. In an addendum to the third edition of *Counter-Statement,* Burke explains that his prospective *Symbolic of Motives* would concern "the study of individual identity," as opposed to "universal relationships" (*Grammar of Motives*) and "partisan relationships" (*Rhetoric of Motives*). He then elaborates: "This third volume would include both poetic and ethical dimensions, inasmuch as both the character of the individual poem and the character of the individual person embody 'equations' (explicit or implicit assumptions as to what fits with what)."[26] Thus the locus, the "dwelling place," of the convergence of ethics and aesthetics lies for Burke in the intersections or "equations" between language and subject that generate the *ethos* of invention. And in making such a statement, he was paralleled, unbeknown to himself and halfway around the world, by the project of Mikhail Bakhtin.

The Dialogue of Ethics and Aesthetics in Bakhtin

Kenneth Burke and Mikhail Bakhtin, although unknown to each other, were both well read in the philosophy and social theory coming out of late-nineteenth-century Germany. Both were profoundly shaped by Kant and Nietzsche, and both had absorbed at second hand the psychology of Wilhelm Wundt.[27] Bakhtin's early works are thoroughly neo-Kantian; he was particularly influenced by the project of Hermann Cohen at Marburg, yet his writings in *Toward a Philosophy of the Act*,[28] especially "Author and Hero in Aesthetic Activity," take a unique turn on the problem of subjectivity, expressed in the concept of *outsideness* as discussed below. Another important influence on both theorists was Henri Bergson. Burke credits Bergson with "opening his eyes" to one of his first psycho-linguistic principles, the "Idea of the Nothing."[29] Bakhtin discusses Bergson as "the most significant" exponent of *Lebensphilosophie* and seems to endorse, with certain reservations, his emphasis on process and subject.[30] Further exploration of these and other such intersections might suggest a common thread of vitalism in both Burke and Bakhtin. This vitalist leaning can be further supported by noting how both theorists opposed, yet also borrowed from, the principal formalisms of their place and time. If Burke opposed objectivism, Bakhtin both opposed and drew from structuralism and Russian formalism.

Bakhtin's insistence on the coordination of ethics and aesthetics is explicit and runs throughout his corpus. It is most prominent in his early writings. A remarkable early essay, "Art and Answerability," from 1919, captures his lifelong concern. In it, he initiates a central idea: "the three domains of human culture—science, art, and life—gain unity only in the individual person who integrates them into his own unity."[31] If Burke described a dialogue between form and society by showing that form is motive and motive is form, Bakhtin introduces the person as an intersection of languages—not in the sense of being determined by language as social code, but in the sense of a consciousness brought into self-awareness by other consciousnesses, created by language but also creating it. Without this intersection in the individual consciousness, "art is too self-confident, audaciously self-confident, and too high-flown, for it is in no way bound to answer for life."[32] On the other hand, life, unable to catch up with "high" art, lapses into vulgarity. It is this focus, on the individuum as constructed dialogically, that enables once again a shift from the aesthetic of the viewer to that of the inventor/enactor of language.

Bakhtin elaborates on this collusion of ethics and aesthetics in his construction of the novelistic "hero." Bakhtin's focus on language mediates between the domain of ethics and that of aesthetics, rendering the psycho-social individual and the literary character or hero virtually interchangeable. "Aesthetic contemplation and ethical action cannot abstract from the concrete uniqueness of the place in being that is occupied by the *subiectum* of ethical action as well as by the *subiectum* of artistic contemplation."[33] What Bakhtin means by this, in part, is what he terms "excess of seeing": each individual is irreplaceable and unique, for each occupies a unique point in the intersection of language and circumstance. While individual cognition, being indeterminate, can surmount this concreteness, it by that very fact cannot perceive itself as complete against the ground of its own environment. We literally cannot see ourselves as aesthetic objects, from the outside. Others, however, can see this for us. Thus, Bakhtin's intersection of language and subject begins with a discussion of individuals as constructed by language, whether they are personalities in the world or characters in a novel:

> Let us say there is a human being before me who is suffering. The horizon of *his* consciousness is filled by the circumstance which makes him suffer and by the objects which he sees before him. The emotional and volitional tones which pervade this visible world of objects are tones of suffering. What I have to do is to experience and consummate him aesthetically. . . . The life situation of a suffering human being that is really experienced from within may prompt me to perform an ethical action. . . . But in any event my projection of myself into him must be followed by a *return* into myself . . . for only from this place can the material derived from my projecting myself into the other be rendered meaningful ethically, cognitively, or aesthetically. . . . Aesthetic activity proper actually begins at the point when we *return* into ourselves and start to form and consummate the material we derived . . . and these acts of forming and consummating are effected by our *completing* that material (that is, the suffering of the given human being) with features *transgredient* to the entire object-world of the other's suffering consciousness.[34]

Bakhtin insists that these "constitutive moments of projecting oneself into the other and of consummating the other" are not ethical but contemplative, aesthetic acts.[35] What he means by this, however, is that the end of such contemplation is not necessarily, or not yet, "directed toward the actual modification of the event and of the other as a moment in that event."[36] It is the role of the author to project and consummate the lived experience of the other. If Bakhtin were to allow that thus far such an act is ethical, he would be in the realm of traditional ethics and spirituality. Instead, he insists such an act of putting oneself in another place is *aesthetic.* What follows from that act of contemplation is essentially a task of *translation,* whether of responding ethically to the needs of another, or of representing another in the form of a novelistic character seen against those features of plot and background that are transgredient to the other as an aesthetic subject. Akin to novelistic translation is the process one goes through in order to express oneself aesthetically; for since I cannot perceive myself directly from the outside, I must see myself through the screen of the other possible emotional–volitional reaction to my outward manifestation—his possible enthusiasm, love, astonishment, or compassion for me.[37]

This process does not differ in kind from that described by Bakhtin in *Problems of Dostoevsky's Poetics,* where his Dostoevsky solves the task of "'portraying all the depths of the human soul'—with 'utter realism,' that is, he sees these depths *outside* himself, in the souls of *others.*"[38] It is this concept of human subjectivity as begun and consummated by the language and significant gesture of others that underlies all Bakhtin's future work on genre and dialogics.

The concepts of polyphony, double-voicedness, and heteroglossia that form the nucleus of Bakhtin's major writings on the novel are all built around this unstable intrapersonal dyad, now resolved into a coherent theory of language. It appears to be relatively late, in "The Problem of Speech Genres," that Bakhtin mounts his direct opposition to formalism. Here behaviorists and Saussurians are alike critiqued. The "general problem of speech genres has never been raised," for instance, since literary genres have been studied only in terms of their particular features, while everyday speech genres have been studied by "the American behaviorists," among others, but was limited to the specific features of everyday speech, and so "could not lead to a correct determination of the general linguistic nature of the utterance."[39] A longer treatment of formalists attempts to isolate the basic unit of language ensues in which Bakhtin insists that the failure of formalism lies in its reduction of the active role of the *other* in the process of speech communication.[40] Thus, the entire ethical-aesthetic *subiectum* as constituted through the possibility of another's response is now fully embedded in the basic unit of discourse, which for Bakhtin is not the word but the utterance.

The utterance is the indivisible monad of discourse. Consequently, to say that "the boundaries of each concrete utterance . . . are determined by a *change of speaking subjects,* that is, a change of speakers" means that the dialogue of *at least* two consciousnesses goes through discourse all the way to the bottom.[41] While Bakhtin's psychological theory, his "excess of seeing," had an entelechy, an aesthetic completion as a creative act between consciousnesses, the utterance has its entelechy as well, a completion signaled by the possibility of response.[42] Thus for Bakhtin as well as Burke, in a sense, form is psychology. Contra the formalists, language cannot be divided into a purely free (and therefore arbitrary) individual act as opposed to a "purely social" (and therefore determined) linguistic system.[43] And since consciousness is both constructed of and constructed by language, the "dwelling place" of consciousness begins in an act of ethical and aesthetic invention, an ordering of chaos on the plane of the individual subject as well as on the plane of language.

Synthesis

Taken together, Burke and Bakhtin show us the way to construct a theory of aesthetics that enlivens rhetoric rather than cutting it to the quick. They point to the intersection of language and subject as locus of the dialogue of ethics and aesthetics.

Both resist placing metaphysics out of reach of the *physis.* Simultaneously, both resist reducing action to motion. Individuals are preserved as unique and irreplaceable loci for the intersection and invention of language and symbol. For both, human consciousnesses are constructed by means of language but not reducible to a single predetermined linguistic code—there are no words that belong to no one; there are no singly owned words.

By coordinating the ethical and the aesthetic in the act of invention rather than the act of reception, they leave open the possibility for a reinvention of ethics in the thick of discourse. Ethics becomes aesthetic, not merely as a desire for the good but as an integrated inventional act, by virtue of which we are never playing an end game with all the remaining moves plotted, but instead there is always the possibility of a new gambit opening up the board, the possibility that a solitary voice may yet alter the balance of power.

Both theorists were lovers of chaos and took the measure of the unpredictable in life, art, and society. Both, while embracing materialism, yet acknowledged in language the more-than-verbal as a loophole predicated by the fiat of language itself. It is perhaps indicative that each theorist adopted a paradigmatic genre—for Burke, the drama, for Bakhtin, the novel. For the ethical/aesthetic aim of both forms is to recreate life—verbal life, reflected in all its complexity. The ethical imperative implied here is not opposed to, but achieved by means of the aesthetic voicing of language—the idea that the vocation of the artist is to enact a form of *imitatio Dei,* but translated into humanist terms. So for Bakhtin, the author who is able to give voice to the "image of a language" is perhaps enacting the verbal mirror of the fiat of creation, an end that is ethical and aesthetic at once. A parallel to this notion of the author as sovereign of verbal creation can be found in Bakhtin's notion of *great time.* For, although heteroglossia reigns outside the boundaries of the novel, in the social world of language, *great time* is a dialogic process by which a historic community sorts through its past texts and repeatedly brings some to the fore, to acquire more and deeper layers of embedded meaning over time.[44] Thus the hand of a "creator" is at work in the generative activity of language and collective subjectivity over time, apart from any single authorial hand.

Throughout *The Rhetoric of Religion,* Kenneth Burke also touches on verbal creation, and nowhere more pointedly than in coining the term "Logology."[45] He takes the creative fiat of God in Judeo-Christian theology and rehabituates it in the realm of language: "things become the signs of the genius that resides in words."[46] At the close of his essay on "Terministic Screens," Burke offers his "Dialectician's Hymn":

> Hail to Thee, Logos,
> Thou Vast Almighty Title,
> In Whose name we conjure—
> Our acts the partial representatives
> Of Thy whole act.[47]

The dialectic of verbal creation merges with the dialectic of spirit, not through deifying the word but through verbalizing the deity.

This posture I have just described, once again, I would call "magic humanism" until I think of a better term. Its secret is that the *mysterium,* for better or worse, is not gone. We simply have to get used to the realization that we create it—both the product and the byproduct of language—and we go on inventing it.

I began this essay with a "representative anecdote" from the side of the aesthetic. Let me end with an example that leans toward the ethical. The power of imagination required for art is also the faculty required for ethics—the ability to imagine oneself in the position of the other. Hannah Arendt paints Adolf Eichmann in the character of one who fatally, but ordinarily, lacks such imagination. She mentions his "heroic fight with the German language," his habit of speaking almost entirely in stock phrases, and most tellingly his inability to adjust his rhetoric to his audience.[48] "The longer one listened to him," she concludes, "the more obvious it became that his inability to speak was closely bound up with an inability to *think,* namely to think from the standpoint of someone else. No communication was possible with him, not because he lied but because he was surrounded by the most reliable of all safeguards against the words and the presence of others, and hence against reality as such."[49]

Of course, the key to Arendt's book is that this failure of imagination is not extraordinary. Eichmann was an ordinary man who followed the rules of a deformed system. He had read and internalized Kant's rendition of the golden rule. "I meant by my remark about Kant," Eichmann states, "that the principle of my will must always be such that it can become the principle of general laws."[50] But for him, according to Arendt, this merely meant "Act as if the principle of your actions were the same as that of the legislation or of the law of the land" or, in other words, "Act in such a way that the Führer, if he knew your action, would approve it."[51]

It was precisely the sense of honor and devotion to duty practiced by the functionaries, the bureaucratic rank and file of the Reich, that given a twisted object allowed them to execute it with all the bureaucratic zeal to which they were dedicated. In their devotion to duty, they failed in the capacity to see their acts from the outside, to see how they would look from the perspective of the other, or even simply to extend sympathetic imagination to those they were sending to their deaths.

And this is why ethics without aesthetics loses the voice that gives it life, while aesthetics without ethics loses the life that gives it voice—and the two can become one only in the *ethos* of invention.

Notes

1. Martin Heidegger, "Letter on Humanism," in *Martin Heidegger: Basic Writings,* trans. David F. Krell (New York: Harper & Row, 1977), 233. For a brief discussion of the ambiguities involved in the translation of ηθος ανθρωποι δαιμων (Heraclitus fragment 119), see Thomas M. Robinson, ed., *Heraclitus: Fragments: A Text and Translation with Commentary* (Toronto: University of Toronto Press, 1987), 159–60.

2. Charles Chamberlain, "From Haunts to Character: The Meaning of Ethos and Its Relation to Ethics," *Helios* 11 (1984): 97–108.

3. Thomas Merton, *The Way of Chuang Tzu* (New York: New Directions, 1965), 110–11.

4. Peter Jackson, "Interview with Peter Jackson," interview by Charlie Rose, PBS's *Charlie Rose,* aired 22 February 2002. Transcript reprinted on TheOneRing.net, http://www.theonering.net/perl/newsview/8/1014699722, accessed 26 February 2002.

5. Plato, *Republic* 598b–608b.

6. Plato, *Phaedrus, Symposium;* Plotinus, *Ennead* 1.6, 60.

7. David Hume, "Of the Standard of Taste," in *Aesthetics: The Classic Readings,* ed. David E. Cooper (Oxford: Blackwell, 1997), 80.

8. Ibid., 87.

9. Immanuel Kant, *The Critique of Judgment,* trans. J. H. Bernard (New York: Prometheus, 2000), 47–50.

10. Arthur Schopenhauer, *The World as Will and Representation,* in *Aesthetics: The Classic Readings,* ed. David E. Cooper (Oxford: Blackwell, 1997), vol. 1, sec. 52, p. 153.

11. Marcus Tullius Cicero, *De Oratore* I.30.134–35.

12. Cf. Ross Wolin, *The Rhetorical Imagination of Kenneth Burke* (Columbia: University of South Carolina Press, 2001), 33–34.

13. Kenneth Burke, "Psychology and Form," in *Counter-Statement,* by Kenneth Burke, 3d rev. ed. (Berkeley and Los Angeles: University of California Press, 1968), 31.

14. Kenneth Burke, *A Rhetoric of Motives* (Berkeley and Los Angeles: University of California Press, 1969), 6.

15. Ibid., 20.

16. Kenneth Burke, "Lexicon Rhetoricae," in *Counter-Statement,* by Kenneth Burke, 3d rev. ed. (Berkeley and Los Angeles: University of California Press, 1968), 1:152.

17. Stan A. Lindsay, *Implicit Rhetoric: Kenneth Burke's Extension of Aristotle's Concept of Entelechy* (Lanham, Md.: University Press of America, 1998), 78–79.

18. Kenneth Burke, *The Philosophy of Literary Form: Studies in Symbolic Action,* 3d ed. (Berkeley and Los Angeles: University of California Press, 1973), 321.

19. Ibid., 322.

20. Kenneth Burke, *Language as Symbolic Action: Essays on Life, Literature, and Method* (Berkeley and Los Angeles: University of California Press, 1966), 420.

21. Ibid., 442–43.

22. Ibid., 455.

23. Ibid., 446.

24. Ibid., 453.

25. David Cratis Williams, "Toward Rounding Out the *Motivorum* Trilogy: A Textual Introduction," in *Unending Conversations: New Writings by and about Kenneth Burke,* ed. Craig Henderson and David Cratis Williams (Carbondale: Southern Illinois University Press, 2001), 4.

26. Kenneth Burke, addendum to "Curriculum Criticum," in *Counter-Statement,* by Kenneth Burke, 3d rev. ed. (Berkeley and Los Angeles: University of California Press, 1968), 222; Williams, "Toward Rounding Out," 5.

27. For example, Burke, *Language as Symbolic Action,* 430; and Michael Holquist, "Introduction: The Architectonics of Answerability," and Mikhail Bakhtin, "Author and Hero in Aesthetic Activity," both in *Art and Answerability: Early Philosophical Essays,* by Mikhail Bakhtin, trans. Vadim Liapunov, ed. Michael Holquist and Vadim Liapunov (Austin: University of Texas Press, 1990), xxxiii and 62.

28. Mikhail Bakhin, *Toward a Philosophy of the Act,* trans. Vadim Liapunov and Michael Holquist (Austin: University of Texas Press, 1993).

29. Kenneth Burke, "Definition of Man," in Burke, *Language as Symbolic Action,* 9; Kenneth Burke, "A Dramatistic View of the Origins of Language," in Burke, *Language as Symbolic Action,* 419; cf. Henri Bergson, *Creative Evolution,* trans. Arthur Mitchell (New York: Henry Holt, 1911), 272–98.

30. Bakhtin, *Toward a Philosophy,* 13; Holquist, "Introduction," xxxiii; cf. Gary Saul Morson and Caryl Emerson, *Mikhail Bakhtin: Creation of a Prosaics* (Stanford, Calif.: Stanford University Press, 1990), 179.

31. Mikhail Bakhtin, "Art and Answerability," in *Art and Answerability: Early Philosophical Essays,* by Mikhail Bakhtin, trans. Vadim Liapunov, ed. Michael Holquist and Vadim Liapunov (Austin: University of Texas Press, 1990), 1.

32. Ibid.

33. Bakhtin, "Author and Hero," 24.

34. Ibid., 25–26.

35. Ibid., 27.

36. Ibid., 24.

37. Ibid., 31.

38. Mikhail Bakhtin, *Problems of Dostoevsky's Poetics,* trans. Caryl Emerson (Minneapolis: University of Minnesota Press, 1984), 61.

39. Mikhail Bakhtin, "The Problem of Speech Genres," in *Speech Genres and Other Late Essays,* by Mikhail Bakhtin, trans. Vern W. McGee, ed. Caryl Emerson and Michael Holquist (Austin: University of Texas Press, 1986), 61.

40. Ibid., 70.

41. Ibid., 71.

42. Ibid., 76.

43. Ibid., 81.

44. Mikhail Bakhtin, "Toward a Methodology for the Human Sciences," in *Speech Genres and Other Late Essays,* by Mikhail Bakhtin, trans. Vern W. McGee, ed. Caryl Emerson and Michael Holquist (Austin: University of Texas Press, 1986), 167.

45. Kenneth Burke, *The Rhetoric of Religion: Studies in Logology* (Berkeley and Los Angeles: University of California Press, 1970).

46. Kenneth Burke, "What Are the Signs of What? (A Theory of 'Entitlement')," in Burke, *Language as Symbolic Action,* 362.

47. Kenneth Burke, "Terministic Screens," in Burke, *Language as Symbolic Action,* 55.

48. Hannah Arendt, *Eichmann in Jerusalem: A Report on the Banality of Evil,* rev. ed. 1965 (New York: Penguin, 1994), 48–49.

49. Ibid., 49.

50. Ibid., 136.

51. Ibid.

Truth as Metaphor
Imaginative Vision and the Ethos of Rhetoric

ROBERT WADE KENNY

The rhetorical tradition has always relied on conceptions of *ethos,* and there is no scholar of rhetoric, today or even twenty-one hundred years ago, who could not wax long on this topic. How is it then that, even now, it calls to us as something to be understood?

We find a clue to our answer in the way that other words have called for and received reexamination, in particular by the philosopher whose critical method regularly follows this path, Martin Heidegger. Consider, for example, the essays "On the Grammar and Etymology of the Word 'Being'" and "Building Dwelling Thinking." In the former, he shows us that the word "Being" has lost its meaning for us, a truth (*aletheia*) he thereby uncovers as "to live, to emerge, to linger or endure." Similarly language has retracted "the proper meaning of the word *bauen,* which means dwelling,"[1] which appears in the second essay not only as a description of mortal existence but also as "to cherish and protect, to preserve and care for."[2] Dwelling, in other words, is something that people *do;* it characterizes, in particular, the project of making a world for the sake of ourselves, other people, and other beings: to free these things, "in the proper sense of the word into a preserve of peace ... the free sphere that safeguards each thing in its essence."[3] And since only humanity is capable of dwelling in this sense, this caretaking of Being is the specific *telos* of humanity.[4] Taking care of the world and the people in it is, by this account, the specific character or project of human beings, and the *ethos* of personhood is accountable to this project.

People often turn from their roles as caretakers of life, however, and get caught up in a hurried and unreflective existence, which Heidegger describes at length in *Being and Time.* Nevertheless, it is always possible for them to take up a more meaningful and caring engagement, and that caring attitude can be recognized when it occurs. Such a commitment to care can be seen in the popular film *It's a Wonderful Life,* directed by Frank Capra. In it, George Bailey renounces what he apparently conceives as a solipsistic existence. The wish that he had never been is granted to him; he returns to his town from the bridge where he made the wish, and suddenly upstanding citizens are corrupted, successful businessman are homeless wretches, and a cherished brother is a bare memory to the residents, for in a world without George Bailey that brother died in childhood. In making Bailey a man who had never been (taking away his Being), Capra creates dramatic circumstances by which the character can be inserted within his world without having the status of one who dwells within that world; showing us that *to be* is *to dwell* and (through the device) that Being without dwelling is existential hell.[5] Thus, Bailey learns that his "wonderful life" was fashioned in those critical moments when he was compelled to make decisions *against* what he conceived as his self-interest. And this discovery does not rob him of his freedom; rather, it frees him from the illusion that the real George Bailey was betrayed by circumstance. The discovery allows him to recognize that by caring for his world and for others he had not sacrificed anything, for this was the only manner that genuine care for his *own* existence was possible.[6] In fact, to simply be *there,* without a history and destiny of obligations to his world and others, to be there in the manner of a thing (which was the manner Capra made him present to his town during the narrative segue), was the opposite of freedom.

A human as a thing is almost possible, we find it dead in a ditch with no identity papers. Between that extreme and the possibility that still awaits us is the challenge of emerging, of coming into the world as a preserve of peace, for our selves and for others. This is the challenge of existence—it is the very way that existence calls to us. But it is not a call we all or always answer. The alternative, of treating the world and others as things at our disposal, is always possible. Or we might just shut ourselves into everyday unthought routines. For Heidegger, such dismissive, exploitative, and mechanical orientations to people and things represent failures to take up human existence as a destiny. They would nevertheless, however, be failures in a person. And so the challenge to humanity is not "to be or not to be" in any absolute sense; for we will, to some extent or other, be (essentially in whatever type and degree of hell that we fashion for ourselves). Rather than a question of our absolute being, then, it is a question of the quality of our being. Can we take up the challenge that existence presents to us—the challenge to fashion this world as a dwelling place for our selves and for others, as a preserve of peace? And can we find a way to see this challenge not simply as a diversion from our lives but as the very existential meaning of our lives? As a character, George Bailey always took up this challenge, without ever knowing it. He came into the fullness of his existence when he recognized, at the end, that his participation in the making of his world was not the diversion or distraction that he had always taken it to be, it was the very meaning (in an existential sense) of his existence. This self-understanding transformed him from a man into a philosopher, but it did not initiate the practice of genuine *ethos* in his life. That was there all along.[7]

In this essay, then, *ethos* is understood as the quality of personhood that calls humanity to care for its self, its world, and its others in such a manner that the dwelling Heidegger regards as fundamental to our Being is made possible. It is not, however, a quality that is simply *in* us, like our liver or a bone; rather, it is behind us and ahead of us, and it only enters us to the extent we take it upon ourselves in the things we do. And, therefore, it is possible to distinguish a disposition toward being that is genuine from one that is not. The genuine disposition toward life is the caretaking disposition, and this is the meaning of *ethos*. It is not part of what we are, but rather *how* we are in the world. It is not an internal faculty that a person performs, nor is it a quality that an audience must discern; it is the manner one takes on responsibility for life.

The distinction between a genuine disposition toward being and one that is not also appears in speech, which "is the basic mode of access to the world . . . and not only the world but also other people."[8] Heidegger identifies inauthentic speech as idle talk and reminds us that to speak badly is to speak in a manner that diverts or subverts the possibilities for genuine engagement in the world.[9] This is why he regularly attacks sophistry, in which "the emptiness of the speech is equivalent to an ungenuiness and uprootedness of human existence."[10]

But Heidegger does not attack rhetoric in this way, as Professor Hyde's introduction to this text reveals, because he recognizes how rhetoric can bring humanity into its destiny.[11] But that can only be the case if *ethos* drives rhetoric, not if it is conceived as something to be performed for advantage. The *ethos* of rhetoric, in this way of seeing things, is not something that a rhetor uses, it is something that uses him.[12] In varying degrees, rhetorical scholarship has recognized or accepted this point. It seeks to demarcate a boundary between the idle talk that floods the public sphere and the authentic rhetorical resources that make possible Being, as the ongoing *dwelling* of humanity. And because it does this, such scholarship establishes the *ethos* of our own community as well.

This essay is offered, then, with a hope. For I believe that, if we continue the *ethos* of rhetoric along the path that Heidegger has fashioned, we can efface the "just" and "mere" that occasionally find themselves the adjectival modifiers of our field. Conceived in the light of what Heidegger has given us, rhetoric plays an *ethical* role in the fundamental project of genuine living.[13] With that turn, comes a new pathway ahead of us, and I take this opportunity to travel some distance along it.

With the principle of rhetorical *ethos* in front of us, the foci for the structure of rhetorical analysis and practice shift. Rhetorical *ethos,* as a sense of commitment to one's dwelling place, brings to the forefront relatively unexamined issues. One of them, the one I intend to discuss in this essay, is the rhetorical imagination. I hold that the rhetorical imagination is a critical dimension of rhetorical scholarship that comes under the sign of *ethos* because just this sort of imagination, realized in speech, is necessary in order to make the processual character of dwelling possible. An architect cannot design a dwelling place without imagining it, and similarly a rhetorician cannot articulate the communal dwelling place without being able to imagine that.[14] Clearly, the term fits logically into a discussion of persons, their dwelling, and rhetoric. How it functions within this abode is what I would like to address in this essay.

The concept of imagination has received limited explicit attention in rhetorical studies. George Kennedy describes how, through Bacon, "[i]magination . . . reenters rhetoric," tracing Bacon's use of Quintilian and Longinus, even drawing some associations with Plato and Aristotle.[15] But no tradition of imagination and rhetoric follows Bacon. George Campbell gives it significant status as an associational faculty that might "aid in promoting nobler ends" than fancy, ultimately functioning as a significant stage in moving the will because of its effects on passion.[16] Whately regarded it useful in reflection when engaging in judgment.[17] Blair regarded the imagination as a source of pleasure that realized beauty, sublimity, and novelty.[18]

All this amounts to incidental commentary, however. And something else will be noticed if we read these authors carefully: when they are speaking of imagination, they are each talking about a different thing. There is nothing wrong with this, for while it is the case that rhetors gain good service from the creation of a new term, such as Michael McGee's *ideograph*,[19] they also find it fruitful to simply develop another manner of thinking about a term already in use—what Walter Fisher does in his study of *narrative*.[20] We might find, then, that the manner we come to see the term *imagination* will play a crucial role in our willingness to use it and our capacity to use it to good effect in rhetorical studies. On this occasion, with the issue of *ethos* central to our consideration, I would like to put forward a theory of imaginative vision that was developed by Northrop Frye, who considers this faculty the critical condition for being in the world, much in the manner that Heidegger describes it.

If we envision knowledge objects as pieces of a puzzle, imagination would have two identities: on the one hand, it would be a piece of the puzzle, and on the other, it would be a color that is also in many of the separate pieces. I intend to deal with both, identifying imaginative vision as a singular concept and a dimension of other rhetorical concepts, in particular rhetorical exigence and eloquence.

The Character of Blake and Frye's Imaginative Vision

Frye's most thorough analysis of imaginative vision is in his first book, *Fearful Symmetry: A Study of William Blake*.[21] There he identified Blake's dislike for a thing-like characterization of humankind—the view that characterized people in terms of observed animal features, what he calls the *vehicular form*.[22] For Blake, a human being was not the thing pointed at, prodded, or dissected, not the dead thing on the medical slab, because human reality is much vaster from the inside than from the outside. For example, as someone looked at, my existence takes up a spot on the lake, but as someone *looking,* my existence takes up the entire lake and every star I can see in the firmament above. This is how Blake saw it. In his thinking, people were a universe within. He called that their "Poetic Genius" and even claimed a human being really did not have a body, "if by 'body' we mean man as a perceived form."

Blake, however, did not believe that this universe within arises as a compulsory image forced upon us by our sense organs. This Lockean conceptualization "is constantly in Blake's poetry a symbol of every kind of evil, superstition, and tyranny."[23] Grounded in the assumption that all people must and do see the same "real" world, this view suppressed the unique quality that each person brings to experience, in terms of both perspective and relationship. Two people look at a tree, for example: perspectively speaking, one sees the trunk, the other the leaves; relationally speaking, one sees her childhood playground, the other sees lumber. For Blake, regarding these things as less than real is a regression "to the level of the dull-witted Philistine who in the first place saw 'just a tree' without noticing whether it was an oak or a poplar."[24] Such a view does not make abstraction as an activity impossible or useless, but it does caution against a tyranny of categorical reasoning. To answer the question what is the essential nature of this thing, Blake would simply say, *the immediate experience you are having with it.* His answer liberates the person because it validates the qualities of a unique human vision. No wonder Blake thought Locke's conceptualization a tyranny. To be compelled to limit one's imagination of reality in exactly the same way as everyone else is to shut the imagination into a categorical dungeon. By contrast, once one is open to one's imaginative experience, one is open to the possibility of freedom. There is more than a hint of existentialism anticipated in this, and indeed Frye shows genuine respect to that tradition, in particular Heidegger, in his later work.[25]

If recognition, forced upon us by sensation, was not the fundamental feature of human experience for Blake, what was? The answer, according to Frye, is imaginative vision, so that "'imagination' is the regular term used by Blake to denote man as an acting and perceiving being."[26] For Blake, "nothing is real beyond the imaginative patterns men make of reality, and hence there are exactly as many kinds of reality as there are men."[27] Genuine human existence does not passively experience a reality external to it but rather *ongoingly fashions* its reality through the imagination of experience, and this means that human existence itself "is a work of art."[28] For Blake, the reality we experience as ahead of us is the canvas of existence that we ourselves are painting. And, therefore, when Blake is asked if he does not, like all the rest of us, see a round disk shaped like a guinea when he looks at the rising sun, he answers, "Oh no, no. I see an Innumerable company of the Heavenly host crying, 'Holy, Holy, Holy is the Lord God Almighty.'"[29] Thus imagination, as Blake conceives it, can be an act of will by which a person brings forth the reality within which to dwell. People who look at the rising sun, willing to see a round guinea, create that experience and dwell in it. Frye reminds us that "Blake can see it if he wants to, but when he sees the angels, he is not seeing more 'in' the sun but more of it."[30]

Of course, Blake recognizes that two people, or even groups of people, should be able to share common ways of seeing a thing; nevertheless, he denies this is done by reducing the thing to a name or a property associated with it. We share the world by sharing, not ignoring, our imaginative experiences of it. To illustrate, two children may not yet know a dozen words, but when they see a ball, they do not need to think it *as one member of the class of spherical objects* and so on in order to coordinate their experiences with it—if one has enough imagination to throw, and the other to catch, that is enough.

Language plays a critical role in this process, for language can beat down the imagination, so that reality does seem to be nothing more than a sensory surface shared by all. However, language can also be used to expand human vision. You might tell a five year old, for example, that a go-cart likes to go fast. And indeed, this claim would not be without truth, for that desire is carried by the toy as the externalization of your desire in crafting it. Similarly, one could describe the exhaustion, poverty, and agony of a pair of sneakers, and this would have its "truth" in the labors of the sweatshop workers who made them.

Coming into language is coming into our world, and in this sense language gives us our world. But as we ourselves develop language, we bring more and more of that world out for each other in the language that we use. Consequently, for Frye, the poetic is not reducible to verbal metaphors that create fantastic mental images. Rather, poetry brings to light the "existential metaphor,"[31] a metaphor that *speaks into existence* an arrow's desire to fly to its target, a tree's desire to give shade, the written word's desire to speak. By characterizing metaphor as existential, Frye rejects the notion that poetic (and for that matter rhetorical) language generates a pseudo-reality. Rather, it is through existential metaphor that "the imagination creates reality, and as desire is part of the imagination, the world we desire is more real than the world we passively accept."[32] For Frye, language *makes the real,* and struggles to overcome the popular imagination of the real as nothing more than the physical. Our desiring imagination can see and say that a tree is a song, a shelter, a desperate hand, a water-walker, or a savior, and when we do this in a way that exceeds analogy, we release ourselves into the possibilities for innovative dwelling that can only come to us through an imagination that transcends the everyday. Such metaphors, for example, allow us to release the tree into our world in terms of its actual possibilities as (1) a guitar, (2) a house, (3) a sculpture, (4) a boat, and (5) a medicine.[33] Practically speaking, the power of imaginative vision is revealed in its potential to overcome the common way of seeing things, to transcend the everyday and the familiar and thereby grow toward the sort of dwelling that Heidegger characterizes. Metaphor is in this sense the truth of what we can be, the forthcoming reality that we pursue as the very meaning of our lives.

Fundamental in everything that Frye has written is a faith in a notion of human progress as destiny. Imaginative vision initiates and drives a process that turns stones into airplanes, trees into pianos, oil into plastic. It thereby frees, from what otherwise would be the unfreedom of the Earth,[34] flight, music, and design. At the same time, it frees us *into* these things, which would otherwise not be part of our existence—as pilots, musicians, and engineers. Heidegger believes a distinguishing feature of human existence is that we are *open* toward Being.[35] It should be apparent that this notion of imaginative vision is a critical dimension of that openness; it names the *how* of human existence and characterizes that special quality of human being that makes dwelling possible. Thrown into this world, yes, but thrown as imaginative existence. And this means we can take up our residence in the distinct manner that is dwelling. We can call the world and even our selves into question because we can imagine better. And as we hold out the possibility of a better life we choose our *ethos.* Thus Frye can say that "the imaginative mind, therefore, is the one which has realized its own freedom."[36]

The capacity to imagine beyond the everyday characterization of the world of things is the talent that Blake particularly attributes to artists, the authors of the Bible being exemplary cases. But Blake also held that anyone could exercise the imaginative vision by willing to see beyond the surface of things as we tend to be comfortably familiar with them. One might suspect that such an imaginative vision is the talent of childhood, and indeed, Blake thinks it so, for a child's sense of experience "is often more open than the dulled-down reason of adults that surround them."[37] Indeed, the child "who can transform the most unpromising toy into a congenial companion, has something which the adult can never wholly abandon without collapsing into mediocrity."[38] Frye notes that this ability to see one thing many ways plays a role in a child's fascination with the idea that a word can have more than one meaning; and he says, "One would hope that this amazement would last the rest of their lives."[39]

Thus Frye develops out of Blake a notion of human imagination that accounts not only for the quality of immediate experience but also for the possibilities of human experience toward which humanity grows. This is because imagination can see what is around the corner (in the sense that a mechanic hears a noise and "sees" a loose timing belt) and what is yet to come (as when I "see" a rundown house restored).[40] Let us begin to examine how this conceptualization of imaginative vision can play a role in rhetorical studies, particularly under the sign of *ethos,* or dwelling place.

The Significance of Imaginative Vision to Rhetorical Theory and Practice

"As the artist (read rhetor) is the shaper of myth," Frye states, "there is a sense in which he holds in his hands the thunderbolts that destroy one society and create another."[41] Rhetoric, Frye claims, has always been concerned with two types of speaking: ornamental and persuasive. There is, it must be noted, a fundamental union between these practices, for a speech that is beautiful should also be effective. When we say that a speech is persuasive, however, we are implying that the speaker has a vision not yet shared by an audience, which suggests to me the familiar notion of rhetorical exigence. Similarly, a speech that is ornamented we would think eloquent. For that reason, I will examine the role imaginative vision plays in matters of exigence and eloquence.

Imaginative Vision and Exigence

He repeatedly draws our attention to the topic of *concern,* by which he refers to our orientation toward how we can survive on this planet and in our particular societies: "something which includes the sense of the importance of preserving the integrity of the whole human community," in other words, how we can come into a preserve of peace.[43] Ultimately, concern points out the insufficiency of the world as we find it, a world in which everything survives by cannibalizing everything else. The insufficiencies *concern* recognizes are the product of, and a call to, imaginative vision. "As long as a single form of life remains in misery and pain the imagination finds the world not good enough," Frye notes.[42]

In Blake's time, nature had not been disciplined in the thousand ways that we now take for granted. For him, nature was a fallen realm, and he regarded the accomplishments of humanity as triumphs over it. Imaginative vision turns mud into homes, rocks into airplanes, plants into clothing. It does not allow us to "escape nature: it enables us to undertake the imaginative conquest of nature."[44] Some of us might reasonably recoil from references to the "conquest" of nature, for such expressions conflict with the environmental rhetoric of our time. Still, if we take the expression in the spirit from which it was offered, we can meditate for a moment and realize that many of the limits that are imposed on us as organisms have been overcome through acts that were initiated by imagination. It is within this context that Frye says, "All works of civilization, all of the improvements and modifications of the state of nature that man has made, prove that man's creative power is supernatural."[45] This view must be discounted, of course, to accommodate the fact that man's creative power has often made a mess of things, but no society is perfect, and one might hope that imaginative vision could work to dissolve "the inequities of class structure and the dismal and illiberal ways of life that arise when society as a whole does not have enough vision."[46] If indeed humanity is no more than a rough beast slouching toward its own birth,[47] it nevertheless does struggle, with every step, to walk more upright. "Man's destiny is not predetermined," Frye declares. "It's his heritage, it's his birthright, it's something he can fulfill if he wants to."[48] Humanity is open toward Being, and even in the most everyday illustration we see the point: "Man has caught and trained the dog; he has developed the dog's intelligence and has projected his own imagination onto him. . . . We get out of nature what we put into it, and the training of the dog is an imaginative victory over nature."[49]

The imagination is not a local product of an individual mind. Rather imagination objectifies itself in social practices, things, and processes. When we look at an airplane, we think we see a thing, but we also see the human imagination. When we watch a small child swim we think we see an event, but we also see her coach's (and her own) imagination. When we see a field of corn we think we see a crop but we also see the farmer's imagination. All the things that we could see in the world if we opened ourselves to the imagination are exactly like the things we have brought into the world already—not simply inert matter shaped to provide a service, but universes of possibility, both realized and yet to be fulfilled.

No solipsistic theory of the imagination could account for such collective human progress, however. That is why it is interesting to note the critical role that communication plays in Frye's ordering of the imagination, for Frye believes that the imagination is transmittable in communicative action. Consider, for example, what happens when a couple goes house hunting. As they talk about who will get the bigger closet, or how they could add a back patio and thereby expand the kitchen, they are passing imaginative visions back and forth while influencing their experience and their attitudes toward the property at the same time. One partner may walk into the house and see nothing more than worn carpets and brown walls. The other may see the hardwood floors beneath, the brass under the painted fireplace, and the picture window in a now-windowless wall that blocks a view of the ocean behind. All she has to do at that moment is *speak,* and a rhetorical process that begins with the sharing of imaginative vision through language culminates as an elderly couple holding hands on a backyard patio, gazing out upon the sea. It is a process that takes place between two people, but also expands to take up responsibility for entire communities, for wherever there is rhetoric "there is a community of shared imaginative experience."[50] Communicative action acts within the Frye/Blake vision as a collecting and filtering of everyone's imaginative visions, the totality of which represents a culture. For Frye, culture is nothing other than "a total imaginative vision of life."[51]

Imagination can only gather such a collective world, however, if people see and work together; and this implies a critical role for rhetorical action in humanity's concernful dwelling. Such rhetorical action will not take place, however, unless the *ethos* of rhetoric is there as well. For example, if I should walk by when the couple I mentioned in the above paragraph were standing on the sidewalk in front of the house, complaining about the condition of the property, I would probably not stop and give them ideas about how they could turn it into their dwelling place. I might never even think how it could be done. This is, at least in part, because I do not care—the couple play a very small role in my world. Certainly no one would fault me for that, but it would be totally another thing for me to go to my own home and ignore my partner's dissatisfaction with the town where we live or the state of the front lawn. In the second case, I am clearly in the midst of my own dwelling place, and my *ethos* is called into question to the extent I disregard how it calls to me. *Ethos* is a concern for how one dwells, and it needs be present if genuine speaking is to occur because "you can't cultivate speech, beyond a certain point, unless you have something to say, and the basis of what you have to say is your vision of society."[52] *Ethos* needs a fiery imaginative vision when it creates dwelling, but imaginative vision equally needs *ethos* if it is to burn bright.

A rhetoric that emerges from imaginative vision and *ethos* fires the imagination of a public, allowing them to share the imaginative vision of the rhetor. And, according to Frye, that imaginative vision is formed out of a concernful regard toward the manner that our community dwells and might yet dwell. In this sense, imagination is also closely associated with exigence, understood as "an imperfection marked by urgency."[53] The rhetor's imagination is a vision that sees *through* the incommensurability and contingency that marks the bare surface of extant circumstances, for the "real world, that is the human world, has constantly to be created, and the one model that we should not make it out of is the world out there. The world out there has no human values, hence we should think of it primarily not as real, but as absurd."[54]

Frye's statement here assures us that the rhetor must possess sufficient imaginative vision to see within circumstances that have passed or are yet to come dimensions of experience too easily overlooked by the public—to use imaginative vision in order "to produce, out of the society we have to live in, a vision of the society we want to live in."[55] Just knowing the facts would never be enough to create that vision. Rather, the rhetor must transcend the facts and their existential circumstances through a will that drives toward the possibilities for becoming. Similarly, the person who develops imaginative vision is not simply someone who can make an impression of Elvis Presley on a sheet of black felt. The developed imagination experiences "a social and moral development too," which is to say, an *ethos* that is gathered out of one's communicative world much in the way that imagination is cultivated.[56] For Frye, the "imagination, which conceives the forms of society, is the source of the power to change that society."[57]

Frye draws our attention to the role of imaginative vision in rhetoric, saying, "In a modern democracy, a citizen participates in society mainly through his imagination."[58] The production of that imagination, however, is always a consequence of the language that goes between people. What brings people of diverse backgrounds together is the fact that they are all "citizens of their society with a common stake in that society."[59] Thus it appears that the sense of exigence, which moves humanity to speak well, is contained within the imagination of the one who would draw together the disparate, bewildered, or even discordant voices of her community under the sign of a single vision. Whereas prophecy is another term for imaginative vision in Blake, the rhetor cannot achieve this effect through creativity alone. Imaginative vision must arise instead as the nascent form of existence, as an *ethos* that calls us to dwell.[60] In other words, to give birth to our true imaginative possibilities is to enter being fully, as persons. Frye believes that human existence is a project, something that is yet to be fulfilled. And this means that any rhetor who is "deeply impressed by things as they are is apt to suffer from imaginative claustrophobia."[61]

When we apply imaginative vision to rhetorical studies, then, we should attend to the fact that it is developed and cultivated within a certain setting. A child is born who cannot read but eventually will write the "1812 Overture," or perhaps *War and Peace*. In the period between birth and authorship, the capacity to imagine these things will be shaped by both experience and the guidance of others. At the same time, a concern for the environment in which this development occurs will also arise, as a fundamental characteristic of the human condition. This concern will shape the rhetor's imaginative vision, when it is experienced as an exigence. And only one whose speech arises from this concern can be understood in terms of the sort of *ethos* that we have before us—a speaker who is the caretaker of self, world, and others,[62] and whose imaginative vision is always turned toward these things.

Notice, however, that this view of rhetoric discounts any speechmaking intended to exploit the audience, irrespective of whether a certain turn of phrase or force of voice is used. When toxic dumping occurs, or hundreds of employees are laid off, or soldiers are called to take part in a massacre, one cannot find the rhetorical *ethos* discussed here within the speaking events that made such actions possible. Conceived as it has been within this essay, *ethos* is entwined with dwelling place. Speech that intentionally brings greater harm to that dwelling place lacks *ethos* and is not regarded as good speech for this very reason. One might argue that Hitler was able to *perform* intelligence, and character, and goodwill toward the German people; but the argument made here leaves space to claim that he was not a great speaker, specifically because he lacked *ethos*. The Führer's inability to experience the existential responsibility to care for his world ultimately destroyed his dwelling place, and him with it. Indeed, any smooth talker with a talent for controlling others has no special gift for himself or his community if he lacks the concern at the heart of the *ethos* addressed in this essay.[63]

Exemplary illustrations of the relationship between imaginative vision and exigence are found in the speeches of Sir Winston Churchill: statesman, historian, writer, and even artist.[64] The sense of urgency that marks the rhetorical situation is easy to recognize in Churchill's war speeches, as is the concernful disposition toward the dwelling of his people. While many others saw only the immediate surface of international events, Churchill's imaginative vision could see beyond the surface and outside the immediate. This vision generated concern and was the source of the anticipation we hear in the words from 1932: "Do not let His Majesty's Government believe . . . that all Germany is asking for is equal status. . . .

That is not what Germany is seeking. All these bands of sturdy Teutonic youths, marching through the streets and roads of Germany, with the light of desire in their eyes to suffer for their Fatherland, are not looking for status. They are looking for weapons . . . and possibly to shatter to their very foundations every one of the countries I have mentioned."[65]

Indeed, there is much of what Blake called the prophecy of imagination in this passage. It serves as an ideal illustration of how this rhetor's imaginative vision was able to foresee and forewarn his people in a matter that radically concerned how they would dwell for more than a decade, and in some senses, till the end of time. If we think back for a moment to *It's a Wonderful Life,* we might recall each time Bailey's life ambitions were interrupted by an event that sparked his imaginative vision and his *ethos*—when his brother went off to college, when his father died, when the bank threatened to take over the savings and loan. Like Churchill, Bailey's vision of his world was challenged by these events and his *ethos* was such that he took up the challenge to bring his community into being, even when that challenge was rhetorical (for example, when he spoke to the panicking shareholders). For a moment in the film, we see what might have happened, had he not been there to take up these challenges. What would it be like to go, in the manner that George Bailey went, into a world where Winston Churchill had never been born? If one could see that, then one could know the force that a rhetorical *ethos* guided by the imaginative vision brings into the world.

Other specific voices, such as Charles Dickens, Abraham Lincoln, and Gandhi come to mind, yet one can also recognize the relationship between imaginative vision and exigence in broader strokes that cut across an entire region of rhetorical action. Feminist discourse, for example, is predicated upon a panoramic vision that, even at this historically early stage, has reordered everything from labor to morality for all of us. This does not suggest that progress is always a good thing, and in fact, Blake is more sophisticated on this than I have thus far indicated. At the same time, we should recognize the fundamental relationship between imaginative vision, concern, rhetorical action, and change. The conceptualization Frye offers us allows us to engage in analysis of a spoken text with these issues in mind. As well, the way that these principles are associated with *ethos* aids us when we distinguish an *ethos* that is performed and lived from one that is a fraud—whether that fraud be the action of a con artist, a corporate executive, a politician, or a cheating spouse. In all such cases, the lack of *concern* for the very dwelling place from which the act is spoken makes it reprehensible to Frye, and places it outside the *ethos* of rhetoric that we are discussing here.

Imaginative Vision and Eloquence

In order to discuss the relationship between imaginative vision and eloquence, we must recognize that the function of speech (from this point of entry into the topic) is to create in the audience the imaginative vision the rhetor intends. When a rhetor uses speech in this way, "the poet (read rhetorical) imagination constructs a cosmos of its own."[66] Thus when a poet says, "The rain of London pimples the ebony street,"[67] something of that street appears before our eyes and this is because of the poet's imaginative eloquence. However, since imaginative vision is something that sees not only with the eyes but also with the soul, the eloquence it offers can be much richer than such mental pictures. For example, when W. H. Auden says that "Time watches from the shadow and coughs when you would kiss,"[68] he awakens an imaginative capacity that cannot be reduced to any image the words might evoke; rather, he calls up that state of mind or mood so hauntingly reminiscent of the childhood anxiety we felt toward the eyes that secretly watched us from the closet.

Of course, this sort of evocative and imaginative act is also eloquent. It releases to the imagination something that is not merely seen but something that can be lived in its full emotional and moral context. To do this, imaginative vision must give birth to new relations in language in order to adequately represent the part of the experience that is unique. These relations are figurative dimensions of speech; they are the result of a speaker's practical knowledge of the formative features that will be expected by a given audience, as well as a sense of how such features can be stretched to create new imaginative experiences for that audience, experiences that were unique to the speaker's world up to that moment—experiences that could not be reduced to an image yet could be shared through images. The last lines of T. S. Eliot's "Love Song of J. Alfred Prufrock," for example, read, "We have lingered in the chambers of the sea by sea girls wreathed with seaweed red and brown till human voices wake us, and we drown."[69] The lines give us a visual image—people, like us, underwater, perhaps in some sort of cave, alongside seaweed covered mermaids. But then it collapses (deliberately of course) as a mere image, partly because of descriptive inconsistency. Apparently we were only dreaming, when we lingered, but then why are we still underwater when we awaken?

The poet relies on an unstated convention in discourse, one that assures us that a confounded image within a poem can be resolved if we refuse to treat the description as if it is just an image. Now reading it with imagination of the soul, rather than the eye, we feel as if we have been hypnotized and told, *You are absorbed in that cavern of silence that is your own reverie and desire, surrounded by the perfection that is present in such ideal worlds of sleep and dream, but you must juxtapose this reverential world to the frustration of your actual existence, which lacks the ideal qualities of your perfect waters; hence you are exiled from paradise, and the memory and longing for it suffocates you in what is your "real" life.* No reader parses out the lines in such a fashion, thankfully. But when they read it effectively they get the feeling of such an experience, when the image takes them to a point at which it surpasses itself and becomes a despair that hovers around the edges of repressed desire. Of course, one does not have to be able to name this feeling in order to experience it, nor to write the words that evoke it. Eliot, as a great poet, has the talent to speak (through images and the juxtaposition of images) moods that cannot be reduced to the image itself. That is one way that imaginative vision is transcendent—it surpasses anything that can be practically described because it can also evoke. Such evocation is the height of eloquence.

For Frye, eloquence is created through identification, which can be most simply described as the revelation of a truth about a thing, through metaphor. To say that Churchill is a lion, or that George Bush is a lion, or that Al Gore is a lion, is to engage in the process of identification as Frye conceives it—and one need only reflect in the three examples I have just given to see that identification as a rhetorical practice orients the imaginative vision of an audience, in one way or another, toward the topic. By contrast with reason, which has a subtractive effect on the operation of day-by-day experience, imaginative vision is additive, for it does not reduce a thing to a sum or a fraction of its known attributes (as when we say George Bush is the president) but adds something to the thing by showing a new light of its truth.

It would not make sense, however, to say that the president is an aardvark or a cantaloupe, and this suggests that we need to distinguish between the imaginary and the imaginative. Imaginative vision speaks *into* its community, and (because it is developed) speaks *as* its community, even as it goes beyond the vision its community has gathered. Consequently, it does not merely see and say anything that is simply different, rather, it reveals a difference that is also a truth, and it is eloquent to the extent it reveals both these things. This means that the imaginative vision will be steeped in the images and associations of its culture. In 1999, for example, it would not have made any sense to most Americans to say that George W. Bush was anything at all, because most Americans did not know who he was. Attempts to frame a vision of him now are associated with the fact that he has emerged upon the stage of the national experience. Language attempts to keep up with what he does by creating a vision of what he is.

Because Frye was a literary critic, he tends to take a less than satisfying position in terms of the relationship between eloquence and reason, holding that it would be "far better if the moral of *Aesop's Fables,* the signposts pointing from art to ethics, were snipped off, because all the morality worth having is already in the story, heightened by the fact that we are not bound down to a single conclusion."[70] Rhetoric cannot disregard such signposts, however, for in public address it is often a rhetor's moral duty to *place reason in the argument,* if not at the very center. Auden's "As I Walked Out One Evening" may carry and evoke a moral sentiment associated with romantic love, but it is not presented in a satisfying form for public address. Although it does function rhetorically and could thereby change the attitudes of a reading public, it is not structured to invite their deliberative skills. Frye may believe that the tools of analytic reason "are aggressive; they think of ideas as weapons; they seek the irrefutable argument, which keeps eluding them because all arguments are theses, and these are half truths implying their own opposite;"[71] nevertheless, in civil matters, public duty *commands* the presence of analytic reason because the choices made by a state or any civil body are based, at least in part, on economic and political considerations that exert an influence independent of the poetics of presentation.

At the same time, it remains true that "political action, again, has to be action in light of the vision,"[72] and political arguments also contain aesthetic properties for "the art of words has a similar relation to the other verbal disciplines . . . [and] the shape of the arguments . . . is ultimately a poetic shape."[73] Consequently, even when we are presenting an audience information to aid them in the deliberative process, we must do so with regard to the fact that "[p]oetic language is closely associated with rhetorical language, as both make extensive uses of figures of speech."[74] The question then amounts to this: What is the effective balance between reason and poesy in rhetorical delivery? This is not a question that can be answered directly, rather it is a question that the critic must ask whenever assessing a text.

Thus there is a distinct challenge to the rhetorical critic, who must evaluate a public text in terms of how it balances the rational and the aesthetic properties in its delivery in order to fulfill its ambitions. One cannot overlook aesthetics in a public delivery, and they must be of a certain quality because the rhetor needs to "distinguish genuine dramatic imagination from the conventional cliches of dramatic rhetoric."[75] The tension that exists between the reasonable and the beautiful in a speech are critical dimensions of its analysis and its effectiveness.

We can see this dynamic in the wartime speeches of Winston Churchill. The prime minister was aware that the experience of the military events in Europe was first shown to his people through his own words. This meant he needed to generate a vision of the movements of great numbers of people across the European continent. The eloquence of that vision can be understood as having two primary dimensions: (1) Churchill's words must have a cinematic quality giving the audience an angle of vision not held by any of the actual combatants, as if one looked at the arena of battle in the way one looks at a chessboard; and (2) Churchill cannot create this image as a mere map for the sake of sight; he must create a vision that is at the same time moral, a vision for the English soul, like the Eliot and Auden poems cited above.

Thus, in the speech that describes the extraction of British and French forces from Dunkirk, Churchill not only painted a picture that described the path of the retreating force as a military maneuver but also used language that would make that maneuver a noble and even heroic gesture; he needed to do so, for it was in the nature of that image that the British people imagined an act of military sensibility as opposed to an act of defeat or cowardice. With these considerations in mind, Churchill's panoramic rhetoric casts his entire army into the body of a single man "holding the right hand of the Belgians and to give their own right hand to a newly created French army which was to have advanced across the Somme in great strength and grasped it."[76] The German attack is then compared to the sweep of a scythe that cuts through these forces, followed by the plodding dull brute mass of ordinary German soldiers "always so ready to be led to the trampling down of other lands of liberties and comforts which they have never known in their own."[77] Thus in Churchill's words one hears a vision of battles from an angle that no eyes ever saw; for Churchill gathers the continent as an imaginative expression in discourse—one that carries morality within the perceptual ordering.

Churchill's major war speeches occurred in a particular and short-lived historical period in which a citizenry could be best realized in a speech that was read in a newspaper, heard on a radio, or observed in a newsreel. Churchill used that opportunity to gather the ambitions of his people, drawing on the chivalric history of his nation and reframing it as something that could once more arise, saying, "There never has been, I suppose, in all the history of war, such an opportunity for youth. The Knights of the Round Table, the Crusaders, all fall back into the past—not only distant but prosaic; these young men, going forth every morn to guard their native land and all that we stand for, holding in their hands these instruments of colossal and shattering power, of whom it may be said that 'Every morn brought forth a noble chance and every chance brought forth a noble knight,' deserve our gratitude."[78]

In this same speech, having given the youth of the British military a vision of the meaning not only of their lives but also in many cases their deaths, he places the entire people of his island in relation to the forthcoming struggle by identifying them in a radical vision of themselves with the words "We shall fight on the beaches. We shall fight on the landing grounds. We shall fight in the fields, and in the streets, we shall fight in the hills. We shall never surrender."[79] History tells us that the British people experienced no immediate relief from their dire circumstances. But Churchill gave them more than that: he gave them a vision of their relation to this circumstance, one that connected them with the history of their ancestors. And it was through his rhetorical imagination that Churchill was able to fire the imagination of the British people, so that they could make it so.

This is also the rhetorical meaning of the words he used to conclude his address to the nation fourteen days later, when he said, "Let us therefore brace ourselves to our duties, and so bear ourselves that, if the British Empire and its Commonwealth last for a thousand years, men will still say, 'This was their finest hour.'"[80] Carrying his people to a vision of themselves as seen by people of the next millennia, he puts the events of the day in the context of a history yet to be written and carries the people of his time to *that time,* to give them a perspective that the people of those islands would imprint into their channel, their soil, and their history with sacrificial blood. Churchill had a reasoned plan of action for stopping Hitler, and that plan was brought before the House of Commons and the British people. But notice that he also situated that plan within a vision that the audience could see and share—could live and even die for. Churchill's words were eloquent not merely because of the metaphorical devices that he used, but because he was able to use these devices, during a time of crisis, to call forth the imagination of the British people in such a way that they could take a stand for their dwelling place, and for dwelling, and, by extension, for themselves.

Today, by contrast with Churchill's time, we exist in a culture of images, and the most powerful of contemporary record (the September 11 flights) played hourly on television during the early drafts of this essay. Such images have caused irreversible damage to one of the foremost elements of rhetorical address: the eloquence of verbal panorama in public discourse. In this illustrative case, announcers spoke flatly about the event while the images of the planes and the falling buildings played constantly in the background—a news-media method that turns the human voice into a footnote of history. When such images come first, they come without the salvation of language, the sort of salvation Churchill was able to bring to the Dunkirk extraction. As Frye says, "If you're totally dependent on visual images, it causes a good deal of confusion.[81] Rhetors should not, therefore, surrender this part of their speaking obligation to photography, despite its powers. Something will be lost."

I began discussions of the role of imaginative vision in my public speaking class a year ago, using the notion to orient students toward imagining their own lives as destinies that could be fulfilled. A few weeks into the course, one of the students handed me a long note in which she said, among other things, that imagining the possibility of her life as a destiny caused "this dormant lump inside of my head . . . to become stimulated. I still am very unsure about what I know and what I don't know, but I will no longer let that be my weak excuse. I am always saying, 'Sara you couldn't do that, you'll never be smart enough or capable enough.' That thought continues to flash through my mind, but I will not let it get the best of me."

I later learned that Sara had been drugged, raped, and left for dead in a basement while still a high school student. For many of us, it is impossible to grasp the crippling effect such violence inflicts upon the human will; and, in Sara's case, the event had caused her life to shrink small enough to fit into the chamber of fear it had created for her. Through her own determination, however, and through her own imagination of what she could become, she managed to gather the emotional resources necessary to testify and endure cross-examination at the rape trial. The experience represented a transformative moment in her life because it marked the occasion on which she took possession of her world. It was an act that demonstrated "a quality of courage; a courage that is without compromise in a world full of cheap rhetoric, yet uses none of the ready-made mixes of rhetoric in a world full of compromise."[82] Thus, in this most regional of action, out of the sort of horrible event that happens to young women far too often, we see the possibility for the same kind of commitment to existence that George Bailey and Sir Winston Churchill have brought to our attention in this essay. We see an occasion upon which a random student in any classroom in America can take up a commitment to the manner that she dwells within the world. She can claim her *ethos* by this commitment and thereby come into Being. But the fulfillment of this possibility requires an imaginative vision that can transcend the images that are handed to her by the everyday. Sara found her way at a very early age. Many others can as well. And though I shudder to think of the teacher as a sort of pop messiah, it is worth noting that this transformation occurred in a public speaking classroom because this transformation is at the heart of what it means to receive a liberal education, and it shows that the human heart can find itself not just in philosophy or religion or psychology classrooms, that human potential can be discovered and realized in rhetoric itself. I believe this faith in the potential for humanity underlies any project such as *The Ethos of Rhetoric,* and I hope that what I have offered here is a worthy contribution to that project.

Notes

1. Martin Heidegger, "Building Dwelling Thinking," in *Martin Heidegger: Basic Writings,* ed. David Farrell Krell (New York: Harper & Row, 1977), 323–39.

2. Ibid., 325.

3. Ibid., 327.

4. If the being of a thing is examined teleologically, then, for example, an acorn comes into selfhood as a tree, a calf comes into selfhood as a steer, and a person comes into selfhood as the caretaker of the world and the people in it.

5. It should be noted, however, that since proper dwelling is an accomplishment (and therefore something that we can undertake or disregard or even abandon), we are all, to one degree or another, in that hell even as I speak.

6. Given dwelling is a pivotal term here, it is fascinating to note that George Bailey was directly involved in the building of homes. I am also reminded of the occasions on which he wanted to travel or go to college but did not because of unexpected circumstances in his community. These interruptions in his life illustrate what Michael Hyde describes in his text *The Call of Conscience: Heidegger and Levinas, Rhetoric and the Euthanasia Debate* (Columbia: University of South Carolina Press, 2001). Hyde argues that the pathways one lives causally, almost habitually, are sometimes disturbed by unforeseen circumstances. He identifies these disturbances as interruptions because they slow, or even close off, certain trajectories of existence; and he finds in them the possibility for an authentic response—specifically when one turns toward the call that comes from other people, in the midst of such events. Whereas Bailey regularly turned away from the path he expected to live, when that path was interrupted by events that affected the people he cared for, his story fits Hyde's characterization of authentic existence so well that it could be his exemplary case.

7. Still, there is something to be said for a self-realized relationship with one's world. It surely made a difference to George Bailey. In that sense, the film also provides an

illustration of how and why it is that philosophy plays an important role in a healthy life.

8. Martin Heidegger, *Plato's Sophist,* trans. Richard Rojcewicz and Andre Schuwer (Bloomington: Indiana University Press, 1997), 159.

9. By way of example, I recently was stopped at a gas station by a self-identified Christian man who initially said he wanted jumper cables but quickly changed the story to $1.98 to complete payment on a car battery, then $5.00 for the old battery core, then $5.00 to borrow tools, then a drive to his place of work, where he would refund me. At the last stop, he bolted into a space between houses and I never saw him again. Much like the occasions when people have walked up to me in parking lots, shaking a set of keys and asking for a few dollars for gas, the entire event was a scam. Ultimately he got $20.00 from me, and in that sense he was effective. Nevertheless, what he did is no example of effective speech because it made me more cynical toward others and allowed him to continue the sort of self-destructive spiral that requires $20.00 a day to perpetuate itself. Effective speech, according to the argument put forth in this essay, proceeds from a commitment to a better world. Events like the one described here, by contrast, bring harm into the world.

10. Heidegger, *Plato's Sophist,* 159.

11. Although his tendency is to talk about that possibility for language in terms of poetry in a manner that, I think, stretches the mantle of poetry over rhetoric.

12. Or *her,* of course. I use the one gender for stylistic purposes only.

13. Already Hyde's *Call of Conscience* has demonstrated how this is possible. See Robert Wade Kenny, "Resituating Rhetoric, Philosophy, and Poetics through Michael J. Hyde's *Call of Conscience,*" *Quarterly Journal of Speech* 88 (2002): 245–58.

14. The issue addressed here is perhaps best considered through Hyde's *Call of Conscience,* which makes clear that rhetoric does not proceed as the handmaiden to philosophy or politics but is a wisdom in itself.

15. George A. Kennedy, *Classical Rhetoric and Its Christian and Secular Form from Ancient to Modern Times* (Chapel Hill: University of North Carolina Press, 1980), 217–18.

16. George Campbell, *The Philosophy of Rhetoric* (Carbondale: Southern Illinois University Press, 1963), 3–4.

17. Richard Whately, *Elements of Rhetoric* (Carbondale: Illinois University Press, 1963), 194.

18. Hugh Blair, *Lectures on Rhetoric and Belles Lettres* (Carbondale: Southern Illinois University Press, 1965), 44. Lecture 3 is largely devoted to an elaboration of these effects.

19. Michael Calvin McGee, "The 'Ideograph': A Link between Rhetoric and Ideology," in *Readings in Rhetorical Criticism,* 2d ed., ed. Carl R. Burgchardt (State College, Pa.: Strata, 2000), 456–70.

20. Walter Fisher, "Narration as a Human Communication Paradigm: The Case of Public Moral Argument," in *Readings in Rhetorical Criticism,* 2d ed., ed. Carl R. Burgchardt (State College, Pa.: Strata, 2000), 338–49.

21. See also Northrop Frye, "The Developing Imagination," in *Learning and Language in Literature* (Cambridge: Harvard University Press, 1963). See also Northrop Frye, "Imagination and the Imaginary," in *Fables of Identity: Studies in Poetic Mythology* (New York: Harcourt, Brace & World, 1963), 151–67.

22. Northrop Frye, *Fearful Symmetry: A Study of William Blake* (Princeton, N.J.: Princeton University Press, 1969), 14. Consider Heidegger's similar dissatisfaction when he says, "Expelled from the truth of Being, man everywhere circles around himself as the *animale rationale.*" Martin Heidegger, "Letter on Humanism," in *Martin Heidegger: Basic Writings,* ed. David Farrell Krell (New York: Harper & Row, 1977), 21.

23. Frye, *Fearful Symmetry,* 14.

24. Ibid., 16.

25. See, for example, Northrop Frye, "Speculation and Concern," in *The Stubborn Structure,* by Northrop Frye (Ithaca, N.Y.: Cornell University Press, 1970), 38–55.

26. Frye, *Fearful Symmetry,* 19.

27. Ibid., 19.

28. Ibid., 248.

29. Cited in Frye, *Fearful Symmetry,* 21. We can better grasp the meaning of Blake's words if he cried, "Holy, holy, holy is the authentic human experience of Life." Blake did not believe that God is a thing.

30. Frye, *Fearful Symmetry,* 21.

31. Northrop Frye, *Words with Power: Being a Second Study of the Bible and Literature* (San Diego: Harcourt, Brace, Jovanovich, 1992), 76.

32. Frye, *Fearful Symmetry,* 27.

33. Tree bark was once used to prevent scurvy and is now used to extract a powerful antioxidant called pycogenol.

34. Earth is unfree in that its *telos* was ordained ahead of it except through its human children.

35. Heidegger, "Letter on Humanism," 228–29.

36. Frye, *Fearful Symmetry,* 23.

37. Ibid., 236.

38. Ibid., 43. We also should note that much of this argument has been verified in Piaget's stages of cognitive development. See, for example, "The Child's Conception of Physical Causality," in *The Essential Piaget: An Interpretive Reference and Guide,* ed. Howard E. Gruber and J. Jacques Vonèche (New York: Basic Books, 1977), 140. There Piaget states that for children at a certain stage, "[c]louds and the heavenly bodies move along because they are alive."

39. Frye, *Stubborn Structure,* 96.

40. The following are the primary characteristics Frye gives to imaginative vision:

Imagination vision is pre-predicative. Sensation does not come before imagination in this view. Even in chaotic experience, the imagination is operating, attempting to make sense of the event while nevertheless imagining it as a chaotic event.

Imaginative vision is transcendent. It is not spatially or temporally constrained. In space, for example, though I am sitting inside my car when I hear a squealing noise, my imaginative vision allows me to see, even from there, the excessively loosened alternator belt under the hood. In time, for example, I may stand on the front porch of a rundown house yet see it, through imaginative vision, completely restored.

Imaginative vision is transmittable in communicative acts. For example, one Christmas I gave my mother a Royal Dalton figurine because she was collecting them. As she opened the present, however, I told her that it was an unbreakable ornament made by a company called Roy L. Dalton. She showed no sign of pleasure in the gift until she saw the stamp of (I shudder to use the term in this context) authenticity underneath.

Imagination is culturally specific. There are any number of cultural entities whose people would neither be impressed by the ornament I gave my mother nor by the tag underneath it. Mother's imagination of the figurine occurs in a specific imaginative culture, one that, although it does change, has regions of relative consistency that allow people to share common visions.

Imaginative vision is developed. This should be clear, especially if one gives regard to the fourth characteristic. For if the imagination of a Royal Dalton figurine depends upon a specific cultural milieu, then one must spend time relating to that culture in order to share the imaginative experiences it offers. My favorite example of a failure to develop a shared imaginative vision comes from a televised episode of *The Beverly Hillbillies.* The family was under the impression that the billiards table was a special dining table, and they used the cues as pot-passers. No one ever challenged this vision, so they held it and did not develop their imagination of the table in any other way throughout the seasons that the program ran.

Imagination is concerned. Frye uses this term to distinguish imagination from the imaginary and from flights of fancy. As he characterizes imagination, the quality plays a fundamental role in the management of existence and participates meaningfully in the creation of our society. Guided by an existential "conviction that life is better than death, happiness better than misery, freedom better than bondage," imaginative vision is a force that drives human life toward its own improvement.

41. Frye, *Fables of Identity,* 147.

42. Frye, *Fearful Symmetry,* 236.

43. Frye, *Stubborn Structure,* 26.

44. Frye, *Fearful Symmetry,* 265.

45. Ibid., 41

46. Northrop Frye, *The Well-Tempered Critic* (Bloomington: Indiana University Press, 1963), 154.

47. "And what rough beast, its hour come round at last, slouches towards Bethlehem to be born?" William Butler Yeats, "The Second Coming," in *The Norton Anthology of Poetry,* ed. Arthur M. Eastman (New York: W. W. Norton, 1970), 914.

48. David Cayley, *Northrop Frye in Conversation* (Concord, Ont.: Anansi Press, 1992), 96.

49. Frye, *Fearful Symmetry,* 41.

50. Northrop Frye, *Spiritus Mundi: Essays on Literature, Myth, and Society* (Richmond Hill, Ont.: Fitzhenry and Whiteside, 1976), 60.

51. Frye, *Well-Tempered Critic,* 154.

52. Northrop Frye, *The Educated Imagination* (Bloomington: Indiana University Press, 1964), 149.

53. Lloyd Bitzer, "The Rhetorical Situation," in *Readings in Rhetorical Criticism,* 2d ed., ed. Carl R. Burgchardt (State College, Pa.: Strata, 2000), 63.

54. Frye, *Stubborn Structure,* 51.

55. Frye, *Educated Imagination,* 140.

56. Ibid., 152.

57. Northrop Frye, *The Critical Path: An Essay on the Social Context of Literary Criticism* (Bloomington: Indiana University Press, 1971), 97.

58. Frye, *Stubborn Structure,* 104.

59. Ibid., 15.

60. Northrop Frye, *A Study of English Romanticism* (New York: Random House, 1968), 128.

61. Frye, *Spiritus Mundi,* 289.

62. "Man is not the Lord of beings. Man is the shepherd of Being." Heidegger, "Letter on Humanism," 221.

63. See, for example, Michael Hyde's discussion of B. J. Nelson and his mother Marie in Hyde's *Call of Conscience,* 178–86. The fact that Nelson was able to publish an article about his mother's death in *Harper's Magazine* is no indication to Hyde, or me, that Nelson's writing demonstrated the *ethos* referred to in this essay.

64. For a remarkable analysis of Churchill's rhetoric, see Manfred Weidhorn, "Churchill the Phrase Forger," *Quarterly Journal of Speech* 58 (1972): 161–74.

65. Winston S. Churchill, "European Dangers," November 23, 1932 (House of Commons), in *Winston S. Churchill: His Complete Speeches, 1897–1963,* ed. Robert Rhodes James (London: Chelsea House, 1974), 5199–5200.

66. Frye, *Words with Power,* xxii.

67. Louise MacNeice, "London Rain," in *The Norton Anthology of Poetry,* ed. Arthur M. Eastman (New York: W. W. Norton, 1970), 1082.

68. W. H. Auden, "As I Walked Out One Evening," in *The Norton Anthology of Poetry,* ed. Arthur M. Eastman (New York: W. W. Norton, 1970), 1078.

69. T. S. Eliot, *The Love Song of J. Alfred Prufrock,* in *The Norton Anthology of Poetry,* ed. Arthur M. Eastman (New York: W. W. Norton, 1970), 996–99.

70. Frye, *Fearful Symmetry,* 116.

71. Frye, *Critical Path,* 94–95.

72. Cayley, *Northrop Frye in Conversation,* 215.

73. Frye, *Stubborn Structure,* 17.

74. Northrop Frye, *Myth and Metaphor: Selected Essays, 1974–1988,* ed. Robert Denham (Charlottesville: University Press of Virginia), 232.

75. Northrop Frye, *Fables of Identity,* 253.

76. Winston S. Churchill, "Wars Are Not Won by Evacuations," June 4, 1940 (House of Commons), in *Winston S. Churchill: His Complete Speeches, 1897–1963,* ed. Robert Rhodes James (London: Chelsea House, 1974), 6225.

77. Ibid.

78. Ibid., 6231.

79. Ibid.

80. Winston S. Churchill, "Their Finest Hour," June 18, 1940 (House of Commons) in *Winston S. Churchill: His Complete Speeches, 1897–1963,* ed. Robert Rhodes James (London: Chelsea House, 1974), 6238.

81. Cayley, *Northrop Frye in Conversation,* 164.

82. Frye, *Fables of Identity,* 254.

The *Ethos* of Rhetorical Criticism
Enlarging the Dwelling Place
of Critical Praxis

BARBARA WARNICK

What might it mean to form and sustain a community of scholars who explore important social phenomena and whose work has currency and intellectual substance? This question has been asked about the practice of rhetorical criticism by my predecessors and colleagues for some time now. Many of them have voiced concerns about rhetorical criticism—its viability, worth, and specific contributions —in a number of venues, including disciplinary conferences, book-length publications, special issues of national and regional journals, convention panels, and retrospective and prospective views of the discipline of speech communication.

Apparently, these authors and speakers are not be fully satisfied with the answers they have found, because they continue to raise the same issues. How can rhetorical critics maintain a scholarly stance and at the same time act as engaged and committed spokespersons on the major issues of our time? How can they study how texts bring unity to thought while keeping in view the discursive formations that condition those texts? In the absence of any culturally unified standard of truth or knowledge, how are critics to approach their work? What standards should they apply, to either the rhetorics they study or their own critical production? Reintroducing such questions here might be interpreted as yet another call for unification in the face of threats to disciplinary identity. Yet I intend nothing so hegemonic as that.

Rather, I would like to make a modest proposal for a rhetorical critical praxis that suits the needs of our age and its social and political circumstances. I suggest that we turn away from preoccupation with disciplinary identity and toward our reading publics and each other. What if we enlarged the abode or dwelling place for criticism and began producing work that is evocative rather than primarily analytical and prescriptive in nature?

The form of criticism I propose would be evocative in the sense that it would reach out to readers and other critics and call forth thought about the issues that rhetoric engages. Its readers would be viewed as participants in a rhetorical process of deliberation rather than as passive admirers of critical prowess. Evocative criticism would leave openings for views other than those of the critic and would be enacted so as to provoke thought and dislodge habitual ways of thinking about social issues. It would not shy away from questions of value in the interest of scholarly dispassion, and it would take pains to recognize and reveal forces that constrain what can be said and limit who can speak. It would continue to be grounded in a minimal consensus among its practitioners about its nature, form, and mission, but it would become more open to a wider range of critical practices and more accessible to a broader general reading public. While this might mean setting aside some of the scholarly conventions and commitments to which critics have subscribed, the benefits to be gained could be substantial.

To lay out this proposal for enlarging the space for critical practice, first it is necessary to discuss four major theoretical issues that have impeded rhetorical critics in their work and then revisit an idea that was broached some thirty years ago but that has been insufficiently considered since then. Finally, consideration needs to be given to how this idea might be taken up to form an *ethos* of rhetorical criticism. The work of some contemporary critics already embodies the model to be described here; however, efforts to develop an *ethos* of rhetorical criticism have been hampered by theoretical controversy over these four issues related to the practice of criticism and to standards for judging its quality.

Four Divisive Issues

For the past two decades, work in rhetorical criticism has been troubled by these four divisive issues: (1) whether the critic should be positioned as scholarly observer or should be politically engaged, (2) whether criticism's starting point should be the intention of the author and the strategic design of the text or the conditions that shaped the text, (3) whether rhetorical texts should be judged according to traditional standards of Western rationality or by some other means, and (4) whether criticism should be method-driven or evocative. The first option in each of these represents the point of view of traditional humanism as custodian of values and preserver of the intellectual and social order.

In his *Communicative Praxis and the Space of Subjectivity,* Calvin O. Schrag argued that, since Nietzsche, traditional humanism has been confronted by the end of theism and the demise of a metaphysics of value. In particular, it has been challenged by a new humanism—a humanism of decentered subjectivity that "illustrates not the theoretical reflection of cognitive detachment but rather the practical engagement of concrete involvement."[1] In Schrag's view, the praxis of this new humanism arises in the *ethos* of rhetoric. In this framework, the rhetor (in this case, the rhetorical critic) seeks to evoke from readers a response that takes place in a rhetorical space of self/other encounter. To describe the quality of this encounter, Schrag invokes the idea of an abode or open region of freely accepted obligations in which participants encounter and respond to the ideas and values of others.

The view of rhetorical criticism I will put forward aligns with Schrag's idea of opening a space where various audiences and subject positions can dwell and are welcome. To show how this idea is problematic, what is at stake here, and where the lines of division in the field have been drawn, I will consider the issues that have so divided rhetorical critics and theorists for so long.

Issue 1: How can we reconcile the need for scholarly distance and dispassion with a commitment to consider political and social issues related to the text?

Raised most clearly in Philip Wander's 1983 essay "The Ideological Turn in Modern Criticism," the issue of critical engagement with significant social issues continues to be raised nearly twenty years later.[2] How does a critic negotiate two seemingly incompatible roles—scholar and public spokesperson? The posture of the critic as scholar is one of objectivity in which more or less clearly understood standards for judging public discourse are applied to the rhetorical text, whereas the critic who seeks to engage the larger social and political framework has a task that is much less well defined. As Wander noted, the politically engaged critic "would confront ideals professed [in the text] with what they obscure in either theory or practice in light of possibilities for real or 'emancipatory' change."[3]

It could be said that the argument for critical dispassion and scholarly decorum has much to recommend it. First, in the critic-as-scholar model, the critic is judged by the extent to which her claims about the text and/or its effects are explicitly shown to be supported by the substance of the text and audience reactions to it. These elements are either accessible to the critic's readers or can be made accessible through her research into the material conditions surrounding the text. The downside of departing from these standard critical practices was perhaps most clearly stated by Forbes Hill in his response to Wander: "Professor Wander leads us with his critiques away from the art of rhetoric. He tells us almost nothing about the work, the traditional topoi drawn on, the unique or unusual strategies developed, the pathe employed, or the kinds of audience it creates or seeks to persuade. These matters I take to be the very essence of an art [of] rhetoric; the rest is peripheral."[4] The assumption here is that, in relinquishing recourse to what is disclosed in the text and to the material conditions that corroborate the critic's analysis, the critic loses those sources of argument and evidence that license and support her work. As Nothstine, Blair, and Copeland noted, on this view, "the proper stance for the researcher is one of objectivity—practical, ethical, and intellectual distance from the object of study."[5]

Second, in venturing into the realms of dispute and deliberation, the critic may have to desert the genre of scholarly writing that so dominates material in peer-reviewed journals and academic publishing. Advocacy does not align well with the requirements to situate criticism in light of earlier scholarship, present complex critical analysis, and show why one's work contributes to disciplinary knowledge. These comprise a set of practices that Michael McGee has referred to as "the culture of critical discourse," one that authorizes itself as the "standard of all 'serious' speech."[6] The rhetorical critic wanting to connect his criticism to the issues of the material social world loses this advantage of self-authorizing serious speech.

There is much to be said, however, for attempting to negotiate the tensions between scholarly dispassion and political engagement. Academics are also citizens, and one might argue that they have an obligation to bring the fruits of their learning and research to the public consciousness and to disclose the complexity and many-sidedness of the issues pertinent to the texts they analyze. Some critical theorists have argued that, instead of being judged purely by the standards of scholarly objectivity, critics should be measured by the extent to which their work engages and extends thinking about the issues relevant to it. Richard A. Cherwitz and John Theobald-Osborne stated this most compellingly: "After reading highly specialized rhetorical accounts of messages, one is left with the question: Of what value is such criticism to those in society who transmit and receive communication? Or more specifically, to what extent can the insights gleaned by scholarly criticism be used constructively to promote better policies?"[7] It seems to me that it is quite fair to ask such questions of the scholars studying public discourse, many of whom argue assiduously for preservation and maintenance of the public sphere but whose scholarly work seems so distanced from it.

As to those who worry about the consequences of deserting the conventions of scholarly writing and taking up polemics, there are reassurances that can be made. As I will argue below, it seems to me that, so long as the critic positions her audience so as to feel comfortable in reasoning along with the critic, she has fulfilled her scholarly commitments and, at the same time, appealed to a more broadly distributed and general public audience than that of the specialized critic.

Issue 2: Should the locus of criticism continue to be focused on the rhetor as origin and the strategic design of the text, or should it bring into account the ways in which the text is conditioned by its discursive environment?

It is well recognized that during the first fifty or so years of the twentieth century, rhetorical criticism in speech communication was centered on the rhetor—his intentions, purpose, strategy, verbal skill, and effectiveness. Within this critical paradigm, the critic stayed within the world view of the speaker, and critical activity was through and through speaker-centered. (And, it must be admitted, this made the task of judging critical production rather straightforward.) When criticism in the field came under the influence of the New Criticism, the emphasis on the speaker was less obvious; it seemed instead to concentrate on the text's artistry and design thereby drawing attention to the artistry of the critic who revealed the artistry of the original and now idealized text.[8]

John Campbell explicitly and unequivocally defended the notion of speaker-centeredness when he argued that agency is the mechanism by which communication becomes intelligible, the means by which readers make sense of what is said: "To say that the invocation of 'agency' is an 'ideology' and we can set it aside in favor of an alternative that dispenses with it is not merely false. It is nonsense. Talk about agency, responsibility, intentions, and community is more secure than anything that could question them, precisely because they are practices in which we are all complicit."[9] Critics subscribing to a speaker-centered view of criticism consider the speaker as the starting point and origin of the text, and they examine the critical artifact within that context. Many of them evidently feel that there is no more appropriate anchor for critical readings. Hill, for example, asked whether it is "worse for a critic to lock himself or herself into the worldview of the rhetor as set forth in the discourse, or, on the other hand, to treat the rhetor from the point of view of a hostile ideology and never sympathetically understand what the discourse is all about."[10]

Commitments to speaker-centeredness and idealized text in rhetorical criticism seem to be part and parcel of an identity that is disciplinary in nature and was characterized as an "ideology" by Gaonkar, who described it as a "view of speaker as the seat of origin rather than a point of articulation, a view of strategy as identifiable under an intentional description, a view of discourse as constitutive of character and community, a view of audience as positioned simultaneously as 'spectator' and 'participant' and finally, a view of 'ends' that binds speaker, strategy, discourse, and audience in a web of purposive actions."[11] A large part of the rhetorical critical tradition has its origin in a model of criticism aligned with this view of rhetorical action. The fact that some of the finest critics in the field were educated and have educated their students in this view should not prevent us from seeing it as one possibility among many others.

Many critical theorists have viewed the speaker-centered orientation as limited and circumscribed.[12] Miller noted that such a view of rhetoric and critical action is an "incomplete and inadequate translation of classical rhetorical theory" and cited Bender and Wellbery's observation that "rhetoric today . . . is a transdisciplinary field of practice and intellectual concern."[13] Intense focus on the text as an instantiation of the rhetor's strategic design may prevent critics from considering the extratextual field of discourse in which discursive event intervenes.

As Goankar has noted, work by contemporary critics should investigate the relationship between "the public sphere, where rhetoric does its business of ideological integration, and social formations like the economy, technoscience, and bureaucracy that are run on a non-dialogic, systemic logic."[14] Excellent work of this kind can be found in authors in fields such as English and women's studies who examine the persuasive dimensions of circulating texts. What I am calling for here was simply described by Cyphert as a move from "judg[ing] rhetorical practice" to "reading discourse as rhetorical."[15] In the field of speech communication, there are various models of this sort of work. As examples I would note Smith and Windes's account of pro- and antigay issue clusters in public discourse and Rushing and Frentz's studies of mythic structures in contemporary films, but such works have not yet become a part of what some scholars view as the canon of critical production.[16]

Issue 3: Should rhetorical texts be judged according to the traditional standards of Western rationality or by some other means?

As a vein of scholarly practice, both rhetorical criticism and its texts have historically been judged according to Eurocentric standards of rationality. One aspect of this is that rhetorical criticism itself functions as an argument, and the critic's work is judged by how closely and thoroughly the claims made about the text are supported by evidence available to the critic's readers. On this view, adherence to consensually recognized standards for inductive and deductive logical proof is an important means for enabling critics and their professional audiences to evaluate their critical work. This requirement was explicitly reflected, for example, in Hill's frustrations about Wander's polemical critique of his work when Hill asked, "How does one verify that? It is difficult to get one's sights on what there is to verify," and in his insistence that the issues at stake were "subject to argument in a scholarly journal [and] can never be settled a priori."[17] Hill claimed that Wander's refutation was "pure partisanship."

Furthermore, tacit adherence to forms of logic originating in the classical rhetorical tradition has deeply imprinted the discipline's teaching of argumentation as well as its critical practice. Rhetorical performances are frequently judged by the complexity and elegance of the logics they employ, and those logics are usually conceived as either inductive or deductive in nature.[18] As Cyphert has noted, "From a Western rhetorical framework, which has carefully defined both sanity and ethics in terms of non-contradictory logic and the articulated perception of external sense data, the dangers of demagoguery could only be prevented with a mechanism of externally grounded 'rational decision making.'"[19] Only relatively recently have rhetorical theorists begun to advocate attention to alternative models of reasoning and logic.[20]

Insistence on the standards of inductive and deductive argument nevertheless systematically privileges only certain culture-bound forms of communication. The classical models for these forms of thought arose in a public sphere very different from the one we experience today—one where audiences of public discourse presumably shared a common cultural experience, premises for argument, and ways of thinking.[21] Broadening our critical perspective may mean including non-Western forms of reasoning as legitimate sources of justification, for both critics and the rhetorics they study. As sociolinguists and argument theorists have noted, people in various cultures who seek to justify their views or communicate ideas do so in various ways. Johnstone, for example, maintained that people may support their views by telling stories, making reference to their own authority, or paraphrasing their position.[22] Studies of contrastive rhetoric and transcultural argument have revealed patterns of parallel and antithetical structure, cooperative or abductive argument, and epideictic reasoning.[23] To create a more habitable discursive abode for a wider audience, traditional critics may need to admit a wider range of reasoning structures into the critical lexicon. A model of what is needed can be found in the work of feminist theorists such as Josina Makau who advocate a broadened conception of critical thinking less dependent on formal logic and canonized forms of reasoning.[24]

Issue 4: Should criticism be judged according to the skill by which it applies its method or the extent to which it provokes further thought?

In most instances of rhetorical criticism, method has had a significant function: to expose to the scrutiny of its readers the rationale for its evaluation and the reasons for the critic's judgment.[25] Whether a critic provides a close textual reading of the style or argument structure of a text, exposes its underlying mythic components or its tacit ideology, or uses some other method, that critic works to make the text nontransparent for readers. In other words, that critic provides a skilled, learned, insightful reading that explains the workings of the text. Critics are judged to be successful by the extent to which their critical judgments resonate with the facts of the text and by the extent to which what they disclose is important or significant and otherwise inaccessible to the lay reader.

Aside from its role in securing the legitimacy of critical interpretation, method-driven criticism has other effects. It is often (but not always) epideictic in nature, viewing its readers as spectators of critical prowess, as fellow professional experts, educated and therefore positioned to admire the critic's skill. When this happens, the critic functions as performer, and if the object of her criticism is an idealized text, the experience of reading or hearing the criticism should be enjoyable and appreciative.[26]

Method-driven criticism has been challenged and criticized for various reasons. Steve Fuller has raised the question of whether "real" audiences and readers actually read texts in the ways that professional critics do. He notes that rhetoricians of science, for example, are "likely to imagine a leisured and learned reader genuinely interested in what the author has to say."[27] He argues that, even in the case of classics in the field of science, "there is little evidence to suggest that [their] impact is the result of people having read [the work] with the sort of critical engagement that would satisfy the rhetorician of science."[28] On Fuller's view, then, the work of method-driven criticism may be intrinsically interesting but often has little relevance in understanding how texts are actually read and appropriated by their real world audiences.

The emphasis on method has also been criticized for its tendency to draw attention toward the technical fine points of criticism and away from the substantive action and social relevance of what the text has to say. In his commentary on published reaction to Wander's essay, McGee noted that of all the other respondents had focused on method and the correctness of their own critical work and that "not once [did they] entertain the possibility that . . . there may be a grain of truth and wisdom in [Wander's] comparison of the relative moral worth of social-rhetorical criticism held over and against that rhetorical criticism which postulates the free agency of the critic."[29] Earlier in this article, McGee argued that "method" itself has become an ideograph, and he maintained that focus on method is a guise for determining what will count as knowledge. He noted that our endorsement of "healthy pluralism" is often nothing more than approval of "methodological pluralism."[30]

Another unfortunate outcome at least partly due to this focus on method was noted by Nothstine, Blair, and Copeland. They argued that insistence upon method is motivated largely by a desire to "scientize criticism," to "ensure against the intrusion of interest or idiosyncrasy."[31] Or, as Klumpp and Hollihan noted, the "dominant interpretation of the rhetorical critic's purpose over the last three decades has formed from the relationship of critical method to social science."[32] The professionalization of criticism has meant reliance on a "frequently opaque language" of the rhetorical critic that renders her work inaccessible and often uninteresting to general audiences. Nothstine, Blair, and Copeland believe that "to the extent that professional critics seem to value the concrete, situated event only as 'data' for theoretical generalizations, as springboards for their feats of scholarly virtuosity, not as interested, consequential discourse, communities outside the academy are unlikely to find their concrete concerns noticed, much less addressed and engaged."[33] The tendency to prioritize criticism that is verifiable, dispassionate, and disengaged, as well as the reluctance to make judgments about policy and social action, may confine critics' audiences to specialists and exclude general audiences who would otherwise be interested in their work. Nothstine, Blair, and Copeland also point out that another audience excluded by critical practice is our students "who may well leave university culture knowing more about how to be citizens of the academic community than they do about ways of being, thinking, and acting in a larger public sphere."[34]

A Modest Proposal

On the whole, then, what seems to be needed is critical praxis less exclusively focused on purely academic concerns and more prone to reach larger audiences in an inclusive, less specialized, and more accessible way. In considering the *ethos* of rhetorical criticism, we should consider enlarging the dwelling place for critical work from a specialized audience of the disciplinarily like-minded to a larger public of concerned and attentive citizens.

Any new form of rhetorical criticism must nevertheless negotiate the tensions I have just described. That is, somehow it must broaden the critic's role without making her into a polemicist, integrate the rhetor/text-centered focus with productive consideration of forces that condition the text, move away from exclusively logocentric standards of judgment, and result in criticism that invites audiences to discuss and ponder major social issues.

To meet these challenges, I will argue, we should shift the focus of concern from method to the critic's responsibility to engage the larger issues with which rhetoric concerns itself. While an emphasis on the critic's responsibilities has been proposed by various theorists during the past three decades, as yet it has not been widely taken up. Foss has speculated that reluctance to emphasize the critic as agent (as opposed to method as agency) may be due to the aforementioned concern that the critic's role as advocate may be incompatible with "criticism [that is] rigorous or legitimate,"[35] but I concur with her view that if there were more emphasis on the critic's role as member of the larger society, we "would find various alternative conceptions of rhetorical criticism, including greater diversity of methods, more nearly equal participation by critic and audience in the creation of rhetorical knowledge, and a reconsideration of the role of objectivity in criticism."[36] What I have in mind is a shift in the critic's role from performer and expert to one of co-arguer and supposer, one who makes it his primary aim to invite his audience to think in new ways. In the words of Klumpp and Hollihan, this is a critic who "listens to what has been said, and even hears what will be said, and offers his/her commentary woven into the emerging fabric of understanding."[37] By this means, such a critic would enlarge the circle of rhetorical critical praxis to include the concerns of any number of groups and audiences, among them disciplinary colleagues but also members of the general public attentive to and concerned about issues relevant to the rhetoric and rhetorical situation studied by the critic.

While instances of criticism that follow this model are not readily found in communication journals, they do exist in the communication field and in English, women's studies, sociolinguistics, and elsewhere. To clarify what I have in mind, I will describe a few examples that put forward a point of view while at the same time being circumspect, thoughtful, and accessible to academics and the general reading public.

N. Katherine Hayles's book, *How We Became Posthuman,* recently contemplated the loss of embodiment and the material in light of the rise of information and virtuality in contemporary culture. Hayles described her work as a recovery effort —to "show what had to be elided, suppressed, and forgotten to make information lose its body."[38] Hers is a threaded narrative that draws on literatures in cybernetics, artificial intelligence, and cyberpunk fiction to reveal the visions that celebrated embodiment along with the erasures that enabled the creation of virtuality. Her work is multivoiced and her presentation inductive; it eventuates in an indefinite outcome, inviting its readers into a dialectical process of reasoning and knowing together that seems primarily designed to produce further thought about "the complex cultural, social, and representational issues tied up with conceptual shifts and technological innovations."[39]

In her book *Modest_Witness@Second_Millennium.FemaleMan©_Meets_Onco-Mouse™: Feminism and Technoscience* feminist scholar Donna Haraway explored themes similar to those examined by Hayles: the cyborgization of the human, computer-mediated virtuality, manipulation of the body through reproductive technologies, and genetic engineering. She sought neither to advance a dystopian view of transnational capital and technoscience on the one hand nor to deny the existence of distributed patterns of domination on the other. Rather, her aim was to show the "dense nodes of human and nonhuman actors that are brought into alliance by the material, social, and semiotic technologies through which what will count as nature and as matters of fact get constituted for—and by—many millions of people."[40]

She thus sought to dislodge our habitual ways of experiencing conventional constructions of race, technology, science, and the human body. *Modest Witness* is a frame-shifting book intended to diffract our perceptions and to introduce "more promising interference patterns in the recording films of our lives and bodies."[41] To this end, Haraway made use of many kinds of discourses—news reports, feminist science fiction, charts, iconic photographs, advertisements, bodily representations, textbooks, pedagogical practices, and other public texts—that illustrate how the constitutive practices of technoscience and racial discourse have come to inhabit the collective psyche. Her novel uses of language and her re-presentations and exegeses of iconic material do not lead to particular conclusions but to new ways of thinking about feminism, racism, democracy, and justice in society. Her heteroglossic restatement of ideas invites her readers to contemplate the implications of her work in their terms.[42]

A fine model of morally engaged criticism can be found in Michael J. Hyde's text *The Call of Conscience: Heidegger and Levinas, Rhetoric and the Euthanasia Debate.* Insofar as questions and issues about euthanasia could be said to become more pressing as the technological means for extending and supporting life develop, Hyde's book indirectly concerns issues related to those that preoccupy Hayles and Haraway. Hyde works more actively and explicitly than they do to consider the implications raised in discourse about euthanasia, however. As he says, his goal is to "begin clarifying how texts mean as announcements of conscience."[43] To that end, he draws on the articulated views of philosophers, physicians, judges, and students, as well as disabled and dying people, as resources for rhetorical analysis and commentary. To recall the words of Klumpp and Hollihan, this is a critic who "listens to what has been said, and even hears what will be said, and offers [his] commentary woven into the emerging fabric of understanding."[44]

Whatever a reader's views on euthanasia might be, they are almost surely to be changed, enriched, rethought, and extended by reading Hyde's book. This is because Hyde draws on his personal experience to speak authentically about choices and decisions nearly everyone has had to make or will someday have to make. He opens questions of value and knowledge by contrasting opposing views—his own

and those of his sources. By holding various possibilities in suspension and in tension with one another, he provokes his readers' thinking. While his positions are
fairly clear, Hyde self-consciously leaves openings for other ways of viewing and
thinking about the processes of death and dying. He finds in his texts what is there
to be appropriated without idealizing them or treating them as objects. This
engaged, disquieting work entails risk—for the critic who puts himself on the line
on a topic that many of us would rather not think about, and for his readers who
may very well be profoundly changed in the process of reading it.

These three works are concerned with major issues and have themes and
points of view, but they expand the thought of their readers by making use of the
discourses of a wide range of sources, among them, narratives, examples, and personal experiences, to develop their themes and ideas. There is argument and a
viewpoint embedded in their work, but the ways in which they go about it open
a dwelling place in which their readers can extend, disagree with, and further
ponder their ideas.

The model of criticism exemplified in these works has actually been proposed
in the communication field for some time. Its advocates include Brockreide, Wander, and Klumpp and Hollihan. Wayne Brockreide's views were expressed in the
1970s, and while they were well and articulately presented at the time, they have
been largely ignored in the rush to method-centered criticism. Wander's contribution was widely criticized immediately after its publication by writers who
seemed more concerned with defending their own work than with seriously
engaging his.[45] As to the impact his essay might have had on critical practice, Wander commented to me recently that criticism instead turned from ideology to
"interpretive strategies which, over the last twenty years, have turned . . . 'ahistori-
cal and text immanent.'"[46] Klumpp and Hollihan's work has had the most notice-
able recent impact, in part inspiring Rushing, Frentz, Morris, Crowley, and others
to consider the moral implications of the rhetorical critic's role.

Brockreide's Idea

Although Brockreide's proposal is argument-centered and therefore somewhat
analytical and deductive (and thus subject to dismissal by some present-day readers because of its apparent logocentrism), Brockreide was a fine theorist and gave
us a greatly expanded conception of argument that viewed it as dialectical and
even dialogic and thus amenable to a more enlarged and inclusive rhetorical criticism. That Brockreide did not have a narrow view of argument is immediately
established in his essay by his definition of "argument" as "the process whereby a
person reasons his way from one idea to the choice of another idea."[47] He then
noted five characteristics of argument and, in two significant footnotes, said that
he considered argument to be an open concept, one "capable of input, change, or
growth."[48]

I will take up this statement here by rephrasing his five characteristics in a way that best develops the idea I have in mind. They include (1) the invitation to the reader to move from existing beliefs to the adoption of a new belief (or reinforcement of an old one), (2) a rationale for the critic's appeal, (3) a choice between two or more alternatives, (4) a regulation of uncertainty in regard to the view expressed, and (5) a willingness to risk one's views by expressing them publicly.[49] Rhetorical criticism as argument means that the critic takes a position, supports it by various means, and does so in ways that invite response and engagement by readers. Brockreide argues that criticism that is purely aesthetic, descriptive, or classificatory does not fit this model. Aesthetic judgments do not offer support in such a way as to regulate uncertainty and so do not position readers to consider the reasons for the critic's views as compared to their own. Descriptions do not indicate to readers what the critic's work is supposed to tell them, and so they are not designed to move readers from an existing to a new belief. Classificatory criticism (usually the application of a preselected method or framework) becomes a form of self-fulfilling prophecy in that the critic commences with what she expects to find and thus does not risk herself or her views in her criticism.

Brockreide's idea makes rhetorical criticism into a process of discovery in which what the critic surmises to be the case might turn out not to be. He argues that "when a critic assumes the responsibility and risk of advancing a significant argument about his evaluation or explanation, he invites confrontation that may begin or continue a process enhancing an understanding of a rhetorical experience or of rhetoric."[50] Rhetorical criticism as practiced in this way involves critics who themselves should be led by the process to discover something that they otherwise would not have learned. It does this because it actively invites readers to consider and respond to the substance of the issues that the discourse is about.

Brockreide's essay on rhetorical criticism may best be read in light of another of his articles, "Arguers as Lovers," published two years earlier in 1972.[51] In it, Brockreide considers an ideal of scholarly argument as practiced by philosophers and scientists, but many of its points could be made equally well of argument as practiced by rhetorical critics. He begins his piece by saying that how one arguer relates to another is a very important factor in the practice of argument, and to illustrate this idea, he proceeds to consider the arguer in three roles—as rapist, seducer, and lover. Both the rapist and the seducer treat the situation unilaterally; their goal is to persuade their audience to their point of view. The rapist will seek to gain superiority by giving prominence to the views he favors and ignoring, discrediting, or ridiculing opposing ideas. The seducer, on the other hand, seeks to charm or trick the listener through misrepresentation, flattery, and exploitation.

The arguer as a lover is a lover of wisdom and seeks it rather than the establishment of his own view as right. To this end, arguers as lovers acknowledge and respect ideas that differ from their own, and they consider their audiences as co-arguers and seek to include them, thereby enabling them to find their own way to a change in their beliefs. Brockreide concludes his essay by noting that "argument has another function as important as any intellectual creation of the 'truth' of a situation, and that is the personal function of influencing the fulfillment and growth of the selves of the people in the transaction."[52]

Furthermore, Brockreide's view of argument in this essay sets another requirement for the arguer as lover that he had mentioned in his argument on criticism: the arguer's praxis should involve risk of self. This might mean recognizing that what the critic discovers in the course of her work may be unexpected, that she may encounter audiences that remain ambivalent and indifferent to her work, that the issues she addresses may be unresolvable, and, most important, that she herself may be changed in some fundamental way as part of the critical process. Without this risk of self, neither the critic nor her readers can really be positioned to consider the grounds of judgment.

In an aside in his notes, Brockreide observes that "the three speeches by Socrates [in Plato's *Phaedrus*] aptly illustrate the three kinds of interpersonal relationships among arguers discussed in . . . this essay."[53] While some aspects of the *Phaedrus* do not align well with Brockreide's idea, the behavior of its three speakers does reflect the contrast he is making in regard to the critic's persona.[54] The attitude of the first speaker (the "rapist") in the supposedly Lysian speech is one of "cold, prudential calculation."[55] This speaker considers his subject only from a utilitarian position of enlightened, advantage-seeking self-interest. The attitude of the second speaker (the "seducer") is also insincere, even though it is seemingly concerned with the boy's welfare. It does not reflect Socrates's real views and is labeled as "blasphemy" later in the dialogue. While well crafted and vivid in its portrayals, skillful, and stylistically well expressed, it is designed for show, to reveal the skill of Socrates as compared with Lysias, and to set a framework for the rest of the dialogue. As such, it functions as a rhetorical device rather than an opportunity to contemplate the problem at hand.

The third speech (that of the "lover") arises in part within the context of the relationship between Socrates and Phaedrus. In suggesting a relationship between speaker and listener that is mutually empowering and potentially reciprocal, this speech enacts Brockreide's requirement for *ethos*-centered criticism. Through its consideration of theological context, personal commitment, and responsibility to the other, the speech adjudicates issues "with reference to a whole universe of discourse."[56] It thus undertakes what Weaver has called the principal duty of the rhetorician—"to represent to us the as yet unactualized future."[57] Furthermore, the speech is morally infused, concerning itself with choice making and right behavior, and espousing such values as chastity, altruism, self-control, and wisdom. Because of these characteristics and in spite of its elitism, the speech is often viewed as a model of composition and thought.

The Challenge to the Critic-Centered Model

More than a decade after Brockreide offered his proposal for a critic-centered *ethos* of rhetorical criticism, Klump and Hollihan noted a challenge to critical practice that they believed had not been met. They argued that despite repeated calls for critics to realize that work celebrating civility and prudence implies complicity in the dominant social order, the theory and practices of many critics had not changed. They maintained that "the charge remains that [these critics] are captive to a perspective on the critical act that leaves them naïve to the very force of the rhetoric which they purport to study."[58] Rhetorical criticism, Klumpp and Hollihan concluded, should move beyond its emphasis on structure and design of the text and "expos[e] the strategies through which rhetoric transforms the material events of the world into sociopolitical power."[59]

Klumpp and Hollihan observed that rhetoric often intervenes at a time when response to it can either support dominant values or lead to social change. Within this context, the rhetorical critic as moral agent can "illuminate the moral force of a rhetorical moment" and thus create a dwelling place for moral deliberation.[60] Here I see Klumpp and Hollihan as endorsing a view also stated by Gaonkar when he noted that the "proponents of the 'prudence/decorum' paradigm, preoccupied as they are with the immediate pragmatics of agent-centered text-composition and deliberative performance, have not devised an adequate strategy for signalling the constitutive presence of larger historical/discursive formations within which a given text or performance is embedded."[61]

In the opinion of these and other theorists, what rhetorical criticism must do is to view the discursive field as comprised of irruptions of discourse that intervene in that field and as the site of larger formations that condition that discourse and preclude the voicing of what is not, cannot, or "should not" be said. Furthermore, these theorists believe that rhetorical criticism should not be circumscribed by a speaker-centered view (which remains within the world view of the speaker) or a text-immanent view (which focuses on the internal operations of the text) or a method-centered view (which applies a theorized framework to the rhetorical text). The *ethos* of criticism calls upon us to enable consideration of the content and contexts of public discourse and to meaningfully engage the substance of what we study so as to bring about meaningful thought about it.

The social field is permeated through and through by administrative structures, corporate interests, tacit racism, pro-technology bias, and other forces that constitute what Klumpp and Hollihan call "the mystery of the social order."[62] These forces "sublimate experience into acceptance," and the critic who exposes them brings them into consciousness. "Illuminate the mystery," Klumpp and Hollihan say, "and you introduce the possibility of change. Experiences are transformed into issues only in the bright light of exposure that follows from the awareness of mystery."[63] Doing this involves the risks implied in Brockreide's view of criticism of argument—disclosure, self-risk, indifference, and hostility—but the benefits to be gained from an enlarged conception of critical practice are substantial.

A Future for Rhetorical Criticism

What is to be gained by a critic-originated, multivoiced, authentic rhetorical criticism that considers the substance of what it studies as well as the manner of its expression? If the criticism is considered as an invitation to further reflection about social issues rather than as a closed circle of critical performance, much is to be gained. By resisting univocality and essentialism, critics open their work to engagement by a wide range of audiences. These include not only the critic's professional peers but also the general publics who are positioned to take up the issues that the critic addresses and to consider them in light of forces that suppress dissent as well as those that promote consensus.

Criticism practiced in this way in the models of criticism that I've described calls on rhetorical critics to bring the texts they study into conversation with the larger cultural intertext. For example, such discourses might include work of other authors pertinent to the studied text, commentaries and reviews of the text, considerations of what the speaker or author said elsewhere, public discussions of the work, personal experiences of the critic and the speaker or author, surrounding texts and conditions that reveal the limits on and possibilities for what can said, and other discourses. By drawing on so many sources, critics can open an abode or dwelling place where various orientations can be brought to bear on each other, so that what is unseen or bracketed in one orientation can be illuminated by another. Including other texts keeps the critic's readers focused on the substance and orientation of the studied text but at the same time acts as a terministic screen that makes what might be invisible or barely perceptible on one reading visible and apparent on another.[64]

Multivoiced critical practice such as this can be incorporated into rhetorical criticism by revealing the critic's point of view while at the same time leaving space for other ideas that might qualify the critic's claims. By conveying her own views as well as those of other people, the critic replaces the "truth standard" of "objective" criticism with a reasonableness standard.[65] Reasonableness, as I understand it in light of Perelman's discussion of it, is a sense of what is correct, right, and proper that has been internalized from the deliberator's culture and from an internal deliberation with oneself (what Hyde might mean by "the call of conscience"). Reasonableness exists in that space that emerges from cultural practices, individual conscience, personal experience, and what Wintgens labels a "dialogue between the generalized other and [her] 'I.'"[66] The critic's considered inclusion of the many discourses that bear on her text ensures a judgment of reasonableness, both of her criticism and of the rhetoric that she considers.

Critical praxis of this sort works against the practice of disqualifying others' readings of a text because they are viewed as inexpert or wrong. It acknowledges that objectivity itself is an ideologically infused term, one directed toward main-taining academics' preferred texts, methods, and points of view in positions of dominance and privilege.[67] Multivoiced, inclusive rhetorical criticism would keep its readers focused on the substance of the issue rather than on the correctness of its author's critical interpretation. It would affirm the possibility of effective criti-cal praxis by transforming criticism and enacting an *ethos* open to critical response and contemplation.

To practice rhetorical criticism as Brockreide, Klumpp, Hollihan, and others have described it, rhetorical critics would need to reconsider some of their schol-arly conventions, epistemological loyalties, and common practices. This would free a portion of rhetorical critical practice from the constraints that keep it sequestered from the general public sphere and from meaningfully influencing public discus-sions about policy and social action. But in a time when humanity is so affected by environmental degradation, extremely rapid technological development, accel-erating alterations in the means and modes of communication, globalization of corporate capital, terrorism, and oppression, it is our responsibility, I believe, to seek out a critical praxis that aims at wisdom, empowerment, and protection of the public interest.

Notes

1. Calvin O. Schrag, *Communicative Praxis and the Space of Subjectivity* (Bloomington: Indiana University Press, 1986), 198.

2. Dale Cyphert, "Ideology, Knowledge and Text: Pulling at the Knot in Ariadne's Thread," *Quarterly Journal of Speech* 87 (2001): 378–95.

3. Philip Wander, "The Ideological Turn in Modern Criticism," *Central States Speech Journal* 34 (1983): 2.

4. Forbes Hill, "A Turn against Ideology: Reply to Professor Wander," *Central States Speech Journal* 34 (1983): 122.

5. William Nothstine, Carole Blair, and Gary A. Copeland, eds., *Critical Questions: Inven-tion, Creativity, and the Criticism of Discourse and Media* (New York: St. Martin's Press, 1994), 23.

6. Michael Calvin McGee, "Another Philippic: Notes on the Ideological Turn in Criticism," *Central States Speech Journal* 35 (1984): 44. McGee cites as the source of this phrase Alvin W. Gouldner, *The Future of Intellectuals and the Rise of the New Class* (New York: Seabury Press, 1979), 28–29.

7. Richard A. Cherwitz and John Theobold-Osborne, "Contemporary Develop-ments in Rhetorical Criticism: A Consideration of the Effects of Rhetoric," in *Speech Communication: Essays to Commemorate the 75th Anniversary of the Speech Communication Association,* ed. Gerald M. Phillips and Julia T. Wood (Carbondale: Southern Illinois Uni-versity Press, 1990), 73.

8. Barbara Warnick, "Leff in Context: What Is the Critic's Role?" *Quarterly Journal of Speech* 78 (1992): 232–37.

9. John Campbell, "Strategic Reading: Rhetoric, Intention, and Interpretation," in *Rhetorical Hermeneutics: Invention and Interpretation in the Age of Science,* ed. Alan G. Gross and William M. Keith (Albany: State University of New York Press, 1997), 121.

10. Hill, "Turn against Ideology," 123.

11. Dilip Parameshwar Gaonkar, "The Idea of Rhetoric in the Rhetoric of Science," in *Rhetorical Hermeneutics: Invention and Interpretation in the Age of Science,* ed. Alan G. Gross and William M. Keith (Albany: State University of New York Press, 1997), 32–33.

12. Wander, "Ideological Turn"; Cyphert, "Ideology, Knowledge and Text."

13. Carolyn R. Miller, "Classical Rhetoric without Nostalgia: A Response to Gaonkar," in *Rhetorical Hermeneutics: Invention and Interpretation in the Age of Science,* ed. Alan G. Gross and William M. Keith (Albany: State University of New York Press, 1997), 161. Miller cites the source for this statement as J. Bender and D. E. Wellbery, "Rhetoricality: On the Modernist Return of Rhetoric," in *The Ends of Rhetoric: History, Theory, Practice,* ed. J. Bender and D. E. Wellbery (Stanford, Calif.: Stanford University Press, 1990), 25.

14. Gaonkar, "Close Readings of the Third Kind: Reply to My Critics," in *Rhetorical Hermeneutics: Invention and Interpretation in the Age of Science,* ed. Alan G. Gross and William M. Keith (Albany: State University of New York Press, 1997), 343.

15. Cyphert, "Ideology, Knowledge and Text," 389.

16. See, for example, Ralph R. Smith and Russel R. Windes, "The Progay and Antigay Issue Culture: Interpretation, Influence and Dissent," *Quarterly Journal of Speech* 83 (1997): 28–48; Janice Hocker Rushing, "Evolution of 'The New Frontier' in *Alien* and *Aliens:* Patriarchal Co-Optation of the Feminine Archetype," *Quarterly Journal of Speech* 75 (1989): 1–24; Janice Hocker Rushing and Thomas S. Frentz, "The Frankenstein Myth in Contemporary Cinema," *Critical Studies in Mass Communication* 6 (1989): 61–80; Janice Hocker Rushing and Thomas S. Frentz, *Projecting the Shadow: The Cyborg Hero in American Film* (Chicago: University of Chicago Press, 1995). Despite the quality and quantity of studies that Rushing and Frentz have produced, their work has not been treated in most of the discussions of rhetorical criticism I examined. It was not cited, for example, in Gross and Keith, *Rhetorical Hermeneutics;* Cyphert, "Ideology, Knowledge and Text"; or Sharon Crowley, "Reflections on the Argument that Won't Go Away: Or, a Turn of the Ideological Screw," *Quarterly Journal of Speech* 78 (1992): 450–65.

17. Hill, "Turn against Ideology," 123.

18. See R. B. Kaplan, "Cultural Thought Patterns Revisited," in *Writing across Languages: Analysis of L_2 Text,* ed. U. Connor and R. B. Kaplan (Reading, Mass.: Addison-Wesley, 1966); Barbara Johnstone, "Arguments with Khomeni: Rhetorical Situation and Persuasive Style in Cross-Cultural Perspective," *Text* 6 (1986): 171–87; and Chaim Perelman, "The New Rhetoric: A Theory of Practical Reasoning," in *The Rhetorical Tradition,* ed. Patricia Bizzell and Bruce Herzberg (Boston: St. Martin's Press, 1990), 1077–1103.

19. Cyphert, "Ideology, Knowledge and Text," 383.

20. Sonja K. Foss and Cindy L. Griffin, "Beyond Persuasion: A Proposal for an Invitational Rhetoric," *Communication Monographs* 62 (1995): 2–18; Michael A. Gilbert, *Coalescent Argumentation* (Mahwah, N.J.: Erlbaum Associates, 1997); and Nancy V. Wood, *Perspectives on Argument,* 2d. ed. (Upper Saddle River, N.J.: Prentice-Hall, 1998).

21. See Warnick, "Leff in Context," and her "Two Systems of Invention: The Topics in *The Rhetoric* and *The New Rhetoric,*" in *Rereading Aristotle's Rhetoric* ed. Alan Gross and Arthur Walzer (Carbondale: Southern Illinois University Press, 1999), 107–29.

22. Barbara Johnstone, *The Linguistic Individual: Self-Expression in Language and Linguistics* (New York: Oxford University Press, 1996*)*.

23. Kristine L. Fitch, "A Cross-Cultural Study of Directive Sequences and Some Implications for Compliance-Gaining Research," *Communication Monographs* 61 (1994): 185–209; Patrick McLaurin, "An Examination of the Effect of Culture on Pro-Social Messages Directed at African-American At-Risk Youth," *Communication Monographs* 62 (1995): 301–26; Barbara Warnick and Valerie Manusov, "The Organization of Justificatory Discourse in Interaction: A Comparison within and across Cultures," *Argumentation* 14 (2000): 381–404.

24. J. M. Makau and D. L. Marty, *Cooperative Argumentation: A Model for Deliberative Community* (Prospect Heights, Ill.: Waveland Press, 2001).

25. Wayne Brockreide, "Rhetorical Criticism as Argument," *Quarterly Journal of Speech* 60 (1974): 167.

26. Warnick, "Leff in Context."

27. Steve Fuller, "Rhetoric of Science: Double the Trouble?" in *Rhetorical Hermeneutics: Invention and Interpretation in the Age of Science,* ed. Alan G. Gross and William M. Keith (Albany: State University of New York Press, 1997), 290.

28. Fuller, "Rhetoric of Science," 291.

29. McGee, "Another Philippic," 49.

30. Ibid., 47.

31. Nothstine, Blair, and Copeland, *Critical Questions,* 37.

32. James F. Klumpp and Thomas A. Hollihan, "Rhetorical Criticism as Moral Action," *Quarterly Journal of Speech* 75 (1989): 92.

33. Nothstine, Blair, and Copeland, *Critical Questions,* 43.

34. Ibid.

35. Sonja K. Foss, "Constituted by Agency: The Discourse and Practice of Rhetorical Criticism," in *Speech Communication: Essays to Commemorate the 75th Anniversary of the Speech Communication Association,* ed. Gerald M. Phillips and Julia T. Wood (Carbondale: Southern Illinois University Press, 1990), 42.

36. Foss, "Constituted by Agency," 43.

37. Klumpp and Hollihan, "Rhetorical Criticism," 93.

38. N. Katherine Hayles, *How We Became Posthuman: Virtual Bodies in Cybernetics, Literature, and Informatics* (Chicago: University of Chicago Press, 1999), 13.

39. Hayles, *How We Became Posthuman,* 24.

40. Donna J. Haraway, *Modest_Witness@Second_Millennium.FemaleMan©Meets_Onco-Mouse™: Feminism and Technoscience* (New York: Routledge, 1997), 50.

41. Ibid., 16.

42. See Mikhail M. Bakhtin, *The Dialogic Imagination: Four Essays,* ed. Michael Holquist, trans. Caryl Emerson and Michael Holquist (Austin: University of Texas Press, 1981), xix–xx.

43. Michael J. Hyde, *The Call of Conscience: Heidegger and Levinas, Rhetoric and the Euthanasia Debate* (Columbia: University of South Carolina Press, 2001), 256.

44. Klumpp and Hollihan, "Rhetorical Criticism," 93.

45. McGee's criticism applies to the following responses: Hill, "Turn against Ideology"; Alan Megill, "Heidegger, Wander, and Ideology," *Central States Speech Journal* 34 (1983): 114–19; and Lawrence W. Rosenfield, "Ideological Miasma," *Central States Speech Journal* 34 (1983): 119–21.

46. Philip Wander, e-mail to author, 23 January 2002. Wander noted that he drew his characterization from Richard Wolin, *Heidegger's Children: Hannah Arendt, Karl Löwith, Hans Jonas, and Herbert Marcuse* (Princeton, N.J.: Princeton University Press, 2001).

47. Brockreide, "Rhetorical Criticism," 166.

48. Ibid., 166. In the first of these notes (no. 4), he states that while some observers might say that his enumeration of characteristics might imply that he has a closed concept of argument, he responds, "I do not wish even to suggest the possibility of such an implication." In the second note (no. 5), he draws on Wittgenstein's philosophy to show that his view of argument is not reductive: "These characteristics are not usefully applied one-by-one as a kind of checklist to help one see if something 'adds up' to an argument. Rather, they are interrelated dimensions of the concept of argument and may, each of them, serve usefully as an entry point or as a mode of emphasis in criticizing a rhetorical experience. They do not 'add up' to an argument. Rather, they bear holistically the marks of family resemblance, they achieve a gestalt, they justify the surname of argument."

49. Brockreide's wording of these characteristics is as follows: "(1) an inferential leap from existing beliefs to the adoption of a new belief or the reinforcement of an old one; (2) a perceived rationale to justify that leap; (3) a choice among two or more competing claims; (4) a regulation of uncertainty in relation to the selected claim—since someone has made an inferential leap, certainty can be neither zero nor total; and (5) a willingness to risk a confrontation of that claim with one's peers" ("Rhetorical Criticism," 166).

50. Brockreide, "Rhetorical Criticism," 174.

51. Brockreide, "Arguers as Lovers," *Philosophy and Rhetoric* 5 (1972): 1–11.

52. Ibid., 9.

53. Ibid., 11.

54. The *Phaedrus* involves a number of ideas that do not align with the model of rhetorical communication I advocate here. For example, it assumes a single conception of truth, celebrates an idea of "the best" that can only be had by people positioned to achieve it, and does not allow for a diversity of values, culture, and experience.

55. R. Hackforth, trans., *Plato's Phaedrus* (Cambridge: University Press, 1952).

56. Richard Weaver, "The *Phaedrus* and the Nature of Rhetoric," in *The Rhetorical Tradition,* ed. Patricia Bizzell and Bruce Herzberg (Boston: St. Martin's Press, 1990), 1065.

57. Weaver, "The *Phaedrus,*" 1062.

58. Klumpp and Hollihan, "Rhetorical Criticism," 86.

59. Ibid., 90.

60. Ibid., 90.

61. Gaonkar, "Close Readings," 343.

62. Klumpp and Hollihan, "Rhetorical Criticism," 93.

63. Ibid., 93.

64. Kenneth Burke, *Language as Symbolic Action* (Berkeley and Los Angeles: University of California Press, 1966).

65. Chaim Perelman, "The Rational and the Reasonable," in *The New Rhetoric and the Humanities,* by Chaim Perelman (Dordrecht, Holland: D. Reidel, 1979).

66. Luc J. Wintgens, "Rhetoric, Reasonableness and Ethics: An Essay on Perelman," *Argumentation* 7 (1993): 457.

67. See Crowley, "Reflections."

Sweating the Little Things in Sidney Lumet's *12 Angry Men*

WALTER JOST

> The greatness of true art . . . [is] to find, grasp, and bring out that reality
> which we live at a great distance from . . . that reality which we run the risk
> of dying without having known, and which is quite simply our own life.
> Marcel Proust, *In Search of Lost Time*

Taking my point of departure from the concept of *ethos* as "dwelling place," I would like us to travel for a short distance first in one direction, on what we might call the Rhetorician's Way, then quickly backtrack (by shortcut) to set off in the opposite direction, let us call it the Philosopher's Way, and thereby, in that admittedly oblique fashion, discover that, notwithstanding the contrasts in landscapes and people and activities we have encountered, our two paths have in fact described a single large circle, and we have circumscribed a place that others identify with expressions such as "Nature" or "la condition humaine" or "human habitation" or even "dwelling place," but that, in the end, we may simply want to call "home."

Two Ways

Not by accident, the provisions we need for these essayings can be found ready to hand in that notion of "*ethos* as dwelling place." First, the notion of "dwelling place" ought to remind us of rhetorical places or topoi, more or less undefined terms, categories, cases, and the like useful for exploring the relevant aspects of some indeterminate practical problem. Thus, to make our way in the following section, I will draw on a topical schema from Boethius's *De topicis differentiis* (a chapter of which is heavily indebted to Cicero's *De Inventione*) to show how topics are used by the jurors in *12 Angry Men* to explore the murder case before them; and then (still in the second section) I will examine how we ourselves can use those same topics to ask questions about the question before us, which is not the murder case per se but the nature of these jurors themselves, our interest in them as people, as protagonists and antagonists engaged in the action. In short, we will use rhetorical topics to illuminate how the jurors ask questions about a murder suspect and to ask ourselves questions about a jury of his peers. The purpose in the first part of the essay is to show students of film, and of rhetoric, how one goes about "thinking like a rhetorician," and to show that some of the fundamentals of the art (of rhetoric—hence of film) have not changed much since the Middle Ages, indeed, since ancient Rome and Greece.

Changing emphasis in the second section of this essay, taking "dwelling *place*" as "*dwelling* place" also ought to remind us that topics, no matter how complex or simple their possibilities, always themselves *already* encompass *ethos.* That is, they encompass not only the "characters" of the characters under scrutiny here (the suspect, the jurors) but also the characters of the ones who are thinking topically, namely (in addition to the director and writer and actors), us viewers, *our* characters, *ourselves* and how *we* live or "dwell" in the world (including how we view intelligent films and talk about them afterward). For that reason, in the third section of the essay, rhetorical matters will have already begun to shade over into ethical, political, and even ontological matters, reaching out from the characters in the film to ourselves, raising philosophic questions: Why? To what end? What good is it to be trained in the way of topical thinking? Now fundamental concepts such as *ethos* itself, and related issues of language, meaning, talk and the contempt of talk (a variant of misology), knowledge of the world and of others, the importance of ordinary language and everyday life, what it is to teach and to learn, and acknowledging others—these and other issues will help us to see just how probing a Hollywood movie can be.[1]

Naturally, I hope that readers are familiar (or will want to get familiar) with director Sidney Lumet's famous film, which stars many excellent actors, among them Henry Fonda, Lee J. Cobb, Jack Warden, Ed Begley Sr., and E. G. Marshall. For those unfamiliar with it, however, let me begin with a brief synopsis of the story.

In the film, a teenager, poor, possibly Jewish, is accused on a capital murder charge of having knifed his father to death in a tenement apartment. Except for several interesting shots at the opening—the exterior of a big-city courthouse with traffic noise in the background; the courthouse interior with worried and distracted people hurrying about; the interior of a courtroom, where the judge summarizes the case just mentioned and drones out, obviously bored, his instructions to the jury—and except for a final exterior shot of the courthouse at the end, virtually all of the scenes take place in a small jury room. This room is exceedingly plain. There are windows on one wall opening out onto the heard but mostly unseen city, a water cooler and a closet without doors on another wall, two doors leading to men's and women's restrooms on a third, an unadorned fourth wall, and a simple wooden, rectangular table in the middle, around which these twelve angry men alternately sit, stand, or restlessly move about. The room is without air conditioning on this hottest day of the summer, and the characters sweat profusely.

Reginald Rose's story and screenplay are straightforward enough: all the evidence seems to point to the boy, and not ten minutes into the movie, our jury of twelve angry men has lost no time voting "guilty" eleven to one (Fonda is the holdout). The remainder of the film charts the halting progress of these twelve reconsidering their initial inclinations, arguing, and eventually becoming eleven to one in favor of "not guilty" (Lee J. Cobb's character, the angriest of the twelve, is now the holdout) until they conclude unanimously, twelve together, in favor of an acquittal—not because they think the boy is innocent but because each juror has come to a "reasonable doubt" about his guilt.

Of course, many aspects of the story and film are obvious enough even on a first viewing. There is, for example, Fonda's quintessentially American "individualist" character standing against the crowd. Also obvious is that the film performs in part as political allegory in which the judicial institution of a free democracy is itself put on trial and found not guilty—not, again, because it is innocent (for, had the Fonda character not been there, this jury might well have remained blithely unquestioning in its deliberations) but because, let us say, it is found to be naïve as an institution, acquitted this time of the mindless conformism of the 1950s. This conformism, too, is obvious, represented most blatantly by the wishy-washy advertising man who doodles cereal boxes ("I have this habit of doodling—keeps me thinking clearly"), by the social anomie of the characters and their relative alienation from each other, by their thinly disguised personal insecurities, and by the unthinking reactions of most of the jury to the case before them. (Also obvious, when we think about it, is our own interest in courtroom dramas, in detective fictions, in whodunits, all of which genres *12 Angry Men* enfolds into its focus on these twelve characters in a locked room.) These things, and many others, are, I think we can agree, obvious.

What interests me, however, is what is not obvious, not because it is hidden but because it is made so palpably visible and audible to us, right in front of our noses, in our ears: water to fish. I mean the way this film dwells at such length, now languorous, now laser-focused, on perfectly ordinary matters. True, this is a murder trial, something in itself extraordinary. But within this unusual framing event resides the far more ordinary activity of people simply talking to each other, saying what they think, making claims, refuting these claims, following a line of argument or digressing, insulting each other, getting their feelings hurt, and much else. As unlikely a figure as Boethius (with a little help from his friends, Cicero and Aristotle) can help us sort all this out. After all, for the characters, what is immediately at stake is the conjectural question ("stasis") of a legal case: Did the boy commit the murder? (cf. *De Inventione,* 2.4.15).

For us viewers and rhetorical critics and thinkers, on the other hand, what is at stake are just these rhetorical activities themselves, and the concepts that organize and confuse them—among others, "talking," "listening," "proving," "knowing," "telling stories," "supposing" possibilities and alternatives, being "biased" in various ways, and the like. These issues grow more complicated the closer we look, so I would like to begin by suggesting how the characters use familiar rhetorical topoi to examine their case and then show how we can examine them in a similar way. Both investigations can afford to be brief, returning us to our starting point—our interest in *ethos* as dwelling place—more determined, I hope, to address questions more baffling than who the murderer is or even what sort of guy (e.g.) the Cobb character is. The real question is, Who are *we?*

Topical Invention

The editor of Boethius's treatise has devised a handy topical "tree" that exfoliates into various topoi familiar to rhetoricians. This tree (or map or blueprint) is hardly exhaustive, since any one of its terms could branch out into further possibilities, but it is enough to help put us on our way. Notice that the topics are organized by "attributes of persons or of actions" (cf. *De Inventione,* 1.24.34). The latter is divided into "attributes" of the action and "things associated with it," these two in turn generating four additional divisions, also familiar to Cicero, and so on. But here we might add (thinking of Aristotle), perhaps placing it under "things associated with the action," the topos of "witnesses." Aristotle called witnesses "atechnical" persuasives, meaning that their testimony comes ready-made and need not be "invented" by the speaker the way arguments need to be invented. But of course witnesses can be impugned, in great measure by reapplying to them the entire topical schema—"attributes of persons or of actions" and all that that entails—that we began with. There is method, after all, to such rhetorical madcap, and the jurors know instinctively what we see discursively here, namely, that commonsense topics like "means, motive and opportunity" exfoliate into such a wide range of possible considerations.

Unfortunately, teaching or showing how topics work is a lot like explaining a joke: it tends to make artificial and flatfooted what is instinctive, fluid and tacit, as the dialogue of this film is.[2] But making topics explicit is also like interpreting a poem, which, though analysis carves up someone's integral vision of a truth or insight while it belabors whatever beauty or sublimity it possesses, nevertheless deepens our appreciation of the native intelligence and vision otherwise hard at work in the poem. As for the film, if we were simply to begin to list the topoi that arise spontaneously once the jurors themselves, after their initial vote, get down to work, we would get something like the following over the course of ten minutes or so of discussion:

> The "fortune" and "luck" (i.e., bad luck) the boy suffered growing up (he's been "kicked around all of his life," "born in a slum," his mother died when he was nine, he was in several orphanages, his father was in jail);
>> "Witnesses" ("I mean, somebody saw him do it");
>> "Witnesses" again (an old man heard the boy shout, "I'm going to kill you" and saw the boy run away);

Rhetorical Topics

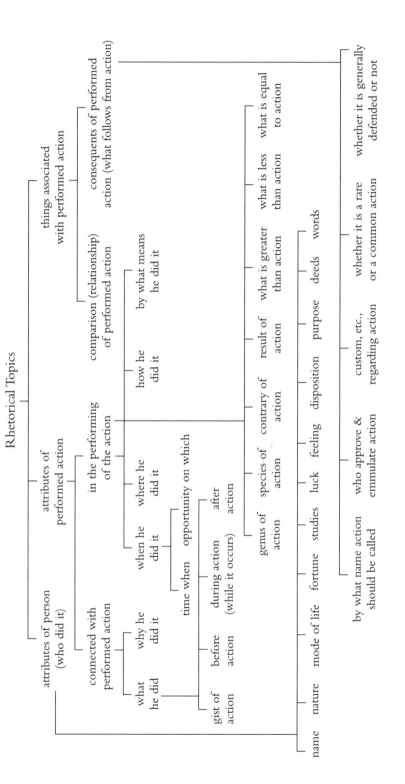

Source: Boethius, *De topicis differentiis*. Translated, with notes and essays on the text, by Eleonore Stump (Ithaca: Cornell University Press, 1978), insert.

"Attributes of the action" (according to the boy's account), including "what," "why," "when," "where," "time when," "before, during and after" the murder occurred;

"Motive" the boy may have had ("why");

"Feeling" (the two slaps the boy received from his father "may have been two too many");

The "nature, disposition, and deeds" of the boy (related by Warden);

The boy's "mode of life," "disposition," and "deeds" (reframed by Marshall);

The "means" the boy is said to have used in the killing (the knife, including "where" and "when" it was bought) and "how" he would have used it (an upward thrust);

The topic of "possible/impossible," not listed by Boethius but central to Aristotle and indeed presupposed as basic to any indeterminate situation (this topos is frequently invoked, not accidentally, by Fonda's character, who has a solid sense of fundamentals and a feeling for limits);

And so on, later including the boy's "words" ("I'm going to kill you"), "by what name" certain actions should be called, the "result" of actions, "how he did the act" (how a switchblade is used), and more.

How do these topics work? It is simple enough—everyone knows it instinctively —although we might take note of an observation by one of the characters, challenged by Fonda to explain what the boy's being hit twice "proved," when he answers (correctly, for certain purposes) that "it doesn't *prove* anything, it's just part of the picture." Arguments generated by topics do not, when isolated from each other, usually prove anything, at least not anything larger than themselves; rather, when taken together they create a picture that may be clear *enough,* even if one part of the picture is out of focus, another part faded, another torn away, and a fourth smudged with dirt. Held up to a strong light with logical tweezers, a single argument may be a flimsy thing, of consequence, no doubt, but how much? Only the expression and juxtaposition of arguments (Cicero calls this "amplification") inject rhetorical significance into merely logical consequence.

In whatever manner psychologists might set about describing the process of topical invention, as a deliberative act available in word and deed we rhetoricians find generally what we find in this film. It may happen that something occurs to someone, a person takes notice of some fact (e.g., a certain kind of knife is the murder weapon), which then suggests a line of argument (under the topics "how he did it" and "by what means"), to wit: This is the murder weapon; the boy had a weapon exactly like this; ergo, this may be the boy's means of killing. Such an argument and/or fact(s) may lead, sooner or later, to further inquiries: how "rare or common" are such knives, that is, how likely is it that someone else owned this knife; how "often" has this boy used such knives; and so on. In the film, these questions occur later on: the man who sold the knife said he had never seen one like it before, in which case—what? (As Cobb's character asks repeatedly, "But

what does it *mean?*") Well, by one reckoning it means, as the stockbroker character points out to Fonda, that it is possible, but "not probable," that the knife belonged to someone else.

Or it may happen another way: someone else starts out explicitly (if not self-
consciously) examining a topos rather than a fact—for example, "motive" ("why")
—which topos in turn may suggest subtopics such as the usual causes or reasons
for crime (Aristotle is succinct for our purposes, stating that "every action must
be due to one or other of seven causes: chance, nature, compulsion, habit, reasoning, anger, or appetite"; *Rhetoric,* 1369a). In the crime in this film, "chance" is discarded at once, as is "appetite" (appetite for what is "useful" or "pleasurable"), and
the possibilities are quickly whittled down to a combination of "nature," "habit,"
and, especially, "anger." Many facts support this last topos (or this last topos generates the notice of many facts), each of which, combined with a more or less
probable major premise, produces an argument, which argument, by the way,
often falls on both sides of the issue, since the issue is indeterminate and probable. For example, pro: "The father punched the boy twice; punches like that can
spark an anger resulting in such an act; ergo killing, here murder;" con: "The
father punched the boy twice; But a kid brought up like that, often kicked around
and abused, is used to such treatment and hasn't killed in the past; ergo—what?
He's not likely to have killed this time." And so on.

I say "and so on" because anyone can proceed to unpack the jury's arguments
in this way, analyzing the interplay of topoi and facts, facts and premises, premises
and further topics, in that way better enjoying just how the characters one by one
are persuaded that a reasonable doubt exists in one or more aspects of the prosecutor's case.[3] And I say "one by one" because each character is, not always obviously, different; what sways one person may not always sway another. The
stockbroker Marshall, a cool head and a clear thinker, holds out almost as long as
the simmering businessman Cobb, who finally erupts in incredulity having had to
watch the others fall away from what to him has from the start been *res ipsa
loquitur.* This variability of the characters in the film is susceptible to the same kind
of topical analysis presented above; the trick of using them is simple enough, since
we use Boethius's checklist—a version of the reporter's who-what-when-where-
how-and-why and their possibilities—all the time, trying to get clearer about
what people say and think and do, hence who they are, the *ethos* they show us.
At the risk of belaboring the obvious, I want briefly to take three easy cases—
Warden, Marshall, and Cobb—in order to suggest that our topoi actually help us
to discover something that is easy to miss and will lead (in the next section) to a
deeper line of inquiry.

The Warden character is virtually transparent, but consider three brief "deeds"
of his that go by quickly and yet speak volumes about his character. First, to give
one tiny example of how thoughtful director and actors are in this film, as the
opening credits roll and the jury members trail into the jury room, watch Warden

in the background. He plucks a paper cup off the stack of cups at the water cooler, gets himself a drink, then replaces the cup on the stack! A brilliant touch. Moments later, looking out of the window and taking a piece of gum into his mouth, he tosses the wrapper out onto the street below. Later, when the jury has paused in its work, he tosses wads of paper at the wall fan over his shoulder, ricocheting one of them off the forehead of another juror. Are there any questions about this character?

Marshall is far more complex, but using the topos of "comparison" (of performed action with other actions) and several of its subtopics, everyone notices that simple but telling moment when one of the jurors (Jack Klugman), sitting next to him, turns and says (recall that it is very hot day), "Pardon me, but don't you ever sweat?" Marshall takes a beat and responds, "No, I don't." This point (shall we place it under "contrary of normal actions"?) comes into play again later, when his cogent arguments against the boy finally fail to hold up. He changes his vote—and with a handkerchief lightly wipes his brow, a "sign" (Greek *semeia*) telling us that something significant has occurred. A trivial point, perhaps, nothing more than a writer's trick to show *ethos* or character. But we will see such trivia return in different guise below.

Notwithstanding the obvious importance of Fonda in the story, in a sense the film begins and ends with Cobb, who is the first to comment on the trial ("I was pretty bored") and the last to change his vote (sobbing, "Not guilty"). Why the last? Everyone recalls how, at a lull early in the deliberations, he narrates (to Fonda, interestingly) the story of his "making a man" out of his son by teaching him to fight. "When he was sixteen we had a fight. Hit me in the jaw—big kid. I haven't seen him for two years." Now, what do we suppose that proves about his character? Of course, we find out at the end, when he breaks down in tears and we realize that his "Guilty!" vote had been predicated all along on an unconscious cache of tortured emotions about his own teenage son.

Again, I make no special claim for my interpretation of these observations about the characters beyond what everyone knows. Rather, it is just that point— what everyone knows—that I find so compelling about this movie. To clarify this point, to bring out its importance, I want to consider one last topos, "words," in order to introduce a new line of argument, namely, that many of the jurors' words are words about words—about talk, deliberations, trials, persuasion, and related matters that I propose the film asks us to consider (not to put too grand a word on it) philosophically.

Toward a Philosophy of Rhetoric

Allow me to approach this large claim about philosophy gradually, by treating the centrality of words by way of some of the characters' attitudes of dismissal of words, or their skepticism about them, or their relativizing of their import. To say this another way, early in the proceedings Fonda's character, challenged to account for his reluctance to vote with the other eleven, makes a point about the legal case that I want to make about this film and our own critical reception of it: "I think the defense let too many *little things* go by." I want to suggest that in this film, Lumet himself (and the writer and actors, too, as I have hinted) does not allow little things to go by, just as Fonda's character does not. Both are attuned to the myriad background facts and assumptions and premises that make up his and the others' lives. As a result, while we may all agree that this is a mid-1950s political allegory about the importance and fragility of democracy, it is, in my view, more importantly a rhetorical and even philosophical education of us, the viewers.[4]

Suppose, as a kind of thought experiment, that the actors are our alter egos projected on the screen as ordinary characters whose lives we know well—because they are our lives. While it may be objected, rightly I think, that most of the characters in the jury room aspire to nothing more than deciding a legal case and themselves undergo no lasting higher education, we in the audience do. But how so? And why would we need an education about the little things that make up our own lives? As far as that goes, how could the little things we already know even count as an education? And why should men in particular (perhaps we would better say the masculine in all of us, men and women) require this? These are the questions I would like to try to answer.

Let me give two examples of the kind of little thing that I think Lumet has in mind and does not let go by. Twice the stockbroker played by E. G. Marshall impatiently interrupts two characters arguing over words—did the old man in the apartment below (one of the witnesses to the murder) "run" or "walk" to his door?—and dismissively settles the question with the more abstract "He *went*." Again, was the boy on trial "punched" or "slapped" by his father? "There's a difference between a punch and a slap," Marshall is reminded, but, impatient with what seems a trivial point, he says, "He was *hit*." Now my point (again, what everyone knows) is that struggling to choose the right concept sometimes turns on little differences. In J. L. Austin's formulation, it is a matter of "what we say when." And when it does matter, as it does in a murder trial, if someone like the stockbroker ignores a distinction, he does so potentially at his (and, more pointedly, at the defendant's) peril. Two other times the stockbroker—who, incidentally, is every whit as intelligent and well intentioned as Fonda—is shown having trouble with words, misremembering a film title as *The Wonderful Mrs. Bainbridge* rather than *The Amazing Mrs. Bainbridge,* and forgetting one of its actors as "Long or Lind, I can't remember." Of course, these latter examples do not make any difference in the abstract or by themselves. But in the specific context of Fonda's line of argument at this point in the deliberations, the stockbroker's easy way with these little things, like his earlier disdain of verbal distinctions, serves precisely to make Fonda's point. They also begin to make my point that this movie is out to show us the difference between taking words abstractly, apart from the practices that make up a form of life, and actually "looking into the workings of our language":[5] "What we do is to bring words back from their metaphysical to their everyday use" (*PI* 115). Thus the cool E. G. Marshall is something of a cold metaphysician in need of a corrective lesson about the difference between words. But then, don't *we* know the difference?

The poet Robert Frost, himself attuned to the everyday and ordinary, the tacit background of our feelings and values and beliefs, once remarked, "Being reminded of something you hardly knew you knew—by something that's in front of you, something that's happening to you, or the past emerging out of the very levels of your knowledge. Books and life and all that—that's the material."[6] For Frost, the material of our education in books and life is not knowledge as new information but rather what, in some sense, we already know. Wittgenstein points repeatedly to similar matters in *Philosophical Investigations:* "The aspects of things that are most important for us are hidden because of their simplicity and familiarity. (One is unable to notice something—because it is always before one's eyes.)" (*PI* 139; emphasis added).

It is here again that I want to propose that, for Lumet as for Wittgenstein and Frost, *12 Angry Men* educates us in what we, in some sense, already know but have failed to grasp, that which is, as Wittgenstein says, "important for us." But then what is it that we already "know" but "fail to grasp," and how do we "know" and yet "not know" this? What do we learn in life, books, or films that is hidden because it is so obvious, and why is it "most important for us?"

In his book *Making Movies* (1995), Lumet summarizes *12 Angry Men* with one word: "Listen."[7] Again I take it as obvious that Lumet is pointing out how poorly most of the characters in this film listen to each other, an important failure given their appointed roles as democratic citizens, as jurors. But then that much—about the characters' failures to listen to each other, about citizenship requiring good listeners—we moviegoers not only know, but we *know* that we know it (so that my saying it here, my merely repeating Lumet's word "listen," cannot account for the education I am claiming Lumet's film gives us. It is not a civics lesson we need, or get). Something else must be at stake—call it the difference between hearing ourselves or others talk and selectively listening to what counts in a given context: "what we say when." Thus when Lumet says, "Listen," he must mean something perhaps equally obvious that we do not "know," or anyway know that we know. For it may be that we sometimes allow such knowledge to go overlooked, or be forgotten, or undergo repression—allow the human to fall out of our best calculations.

In fact, I suspect that it is unlikely that we viewers have ever really listened, listened not only to what the characters say in this film (or in many other films) but, more important, to how they talk, and listen, and how, specifically, they verbally get in each others' way. And it is unlikely that we have listened to what they themselves have to say about talking and listening.

Consider briefly, for example, the characters played by Begley, Cobb, and Warden, respectively: the bigoted car wash owner who repeats, at least ten times throughout the film, "*Know* what I mean?"; the "excitable" businessman who constantly exclaims, "But what does it *mean?*" and the hopelessly jokey salesman, the one rhetorically addicted to baseball metaphors. As it turns out, regarding Begley, the others do not know what he means, or rather, they come to know very well what he means but recognize that they do not mean the same thing. For what he means, what he stands for, is an arrant bigotry, masquerading as Enlightenment, against the poor, against racial minorities, against a large indefinite "them." (Virtually every topos under "attributes of person" is involved here.) And when we listeners to the film really listen to this bigot (he is later disgraced and shunned), part of the way we come to know what he means is not what he says about "them" but how he complains about his having to listen at all, to talk, to engage with others in the first place—as if somehow he is metaphysically above all that, and as if he expects his co-jurors to declare themselves above the need to talk and listen to each other.

This metaphysical contempt of talk, of conversation, of rhetorical (forensic) deliberation—this contempt is given various skeptical and relativist turns as well. Listen to one of the very first things we hear from one of the jurors, the Lee J. Cobb character, as they enter the jury room. Cobb: "The way these lawyers talk and talk and talk. Did you ever hear so much talk about nothing?" By contrast, when Fonda is asked after his lone not guilty vote, "What do we do now?" he responds, "I guess we talk." To which the dogmatic (bigoted) Begley responds, "You won't change my mind if you talk for a hundred years." Soon Begley is complaining of the others, "You guys can talk the ears right off my head, you know what I mean?" and later, "You can talk until your tongue is dragging on the floor." By this time, the failed father (Cobb) and the salesman (Warden) are also equally contemptuous of talk. Warden: "[A]sking grown up people to believe that kind of jazz"; "I'm getting tired of all this yackety-yacking"; "What are you giving all this mumbo-jumbo for?"

This skeptical attitude toward talk is adroitly blended in with what philosopher Richard Bernstein has called "Cartesian anxiety" about the inadequacies and dangers of talk—anxiety about both their own inexpressiveness as well as the possibility that they have betrayed themselves in speech, been too expressive after all; and blended in with an obliviousness in the characters to the various obstacles preventing them from talking well. About the case at hand, one of the jurors begins, "It's hard to put into words, I just think he's guilty," adding, "What I meant was, I just think he's guilty" (and then adding, only as an afterthought, "I mean, someone saw him do it"). Warden's salesman is himself so rhetorically straitjacketed that he can only use baseball metaphors to assess his situation, and when he tries to avail himself of a boxing metaphor he finds himself obtusely unable to finish the comparison(!). When he tries to argue, he repeatedly, unconsciously, begs the question, and when others argue against him, he dismisses them: "You ought to be at Atlantic City at the hairsplitters' convention." Impatient with Fonda's mindfulness, urging him to cease, he sighs, "It's like talking into a dead phone," perfectly describing himself. And when another juror, an old man, is propounding his view of a matter, Warden rudely walks out; the old man shouts after him, "I'm talking here," and all that Fonda can do is gently touch him on the shoulder, saying, "He can't hear you. He never will." By the end Warden's relativism has been challenged by another juror's demand that he give what he has so much difficulty finding: a real reason for his decision.

When businessman Cobb—he runs a messenger service (of all things!), called the "Beck and Call"—starts to argue, he often quickly explodes in anger, constantly demanding, "What does *that* prove? But what does it *mean?*" When he later needs to apologize to a character whom he's unjustly attacked, he adds in a self-confident aside, "I'm glad you're not one of those who lets emotional appeals influence him." (Earlier this rageful, brokenhearted man is the one who had claimed, "I don't have any personal interest here; I just want to talk about facts.") Throughout the film, Begley and Cobb and even cool-hand Marshall worry about the "fairy tales" others are expounding and attack the stories that "twist the facts." Marshall, for example (about the boy's alibi): "Now, there is a tale, gentlemen." Their fear of words is less the empiricist's preference for "facts" than it is the skeptic's demand for "proof."

I am not suggesting here that it is Fonda's character (an architect) alone who is the exemplary teacher of the others, for he is not the only one, nor is he himself without limitations and faults, for he initially misinterprets Cobb's rage as sadism. Nevertheless, Fonda is an exemplar. When deliberations get under way and he is asked what he thinks, he responds to all of them. "I don't have anything brilliant," he says. "I only know as much as you do." These lines are telling, for they suggest that the discussion will not turn on superior skill or expertise but on what they all already know. The difference is that Fonda, unlike the others, is willing (or more willing) to try to remind himself of what he may know but may have forgotten or overlooked or denied or refused. Having produced a knife just like the murder weapon, he admits that he went walking in the boy's neighborhood the night before and found it easily for sale there. While the other jurors (and perhaps the audience) are incredulous at the find, I am struck at how this character has the wits to return the problem to the scene of the crime, to take a judicial abstraction back to the neighborhood of its action, to what Wittgenstein repeatedly calls (a venerable rhetorical term) its "circumstances" (*Umstanden;* in Greek, *peristaseis,* in Latin, *circumstantiae*). "Our language," he states, "can be seen as an ancient city: a maze of little streets and squares, of old and new houses" (*PI* 18) that we must revisit in order to see how a given word works: "Here the word 'language-game' is meant to bring into prominence the fact that speaking of language is part of an activity, or of a form of life" (*PI* 23). In this instance, Fonda *does* symbolically what Wittgenstein invites us to do grammatically and rhetorically.

Fonda also has the ability to construct (he is, after all, an architect) competing scenarios, alternative possibilities, "intermediate cases" (*PI* 122). Throughout the film he asks the others to "suppose" that such and such happened, to "imagine" something another way: "Isn't it possible, just *possible* that . . ." These abilities of his are common enough and central to the activity of Lumet's film, for they exemplify *ways to think:* citing examples, imagining alternatives, inventing intermediate cases to put extreme views into relief, recalling facts and working out their implications. Above all, because these activities are indeterminate in themselves, Fonda reminds us *that* they must be applied differently in different situations, as well as *how* to identify "little things" and assess their relevance and irrelevance to the particular situation and problem at hand. In a phrase, he thinks like a rhetorician. And Lumet, so I am proposing, thinks like a philosopher of rhetoric.

I have noted several times that Fonda plays an architect, and noted also that the characters, on this hot summer day without air conditioning, sweat throughout the film. I want to conclude my argument on these little details, and end my talk on yet one further little oddity.

Why an architect? At the beginning of the film, before the jury begins their deliberations, Fonda is staring out at the city when he is approached by the advertising man who, following his line of sight, asks, "Isn't that the Warwick Building?" Fonda answers, "That's right," and the ad man continues: "You know it's funny, I've lived here all my life and I've never been in that building." Mentally I can hear your objection to my own line of thinking, "What does *that* prove?" and "What does it *mean?*" It means least of all, I think, that, for all we know, Fonda's architect *designed* that building. More generally and significantly, it means that Fonda's being an architect (like his evening walk the night before) suggests that he knows this city, hence knows something about the unnamed men who come out of it to comprise this jury. Rhetorically we might pun by saying he "knows the premises," meaning not only the physical premises around them but also the argumentative premises, the values and commonplaces that comprise his own, and the others,' lives. In a word, he represents a long line of American artists, what I call "low modernists" (like Robert Frost) who, facing the cultural crises of their age, turn toward what Emerson called the "familiar, the common, the low." In a word, the little things. Lumet himself stands in this low modernist tradition.

When I ask my students, "What's with all the sweating in this film?" I invariably receive the answer that it's a hot day. Of course that does not answer the real question, which is, of course, why does the director make the day a hot day, so hot that the characters must sweat as they do throughout? By now I trust you are confident of the answer: as mortal, fallible, even gullible creatures, the jurors—and here I mean we—are creatures under Adam's curse, those who must toil for their bread, who must "sweat the little things." That it is men who do the sweating suggests that it is men, or rather the culturally inculcated masculine part of all of us, who must learn to attend to the details by talking and listening appropriately.

At the end of the movie, as we watch Fonda at eye level walk down the mighty steps of the courthouse, about to reenter the city he seems to know so well, the character of the old man shouts, "Hey" and hurries over to him. "What's your name?" he asks. "Davis," Fonda says. "I'm McArdle," the old man responds, and then, "Well, see ya!" Invariably my students laugh at this gratuitous moment, this seemingly aberrant detail. What they have not yet understood is the need that these two anonymous characters recognize to acknowledge the other by name, to mark out their anonymity as men who have, momentarily, shared an intellectual friendship, who have learned a lesson, as we all must do, out of school.

Notes

1. Here I am alluding to, and implicitly relying on, several seminal works of Stanley Cavell: *The World Viewed: Reflections on the Ontology of Film* (Cambridge: Harvard University Press, 1971); *Pursuits of Happiness: The Hollywood Comedy of Remarriage* (Cambridge: Harvard University Press, 1981); *Contesting Tears: The Hollywood Melodrama of the Unknown Woman* (Chicago: University of Chicago Press, 1996).

2. For an explanation of why this should be the case, see Thomas M. Conley, "What Jokes Can Tell Us about Arguments," in *A Companion to Rhetoric,* ed. Walter Jost and Wendy Olmsted (Oxford: Blackwell, 2003); and Robert L. Scott, "The Tacit Dimension," in *The Encyclopedia of Rhetoric,* ed. Thomas O. Sloane (Oxford: Oxford University Press, 2001), 765–68.

3. For an excellent and discussion of the rhetorical nature of reasoning by courts and juries, see Robert P. Burns, *A Theory of the Trial* (Princeton, N.J.: Princeton University Press, 1999).

4. Cf. Ludwig Wittgenstein, *Culture and Value,* ed. G. H. von Wright in collaboration with Heikki Nyman, trans. Peter Winch (Chicago: University of Chicago Press, 1984): "A typical American film, naïve and silly, can—for all its silliness and even by means of it—be instructive."

5. Ludwig Wittgenstein, *Philosophical Investigations,* trans. G. E. M. Anscombe (New York: Macmillan 1953), 109. Hereafter cited in the text as *PI.*

6. Reginald L. Cook, *Robert Frost: A Living Voice* (Amherst: University of Massachusetts Press, 1974), 158.

7. Sidney Lumet, *Making Movies* (New York: Vintage Books, 1995), 14.

Special Delivery

Rhetoric, Letter Writing, and the Question of Beauty

JOHN POULAKOS

Oct. 20, 1966

Dear Aunt Fannie:

This morning, my platoon and I were finishing up a three day patrol. Struggling over steep hills covered with hedgerows, trees, and generally impenetrable jungle, one of my men turned to me and pointed a hand, filled with cuts and scratches, at a rather distinguished looking plant with soft red flowers waving gayly in the downpour, (which had been going on ever since the patrol began), and said, "That is the first plant I have seen today which didn't have thorns on it." I immediately thought of you.

The plant and the hill upon which it grew, was also representative of Viet Nam. It is a country of thorns and cuts, of guns and marauding, of little hope and of great failure, yet in the midst of it all, a beautiful thought, gesture, and even person can arise among it waving bravely at the death that pours down upon it. Some day this hill will be burned by napalm, and the red flower will crackle up and die among the thorns. So what was the use of it living and being a beauty among the beasts, if it must, in the end, die because of them, and with them? This is a question which is answered by Gertrude Stein's "A rose is a rose is a rose." You are what you are, what you are. Whether you believe in God, fate, or the crumbling cookie, elements are so mixed in a being that make him what he is; his salvation from the thorns around him lies in the fact that he existed at all, in his very own personality.

There once was a time when the Jewish idea of heaven and hell was the thoughts and opinions people had of you after you died. But what if the plant was on an isolated hill and was never seen by anyone: that is like the question of whether the falling tree makes a sound in the forest primeval when no one is there to hear it: it makes a sound, and the plant was beautiful and the thought was kind; and the person was humane, and distinguished, and brave, not merely because other people recognized it as such, but because it is, and it is, and it is. Beauty, they say, is only skin deep, but true beauty emanates from the soul where it might not be recognized, seen, or appreciated as readily, but nevertheless is there, even more than the skin-deep variety.

The flower will always live in the memory of a tired, wet Marine, and has thus achieved a sort of immortality; but even if we had never gone on that hill, it would still be a distinguished, soft, red, thornless flower growing among the cutting, scratching plants, and that in itself is its own reward.

Love,
Sandy[1]

This letter was written by marine 2d Lt. Marion Lee Kempner (nicknamed Sandy) to his great-aunt Fannie. In her person, it had a particular addressee, a designated interlocutor. Its message was meant for her. But as fate would have it, the letter made only a brief stop in her hands. Continuing its journey, it eventually reached the pages of an anthology. Today, it is exposed to the reading gaze of the unknown reader, much like the name of its writer is on the shiny surface of the Vietnam War Memorial. But unlike the inscription, marion lee kempner, so chilling and final to its beholders, the letter affords us a glimpse at a minute segment of an unknown soldier's infinite thoughts. More important, it serves as an occasion for an introspective glance at the "steep hills" and "impenetrable jungle" of our own predicament. In the light of its example, the letter invites us to reflect on the objects of our attention and the subjects of our writing when finding ourselves in inhospitable places. And it asks us, if we would, to communicate to others those instances of beauty we discover "in the midst of it all."

Soldiers are authorized killers in the service of failed communication. When sent to the theater of the last resort, they are not supposed to contemplate the questions of beauty and existence. Their mission is conquest, and their goal is survival. True enough, Sandy was a certified player in a game in which even the victors emerge scathed and brutalized. Significantly, however, his letter ignores his official role in that game. In a single stroke, he directs our attention away from his soldierly assignment and toward the "distinguished-looking plant with soft, red flowers waving gaily in the downpour." This is rhetoric at its most elemental: highlighting some things and placing others in the shade. Ever mindful of the struggle for prominence in the order of presumptive goods, this rhetoric amounts to a declaration of justified bias, a statement affirming what it glorifies and letting all else wait. For his part, Sandy disavows the role of the warrior and embraces that of the lover of beauty. In this twofold gesture, he reveals his own *ethos* as a man for whom life without beauty is a mistake; at the same time, he grants rhetoric an *ethos* whose authority issues from the principle of topical preference.

One of the remarkable things about this letter is the fact that it was written in the first place. Sandy's arresting encounter with the thornless plant could have easily ended in his own person. His delight in the "soft, red flowers" could have turned into one of those private secrets that yields pleasure time and again, precisely because it is a secret. And his reflection on the isness of one of nature's beauties could have been confined within the borders of his own mental horizon. In short, he did not have to write the letter. But write it he did. And in so doing, he set out to communicate what he had witnessed and thought, thus letting his aesthetic encounter spill outside himself and onto the consciousness of a far away aunt. Presumably, his routine at camp had to be refigured—a letter takes time to write, and capturing a fleeting encounter in the trap of phrases requires effort. But semper fidelis, the marine let his sense of loyalty direct him to the person he had thought of "immediately." His own experience of beauty had to be conveyed to his aunt on the very same day. The matter was urgent. There could be no delay.

Another remarkable thing about the letter is that it departs from the typical letter from the front. Accordingly, it reports precious little about the scene in which it was written. The most Sandy offers is an impressionistic line: "It [Vietnam] is a country of thorns and cuts, of guns and marauding, of little hope and great failure." This is hardly an account of the real conditions of the battlefield, hardly a description of bellicose actions, hardly a story of events, dates, and names. For this reason, it would be a disappointment to researchers seeking materials for a documentary. And it would be useless to biographers interested in the informational verities of the sender's life. Researchers and biographers, however, are seldom the final arbiters of letters. Had Sandy, like so many other warriors do, written about the pervasive horror or the perfect futility of the war, we would have understood. Had he talked about the loss of his boyhood and the discovery of his manhood in the testing ground of battle, we would have made allowances. And had he said that he was missing his family, longing for the quiet luxuries he had taken for granted, or looking forward to the glorious return to his Ithaca, we would have sympathized. But Sandy's letter invokes none of these commonplaces of the typical letter from the typical soldier. Unexpectedly, his topic is beauty, beauty witnessed and beauty contemplated, even in Vietnam when Vietnam was burning. "In the midst of it all" the young marine let "a beautiful thought, gesture, and even person . . . arise among it, waving bravely at the death that pour[ed] down upon it."

Neither the relentless rain, nor the task at hand, nor yet the anxiety over distance and displacement from home, were strong enough to stand in the way of taking notice of something beautiful. The whole encounter could have easily been only a temporary distraction, a stolen moment from the agonizing days and months of killing and being killed. The second lieutenant could have walked around the plant, stepped on it, scolded his subordinate for inattentiveness to the platoon's mission. Or he could have stood there for a second or two, in total sympathy with a natural marvel, enjoyed the aesthetic experience privately, and gone on, busying himself with the cares of the day. But this is not what happened. For a brief moment, the awareness of the war and the duty on the hill lost their gravity. The ugliness of the one and the exertion for the other were no longer burdens.

Miraculously, as it were, their weight was lifted at the sight of the "soft, red flow-ers." This was a moment of freedom, a moment in which the soldier could cry "no" to the wretchedness surrounding and threatening to engulf him. And it was a moment of salvation, a moment in which he could say "yes" to beauty as a life-affirming proposition. In that moment, a presumably armed man was disarmed. Later on that day, he wrote to his great-aunt. His letter tells the story of recogniz-ing beauty at the very center of human hell.

Sandy knew that the flower's future would be short and its end tragic. Its fiery death "among the thorns" was a certainty. But for him, the flower's impending demise was no match for its distinction. Its approaching death could not detract from its splendor. And its imminent destruction could take away nothing from its "very own personality." Yet these approaching threats were not entirely idle. As if to avert them, the soldier let the flower find permanent refuge in himself. Deter-mined to rescue an instance of beauty, he let the flower transplant itself firmly in his memory, a place where it could live always. But even memory has its limits. Hence the letter, a gesture of faith in the capacity of words to communicate something worth communicating, and preserve something worth preserving, a way of disallowing finality from becoming final. To borrow from Heidegger, Sandy's language brought "what is, as something that is, into the Open for the first time."[2] At the same time, it preserved it, which is another way of saying that he stood in the flower's openness, knowing it truly. And for Heidegger, "He who truly knows what is, knows what he wills to do in the midst of what is."[3] Effec-tively, Sandy willed that, in the perennial struggle between being and nothingness, nothingness could not be allowed to have the last word.

By virtue of his letter, Sandy belongs to the tradition of letter writing, a tradi-tion that shares a long history with the rhetorical tradition. For many centuries, letter writing has borrowed, substituted, or extended rhetoric's persuasive, consti-tutive, and evocative functions. For its part, rhetoric has often employed the fig-ure and form of the letter in order to express the kinds of intimacies not readily available to the public orator. The kinship between the two traditions, however, is not only historical. It also extends to topical preferences and the impulse to accord significance to subjects close to the heart. Neither rhetoric nor letter writing has a subject matter of its own—both are capacities for addressing any topic what-soever. Even so, the choice to address one topic rather than another amounts to a declaration that says, At least for the time being, this topic is worthy of attention, more attention than other topics; it must be put ahead of them; it has priority.

This declaration tells us that one of rhetoric's functions is to circumscribe a topos and issue an invitation to dwell in it, if only briefly. What gets said in a piece of discourse often amounts to many utterances whose common aim is to iden-tify, explore, and cultivate a particular place, a specific locus. At the same time, a piece of discourse petitions the audience to visit the place it describes, and in so doing honor it in the manner of the orator. Over time, topical preferences betray standing inclinations and persistent affinities, and to know them is to know a great deal about the *ethos* of the writer. By extension, topical preferences reveal a great deal about the *ethos* of a discipline or the spirit of an age.

In book 3 of his *Topics* Aristotle discusses topical preferences and asserts that certain kinds of topics matter more than others. Specifically, he notes that "that which is more permanent or constant is more worthy of choice than that which is less so, and also that which the prudent or good man would prefer" (116a13–14).[4] His long list of preferences includes the genus over the accident, the end over the means, the divine over the human, and the soul over the body. In his discussion, however, Aristotle does not tell us how to address any one particular topic—this is something he reserves for the *Rhetoric.* But even there, his guidance comes mostly via his own example, an example that hinges on the authority of *ta endoxa,* the commonly held beliefs of a people. For all its wise counsel and staying power, however, Aristotle's *Rhetoric* does little to point us in the direction of renewal and regeneration. Again and again, the authority of his examples issues from the literary tradition he had inherited, a tradition ranging from Homer to his contemporary Isocrates.

Working exclusively from within a tradition carries a price. Too much deference for time-bound requirements, conventions, and occasions prevents a piece of rhetoric from addressing future audiences, audiences living under different signs and dissimilar irresolutions. Thus once perfectly proper orations are often frozen in time and condemned to the silence of irrelevance. The same obtains with letters addressing so narrow a matter that no future reader can hope to read with profit. Such letters have nothing to tell us, their unintended recipients. Yet few letters manage to transcend the authority of the normative and avoid the pressures of the circumstantial. As such, they continue to address a transhistorical audience of addressees. At the same time, they can serve as occasions for renewing and revising our thinking about rhetoric. Sandy's letter is such a letter. And because it is, it can help us rethink several rhetorical notions. In what follows, I focus on two.

The first notion comes from Aristotle's *Rhetoric:* "Individual cases are so infinitely various that no systematic knowledge of them is possible. Accordingly, the theory of rhetoric is concerned not with what seems probable to a given individual like Socrates or Hippias, but what seems probable to men of a given type" (1356b28–34).[5] True, we cannot generalize from an individual case. Generalization requires many instances of the same thing. But this is only part of the story. Another part is what a generalization does *with* or *to* an individual case. On this issue, Aristotle argues that insofar as an individual case does not conform to the general one, it should be regarded as a peculiar oddity. In fact, in the *Metaphysics* he goes as far as to say that when it comes to a unique or accidental case, we may as well say that it did not happen (1026b22).[6] But neither the plant nor the letter about it are instances of the general case. What made the plant on the hill stand out was the fact that it was "the first plant ... which didn't have thorns on it." And what makes Sandy's letter stand out is the fact that it is atypical. Contra Aristotle, then, the letter suggests that an individual case does not need the weighty support of established generalizations. If generalizations are derived from individual cases, and if individual cases are "infinitely various," any one generalization is always premature. But if this is so, it follows that attention to an individual case can make a generalization less premature. Second, the letter suggests that it always takes an individual case to awaken in us something as universal as the idea of beauty. Last, it suggests that the case of beauty is not an appeal reserved for people of a given type but a topos that appeals to all people.

The second notion comes from Lloyd Bitzer's discussion of rhetoric in terms of exigences, that is, imperfections marked by urgency. But as Sandy's letter shows, instances of perfection may have higher claims to urgency. This is so because such instances are so rare and so powerful that when they do manifest themselves, they are simply irrepressible. In Bitzer's view, rhetorical discourse arises in response to exigences, which it tries to modify positively, to fix. In doing so, rhetoric seeks to return a situation to a state of normalcy, a state in which things are as they ought to be. In Sandy's view, however, perfection *also* calls for rhetorical discourse, discourse designed to reveal the extraordinary and remind the audience how stunning things can be *even* in their normal state. Bitzer claims that "in the best of all possible worlds, there would be communication perhaps, but no rhetoric."[7] Sandy's response here would be that this world is the only one we have, and one of rhetoric's functions is to celebrate what there is, and imagine what has yet to be. An uncelebrated world reduces us to disinterested observers, and an unimagined one deprives us of the vitality of hope.

In and through his letter, then, Sandy challenges the assertion of an imperfect world as he communicates an experience of perfection. In this way, he is much closer to Nietzsche, who explains, "Nothing is so conditional . . . as our feeling for the beautiful. . . . In the beautiful, man sets himself up as the standard of perfection. . . . A species *cannot* do otherwise than affirm itself alone in this manner. . . . Man believes that the world itself is filled with beauty—he *forgets* that it is he who has created it. He alone has bestowed beauty upon the world."[8] In the light of this explanation, Sandy emerges not as a repairman of the world's dents and bruises but as a poet and world maker. For him, the world is not imperfect; it is forever incomplete. And because it is incomplete, it urgently needs creative artists who can bring it closer to completion, authors who can realize its unrealizable possibilities. In his belief that he had discovered one of nature's beauties, Sandy may have forgotten that he himself was the author of the beauty he beheld. His letter, however, assures us that indeed he was.

In this regard, Sandy's hellish predicament is instructive if only because it magnifies the value of his message. Here is a twenty-four year old, far from home, outside of his element, separated from family and friends, circulating among mangled corpses, exposed to the stench of human decomposition, mixing with the wounded, the disillusioned and the scared. And what does he do? He stops at a beautiful flower and then writes about his experience of it. Here is Nietzsche once again: "Nothing is beautiful, only man: on this piece of naivete rests all aesthetics, it is the *first* truth of aesthetics. Let us immediately add its second: nothing is ugly but *degenerate* man—. . . . Reckoned physiologically, everything ugly weakens and afflicts man. It recalls decay, danger, impotence; he actually suffers a loss of energy in its presence. . . . Whenever man feels in any way depressed, he senses the proximity of something 'ugly.' His feeling of power, his will to power, his courage, his pride—they decline with the ugly, they increase with the beautiful."[9] If we grant this Nietzschean stipulation, Sandy knew well both truths of aesthetics. As such, he turned to the flower in an act of self-preservation and self-affirmation, in effect challenging and defying those dehumanizing and devitalizing forces that were threatening to unravel him. The result of this turn was his letter, a gesture of supreme generosity, illustrating and reminding us that appreciating beauty privately is not enough. One has to go the extra step and attempt to make it happen for others. To do so is to keep them from degenerating in the face of the adversities of existence.

If Sandy's letter is rhetorical, it is so because it turns our attention away from the war and toward the beautiful plant with "soft, red flowers," away from "the midst of it all" and toward the kind thought, and the humane, distinguished, and brave person. His message assures us that these things, too, are part of the order of the world; so much so that those who ignore them are out of order. And even though Sandy grants existence precedence over experience, his adjectives ("beautiful," "red," "soft," "thornless," "kind," "humane") betray an orientation according to which the world and its beauty need not be two separate things.

We often pride ourselves for being the descendants of the glorious rhetoric of the Greeks. But the chasm between their sensibilities and ours is enormous. Theirs were shaped by Paris's preference for beauty over power or domination; ours are driven by power and domination to the exclusion of beauty. When Paris chose Aphrodite over Hera and Athena, he chose not only for himself but also for generations to come. Thus Isocrates was reiterating the Homeric vision for his own generation when he observed in his *Helen* that it was the beauty of Helen that united the Greeks against the Trojans. Plato was doing likewise when he arranged to have the top of his hierarchy of human types cohabited by the lover of beauty and the lover of wisdom, the *philokalos* and the *philosophos,* respectively (*Phaedrus* 248D).[10] And Aristotle was following suit when he noted that the ways of nature and our search for them are a source of pleasure and delight: "The glory, doubtless, of the heavenly bodies fills us with more delight than the contemplation of . . . lowly things, but the heavens are high and far off, and the knowledge of celestial things that our senses give us, is scanty and dim. Living creatures, on the contrary, are at our door, and if we so desire we may gain full and certain knowledge of each and all. We take pleasure in a statue's beauty; should not then the

living fill us with delight? And all the more if in the spirit of the love of knowledge we search for causes and bring to light evidences of meaning. Then will
nature's purpose and her deep-seated laws be revealed in all things, all tending in
her multitudinous work to one form or another of the beautiful."[11] From Homer
to Aristotle, then, we encounter an orientation that treats the world as an aesthetic
phenomenon and posits an appropriate attitude to go with it. This is an orientation that has the language to go with it. Recall that the Greek word for world is
cosmos which means "fitting order" or "beautiful arrangement." The Greeks also
invented the prefix "eu" and attached it to the four nouns that define all human
beings—life, death, logos, happiness (*eu zein, euthanasia, eulogy, eudaimonia*). But the
Greeks' aesthetic orientation has been neglected for so long that it is nearly forgotten.

This is what Albert Camus had in mind when he wrote in 1948 "Helen's
Exile," an essay lamenting the sorry state of his misguided era:

> We have exiled beauty; the Greeks took up arms for her. . . . Greek thought
> always took refuge behind the conception of limits. . . . Our Europe, on the
> other hand, off in the pursuit of totality, is the child of disproportion. She
> negates beauty, as she negates whatever she does not glorify. And, through all her
> diverse ways, she glorifies but one thing, which is the future rule of reason. . . .
>
> We have preferred the power that apes greatness. . . . We . . . have conquered,
> moved boundaries, mastered heaven and earth. Alone at last, we end up by rul-
> ing over a desert. What imagination could we have left for that higher equilib-
> rium in which nature balanced history, beauty, virtue, and which applied the
> music of numbers even to blood-tragedy? We turn our backs on nature; we are
> ashamed of beauty. . . . This is why it is improper to proclaim today that we are
> the [descendants] of Greece. . . .
>
> [M]an cannot do without beauty, and this is what our era pretends to want
> to disregard. It steels itself to attain the absolute and authority; it wants to trans-
> figure the world before having exhausted it, to set it to rights before having
> understood it. Whatever it may say, our era is deserting this world. . . .
>
> Admission of ignorance, rejection of fanaticism, the limits of the world and
> of man, the beloved face, and finally beauty—this is where we shall be on the
> side of the Greeks.[12]

If there is a difference between Camus's era and our own, that difference lies
in the shift from reason to power. Unlike his "reason," which disregards beauty,
our "power" reduces beauty to a suspect notion to be tracked down and exposed
as a deceptive, because hidden, form of power. This is what Peter Schejdahl meant
when he recently said that contemporary "intellectual fashion demonizes it
[beauty]."[13] Our suspicion toward beauty has been in place so long that it has
become habitual. Effectively, we have developed a second nature with which we
are trying to replace our first nature, the one that could not do without beauty.
And it shows. Our academic prose is crowded with the idea of power and its

synonyms (domination, hegemony, oppression, subjugation, tyranny, exploitation, manipulation). But the more we attend to the topic of power to the exclusion of beauty, the more the *ethos* of rhetoric becomes a site of imbalance, disorder, and disproportion. In this regard, it is worth recalling that Aristotle discussed the *ethos* of the orator in terms of a balance among phronesis, arete, and *eunoia* (good sense, moral excellence, and goodwill). For our part, we would not be far from the mark if we aimed for a similar balance in the *ethos* of rhetoric. If I am correct in asserting that rhetoric derives its *ethos* from the principle of topical preference, it would seem that the topic of beauty can no longer remain unaddressed. It is time that beauty be repatriated.

In a certain sense, we all live in the Vietnam of the 1960s. And because we do, we are preoccupied with "the cutting and scratching plants" of our predicament. There is no wonder here. The wonder begins the moment we take it upon ourselves to acknowledge beauty "in the midst of it all" and resolve to communicate it to others. To do so would mean to reaffirm rhetoric's capacity to articulate visions of perfection and its commitment to communicate subjective feelings as if they were objective truths.

Notes

1. *Letters from Sandy* (Luneburg, Vt.: Stinehour Press), 1967. I am grateful to Harris L. Kempner Jr. for his permission to publish this letter. I am also grateful to Patricia Sullivan and Robert Danisch, who read earlier versions of this essay and made insightful suggestions.

2. Martin Heidegger, "The Origin of the Work of Art," in *Poetry Language, Thought,* trans. Albert Hofstadter (New York: Harper & Row, 1975), 73.

3. Ibid., 67.

4. Aristotle, *Topics,* trans. E. S. Forster (Cambridge: Harvard University Press), 1976.

5. Aristotle, *Rhetoric and Poetics,* trans. W. Rhys Roberts and Ingram Bywater (New York: Random House), 1954.

6. Aristotle, *Metaphysics,* trans. High Tredennick (Cambridge: Harvard University Press), 1980.

7. Lloyd Bitzer, "The Rhetorical Situation," *Philosophy and Rhetoric* 1, no. 1 (1968): 13.

8. Friedrich Nietzsche, *Twilight of the Idols,* trans. R. J. Hollingdale (New York: Penguin Books, 1984), 78.

9. Ibid., 78–79.

10. Plato, *Phaedrus,* trans. H. N. Foweler (New York: G. P. Putnam's Sons), 1933.

11. Edith Hamilton, *The Greek Way* (New York: W. W. Norton, 1993), 32.

12. Albert Camus, "Helen's Exile," in *The Myth of Sisyphus and Other Essays,* trans. Justin O'Brien (New York: Random House, 1955), 134–38.

13. Peter Schejdahl, "Beauty Is Back," *New York Times Magazine,* September 29, 1996, 161.

The *Ethos* of a Black Aesthetic

An Exploration of Larry Neal's Visions of a Liberated Future

ERIC KING WATTS

The Black Arts movement (BAM) ballooned like a mushroom cloud and exploded with fire and force. Seizing the energies of mid-1960s African American discontent and rage, the movement excited the sentiments associated with death and demoralization and through a "critical reexamination of Western political, social and artistic values"[1] articulated for black people "what the world is and what it *ought* to be."[2] Indeed, the BAM sought to make up a new world, a black world. Interestingly, this "new" place for African American living was composed of disparate remains from the past and romanticized visions of the future. Motivated, in part, by the political assassinations of Patrice Lumumba and Malcolm X, and sensing that the civil rights agenda led by Dr. Martin Luther King Jr. would not stave off the eleventh hour for black America, BAM advocates got together to create and destroy, to "raise the level of black struggle to a more *intense expression*" (emphasis added).[3] Imagining black arts as the "aesthetic and spiritual sister of the Black Power concept,"[4] artists and intellectuals proposed, like Stokely Carmichael, that black liberation depended upon black self-understanding and self-determination.[5]

Embracing tenets of cultural nationalism, the BAM dedicated itself to the recollection and explicit fabrication of a black aesthetic—an ideological system constitutive of a distinct "black perspective" on the beauty and on the cruelty of black life. Framed by the notion that "black art *was* black power," that "social and aesthetic values were inextricably wedded," the push to develop black art also involved reflection upon the meaning of "blackness" and about how black folk ought to engage the political sphere.[6] Although the black aesthetic has received sparse scholarly treatment over the years, it is generally understood as referring to a loosely connected set of underdeveloped (and contradictory) theories of artistic production.[7] From this perspective, the black aesthetic is evaluated on its capacity to make sense of how art works reflect the perceptions of black artists. But since the black aesthetic "confuses social theory with aesthetics" and is "predicated upon crude, strident forms of nationalism" that exhibit a "swaggering rhetoric of ethnic and gender chauvinism," it is not surprising that the productions of the Black Arts movement are seen as belligerent and angry and typically are held in "low esteem."[8] In terms of yielding a theory of art, the black aesthetic has not with much confidence been judged a success. But pronouncements such as this lead to conclusions about the viability and value of the black aesthetic based principally on its status as a theory of art, that is, based on its potential to clarify the relationship between the work and the imaginary world of the artist. Generally speaking, such thought is predicated on the belief that incoherence regarding its interpretive rules is a sign of inferior theorizing.[9] I contend that such treatment, debatable even from the point of view of aesthetic theory, does not provide us with an understanding of how the black aesthetic helped its proponents do what they claimed it did, that is, make sense of the world and convey that sense to black people.

Making sense of the world in this fashion has historically enabled black folk in America to cultivate a "dwelling place." My work regarding the Harlem Renaissance has explored the ways black artists and intellectuals during that era exploited white interest in the "exotic" and self-interest in black identity to bring into being tangible and palpable features of a black home or "Mecca."[10] The ontological and ethical implications of such an endeavor are immediately evident as we ask a few simple questions: What should this home look like? How should it be designed and constructed? What should it "feel" like to live there? What are the obligations and commitments of its residents? How should it be governed? These questions underscore for critics the rhetorical characteristics of a black aesthetic precisely because such questions are given graphic demonstration in works and are subject to public scrutiny as folks work collectively to "know-together" the "proper" practices for constituting black art and culture. This is why scholarship shaped by questions about traditional aesthetic theory neglects the black aesthetic's capacity to function as a mode of interpretive understanding and rhetorical invention. Moreover, since varying conceptions of a black aesthetic index significant development in black American public expression and creativity, shaping the character of a black rhetorical voice,[11] such disregard prohibits us from appreciating how this particular characterization contributes to African American rhetoric and influences our broader predicament regarding how race and culture matter in civic life.

This chapter, therefore, explores the reinvention of a black aesthetic during the Black Arts movement in order to understand its role in the reconstitution of an African American *ethos*. I assert that as black nationalism gained momentum during the mid-1960s, black artists and intellectuals of the movement rationalized the "purification" of "blackness" by characterizing the "proper" relations between "blackness" and "whiteness" as fundamentally oppositional and antagonistic. Also, Black Arts advocates invented a discourse positing an "authentic" black homeland through appropriations and revisions of anticolonialism, premodernism, African mythos, and black folk culture. I argue that the black aesthetic is constitutive of a hermeneutical rhetoric and is a topical resource shaping further interpretive acts. Since the BAM describes an ideology more than a collective action and can be pieced together from a panoply of discourses, no one work can adequately account for its rhetoric. This chapter focuses, therefore, on *Visions of a Liberated Future,* a collection of Larry Neal's Black Arts movement writing. Neal was a principal intellectual spokesperson for the movement, and his writing displays an aesthetic praxis that animates and structures intense emotions associated with the liberation of "blackness" and the destruction of "whiteness." Such emotions, I argue, shape the character of this hermeneutical rhetoric by correlating its interpretive acts with the fear of nihilism. In this way, a black homeland is, in part, conceived as a place where the gratification of self-determination and the edification of self-definition are deepened by dramatizing the devastation of the source of that fear —the white other. Thus, nationalism and nihilism arouse feelings supporting both the construction and constriction of an African American *ethos.* The chapter concludes with some observations regarding the liabilities of a rhetoric employing abstract concepts of "race" and the potentialities associated with an aesthetic praxis governed by concrete emotions regarding community.

The Senses of a Black Aesthetic

Hermeneutical rhetoric involves the location and application of the topical materials of speech. When one decides to speak about a thing, one usually chooses certain features of the thing to be expressed; more than involving the picking out of what one wishes to say, hermeneutical rhetoric concerns the interpretation of the "truth" of that which will be spoken—one must "find the *right* words."[12] Since our self-understanding and our relations to others condition our interpretive acts, the application of interpretive understanding is constitutive of a form of social knowledge. I have argued elsewhere that this process requires an interpretive competence that is mediated by an aesthetic praxis.[13] Identifying the "proper" words is not simply a calculative or instrumental activity; it is enveloped by sensuality, a feeling toward (or away from) the topic, its history and traditions, its values as one perceives them, and its status as a historical being in the world. Roger Scruton argues that as we participate in public culture, we are educated about our community's attitudes and sentiments regarding ourselves and regarding the artifacts that make up our culture.[14] We are trained to feel a certain way (and not to feel otherwise); such civic lessons constrain our sense of what is and what ought to be. We can see, then, that this aesthetic understanding is ethical because it implicates the negative, that which is not and *should* not be. It also requires adjudication by interested others; it needs to be affirmed as appropriate and valuable (or not) and, hence, cannot come into being in private. Involved in the work of *sensus communus,* our interpretive acts not only constitute a world view but also instruct us on how to feel about the world and our place in it. It is in this respect that "truth" and knowledge have sensual dimensions that cannot be adequately explained by reason; as we seek to get to the "heart" of the matter[15] and seek to effectively convey that "truth" to others, our palpable existence preconditions our perspective on propriety. We know what is proper not just because we *perceive* it to be so; we also *feel* it to be so. Furthermore, our emotional judgments about what we should do and say (and how we should do and say) display our rhetorical and hermeneutical competence to others.

In terms of exploring how the black aesthetic functioned as a mode of interpretive understanding and rhetorical invention, one must first recognize that even among its most ardent supporters and at the peak of the movement, there was "no real agreement about [its] meaning."[16] Hence, the attempt to "create values"[17] and to "carry the past"[18] forward is itself shaped by a desire to reduce this equivocality by appealing to what black arts advocates thought to be the "heart" of the black experience: oppression. Contrasting themselves with the artists of the Harlem Renaissance, now indicted for having failed to produce a lasting or serviceable cultural agenda due to inner "confusion" and a penchant for appealing to the conscience of white folk, BAM proponents congratulated themselves on their clarity and autonomy.[19]

Inspired by the works of Frantz Fanon and enamored with the concept of an African American colonial subjectivity, the black self is reinterpreted as a historically oppressed and purely objectified body, separated and fixed as not white. The distinction that is made here is not only consistent with the belief that the black aesthetic brings into being "an art which *maximizes the differences* between White and Black culture" but also habituated by the threat of nihilism.[20] In an essay called "Black Arts," Neal declared that "today we bear witness to the moral and philosophical decay of a corrupt civilization. Europe and America are the new Babylons."[21] The depiction of American culture as corrupt and senseless warrants a complete separation from and negation of this threat. Such an interpretive understanding impels artists to "speak" in the voice of the colonized and to instruct the "wretched of the earth" to embrace this *ethos* and wage war on the colonizer.[22] In the introduction to *The Black Aesthetic,* Addison Gayle writes, "The Black Aesthetic . . . is a corrective—a means of helping black people out of the polluted mainstream of Americanism, and offering logical, reasoned arguments as to why [they] should not desire to . . . surrender their history and culture to a universal melting pot."[23] Similarly, essayist Linsay Barrett writes of a scenario in the anthology *Black Arts* in which black music is lethal: "If a black man could grasp a [John] Coltrane solo in its entirety as a club and wield it with the force that first created it . . . the battle would be near ending and in [the black person's] favor."[24] But notice that this confrontation also involves the appropriation and modification of the sort of dialectical transcendence that Victoria J. Gallagher investigates in the rhetoric of Stokely Carmichael.[25]

Using Kenneth Burke's concept of the negative to explore Carmichael's Black Power speech at Berkeley, Gallagher notes that definitions of race have historically been arrived at dialectically in terms of specifying what a thing is not. Moreover, the economy of U.S. racial discourse supports a dialectic that affirms absolute categories of race as well as promotes racial supremacy by establishing the belief that "whiteness" is "categorically different" from (and superior to) all other racial terms.[26] The constitution of "whiteness" requires the isolation and purgation of that which is black, brown, yellow, and so forth. In this discursive process, "whiteness" transcends racial categories altogether and is thus absolved of "ethnicity" and the limitations of "otherness." Since an incongruous perspective is always possible, however, allowing one to see a thing as *not* like something else, this dialectical procedure is an extreme form of negative critique. In the context of culture wars, the search for "purity" can be a powerful tool of the ideologue, obscuring the crucial fact that "difference" is inescapable. This is why Burke understands such "transcendence" as generative of a "paradox of purity."[27]

This paradox is doubly present in the black aesthetic. As artists assume the *ethos* of the oppressed, they appropriate this dialectic and enact it in two revised modes. The first mode posits the "purity" of whiteness but transposes its valence. Rather than synthesizing white goodness, the reinterpreted white/not white pair articulates the *wrongness* of whiteness and specifies why black folk are (fortunately) "not white." But as artists simultaneously turn inward, toward the black community and work to "affirm ourselves—each other[,] . . . affirm the kingdom of heaven within us," the dialectic is translated into its opposite: black/not black.[28] This dialectic demonstrates the "purity" and beauty of blackness by isolating and purging (white) substances that do not properly belong to it; in short, it identifies values and ideas that are "not black." The threat of nihilism in the white world is converted here into a fearful campaign toward the absolute negation of vestiges of white psychology and cultural values that are thought to jeopardize the existence of a black dwelling place. In *Race Matters,* Cornel West describes this sort of logic in terms of the "Pitfalls of Racial Reasoning."[29]

The two structures are mutually reinforcing: whiteness is understood as responsible for the ills of the world while blackness is defined in terms that reclaim a sense of moral agency for black folk in a corrupt world. As Burke points out, such dialectical structures imply one another, like a disease intimates its cure;[30] but these dialectics are also infused with the emotional entailments of racial discourse. The white/not white pair generates demonizing rhetoric and the black/not black dialectic posits blackness as a "corrective." Toward whiteness there is fear and loathing, and associated with blackness one experiences adoration and gratification. The feelings corresponding to each dialectical operation, however, can be carried over into its "other." As such, the racial discourse orchestrated by these dialectical pairs is often manic—expressing a Dionysian rapture associated with the "destruction" of whiteness so that a black self-love may emerge. Such discourse celebrates the raising of a black national flag, but because nihilism is generative of this nationalistic impulse, the dwelling place arising out of it becomes increasingly inhospitable and hostile toward all signs of "difference." Because the constitution of a home is bound up with the elation of negation, the gratification of rising up and dedicating oneself to a "murderous and decisive struggle [with] searing bullets and bloodstained knives,"[31] black self-expression is habituated as a form of "violence."

This latest discussion clarifies the character of the hermeneutical rhetoric constitutive of the black aesthetic. First, "authentic" black experience is understood in terms of oppression. Second, blackness is "purified" and opposed to whiteness. Third, the appropriation and transposition of the process of dialectical transcendence catalyzes a negative racial critique that paradoxically reproduces, alongside "pure" blackness, whiteness as the corrupt "thing" to be destroyed; thus a black homeland is generative of intense emotions associated with notions of racial "authenticity" and suffers from the stress of this paradox. I argue in the proceeding section of this chapter that Larry Neal's hermeneutical rhetoric appropriates and reinterprets anticolonialism, premodernism, and African and black folk culture and captures the imagination of black aesthetic enthusiasts. More important, by being sensitive to the workings of these emotions Neal invents a discourse that points the way out of the paradox of purity.

Visions of a Liberated Future

Visions of a Liberated Future is a posthumous dedication to the life of artist and essayist Larry Neal, considered the chief "theoretician" and spokesperson for the BAM and the self-proclaimed "synthesizer" of movement elements.[32] Neal's writing attempts to bend time and space; it is mythic in the sense of conjuring heroes for black worship; it is humanistic, showing black folk their own faces; it is poetic, syncopating the rhythms and beats of black living; it is apocalyptic, forewarning of racial war and strife; it is chauvinistic, reinforcing the barricades against gendered and sexual others; and it is idealistic, enacting for us an aesthetic praxis that undermines his own bigotry and hubris. Neal's "vision," therefore, is prismatic, refracting the light from a black fire, transforming it into the multifarious colors of life itself. But for the sake of clearly seeing his hermeneutic, let us begin with just two colors—black and white.

Neal's writing expresses the rage and bereavement of black folk following the death of Malcolm X and channels those sentiments into painfully piercing exposés regarding black writers, black writing, and black reading (listening). Blackness is posited as a first principle requiring nothing more than the presence of whiteness to confirm its status as absolute "other"; it is also subjected to critical inquiry regarding its complexity and mutability. Reification, however, precedes transformation in Neal's discourse by a long shot. Hence, in the months following

Malcolm's assassination, Neal proposed that the artist and activist "understand and manipulate the collective myths of the race. Both are warriors, priests, lovers, and destroyers. For the first violence will be internal—the destruction of a weak spiritual self for a more perfect self."[33]

One can hear in Neal the echoes of Frantz Fanon's revolutionary diagnosis of the colonial mentality. Fanon argued that the subjects of colonialism must dedicate themselves to violence in order to realize political movement and reassert political and cultural agency.[34] Even as cultural nationalists "invoked the idea that 'Black is a country' as a sweeping rhetorical claim for Afro-American struggles [and] as 'only a microcosm of the struggle of the new countries all over the world,'" advocates for decolonization recognized the impossibility of secession.[35] Rather than waging literal war against white colonialists, therefore, black writers asserted "a literature that would fight" against the presence of white ideology in the black communal consciousness.[36] This presence has a history shaped, Neal argues, by a pathological desire to be embraced by white folk and signifies a form of collective mental illness. Having internalized the oppressor's "useless, dead ideas,"[37] incorporated an "alien sensibility,"[38] black culture is perceived as schizophrenic, as fragmented by the presence of a "decaying structure" that is "anti-human in nature."[39] From this vantage point, double consciousness is reinterpreted as life threatening and black thinkers' attempts to maintain W. E. B. Du Bois's famous duality, first described in the *Souls of Black Folk,* are understood as marred by an acute "confusion."[40]

Mark Lawrence McPhail correctly points out that double consciousness has manifested itself as a rhetorical trope that is constitutive of an anxiety regarding racial identity. Appropriated and reinterpreted generation after generation, double consciousness is nevertheless consistently explicated within a therapeutic context.[41] Du Bois perceived it as a remedy for the material conditions for black folk as well as for the American political economy because it encouraged openness toward the life world of the other. Du Bois, in part, understood double consciousness as an existential invitation for alterity. But it is precisely this propensity for "second sight" that Neal poses as a problem for black self-preservation. In a sense, being doubly conscious means being able to live and let live; being able to appreciate and respect the living conditions of others. Contending that the black writer is an "oppressed individual" and "an interpreter"[42] of history and social life, Neal argues that the black artist must not live in two places; he "must decide that his art belongs primarily to his own people. This is not to deny that there are some 'universal' factors at work; but we are living in a specific place, at a specific time, and are a specific set of people with a specific historical development. In the confusion of today's struggle for human survival, the black artist cannot afford vagueness about himself and his people who need him."[43]

Neal's repetitive appeal to the specificity of lived experience draws our attention to the particularity of black life (and death) and to the character of his aesthetic praxis. Reinventing an "emotional history,"[44] Neal writes that the black aesthetic "can be read . . . as a rejection of anything that we feel is detrimental to our people. And it is almost axiomatic that most of what the West considers important endangers the more humane world we feel ours should be. . . . This is important to know because the sense of how that history should be felt is what either unites or separates us."[45] There are two aspects of this hermeneutic that warrant brief attention. First, Neal posits that the primary role of the historical for black empowerment is not to constitute moral lessons by which to live; rather, history itself should be *re-lived* so as to inculcate the proper emotions regarding the subjects of history. Second, Neal's "emotional history" arouses severe disdain for the colonizer's world view, so much so that the black artist's "motive is the destruction of the white thing"[46] in order to "be more human,"[47] in order to survive. Shared feelings orient black folk toward a shared past and a shared threat, and occupying the category of the "oppressed," black folk are moved to consistently consider themselves in a state of war. In this state of arousal, black folk are conditioned to see America as a frightful wasteland where folks can easily be lost and emasculated. "Outside of the ethos," Neal states, "you have to become bitchy and perverted, 'cause you ain't holding on to nothing. . . . [C]ut loose from a unified center, we become freaks, confused, driven from without rather than from within. . . . You [can be] squeezed spermless, your seed scattered among the ice and rocks."[48]

Through an appropriation of anticolonialism, Neal is able to characterize "whiteness" as deadly, threatening not only the individual but also the life of a (manly) black homeland. In order to safeguard one's home, black folk are stimulated toward the kind of vigilance in which they are sensitive to the barbarians clamoring at the gate as well as "celebrate" artistic works that, in part, strive "to create fear" in the hearts of an interpretive community.[49] Carolyn Fowler describes the experience this way: "One goes away from the theater, the sculpture, the painting, the novel or poem not drained of emotion and at peace, but troubled, and with no place to hide."[50] And so, the feelings corresponding to a nihilistic threat condition the features of a black aesthetic due to the way that this interpretive practice dedicates itself to an oppositional "rhetoric of the gun."[51] Nihilism becomes a pleasurable doctrine of negation directed toward "whiteness" and, paradoxically, it informs the constitution of "blackness" and of a black home.

This hermeneutical rhetoric is also enabled by Neal's appropriation of elements of premodernism. Karol Berger, in *A Theory of Art,* draws a distinction between the uses and functions of modern and premodern artistry so as to clarify how modern artistry attained autonomy as a reflection of the individual's imagination. In contrast to this development of a market economy for art, Berger describes the art of the premodern era as determined by a social group, community, or clan: "The most distinctive feature of the premodern . . . art was its heteronomy, the fact that the goods one pursued in working at it were primarily not internal to the practice of art itself, but rather internal to other, nonartistic social activities of art consumers."[52] Berger's thesis connects civic goods with aesthetic production and theorizes that the highest achievement for art in any society would be to allow "us to evaluate what actually is and not what might or should be . . . [to make] public deliberation possible."[53] Since Western culture is represented as depraved and antihumanistic, and modern artists as pursuing art for art's sake, detached from questions of civic good, black artists constituted an art that represented its antithesis. This entailed the production of a social art conceived by an artist in intimate relations with her community seeking to perpetuate the civic goods of that group.

According to William Van Deburg, white culture "was said to reveal an unfortunate separation of art from life; artists from their audiences."[54] Given this gulf between the artistic and the body politic attributed to internalized "whiteness," black arts advocates argued that black artists should devote themselves to promoting a spiritual rapprochement between black history, culture, and community life. Neal posits that "artists carry the past and the future memory of the race. . . . [T]hey link us to the deepest, most profound aspects of our ancestry."[55] The black aesthetic is, hence, "radically opposed to any concept of the artist that alienates him from his community."[56] And so, Neal reasons, the "writer must somehow place himself at the center of the community's cultural and political activity and perform the role of interpreter of the mysteries of life."[57] There are two puzzles that Neal tried to solve relating to the immersion of the artist into her community. First, the role of interpreter for the artist suggests a privileged status as knower. Indeed, Neal argues that the most vital black artist will perform priestly rituals on behalf of community spirit. Second, Neal seems to rely on this artist's self-understanding as an "oppressed individual" even as he characterizes individual consciousness as the source of Babylonian chaos.[58] Neal asks writers to be a fount of divine cultural knowledge and yet turn away from the germs of Western corruption—authority and power—ascribed to such sources. Faced with these sorts of philosophical problems, Neal and other movement proponents, as "members of an activist generation . . . [become] more interested in pointing out what the aesthetic could *do* for black people" (emphasis added).[59]

The turn toward premodern notions of art also promoted the understanding of art's purpose and function as community ritual and as the site of programmatic agendas constitutive of the artistic process. The Black Arts Repertory Theater/School (BARTS), established in Harlem in 1966 by LeRoi Jones and Larry Neal, was a working model of this understanding, developing black artistic sensibilities that would reproduce and extend black nationalist ideology. The BARTS was designed to teach and to organize black collective action and was, therefore, posited as a substitute for the black church as the locus of community involvement. Playwright William Kgositsile described the idea this way: "Our theater will be a definitive act, a decisive song. There will be portions of actual life unveiled. All the things we could have been. All the things we are. All the things we will be.

There will be instruction. There will be construction. There will also be destruction."[60] Responding in part to criticisms from the Black Panthers accusing cultural nationalist groups of being a bunch of pacifists who were overly concerned with the symbolic, Neal also affirms the idea that "poetry is a concrete function, an action."[61] The reinterpretation of black art as consistent with premodern artistic practices accomplishes three related tasks. First, premodernism supports the view of black art as a communal endeavor; as a participatory aesthetic generative of cultural practices and shared feelings, nationalist arguments were bolstered regarding its "authenticity." Second, premodernism warrants the claim that black art should not be considered an autonomous object of anonymous consumption in a market economy; rather, black art reproduces and actualizes a specific cultural memory meant to guide ethical action. Third, premodernism allows Neal to orchestrate key features of African mythos and integrate them with black folk culture. It is toward this third issue that we now turn.

In an essay dedicated to the legacy of black folktales called "And Shine Swam On," Neal constitutes the black aesthetic in terms of how black American discursive strategies were informed by an African sensibility. For Neal, African art was essentially ritualistic; it dramatized for community reflection and deliberation the material conditions of everyday lived experience. As a genuine rhetorical community, Africans took part in such dramatizations so that everyone's experiences could shape the social narrative.[62] Moreover, such participation instructed one's emotions regarding one's being in time. Although Neal racializes this aesthetic praxis, not acknowledging that premodern European communities performed similar rituals, it is the irresistibility of community practices and the emotions they arouse that illuminates for Neal (and for us) a way out of the paradox of purity.

Initially following the work of LeRoi Jones in *Blues People*,[63] Neal suggests that quintessential black expression emanates out of a blues idiom. Sharing cultural roots with spirituals, the blues, however, are perceived by Neal to contain the "bad" seed; unlike the sorrow songs' emphasis on transcendence of the material world, the blues dwells in the angst of existence, personifying a "toughness of spirit," a willingness to confront the world as it is.[64] The blues offers a "social history of mental and physical hardships; they lyrically address themselves to *concrete life situations*" (emphasis added).[65] This challenging spirit motivates the blues singer, says Neal, to travel among black communities and urge others to become acutely aware of the harsh materiality of life by inviting them to share his pain. The blues singer is welcomed like a traveling preacher, celebrated as the bringer of a troubled cultural memory. By juxtaposing the blues artist and the preacher, Neal encourages us to see the secular in terms of the sacred. The blues singer is a spiritual leader and demands the congregational practice of "call and response." The blues singer is a reservoir for "oral tradition" because her scripture is made up of the ongoing disclosure of the people's Word. This tradition is of course musical, and Neal applauds black artistry that infused writing with listening. Commenting on Jones's play, *Slave Ship,* Neal asserts, "There is no definite plot (LeRoi calls it a pageant), just a continuous rush of sound, moans, screams, and souls wailing for freedom and relief from suffering. . . . Events are blurred, rising and falling in a stream of sound. . . . It is a play which almost totally eliminates the need for a text."[66] Indeed, the elimination of a text, for Neal, backgrounds the modern artifact and foregrounds performance and action. Thus, the blues is the sound of the oppressed; as an idiom of expression, it dwells in the place occupied by the animation of remembrance and sensation. The blues singer signifies the premodern African griot in a modern world. In terms of a temporal orientation, premodernity is closer to a form of sacred time in which one's past is experienced as always present. It is in contemplation of how the blues serves this sacred function in a secular fashion that leads Neal to a revision of his dismissal of Christianity as a "tool of the oppressor" and to take seriously the perils of an oversimplification of and detachment from the complexity of social life.[67]

In an essay published in 1970, dedicated to the defense of Ralph Ellison's *Invisible Man* as a legitimate example of a black aesthetic, Neal argues that critics should not prejudge how blackness can be performed; rather, they should be open to how black folk culture and a blues idiom can yield complex perspectives on black living. "We must address ourselves to this kind of humanity because it is meaningful and within our immediate reach," he notes. "To do so means understanding something essential about the *persistence of tradition,* understanding the manner in which values are shaped out of tradition, and—what's more important—understanding the values whose fundamental function was to bind us together into a community of shared feelings and memories in order that we might survive" (emphasis added).[68] This kind of emotional bonding encourages Neal to question his own presumptions about the Byzantine constraints on black writing and to assess the values of Ellison's "zoot suit," not from the ideological perspective of other cultural nationalists who reject its putative claims to a "social realist" aesthetic[69] but to appreciate the way that Ellison induces a sense of vertigo in the reader/listener as his nameless protagonist rapidly descends underground. Pulled downward by the poignant gravity of Ellison's narrative and attracted to the sound of Louis Armstrong's horn in Ellison's notes, Neal is impelled to abandon the hubris and arrogance of earlier writing and to exhibit a reflective openness toward alternative possibilities for an African American *ethos.* Importantly, in defense of Ellison, Neal takes up an ongoing polemic regarding the significance of "protest" writing and of Ellison's status as a black writer in particular. Although this essay cannot account for this thorny debate, it is clear that Neal was troubled by attempts made by liberal white critics to police the boundaries of black expression by positing violent "psychological dynamics" as essential to "Negro writers."[70] Neal's involvement with this problem, in part, conditioned his growing skepticism about the propriety of abstract categories of race and culture and to move him toward a fuller appreciation of the courage it takes to write honestly about black living.

In the essay "My Lord, He Calls Me by the Thunder," Neal shifts from an oppositional discourse that, through a negative critique identifying that which is "not black," constricts the circumference of a black homeland to a discourse that closely interrogates local cultural practices that "enabled us to survive spiritually."[71] Chief among such practices was Christianity. Neal's revision begins with a reinterpretation of the relationship between ideology and liberation: "Insecurity frequently leads us to conclude falsely, that all of our problems would be solved if the Black masses would only convert to some specific ideological or theological tenets—namely, the ones *we adhere to.* But in reality, the problem is far more complex than any *one* ideological position because life itself is essentially fluid and changing" (emphasis added).[72] Neal's comment recognizes how philosophical dogma, in any form, desensitizes us to the lived experiences and feelings of others.

In keeping with a renewed attention to the indeterminacy and the authenticity of being there, Neal expresses the joy and the everyday satisfaction of folks who, through Christianity, have their burdens lifted by God. Moreover, Neal implores would-be black revolutionaries to recognize and appreciate the important fact of massive black folk religious practice. "In other words, a life-style exists among black folk that is totally at odds with the attitudes of nationalist intellectuals who instead of denigrating the religion of much of the black body should be trying to understand the influence—past and present—of the black church."[73] Interestingly, for much of his career Neal was conflicted about the status of Christianity in the black community. Two years earlier, in *Black Fire,* his short story "Sinner Man Where You Gonna Run To?" seemed to suspend Christianity between the promise of its ancient radical roots and the practical requirements of black revolution. Radicals, Neal's story suggested, need to draw strength from covert practices that affirm the divine right, not to turn the other cheek, but to spill blood in a liberationist cause.[74]

In "My Lord," however, Neal testifies to a more sensitive understanding of cultural transformation while retaining the deep commitment to vivifying a shared emotional history. Recognizing that in all sorts of localized practices and occasions, African slaves reinvented Christianity in order to make it livable, Neal called the masses of black folk "Christian Africans"[75] who regularly celebrate "Afro-Christian services."[76] This cultural distinction allows Neal to remain antagonistic toward "White Christianity" by opposing it to its black version, but because Neal's rhetoric locates the reproduction of social life and culture within particular group practices and contexts, ideological systems become mutable. "Christianity," Neal contends, "like everything else the black man has touched in the West, has been transformed by the African presence."[77] If by "everything else" Neal includes the character of racial relations, the black aesthetic's racial opposition itself is subject

to revision. Neal begins to dissolve this racial antithesis by reinterpreting the relationship between the Christianity of black slaves and the Christianity practiced by
white slaveholders. Neal argues that the institution of slavery corrupted Christian
ideals and, sounding a little like G. W. F. Hegel in "Master and Slave," posits that
the slave came closer to realizing true Spirit,[78] represented here as the radical possibilities of Christian love. The dialectical tension of the Master/Slave provokes a
movement toward a kind of "purity" or ideal in this essay, but is converted by the
non rational elements of an emotional history, unconditional acceptance, and the
practical requirements of social change into a near perfect faith in the power of a
black *ethos* and its impact on the civic good. By the end of the essay, such devotion seems dedicated to sublimating the "ethics of white Christianity" and saving
—not negating—white America's soul.[79]

The Black Arts movement sought to introduce a way of manufacturing livable
space—a dwelling place—for black folk. The black aesthetic was a powerful concept that helped black nationalists to organize and make sense of the various discursive topics made available by a robust hermeneutical rhetoric. I have argued
that Larry Neal was a principal public intellectual and artist of the movement and
I have explicated the maturation of his rhetoric. Specifically, I contend that Neal's
interpretive acts were habituated by an aesthetic praxis that cultivated in him an
understanding of "liberation" that was not predicated upon the destruction of
whiteness.

Neal's perspective on cultural transformation troubles the presumed "purity"
of "blackness" and of "whiteness" because it denies the possibility of absolute
transcendence inscribed in the dialectical pairs black/not black and white/not
white. In other words, due to the transfusional nature of social life and cultural
reproduction, one cannot absolutely identify that which is "not black" or that which
is "not white." Also, Neal's aesthetic praxis shows us that over time the emotions
that shape our identification with and orientation toward those that we judge to
be "one of us," are themselves reanimated by our continued participation in public culture. Neal's activities as a black public intellectual made available to him intimate contact with alterations in the material world and those activities demanded
that he answer, that is, *address,* those alterations. And so, Neal's hermeneutical rhetoric was conditioned by an aesthetic praxis that produced a sense of claustrophobia as he was suffocated by the pressures of locating that which is "not black."

Neal did not live to complete his turn toward the *ethos* of the other; he did not
provide us with a more fully revised explication of racial identity, art, and culture.
His writing, however, shows us how the practices of building one's dwelling place
can be self-reflexive, that as we figure out how we can know each other and ourselves, we must also know that we *do not know* how to be perfect together. Neal's
early death can itself serve as a testament to the unfinished character of the *ethos*
of rhetoric. For how can we complete such a dwelling place when folks who

would live with us and love us are finite and particular? My comfort here and now implicates another's discomfort there and then. And how can I rest peacefully while others lack adequate shelter? But Neal is helpful here, too. It is clear that, although he no longer maintained a strict oppositional hermeneutical rhetoric, he believed until his death that "nationalism is the central mode of black liberation."[80] Putting aside the specter of separatism for a moment, what Neal suggests is that the *ethos* of rhetoric "naturally" pulls toward the articulation of common interests that allow collective deliberation and action. It is up to its framers, the agents of rhetoric, however, to keep in mind that one's home is part of a neighborhood. Neal's "vision" may not include more than one aesthetic; his sight might in fact focus too much on how folks who "look alike" should see the same way. But what he does give us in his notation about how a black aesthetic can survive its own negative racial critique is a picture of an aesthetic praxis that senses how one's relations to others places and relieves the inevitable stress of living together.

Notes

1. Larry Neal, *Visions of a Liberated Future: Black Arts Movement Writings* (New York: Thunder's Mouth Press, 1989), 8.

2. Neal, *Visions,* 69.

3. Amiri Baraka, in Neal's *Visions,* ix.

4. Neal, *Visions,* 62.

5. Stephen Howe, *Afrocentrism: Mythical Pasts and Imagined Homes* (London: Verso Books, 1998), 92.

6. William L. Van Deburg, *New Day in Babylon* (Chicago: University of Chicago Press, 1992), 171, 177.

7. David Lionel Smith, "The Black Arts Movement and Its Critics," *American Literary History* 3 (1991): 93–110.

8. Ibid., 93.

9. Karol Berger, *A Theory of Art* (New York: Oxford University Press, 2000), 23–40.

10. Eric King Watts, "African American Ethos and Hermeneutical Rhetoric: An Exploration of Alain Locke's *The New Negro,*" *Quarterly Journal of Speech* 88 (2002): 19–32.

11. Eric King Watts, "Cultivating a Black Public Voice: W. E. B. Du Bois and the 'Criteria of Negro Art,'" *Rhetoric and Public Affairs* 4 (2001): 181–201.

12. James Risser, *Hermeneutics and the Voice of the Other: Re-reading Gadamer's Philosophical Hermeneutics* (Albany: State University of New York, 1997), 14.

13. Watts, "African American Ethos," 20–22.

14. Roger Scruton, *The Aesthetic Understanding: Essays in the Philosophy of Art and Culture* (Manchester: Carcanet Press, 1983), 139–42.

15. Michael J. Hyde, "Hermeneutics," in *Encyclopedia of Rhetoric,* ed. Thomas O. Sloane (New York: Oxford University Press, 2001), 330.

16. Smith, "Black Arts Movement," 94.

17. Addison Gayle Jr., "The Harlem Renaissance: Towards a Black Aesthetic," *Midcontinent American Studies Journal* 11 (1970): 80.

18. Larry Neal, "Black Art and Black Liberation," in *The Black Revolution,* ed. John H. Johnson (Chicago: Johnson, 1970), 39.

19. Addison Gayle Jr., *The Black Aesthetic* (New York: Doubleday, 1971), xviii.

20. Gayle, "Harlem Renaissance," 82.

21. Neal, "Black Art," 33.

22. Robert L. Allen, *Black Awakening in Capitalist America* (Trenton, N.J.: Africa World Press, 1990), 247–73.

23. Gayle, *Black Aesthetic,* xxiii.

24. Linsay Barrett, "The Tide Inside, It Rages," in *Black Arts: An Anthology of Black Creations,* ed. Ahmed Alhamisi and Harun Kofi Wangara (Detroit: Black Arts, 1969), 94–95.

25. Victoria J. Gallagher, "Black Power in Berkeley: Postmodern Constructions in the Rhetoric of Stokely Carmichael," *Quarterly Journal of Speech* 87 (2001): 144–57.

26. Ibid., 147.

27. Kenneth Burke, *A Rhetoric of Motives* (Berkeley and Los Angeles: University of California Press, 1969).

28. Joe Goncalves, "Natural Black Beauty," in *Black Arts: An Anthology of Black Creations,* ed. Ahmed Alhamisi and Harun Kofi Wangara (Detroit: Black Arts, 1969), 22.

29. Cornel West, *Race Matters* (Boston: Beacon Press, 1993), 33–49.

30. Kenneth Burke, "Four Master Tropes," in *A Grammar of Motives,* by Kenneth Burke (Berkeley and Los Angeles: University of California Press, 1960), 503–17.

31. Franz Fanon, *The Wretched of the Earth* (New York: Grove Press, 1963), 37.

32. Neal, *Visions,* 131.

33. Ibid., 23.

34. Fanon, *Wretched of the Earth,* 73–86.

35. Howe, *Afrocentrism,* 93.

36. Baraka, *Visions,* x.

37. Neal, *Visions,* 22.

38. Van Deburg, *New Day in Babylon,* 181.

39. Neal, *Visions,* 63, 65.

40. Ibid., 27.

41. Mark Lawrence McPhail, "Double-consciousness," in *Encyclopedia of Rhetoric,* 11–12.

42. Neal, *Visions,* 60.

43. Ibid., 80.

44. Ibid., 69.

45. Ibid., 7–8.

46. Ibid., 64.

47. Van Deburg, *New Day in Babylon,* 134.

48. Neal, *Visions,* 131–32.

49. Lewis M. Killian, *The Impossible Revolution, Phase II* (New York: Random House, 1975), 6.

50. Carolyn Fowler, *Black Art and Black Aesthetics: A Bibliography* (Atlanta: First World, 1976), xxiv.

51. Van Deburg, *New Day in Babylon,* 159.

52. Berger, *Theory of Art,* 5.

53. Ibid., 7.

54. Van Deburg, *New Day in Babylon,* 183.

55. Neal, "Black Art," 41.

56. Neal, *Visions,* 62.

57. Ibid., 60.

58. Ibid., 64.

59. Van Deburg, *New Day in Babylon,* 182.

60. K. William Kgositsile, "Towards Our Theater: A Definitive Act," in *Black Expression: Essays by and about Black Americans,* ed. Addison Gayle Jr. (New York: Weybright & Talley, 1969), 146.

61. Neal, *Visions,* 66.

62. Ibid., 14–16.

63. LeRoi Jones and Amiri Baraka, *Blues People* (New York: William Morrow, 1963).

64. Neal, *Visions,* 110.

65. Ibid.

66. Ibid., 74.

67. Ibid., 120.

68. Ibid., 46–47.

69. Ibid., 30.

70. For example, see Irving Howe, "Black Boys and Native Sons," *Dissent* 10 (1963): 359; also see Ralph Ellison's response to Howe in "The World and the Jug," *New Leader* 46 (1963): 22–26.

71. Neal, *Visions,* 118.

72. Ibid.

73. Ibid., 119.

74. Larry Neal, "Sinner Man Where You Gonna Run To?" in *Black Fire: An Anthology of Afro-American Writing,* ed. Leroi Jones and Larry Neal (New York: William Morrow, 1968), 510–18.

75. Neal, *Visions,* 120.

76. Ibid., 122.

77. Ibid., 120.

78. G. W. F. Hegel, *The Phenomenology of Mind* (New York: Allen & Unwin, 1966), 229–40.

79. Neal, *Visions,* 123.

80. Ibid., 119.

Religious Rhetoric and the *Ethos* of Democracy

A Case Study of the 2000 Presidential Campaign

MARTIN J. MEDHURST

> Whether they are religious or not, most Americans are hungry for a deeper connection between politics and moral values, many would say "spiritual values." Without values of conscience, our political life degenerates. And Americans profoundly—rightly—believe that politics and morality are deeply interrelated. They want to reconnect the American spirit to the body politic.
>
> Al Gore, May 24, 1999

One need not search long for reasons to study the 2000 presidential campaign: one of the closest elections in American history, a contested popular vote in the state of Florida that resulted in counts and recounts, a court challenge that ended up at the U.S. Supreme Court, a win for George W. Bush by five electoral votes coupled with a loss to Al Gore in the overall popular vote—only the fourth time in American history when the popular vote and the electoral vote did not correspond.[1] And then there was the issue of religion: the candidacy of Joe Lieberman, the first person of the Jewish faith to run on a major party ticket; the role of the black churches, particularly in Florida, in turning out the Democratic vote; the support of George W. Bush by the religious Right and his controversial speech during the South Carolina primary at Bob Jones University; and the role of the Catholic vote and its continuing migration toward the Republican Party.

Any or all of these topics are worthy of extended analysis. But I want to focus on a slightly different, though no less important, dimension of the 2000 campaign: what the role of religious rhetoric suggests about the state—the *ethos*—of our American form of democracy. For some time, analysts of both the Left and Right have held that the theory and practice of democratic governance has been in decline. Some point to the lack of participation in electoral politics, the continuing decline in the percentage of people who actually go to the polls and cast a ballot; others point to more abstract problems such as the loss of connection between the people and their representatives, the role of big money in election contests, the interposition of the media between the people and their government, and the feeling of disconnection, disempowerment, and distance—the belief that the government no longer reflects the beliefs and values of the people, preferring instead a form of self-imposed neutrality that has, in the view of some, the effect of stripping religious and moral values from articulation, much less influence, in the public square.

A survey of the titles of some recent books tells the story: *Democracy against Itself* (1993), *Democracy on Trial* (1995), *Fragility of Freedom* (1995), *Democracy's Discontent* (1996), *Dissonance of Democracy* (1996), *Democracy in Dark Times* (1998), *Democratic Paradox* (2000), *Democratic Equality: What Went Wrong?* (2001), and *Democracy—The God That Failed* (2001).[2] If these books are to be believed, we are experiencing a time of trial and testing with respect to the very validity of the American experiment. In retrospectives on the 2000 campaign, some analysts purported to find a nation divided against itself. A map showing how the country voted, red representing the Bush vote in the interior and blue representing the Gore vote in clusters along the East and West Coasts, vividly illustrated this point. One interpretation of this geographical representation of voting patterns was that there existed a basic discontinuity of beliefs, values, and attitudes—a discontinuity so stark, so widespread, and so obvious by the pattern of the dots that it could no longer be denied. If one were inclined to believe some of the more extreme commentators, one might even get the idea that we were on the brink of a civil war, so divided had we become.[3]

Yet despite the books and articles, despite the voting patterns, despite the disenfranchisement of voters in Florida, and despite the ultimate seating of a president who did not receive the majority of votes cast nationwide, the Republic endures. Why? Some will say it is all a matter of simple inertia. Once a system is in place and running it will continue to run until something stops it. Others will claim that it is because those who profit most from the current system still hold all the cards—the reigns of power—and will keep the system going for their own benefit. Still others will cite the conserving qualities of the Constitution and the mechanisms of Constitutional governance as the driving and sustaining force. But the rhetoric of the 2000 campaign—specifically the moral and religious rhetoric in that contest—suggests a different reason. It suggests that Americans may not, in fact, be as divided as the critics claim. It suggests that there is an *ethos* to our democracy—a dwelling place—that is shared across parties, across religions, across geography, across races, and even, to some extent, across ideologies. It suggests a people, a demos, hungry for spiritual values and willing to support those who articulate with clarity and passion the specifically moral, ethical, and spiritual dimensions of public policy choices.

To illustrate my contention, I will survey the use of religious rhetoric by the major party candidates from late 1998 until election day 2000. My survey will be

roughly chronological since much of the meaning attributed to campaign rhetoric is context and situation specific. Unlike the cynics who find any references to
religion or morality to be nothing more than pandering for votes, I read the religious rhetoric of the 2000 campaign as a signal of an emerging consensus over
the nature, purpose, and identity of democracy in America. Such rhetoric becomes,
itself, a sign of something deeper—an *ethos,* an identity, a character, a spirit that
binds Americans together rather than drives them apart. Such rhetoric points to
an abiding dimension of the American character or, better yet, a national character seeking a place to abide, a locus of communal values that transcends parties,
politics, and philosophies.

   The language of religion began even before the candidates made their formal
declarations of candidacy. Speaking to the Democratic Leadership Council's
(DLC) annual conference on December 2, 1998, Al Gore observed, "We began
by inventing a new and vibrant politics of the center—a politics that moved not
left or right, but forward. A politics that allowed us to begin the most important
work of our lifetimes: redeeming the very idea of self-government—and using it
as a force for good in the lives of the American people."[4] Here Gore specifically
links the idea of redemption with the reinvigoration of self-government, the project of American democracy. But there was more. "Beyond the old polarities of
individual choice and national government," Gore said, "lie the subtle connections
that are the matrix of community." And what were those matrixes of community?
As he came to end of his speech, Gore set them forth: "Let us choose the future
that is built on the insight of our mutuality: mutual respect, mutual responsibility,
mutual civility, and, in regards to the weakest among us, mutual kindness and care.
As it is written in the scripture: 'If one part suffers, every part suffers with it; if
one part is honored, every part rejoices with it.' Let us choose that future for your
children—and mine; and for all their brothers and sisters around this country and
around this small, irreplaceable world."[5]

   In what will become a pattern of religious rhetoric over the course of the
campaign, Gore sets forth a vision of democratic community then justifies that
vision with a quotation from the Bible. In this instance, the operative component
of the democratic *ethos* is mutuality. It is important to note that the audience for
this speech is a purely political gathering—the annual conference of the DLC.
This is not religious speech directed to a gathering of believers but the expression
of an ecumenical democratic *ethos* articulated in explicitly religious language.

   Two days later, on December 4, 1998, George W. Bush was interviewed upon
his return from the state of Israel, a visit that rekindled concern in some quarters
about his sensitivity to and respect for minority religions in America. The specific
concern was the resurfacing of a story from 1993 that Bush had once said that
Jews cannot go to heaven because they do not accept Jesus as their savior. After
making it clear that "it's not the governor's role to decide who goes to heaven. I
believe that God decides who goes to heaven, not George W. Bush," the governor

said, "[I believe I have] shown people that I'm a tolerant person. And my job as governor is to use my office to promote dialogue and mutual understanding and mutual respect."[6] He then defined what he meant by compassionate conservatism, which consisted, he said, in "[m]aking sure every child can read, making sure that we encourage faith-based organizations . . . [and] when it comes to helping neighbors in need, making sure that our neighborhoods are safe, making sure that the state of Texas recognizes that people from all walks of life have got a shot at the Texas dream but, most importantly, making sure that government is not the answer to people's problems."[7] Here Bush articulates a central theme of his compassionate conservatism—that the real solutions to our problems as a nation lie somewhere else than in the state or federal government, which has little ability to "promote dialogue, and mutual understanding and mutual respect"—virtually the same dimensions of democratic *ethos* cited by Al Gore only two days earlier.

As the pre-campaign moved into 1999, Bush and Gore continued to sound many of the same themes. Gore, in particular, went out of his way to underscore the essentially religious values that supported his vision of American democratic life. In his commencement address at the University of New Hampshire on May 22, he asked those in attendance, "What can we do, all of us, to build a future in which all children choose good over evil?" He reminded the audience that "we all share a responsibility for changing a toxic culture that too often glorifies violence and cruelty." He then said,

> In my religious tradition, there is a story known as the parable of the sower. . . . In the parable of the sower, some of those seeds fall by the wayside, some fall on rocks, some on barren land, some on land already clotted with thriving plants. But some fall on open, fertile soil, where they take root, and bear fruit.
>
> There is no question in my mind that some portion of those 20,000 simulated murders shown in the minds of each child bear bitter fruit.
>
> There is no question that images not only of violence, but of explicit sexuality, of inappropriate behavior . . . have a powerful effect on children's minds.

Gore then returned to the question of good and evil:

> Of course, for all the many contributing causes to tragedies such as Columbine, we are still left with a basic question of good and evil.
>
> In my faith tradition, I am drawn to the story of the first murder. Cain's offering was rejected, whereas his brother Abel's was accepted. God asked him: "Why are you angry, and why has your countenance fallen? If you do well, will you not be accepted? And if you do not do well, sin is couching [*sic*] at the door; its desire is for you, but you must master it."
>
> On the street-corners of America's cities today, we often hear the word "disrespected." Cain felt "dissed" by God. Those boys at Columbine, according to all the available evidence, and despite all the privileges they had, felt disrespected. Disconnected. Not accepted. Rejected.

Sin came to their door, whether through Nazi hate literature, or violent video games, or a culture of death and destruction. They still had a duty to resist it and master it—but its desire was for them, and they were vulnerable to it because they felt disrespected. . . .

We must make the children of this country less vulnerable to sin by making sure that they feel connected. By nurturing in them a set of values that allows them to find self-respect, self-discipline, and the appreciation of those who care about them.[8]

In this remarkable speech, Gore sets forth a values agenda for the country and he underscores that agenda by drawing on his own faith tradition. It is important, I believe, that he explicitly identifies it as his own tradition, thus implying that there may be other traditions with valuable lessons to teach as well. For Gore, the biblical narratives illustrate timeless principles that can be applied to modern-day life. The linchpins of the narrative are clear: good and evil are real; humans can fall prey to evil unless they are inculcated into the good; humans are responsible for their actions; and all of us, as members of the human community, are responsible for one another, especially the weak and the young. Self-respect, self-discipline, and the appreciation of others are clearly aspects of a democratic *ethos,* for democracy, as Jean Bethke Elshtain writes, "is not simply a set of procedures or a constitution, but an ethos, a spirit, a way of responding, and a way of conducting oneself."[9] Gore makes this clear in the conclusion of his address:

Our unspoken civic values form what Yeats called "the ceremony of innocence."

If we tolerate violence in our culture and silence in our families, we're telling our children it's OK to despair.

If we tolerate selfishness in our hearts and hopelessness in our souls, we're telling our children it's OK to believe life has no meaning.

If we tolerate a decline in the number of people voting in elections, and a decline in the number of parents visiting their children's schools we're telling our children: it's OK to withdraw, to drop out of our body politic, to recoil from the community we seek to build.

The resulting cynicism can transform a normal, healthy balance of faith and skepticism into a stubborn, unwavering disbelief in the possibility of good.

It drains us of the will to improve; it diminishes our public spirit; it saps our inventiveness; it withers our souls. . . .

I believe in hope over despair, striving over resignation, faith over cynicism. . . .

I believe in fulfillment through family, for the family is the true center of a meaningful life. It is in our families that we learn to love.

I believe our communities' purpose is to be there for families the way that families are always there for each other.

I believe in serving God and trying to understand and obey God's will for our lives.[10]

Faith, family, community, hope, the recognition of good and the condemnation of evil, these are the contours of Gore's vision. And it is, at one and the same moment, both a democratic vision and a religious vision. The two are so closely intertwined that it seems reasonable to say that one cannot exist without the other, for the simple reason that the vision rests on the foundation of knowing good, and the good, whatever else it may be, is a philosophical or religious ideal. In this case, the grounding of the good clearly comes from a religious source.

Two days later, speaking to the Salvation Army, Gore extended his vision to encompass faith-based organizations:

> In spite of the cultural soul sickness we've confronted recently, there is a goodness in Americans that, when mobilized, is more than a match for it. . . .
>
> This hunger for goodness manifests itself in a newly vigorous grassroots movement tied to non-profit institutions, many of them faith-based and values-based organizations. A church's soup kitchen. A synagogue's program to help battered women. A mosque's after-school computer center that keeps teenagers away from gangs and drugs.
>
> It's commonplace to say that people are turned off to politics. This transformation shows that in fact people are not turned off to politics—to organized community action; rather, they are turned off to too many of the ways they have seen Washington work.
>
> What many people are struggling to find is the soul of politics. . . .
>
> Ordinary Americans have decided to confront the fact that our severest challenges are not just material, but spiritual. . . .
>
> In this new politics, citizens take local action, based on their churches, synagogues, and mosques, but reaching out to all—to do what all great religions tell good people [to] do: visit the prisoners, help the orphans, feed and clothe the poor. . . .
>
> To the workers in these organizations, that client is not a number, but a child of God.[11]

Gore explicitly links moral and spiritual values to the accomplishment of socio-political goals. In so doing, he echoes Bush's earlier view that often times the federal government in Washington is not the source of all solutions. By continually quoting from the Bible and other religious sources—in this speech alone, he cited Mother Teresa, radical evangelical Jim Wallis, and a Jewish proverb—Gore underscores the values that he sees as necessary to sustain the democratic project. In doing so, Gore is always careful to point out that he strongly believes in the separation of church and state but that "freedom of religion need not mean freedom from religion."[12] In his vision, religious values, religious people, and religious organizations can all have an active part in the democratic polity. Indeed, they are, in many ways, central to what makes that polity democratic insofar as they are grounded in local communities, express values endemic to those communities, and undertake actions in support of the community.

It was about at this point in the campaign, in June 1999, that voices started to be heard expressing a more strategic, perhaps even cynical view of Gore's religious rhetoric. The first such voice came from Gore's own campaign, when his senior policy advisor, Elaine Kamarck, was quoted as saying that "the Democratic Party is going to take God back this time."[13] Later, Democratic strategist James Carville, after the selection of Joseph Lieberman as the vice presidential nominee, offered, "We had to do something about this values stuff."[14] The question of sincerity versus strategy is always lurking around the edges of any political campaign. Do Gore and Bush really mean what they say, or are they saying what they think people want to hear and what will help to get themselves elected? This is, at base, an ethical question—a question of character. But let us suppose, just for a moment, that neither Gore nor Bush really believed what they were saying with respect to the religious language and values being articulated. Why, then, would they be saying such things? For one reason only: because they think that is what the electorate believes and wants to hear. And if the electorate, the democratic polity, really believes in such values, then should not those values be the basis for political action without regard to what the individual candidates may really believe? In other words, if a democracy is, at base, rule by the people, then should not the people's beliefs, values, morals, ethics, desires, and character rule supreme? In short, while the question of the strategic nature of such language choices is interesting from the point of view of a political tactician, someone like a James Carville or Karl Rove, it does not touch on the basic idea of a democratic *ethos* because that *ethos,* whatever its specific dimensions, must necessarily be grounded in the nature and identity of the American people rather than the individuals elected to lead the nation. In this sense, I am trying to read the *ethos* of the people through the symbology of the appeals directed to them during the campaign. I am seeking the dwelling place of the American polity.

That said, there clearly were strategic advantages to each side in utilizing the rhetoric of religion. For Gore, there were two great positives: such moral language tended to separate him from the immorality associated with the Clinton/Lewinsky scandal, and it tended to blur the differences between Gore and Bush, thus preventing large portions of the electorate from associating only one candidate with God, religion, and moral values. Bush, too, derived strategic advantages from his religious rhetoric. Specifically, it allowed him to cultivate the religious Right, a core constituency of the Republican Party, but to do so in language that did not offend other constituencies needed for electoral success. It also allowed him to promote his campaign theme of compassionate conservatism by linking religious values such as care of neighbor, charity, respect for the elderly, and tolerance to his political agenda. Finally, the values orientation of the campaign allowed Bush, by indirection, to contrast himself to the previous administration. Through early 1999, Bush would end his stump speeches with the same refrain: "I know my most important responsibility is when I put my hand on the Bible, I will not only swear to uphold the laws of our country, I will swear to uphold the dignity of the office of the president of the United States."[15]

Yet by focusing only on the strategic advantages to the candidates and their campaigns, analysts have often missed the more important point that whether directly or indirectly, sincerely or insincerely, scripted or unscripted, the language of religion helped to fuse not only the two campaigns but, more important, the American people. There was a common language that both sides were speaking, a language that resonated with large segments of the public because it was based on values widely held and attitudes toward religion and morality broadly shared. Who, after all, would not want to conceive of himself or herself as a member of "the armies of compassion?"

When Bush announced his plan to extend $8 billion in tax credits and grants to faith-based organizations in his July 22 speech in Indianapolis, he painted a broad picture of American pluralism, pledging not to discriminate "for or against Methodists or Mormons or Muslims, or good people of no faith at all." Citing both John Paul II and St. Francis of Assisi, Bush said, "We found that government can spend money, but it can't put hope in our hearts or a sense of purpose in our lives. . . . This is done in churches and synagogues and mosques and charities that warm the cold of life. A quiet river of goodness that cuts through stone."[16] It was in those transcendent values of "hope" and "purpose" that Bush located the dwelling place—the *ethos*—of the American character.

Campaigning in New Hampshire in November 1999, Bush sounded a good deal like Gore: "Our children must be educated in reading and writing—but also in right and wrong. . . . The real problem comes not when children challenge the rules, but when adults won't defend the rules." His speech focused on respect, responsibility, self-restraint, family commitment, civic duty, fairness, and compassion. "Our schools should not cultivate confusion," Bush said, "they must cultivate conscience." Returning to the religious theme, this time with an education angle, Bush declared, "Schools must never impose religion—but they must not oppose religion either. . . . Religious groups have a right to meet before and after school. Students have a right to say grace before meals, read their Bibles, wear Stars of David and crosses and discuss religion with other willing students. Students have a right to express religious ideas in art and homework."[17] Bush clearly sees the religious beliefs and practices of the people as a primary source of civic virtue—the inventional source from which ideas of right and wrong spring and the affectional basis for choosing compassion, commitment, and mutual respect.

Bush further identified himself with this religious *ethos* later in November when he released his campaign autobiography, *A Charge to Keep*. Based on a hymn by Charles Wesley, *A Charge to Keep I Have*, Bush said that the title "speaks of determination and direction; it calls us to a higher purpose."[18] By campaigning as a "compassionate conservative" who was committed to rallying "the armies of compassion," he sought to redefine the conservative Republican agenda away

from the divisiveness of the 1992 and 1996 campaigns and toward the inclusiveness of moral and religious duty.

Given the direction that both the Gore and Bush campaigns had taken for the
previous six months, and given the fact that both Gore and Bush had self-identified as Christians over a period of years in public life, it should not have come as
much of a surprise that Gore spoke of himself as a "born again Christian"[19] on
the December 5 edition of *60 Minutes* or that Bush, on December 13, identified
"Jesus Christ" as the political philosopher who had most influenced his life because,
as he said, "he changed my life."[20] Even so, these revelations sparked animated
debates on the television talk shows and on the editorial pages of the nation's
newspapers.

Adding to the religious rhetoric were the other Republican candidates, Gary
Bauer, longtime leader of the religious Right's Family Research Council; the
straightlaced Mormon Orrin Hatch; the Roman Catholic antiabortion crusader
Alan Keyes; Elizabeth Dole, who had already described herself as a "born-again
Christian" who saw "spiritual starvation" in the land;[21] Steve Forbes, one-time economic crusader now reborn social conservative; and John McCain, who, though
not known as a religious conservative, had, by mid-December 1999, already begun
running a radio ad in South Carolina that featured references to a "sermon" he
composed while a POW in Vietnam and a voiceover by fellow POW Bud Day
that said, "It was certainly a shot to everyone's morale to hear those Christian
words in that very unChristianlike place."[22]

The lone Democratic challenger, Bill Bradley, did not engage in any religious
rhetoric per se, yet even he spoke frequently about "a new world of possibilities
guided by goodness."[23] The difference between Gore and Bradley is that Gore
specifically identified the source of that goodness as the God of the Bible, as did
Bush.

Bush continued to link his religious rhetoric with compassionate conservatism.
In Colfax, Iowa, he visited a Teen Challenge rehabilitation center, where, according to news reports, "he heard stories from three young men about how Christian faith had turned them away from lives of crime and drug addiction."[24] Speaking
in the chapel at the facility, Bush said, "I used to drink too much. I quit drinking
and I believe it was because Billy Graham planted a seed in my heart on time. It
wasn't Billy—he was the messenger."[25] By focusing on compassionate conservatism and visiting faith-based organizations like Teen Challenge, Bush was able
to put the spotlight on those aspects of his agenda that crossed traditional partisan divides and spoke to the need for local action in support of civic goals. Such
an approach also allowed Bush to soft-pedal the most divisive issue of all: abortion.

Although Bush was twice elected Texas governor on a pro-life platform, he
had clearly determined that abortion could not be front and center if he was truly
to run as a compassionate conservative. At the same time, he could not move away
from his basic pro-life stance if he hoped to garner the Republican nomination.

Rather than pick a fight with his pro-life allies, including all the members of the religious Right, Bush allowed the Republican platform to retain its opposition to all abortions and its call for a constitutional amendment to ban abortions. Bush, himself, made clear that his position was softer than that of the platform. He would allow exceptions in the cases of rape, incest, or the physical health of the woman. Furthermore, though he supported a constitutional amendment to ban the procedure, Bush made clear that he did not believe the country was yet ready to pass such an amendment and that until the time came when it was ready, it would not be a high priority on his agenda. His rhetoric reflected these commitments. When pressed on the matter, Bush focused on the way the *Roe v. Wade* decision was made rather than on efforts to ban abortions. Said Bush, "I felt like it was a case where the court took the place of what the legislatures should do in America. . . . It should be up to each legislature."[26] Notice that even the language Bush uses is drawn from the civil realm, not the religious. It is a matter of a case, court, and legislatures. Furthermore, even on this most controversial of issues, Bush was able to transform the debate into one over local control. This fit well with his overall commitment to compassionate conservatism, where action moves from the grass-roots up rather than from the federal government down.

On February 1, 2000, John McCain defeated George W. Bush in the New Hampshire primary. The Bush campaign, fearful that New Hampshire might jump-start a McCain steamroller, decided to pull out all the stops in the South Carolina primary, scheduled for February 19. As part of their strategy, the Bush campaign ran television and radio ads attacking McCain's voting record on military and veteran's affairs issues. McCain was livid and looked for any opportunity to counterattack. He found that opportunity on February 2, when Bush chose to make a speech at Bob Jones University, a well-known fundamentalist enclave where, in previous years, Ronald Reagan, Jack Kemp, and Bob Dole had all made campaign stops. Bush gave his standard stump speech at the school, but he failed to take note of—much less to repudiate—the fact that the university forbade interracial dating and castigated the Roman Catholic Church as "satanic."[27] Seeing his opening, McCain struck hard, immediately demanding that Bush apologize to Catholics. Thus began what would become the worst thirty-day period of the primary season for Bush.

The McCain-Bush battle that took place in the South Carolina, Michigan, and Virginia primaries between February 1 and February 29, 2000, was anything but compassionate. Indeed, the entire episode growing out of the Bob Jones speech threw Bush off of his campaign themes for more than a month. Already hurt by the apparent failure of compassionate conservatism to melt the hearts of Granite State voters, Bush switched his slogan to a "Reformer with Results," a not-so-subtle attempt to undercut McCain's main claim on the electorate. Worse still, McCain's attacks on Bush's appearance at Bob Jones University opened a whole new dimension on the rhetoric of religion. Whereas Bush and Gore had made religious appeals a central part of their efforts to reach across the barriers of race, class, geography, gender, and ideology in an effort to unify the electorate, McCain's appeal was to divisiveness—Protestant against Catholic, black against white, fundamentalist against nonfundamentalist.

Although Bush won the South Carolina primary by a substantial margin over McCain, the damage to his campaign had already been done. As the liberal columnist E. J. Dionne Jr. noted:

> The irony of the South Carolina contest is that it threatens to undermine a useful project Bush undertook at the beginning of his quest for the presidency: an effort to transform the definition of conservative Christian politics.
>
> Bush spoke of rallying the "armies of compassion," of bringing the American dream "to every willing heart." Being a Christian meant not just delivering votes to the ballot box but meals to the poor, mentoring to the young, comfort to the afflicted.
>
> Bush still offers those words, and they sound as good as ever. But the revolution in Christian conservatism that once seemed possible has foundered on the hard rock of the McCain challenge and interest group politics.[28]

The foundering was brought about in large part because of the agonistic nature of presidential campaigning. An unfair attack on McCain's record on military and veteran affairs led to an equally unfair attack on Bush's speech at Bob Jones University. Perceiving an apparent break in what had been, until New Hampshire, a Bush cakewalk toward the nomination, McCain exploited Bush's appearance at the fundamentalist school by using recorded telephone messages targeted to Catholics in states such as Michigan and Washington: "This is a Catholic Voter Alert. Gov. George Bush, Jr. [sic] has campaigned against Sen. John McCain by seeking the support of Southern Fundamentalists who have expressed anti-Catholic views. Several weeks ago Gov. Bush spoke at Bob Jones University in South Carolina. That's the same Bob Jones who said the Pope was 'the antichrist' and called the Church 'a satanic cult.' Sen. John McCain has strongly criticized this anti-Catholic bigotry, while Gov. Bush stayed silent while gaining the support of Bob Jones University."[29]

Bush responded by releasing a letter sent to John Cardinal O'Connor of New York, which said, in part, "Some have taken and mistaken this visit [to Bob Jones University] as a sign that I approve of the anti-Catholic and racially divisive views associated with that school. Such opinions are personally offensive to me, and I want to erase any doubts about my views and values."[30] Even so, McCain's campaign continued to use the Catholic Voter Alerts. The Bush campaign responded with a recorded message of its own from surrogate Pat Robertson, targeted to conservative Protestants, that charged that a McCain campaign official [Warren Rudman] was "a vicious bigot who wrote that conservative Christians in politics are anti-abortion zealots, homophobes and would-be censors."[31] On February 28, one day after Bush released his letter to O'Connor, McCain opened a second religious offensive by associating Bush with the leaders of the religious Right, whom he also castigated. Speaking from Virginia Beach, the home of Pat Robertson's *700 Club* ministry, McCain charged:

Unfortunately, Governor Bush is a Pat Robertson Republican who will lose to Al Gore. I recognize and celebrate that our country is founded upon Judeo-Christian values, and I have pledged my life to defend America and all her values, the values that have made us the noblest experiment in history. But political intolerance by any political party is neither a Judeo-Christian nor an American value. The political tactics of division and slander are not our values. They are corrupting influences on religion and politics and those who practice them in the name of religion or in the name of the Republican Party or in the name of America, shame our faith, our party and our country. Neither party should be defined by pandering to the outer reaches of American politics and the agents of intolerance, whether they be Louis Farrakhan or Al Sharpton on the left or Pat Robertson or Jerry Falwell on the right.[32]

The next day, February 29, in the Virginia Republican primary, those "outer reaches of American politics" effectively ended McCain's presidential campaign, giving Bush a solid 53 to 44 percent victory and presaging Bush's overwhelming victories on Super Tuesday, March 7.

Even as the Virginia tally rolled in, Bush was in Cleveland, Ohio, visiting the Fatima Family Center and trying to return to his message of compassionate conservatism. Once again, he endorsed aid to faith-based charities. But substantial damage had been done. As one analyst noted, "Bush is in trouble with the voters in the magic middle, which is where he was headed with his 'compassionate conservative' campaign until getting sidetracked in the snows of New Hampshire and the false spring of South Carolina. Exit polling in state after state that voted Tuesday points to trouble ahead for Bush as he seeks to reposition himself for the general election campaign."[33]

The McCain-Bush slugfest in the South Carolina, Michigan, and Virginia primaries had shown the ugly side of religion in politics. Yet the very fact that the month of February contrasted so radically with the six months that had gone before pointed to the possibility that appeal to moral and religious sensibilities need not necessarily lead to bigotry and recrimination. As Bush told Jewish leaders at the Simon Wiesenthal Center Museum for Tolerance in Los Angeles, "I believe our nation was chosen by God and commissioned by history to be a model of justice and inclusion and diversity without division. . . . We don't believe in tolerance in spite of our faith. We believe in tolerance because of our faith, and it leads us to condemn all forms of religious bigotry."[34]

As the media pundits continued to debate the role of religion in politics throughout the month of March, the presumptive nominees, George Bush and Al

Gore, started to lay their plans for the coming fall contest. Gore used the McCain-Bush battle to remind voters that Bush was the candidate of the religious Right and a Bush presidency would give Pat Robertson and Jerry Falwell "a working majority" on the Supreme Court.[35] Bush, for his part, tried to steer the campaign back toward his message of compassionate conservatism. Speaking at the National Press Club, Bush surrogate Tom DeLay, House Majority Whip, opined: "What we need is simply a return to the healthy appreciation for religion that has always sustained the nation. . . . Government can't enforce religious teachings or doctrines of specific faiths. But at the same time, federal power must not be distorted into a wedge that splits the vast majority of Americans from the sacred ideals that guide their lives."[36] DeLay, like Bush, could read the polls. And what the polls were telling them was that overwhelming numbers of Republican voters, and a majority of the electorate at large, saw morality and integrity, character issues, as key in the forthcoming general election. As one analyst noted following the Super Tuesday voting, "In several key states that voted Tuesday, exit poll interviews with Republican voters found that "moral issues" were the key concern for the upcoming national administration, often coming in at twice the percentage of taxes or even Social Security and Medicare."[37]

By the summer of 2000, the Gallup Poll was showing similar results on a nationwide survey of likely voters. On the question "How important would you say religion is in your own life?" 57 percent chose the most extreme option, "very important." On the question "Do you believe that religion can answer all or most of today's problems, or that religion is largely old-fashioned and out of date?" 63 percent responded that religion "can answer" all or most of today's problems. Finally, when asked, "How important will your own personal religious beliefs and faith be in deciding your vote for president this year?" 54 percent responded with "extremely important," "very important," or "somewhat important."[38]

The polls reflected the mood of the electorate and so, too, did the candidates' rhetoric. That it also reflect the deeply held beliefs of Bush and Gore added to its appeal. Gore and Bush were not merely playing to the choir; they were members of the choir and were singing their own songs.[39] Bush's compassionate conservatism was not a slogan coined just to make a presidential run. Indeed, it had been years in the making, with substantial input from scholars such as James Q. Wilson, John J. Dilulio Jr., and Marvin Olasky, think-tank intellectuals such as Myron Magnet, and community activists such as Robert L. Woodson. As Stephen Goldsmith, Bush's chief domestic policy advisor during the campaign, put it, compassionate conservatism "means providing help in such a way as to stimulate and reinforce self-governance."[40] And self-governance required a set of character traits grounded in individual morality. As Bush himself noted, "These [faith-based] institutions, at their best, treat people as moral individuals, with responsibilities and duties, not as wards or clients or dependents or numbers."[41]

Gore, too, saw his campaign through the lens of his religious faith. When he announced the selection of Joseph Lieberman as his running mate on August 8, 2000, Gore let it be known that their first act together was to pray. In his first appearance before the press, Lieberman said, "I never dreamed of this. And you know what it says to me—and everyone else—that every day we are lucky enough to be alive by the grace of God is full of possibilities, and miracles happen. And I consider this a miracle for which I am grateful."[42] Lieberman's language of grace, God, and miracles was entirely consistent with Gore's own religious rhetoric throughout the campaign.

One writer for the *San Francisco Chronicle* immediately saw the symmetry in Gore's choice of Lieberman:

> Gore didn't choose Lieberman because he's Jewish; he chose him because the Connecticut centrist is a man of faith. Gore and his advisers understand that the theological and political fault lines in America no longer divide us into camps of Christians or Jews, Catholics or Protestants, Baptists or Methodists.
>
> We live in a post-denominational world, where the commonalities of faith overshadow sectarian differences.
>
> We live in a world where Presbyterian churches host Passover seders, where Pope John Paul II travels to Israel and refers to Jews as "our elder brothers."
>
> Evangelicals complain about Lieberman's pro-choice position on abortion, but they embrace him as a Judeo-Christian brother who believes in God.[43]

Gore's faith was evident not just in his selection of Lieberman but also in his acceptance address at the Democratic National Convention as well. "My parents taught me that the real values in life aren't material but spiritual," he said. "They include faith and family, duty and honor, and trying to make the world a better place." He recalled "citizens lifting up local communities, family by family, block by block, neighborhood by neighborhood, in churches and charities, on school boards and City Councils." Although the address was not nearly as explicit about Gore's values agenda as his New Hampshire speech of 1999, he still spoke the language of morality and religious conviction when he proclaimed, "It's just wrong for seniors to have to choose between food and medicine" and "It's just wrong to have life and death decisions made by bean-counters at HMOs."[44] It was precisely the spiritual values that informed Gore's life that allowed him to make these moral judgments—and to appeal to the American people, whom, he believed, shared those same moral and spiritual values.

Democratic delegate James Wall, who also shared those values, articulated the basis for Gore's religious appeal by noting, "All of us are motivated, driven by, compelled by some kind of center. . . . I am compelled by a moral center conformed by my religious beliefs. Other people have other moral centers, other Christian beliefs, other Jewish beliefs, and so forth. Other people with no religious moral center may have a moral center driven by philosophy or some other principle. We all have some kind of motivation."[45]

And that was precisely the point. On a whole range of issues—from social welfare policy to hate crimes legislation to the death penalty to funding for AIDS research—people's moral, ethical, and religious motivations were, according to the polls, entering into their decision-making processes.[46] Even setting aside the question of abortion, many other issues and policies raised profound moral or ethical concerns—from human cloning and stem cell research to the privacy of medical records and the testing of experimental vaccines, to name just a few. Therefore, much of the criticism of the religious rhetoric in the campaign seemed, at best, misplaced. One of the most consistent critics was Barry Lynn, executive director of Americans United for Separation of Church and State. The Reverend Lynn repeatedly made comments such as "We are having an election for president, not selecting a pastor for a church nor a rabbi for a synagogue. . . . It's important to get off the religion talk and into talk about policy issues."[47] But as James Wall noted, all policy issues are motivated and many of those motivations are moral or spiritual in nature. The religious rhetoric used by the Gore-Lieberman and Bush-Cheney tickets was an attempt to speak both to that motivation and to the kinds of actions each ticket would take with respect to those issues that spring from moral or religious motivations.

No campaigner was more explicit about these connections than Joseph Lieberman. Speaking to a black church in Detroit on August 27, he said, "I stand before you today as a witness to the goodness of God. . . . For me, like you, and like my running mate Al Gore, faith provided a foundation, order and purpose to my life. . . . There must be and can be a constitutional place for faith in our public life."[48] Campaigning in California, Lieberman asked his audience, "Isn't Medicare coverage of prescription drugs really about the values of the Fifth Commandment, Honour Your Mother and Father?"[49] The comment demonstrates, once again, how religious motivation can be directly linked to specific policy issues.

On the airwaves, the Gore-Lieberman ticket touted values in a thirty-second spot titled "Veteran," which concluded with these lines: "Fight violence and pornography on the Internet, helping parents block out what children shouldn't see. Al Gore. He'll put his values to work for us."[50]

On the campaign trail, Lieberman was putting those values to work, too. In West Palm Beach, he noted, "The fact is that we worked for civil rights and we worked, for instance, as we are now, for protections against hate crimes because we are all created by God, and as a result, every citizen deserves to be treated with the same respect and dignity. . . . Our leadership and our laws, at their best, must flow from our values and reflect the basic principles that America is all about."[51] Touting their stand on the environment in Wisconsin, Lieberman explained, "For Al Gore and me, this begins, if you will, by our faith. . . . If you believe in God, I think it's hard not to be an environmentalist, because you see the environment as the work of God." He reminded the audience that God had put Adam and Eve on Earth "to work the garden, but also to guard it."[52] In so speaking, Lieberman was doing nothing more than echoing Gore's views, first published in his 1992 book *Earth in the Balance,* in which he wrote, "As it happens, the idea of social justice is inextricably linked in the Scriptures with ecology. In passage after passage, environmental degradation and social injustice go hand in hand. Indeed, the first instance of 'pollution' in the Bible occurs when Cain slays Abel and his blood falls on the ground, rendering it fallow."[53]

As the campaign moved into its final weeks, Gore joined with Lieberman in appealing to moral and religious values. Proclaiming that "the center of my life is faith and family," Gore lashed out at "cultural pollution" and the "toxic entertainment that too often passes on the wrong values." Speaking at the Potter's House Church in Dallas, Gore said, "I want you to know how deeply I care about strengthening our families. . . . I want you to know that this is not just the heart of an agenda, it is the foundation of my life and my faith."[54]

On October 24, Lieberman gave a major address at the University of Notre Dame, where he called for a "new great American spiritual awakening." He argued that "we have gone a long way toward dislodging our values from their natural source in moral truth" and observed, "Without the connection to a higher law it becomes more and more difficult for people to answer the important day-to-day questions that test us: Why is it wrong to lie or cheat or steal? Why is it wrong to settle conflicts with violence? Why is it wrong to be unfaithful to one's spouse, or to exploit children, or to despoil the environment, or defraud a customer, or demean an employee?" Lieberman told his listeners that to "make a difference, we must take our religious beliefs and values—our sense of justice, of right and wrong—into America's cultural and communal life."[55]

As the final week of the campaign approached, both Gore and Bush sought to solidify their respective bases—Gore with African American churchgoers and Bush with the religious Right. The importance of the African American church vote was underscored when, with less than ten days to go before the election, President Clinton invited one hundred black ministers to the White House and "asked for help in getting out the vote."[56] Although the religious Right in general and the Christian Coalition in particular had been, relatively speaking, quiet throughout the campaign, they nonetheless pulled out all the stops on behalf of their preferred candidate. The Christian Coalition alone claimed that it would distribute 70 million voter guides in churches across America. "This is the biggest get-out-the-vote effort that the Christian Coalition has ever done," said executive director Roberta Combs. "Our phones are ringing off the hook."[57]

Gore began the final push by making what one newspaper called "a series of sermonettes," urging his supporters to "take your souls to the polls."[58] Speaking at a black church in Memphis on November 4, he said:

You know me. You know my heart. You know that God sees on the inside and not on the outside. . . .

Because you know me, you know what is in my heart and you know that however far down we find ourselves we can be lifted up. You know that even in the valley of the dry bones the Lord breathed life into those bones and bone came to bone, and sinew came to sinew, and there rose up a mighty army. . . .

I need your help to breathe life into this campaign. I need you to lift me up.[59]

On the final Sunday before election day, both Gore and Bush started off at church—Gore at the Mount Carmel Baptist Church in Philadelphia and Bush at Old St. Andrews Episcopal Church in Jacksonville, Florida, where he was joined by the Reverend Billy Graham. The symbolism was apropos inasmuch as Gore carried 96 percent of the black church vote and Bush carried 76 percent of the white evangelical vote.[60] But the real news of the campaign was not, as some commentators opined, that Americans were radically divided. Instead, the close election pointed to an electorate that endorsed the moral and religious visions of both candidates, particularly as those visions touched on the rebuilding of civic virtue and community. Both candidates held forth a vision of a renewed democratic *ethos,* one grounded in faith, religion, and moral values and expressed through the language and symbols of traditional Christianity (in the case of Bush and Gore) and Judaism (in the case of Lieberman). This reanimation of the Judeo-Christian rhetorical tradition was not merely a cynical attempt to identify with religiously inclined voters. Instead, it was first and foremost an attempt by both political parties to recognize a hunger on the part of the electorate for purpose and significance and direction in their own lives and in the corporate lives of their communities and nation. It was a recognition of a deep longing to return to a "home" where the values of community, and mutuality, and compassion reigned supreme.

Judged by the rhetoric of their campaigns, both Bush and Gore would appear to agree with political theorist Michael J. Sandel: "But we are beginning to find that a politics that brackets morality and religion too completely soon generates its own disenchantment. A procedural republic cannot contain the moral energies of a vital democratic life. It creates a moral void that opens the way for narrow, intolerant moralisms. And it fails to cultivate the qualities of character that equip citizens to share in self-rule."[61]

In the 2000 presidential campaign, the candidates spoke openly about such "qualities of character" as mutual respect, mutual responsibility, mutual civility, mutual kindness and care, tolerance, dialogue, mutual understanding, self-respect, self-discipline, appreciation of the other, inclusiveness, duties, dignity, and the importance of communal life. These they repeatedly linked with religious values, among them, redemption, brotherhood, goodness, avoidance of sin, faith, hope, love, service to God, obedience to God, truth, purpose, right and wrong, justice, sacred ideals, order, commandments, awakening, and the higher law. Such linkages were used to discuss specific policy issues, including education, crime, school violence, drugs, violence against women, hunger, separation of church and state, HMOs, the cost of drugs for seniors, Medicare coverage, pornography on the Internet, civil rights, and environmental degradation, among other issues.

Far from indicating an electorate hopelessly divided against itself, the religious rhetoric of the 2000 campaign points, instead, to a people in search of a common democratic *ethos,* in search of a dwelling place large enough and accommodating enough to shelter all but the most extreme members of the American community. Such an *ethos* is grounded in the religious history, character, and rhetoric of the American experiment and articulated through the language of biblical truth, a language that constantly reminds us that "the values of the American people are deeply rooted in religion."[62] For as Richard John Neuhaus argues, "[W]hether it is called Judeo-Christian ethic, or Christianity, or the operative social values, or a civil religion, it is the dynamic of religion that holds the promise of binding together (*religare*) a nation in a way that may more nearly approximate *civitas.*"[63]

Notes

1. The other three times were in 1824 (John Quincy Adams defeated Andrew Jackson), 1876 (Rutherford B. Hayes defeated Samuel J. Tilden), and 1888 (Benjamin Harrison defeated Grover Cleveland). In each case, the defeated candidate received more of the popular vote than did the ultimate winner of the election.

2. See Jean François Revel, *Democracy against Itself: The Future of the Democratic Impulse,* trans. Roger Kaplan (New York: Free Press, 1993); Joshua Mitchell, *The Fragility of Freedom: Tocqueville on Religion, Democracy, and the American Future* (Chicago: University of Chicago Press, 1995); Jean Bethke Elshtain, *Democracy on Trial* (New York: Basic Books, 1995); Susan Bickford, *The Dissonance of Democracy: Listening, Conflict, and Citizenship* (Ithaca, N.Y.: Cornell University Press, 1996); Michael J. Sandel, *Democracy's Discontent: America in Search of a Public Philosophy* (Cambridge: Harvard University Press, 1996); Jeffrey C. Issac, *Democracy in Dark Times* (Ithaca, N.Y.: Cornell University Press, 1998); Chantal Mouffe, *The Democratic Paradox* (New York: Verso, 2000); Edward Broadbent, ed., *Democratic Equality: What Went Wrong?* (Toronto: University of Toronto Press, 2001); and Hans-Hermann Hoppe, *Democracy—The God That Failed: The Economics and Politics of Monarchy, Democracy and Natural Order* (New Brunswick: Transaction Publishers, 2001).

3. See, for example, Terry Teachout, "Republican Nation, Democratic Nation?" *Commentary,* January 2001, 23–29; Francis Fukuyama, "What Divides America," *Wall Street Journal,* November 15, 2000, http://www.mugu.com/pipermill/upstream-list/2000–November/000841.html. For a discussion of this topic at a public event sponsored by the Cato Institute and featuring Terry Teachout, Deborah Dickerson, and Andrew Sullivan, see "Divided America," March 27, 2001, http://www.cato.org/events/transcripts/010327 et.pdf.

4. Al Gore, "Remarks as Delivered by Vice President Al Gore: DLC Annual Conference," Gore/Lieberman 2000 web site, wysiwyg://73/http://www.algore2000.com/speeches/dlc.html (1).

5. Ibid., 5.

6. Clay Robison, "Bush Fields Questions about Faith upon Return from Trip to Israel," *Houston Chronicle,* December 4, 1998, http://web.lexis-nexis.com/universe/docum . . . lzV&_md5=b944d98cb9cdf0cb500b5f96050229d8 (1–2).

7. Bush in Robison, "Bush Fields Questions," 2.

8. Al Gore, "Remarks as Prepared for Delivery by Al Gore: University of New Hampshire, Durham," Gore/Lieberman 2000 web site, wysiwyg://95/http://www.algore 2000.com/speeches/speeches_unh_052399.html (1–3).

9. Elshtain, *Democracy on Trial,* 80.

10. Gore, "Remarks as Prepared," 3–4.

11. Gore, "Remarks on the Role of Faith-Based Organizations," 1–3.

12. Ibid., 2.

13. Elaine Kamarck quoted in Linda Feldmann, "Campaigning for President . . . or for Preacher?" *Christian Science Monitor,* June 8, 1999, http://web.lexis-nexis.com/universe/docum . . . lzV&_md5=e201aa52af231f6075cbela3745ec93e.

14. "'Miracles Happen,' Leiberman Says; Gore Running Mate Is Seen as Antidote to 'Clinton Fatigue'; Some in GOP Also Hail Choice," *St. Louis Post-Dispatch,* August 8, 2000, http://web.lexis-nexis.com/universe/docum . . . lzV&_md5+e4aed62f08b2e2cc 957ce034088c4ala (2).

15. Julie Mason, "Bush's 53rd Birthday Takes Bipartisan Tone," *Houston Chronicle,* July 7, 1999, p. 9A.

16. Kim Cobb, "Bush Urges Welfare Role for Faith-Based Groups," *Houston Chronicle,* July 23, 1999, p. 1A; quotation at p. 14A.

17. Bennett Roth, "Schools Need More Morality, Discipline, Bush Tells Voters," *Houston Chronicle,* November 3, 1999, p. 11A.

18. R. G. Ratcliffe, "Bush's Book Slams Some Journalists Who Dig in His Past," *Houston Chronicle,* November 15, 1999, p. 8A.

19. Al Gore, *60 Minutes,* CBS, December 5, 1999. Gore's comment was reported in Richard L. Berke, "Religion Center Stage in Presidential Race," *New York Times,* December 15, 1999, http://web.lexis-nexis.com/universe/docum . . . lzV&_md5=8b957ef 2563fb24426fe29c26bcc4279.

20. George W. Bush, "Remarks at Iowa Caucus." Bush's comment was reported in James O. Goldsborough, "Selecting Jesus as Their Running Mate," *San Diego Union-Tribune,* January 3, 2000, http://web.lexis-nexis.com/universe/docum . . . lzV&_md5= 8cc0ade36635c076c11ac4c394c52312.

21. Feldmann, "Campaigning for President," 1.

22. Berke, "Religion Center Stage," 1.

23. Cragg Hines and Alan Bernstein, "Presidential Race Gears Up in Iowa Today," *Houston Chronicle,* January 24, 2000, 1A; quote at 8A.

24. R. G. Ratcliffe, "McCain's New Ad Accuses Bush of 'Attack Politics,'" *Houston Chronicle,* January 22, 2000, p. 21A.

25. Ratcliffe, "McCain's New Ad," 21A.

26. Glen Johnson, "Bush: Court Overstepped Boundaries," *Bryan-College Station Eagle,* January 22, 2000, p. A3.

27. Wendy Koch, "Both Parties Are Grabbing for Political Soul of Catholics," *USA Today,* March 3, 2000, http://web.lexis-nexis.com/universe/docum . . . lzV&_md5= 2cbd74df6e513cb8c325ef82a5adaf8f (2).

28. E. J. Dionne Jr., "Putting Faith in the Political System," *Bryan-College Station Eagle,* February 18, 2000, p. A10.

29. The text of the Catholic Voter Alert can be found in "Religion Rules as Primaries Approach," *USA Today,* March 3, 2000, http://www.usatoday.com/news/e98/e1287. html.

30. "Kwame Holman Reports on the Republican Primary Race," *Online NewsHour: Hot Context,* February 28, 2000, http://www.pbs.org/newshour/bb/election/jan-june00/ gop_2–28.html (1).

31. David Esp, "Republicans Push for Michigan Votes," *Bryan-College Station Eagle,* February 22, 2000, p. A1.

32. "Kwame Holman Reports," 2.

33. Cragg Hines, "Primary Process Has Weakened Bush Substantially," *Houston Chronicle,* March 9, 2000, 13A.

34. R. G. Ratcliffe, "Bush's Effort Has Been Plagued by Series of Religious Faux Pas," *Houston Chronicle,* March 7, 2000, p. 9A.

35. "Primaries," *Bryan-College Station Eagle,* March 15, 2000, p. A1ff.

36. "DeLay Vows a Return to Religion If Bush Wins," *Houston Chronicle,* May 7, 2000, http://web.lexis-nexis.com/universe/docum . . . lzV&_md5=490997303039e886062 74564d53a7ee5 (1).

37. Hines, "Primary Process Has Weakened Bush," 13A.

38. The Gallup Organization, "Gallup Poll Surveys, August 24–27, 2000," *Gallup Poll New Service,* August 24, 2000, http://www.gallup.com/poll/surveys/2000/Topline000824/ q16t18.asp (1ff).

39. This is my own judgment, but I think it is supported by the record of both Bush and Gore over a period of many years. See Laurie Goodstein, "Bush Uses Religion as Personal and Political Guide," *New York Times,* October 22, 2000, http://www.nytimes.com/ 2000/10/22/politics/22PRAY.html (1–6); "Beliefnet Interviews Presidential Candidate George W. Bush," Beliefnet.com, http://beliefnet.com/story/47/story_4703_1.html? frameset=1&storyID=&boardID=7200 (1–3); "George W. Bush," *Catholic Digest,* November 2000, 56–65; Melinda Henneberger, "Al Gore's Journey: Gore Has Explored a Range of Beliefs from Old Time to New Age," *New York Times,* October 22, 2000, http://www. nytimes.com/2000/10/22/politics/22FAIT.html (1–11); "Al Gore," *Catholic Digest,* November 2000, 70–79.

40. Alison Mitchell, "Bush Draws Campaign Theme from More than 'the Heart,'" *New York Times,* June 11, 2000 http://www.manhattan-institute.org/html/_nyt-bush_draws_ campaign_.htm (1).

41. Mitchell, "Bush Draws Campaign Theme," 4.

42. "Miracles Happen," 3.

43. Don Lattin, "Getting Religion in Battle for the Middle; Candidates Find Faith Is No Longer a Liability," *San Francisco Chronicle,* August 12, 2000, http://web.lexis-nexis.com/ universe/docum . . . lzV&_md5=03d0ba3f896f7d847b126ce6bd3b5729 (2).

44. Al Gore, "Remarks as Prepared for Delivery by Al Gore: Democratic National Convention," Gore/Lieberman 2000 web site, wysiwyg://90/http://www.algore2000.com/speeches/sp_08172000_dnc.html (2–4).

45. Miles Benson, "Politics, Faith and Jefferson," *Minneapolis Star Tribune,* August 26, 2000, http://web.lexis–nexis.com/universe/docum . . . lzV&_md5=0342946539dcc 7c074b02dd560e22db6 (3).

46. The Pew Research Center for the People and the Press, "Survey Reports: Section III: Religion, Politics and Policy," April 10, 2001, http://people-press.org/reports/display.php3?PageID=114 (1–4). Religion, according to the Pew Research Center, "plays an important role in shaping Americans' views on public policy issues. When respondents were asked about several controversial issues—ranging from human cloning to gay civil unions—and what was the most important factor in shaping views on these subjects, religious belief tied with personal experience as the most frequently mentioned influence. Overall, more than six in ten (61 percent) of the survey's respondents said that religion was the most important influence on their opinion about at least one of seven issues probed" (2).

47. Miles Benson, "Religion, Politics Becoming Uneasy Mix, Some Say; Policy Issues Taking a Back Seat to Piety," *New Orleans Times-Picayune,* August 20, 2000, http://web.lexis-nexis.com/universe/docum . . . lzV&_md5=a660201d34c673a945a894bd1891 9546 (2).

48. Ceci Connolly, "Taking the Spirit to the Stump; Lieberman Urges 'Place for Faith in Our Public Life,'" *Washington Post,* August 28, 2000, http://web.lexis-nexis.com/universe/docum . . . lzV&_md5=b2e3780e6e5659b38aeaba35d9aae95c (1–2).

49. Ed Vulliamy, "God Kept Busy by Presidential Race," *New York Observer,* September 3, 2000, http://web.lexis-nexis.com/universe/docum . . . lzV&_md5=bb64229cb209357 d421c51c60ba2b9b4 (2).

50. "The Ad Campaign: Another Look at Gore the Man," *New York Times,* September 28, 2000, http://www.nytimes.com/2000/09/28/politics/28ADBO.html (1).

51. Richard Perez-Pena, "Lieberman Stakes Claim to Basic Values," *New York Times,* http://www.nytimes.com/2000/10/17/politics/17LIEB.html (1–2).

52. Joseph Lieberman, "Lieberman Cites Religion as Foundation of Environmentalism," *New York Times,* http://www.nytimes.com/2000/10/19/politics/19VEEP.html (1).

53. Senator Al Gore, *Earth in the Balance: Ecology and the Human Spirit* (Boston: Houghton Mifflin, 1992), 247. This excerpt from the book also appeared in "Gore on the Bible and Ecology," *New York Times,* October 22, 2000, http://www.nytimes.com/2000/10/22/politics/22EXCE.html (1)

54. Kevin Sack, "In a Texas Church, Gore Campaigns for Morality, Values and 'Prosperity of the Spirit,'" *New York Times,* October 23, 2000, http://www.nytimes.com/2000/10/23/politics/23GORE.html (1, 3).

55. Richard Perez-Pena, "At Notre Dame, Lieberman Revisits Faith's Role," *New York Times,* October 25, 2000, wysiwyg://2http://www.nytimes.com/2000/10/23/politics/25LIEB.html (1–2).

56. Jodi Wilgoren, "Just Before Election, Politics and Religion Mix Easily at a Michigan Church," *New York Times,* November 6, 2000, wysiwyg://3/http://www.nytimes.com/2000/11/06/politics/06MICH.html (3).

57. Matthew Vita and Susan Schmidt, "The Interest Groups; Religious Right Mutes Voice, Not Efforts," *Washington Post,* November 2, 2000, http://web.lexis-nexis.com/universe/docum . . . lzV&_md5=eaba55d0a101ad5b540f787a729b44b3 (2).

58. Kevin Sack, "Gore Urges Votes of Black and Labor Base," *New York Times,* November 5, 2000, wysiwyg://2/http://www.nytimes.com/2000/11/05/politics/05GORE. html (1).

59. Sack, "Gore Urges Votes," 4.

60. James L. Guth, Lyman A. Kellstedt, John C. Green, and Corwin E. Smidt, "America Fifty/Fifty," *First Things,* October 2001, 19–26. See chart on page 21 for specific percentages.

61. Sandel, *Democracy's Discontent,* 24.

62. Richard John Neuhaus, *The Naked Public Square: Religion and Democracy in America* (Grand Rapids, Mich.: William B. Eerdmans, 1984), 21.

63. Neuhaus, *Naked Public Square,* 60.

George W. Bush Discovers Rhetoric

September 20, 2001, and the
U.S. Response to Terrorism

DAVID ZAREFSKY

Where in American culture does rhetoric dwell? That seemingly simple question does not permit an easy answer, because the *ethos* of rhetoric as social practice is both ambiguous and ambivalent. Americans have valorized oratory as the literature of the masses and disdained it as the tool of the demagogue. If a speaker seems too obviously to adapt to an audience, we denounce the behavior as glibness and pandering, just telling listeners what they want to hear. It is a mark against a political candidate that he or she will "say anything in order to get elected." At the same time, we expect leaders to articulate our values and to connect their goals with our needs. We mark ceremonial occasions with speeches, and we note their absence at the moments when we expect them.[1] But when they occur, we may note their existence more than their content. Few can recall what any particular commencement speaker said, and patriotic messages can be conveniently characterized as "Fourth of July oratory," a term that is as likely to evoke scorn as praise.

We have recognized the power of a speech to give voice to our inchoate thoughts and feelings, yet one of the maxims of our culture is that "actions speak louder than words." This maxim suggests that words and actions are distinct, and this very distinction marginalizes rhetoric. At best it is a prelude to action; more often it is a cover for inaction. In ordinary usage, "rhetoric" has negative connotations. It is often described with adjectives such as "empty" and "mere," and it is set in opposition to terms such as "reality," "truth," "genuineness," and "sincerity." These observations suggest that in ordinary times we recognize rhetoric but view it somehow as a necessary evil. It cannot be banished, but certainly it ought not to be celebrated. Even when we lament the alienation of Americans from politics, the weakening of a common culture, the seeming loss of the skills of deliberation, or the atrophy of the public sphere, we typically do not see these maladies as reflections of the very modest and marginal dwelling place rhetoric is assigned in American culture.

In times of crisis and periods of uncertainty, however, we insist on rhetoric. We hear a call to find meaning in the face of unexpected or threatening events, and we in turn call for our leaders to articulate a vision to which we can subscribe. We long for eloquence and acknowledge its power. In these moments, rhetoric has the ability to reshape our world by altering our sense of who we are, by replacing the narrative structure in which we understand events, by changing our hierarchies of value and importance, and by causing us to see old realities in a new light. In these moments we dwell in a rhetorical culture and are glad to do so. We find new meaning and purpose, and we reward the leaders who so skillfully matched rhetoric to occasion.

When the crisis is national in scope, Americans look to the president to perform this rhetorical role. This is not new. Writing about Abraham Lincoln's Civil War leadership, James M. McPherson posits that "communication and inspiration are two of the most important functions of a president in times of crisis."[2] But the rhetorical role of the president has received increased attention in recent years. In his study of qualities that explain presidential success or failure, Fred Greenstein identified "the president's proficiency as a public communicator" first, and he noted that this skill pertains to "the outer face of leadership."[3] Another political scientist, Erwin C. Hargrove, identifies the first task of the president as being "to 'teach reality' to publics and their fellow politicians through rhetoric." This includes, he says, both "the explanation of contemporary problems and issues" and relating them to "the perennial ideals of the American experience."[4] In a well-known formulation, Jeffrey Tulis has argued that the twentieth century so transformed the presidency as to make it largely a rhetorical institution and to define the president's central role as leading the country, not managing the government.[5] Mary Stuckey has described a significant aspect of the president's role as being our "interpreter-in-chief" who helps the people understand what things mean.[6]

In ordinary times, the president's rhetorical performance is constrained by the marginal role our culture assigns to rhetoric. But in times of crisis, this friction is removed and the nation looks to its President for meaning, reassurance, and purpose. Drawing on his own sense of purpose and perhaps on religious inspiration, the president tries to meet these needs through rhetorical leadership.[7] The response of President George W. Bush to the terrorist attacks of September 11, 2001, offers a powerful contemporary example of the suddenly central dwelling place of rhetoric in moments of national crisis.

The Rhetorical Situation

Even as these horrific incidents recede into history, it is still hard to find any words with which to encompass them. Certainly, neither the widely adopted euphemism "the events of September 11" nor the shorthand numeral "9/11" does them justice. To regard the hijacking of airplanes, the destruction of the World Trade

Center, the devastation of part of the Pentagon, and the wasting of thousands of human lives on the airplanes and on the ground in New York, Virginia, and Pennsylvania as an invitation to rhetoric may border on the obscene. Yet surely that, among other things, is what it was. The facts of what happened were clear, seared indelibly in the mind's eye of anyone who watched television that fateful Tuesday. But what these facts meant was anything but obvious. That would depend, largely, on how the president chose to contextualize them in the subsequent days and weeks, particularly in an address to a joint session of Congress and to the nation on September 20.

It can be safely stipulated that rhetorical prowess had not been regarded as one of George W. Bush's great strengths. He had been ridiculed during the 2000 campaign for his mispronunciations and errors of syntax. Although some of his speeches had been well received, such as his nomination acceptance speech and his inaugural address, it is fair to say that they did not reach oratorical heights. Nor did his early pronouncements as president. Some critics dismissed his verbal missteps as idiosyncratic; others saw them as reflecting a deeper underlying problem.[8]

By early September 2001, Bush's public stature had not changed much since his inauguration. His legitimacy as president was acknowledged, but he still labored under the cloud of the disputed election of 2000. Just over half the public, according to the polls, approved of his performance as president, and many were concerned that he seemed out of touch with average Americans, concerned more with large corporations than with "people like me."[9] If the election of 2000 were rerun, polls suggested that the result would be the same virtual tie.

On the morning of September 11, Bush was in Florida to promote his education program. Told of the terrorist attacks, he wanted to return immediately to Washington but was dissuaded from doing so by fears for his safety. He spent much of the day aboard Air Force One or at military facilities in Louisiana and Nebraska. He did not issue public statements and did not return to the capital until evening, after all commercial airspace had been closed and he could be adequately protected. Neither his silence during the day nor his brief statement that night inspired great confidence. His September 11 speech was "too slight," in the words of one commentator, for the magnitude of the great events.[10]

The president's other early remarks also failed to inspire confidence. He had referred to the terrorists as "folks"—hardly the right language for such an alien force—and then had called for a "crusade" against them, only to abandon the term after being told that it conjured up images of eleventh-century European Christians sent to recover the Holy Land from the reigning Muslims.[11] The Defense Department named a planned antiterrorist campaign "Infinite Justice," but this too was changed (to "Enduring Freedom") after it was pointed out that Islam assigned infinite justice exclusively to Allah. Meanwhile, like the sheriff in some old western, Bush proclaimed that he wanted the suspected terrorist leader, Osama bin Laden, "dead or alive," until his father and others urged him to tone down his rhetoric.

Some advisers reportedly were worrying that Bush's exhortations were "headlong and immature," making threats that could not be backed up and promises that could not be kept.[12]

Bush began to find the appropriate voice later in the week. He gave a eulogy at the National Cathedral on September 14. The speech memorialized the dead, proclaimed the goal of answering the attacks in order to remove evil from the world, asserted that the country was united, and sought divine guidance and blessing. The speech was beautifully moving yet in a sense inauthentic. There was a loftiness to it, a sense of the grand style, that did not match the president's persona. He might have spoken the words, but they were not his own voice.[13] The next Monday, he spoke at the Washington Islamic Center and distinguished the terrorists from Islam, noting that Islam was a religion of peace but the terrorists represented evil and war.[14] Bush was working toward the way he would capture the meaning of the events for the American people, but he was not there yet. His early mishaps were failures of rhetoric—failure to find the right proportions between words and the events they describe, between words and the man who uttered them, between words and the paralinguistic message, between words and the emotions they represent. Unless these breaches somehow could be repaired, the president would have difficulty in "teaching reality": explaining the dastardly attacks as a challenge to American ideals and mobilizing his audiences to respond.

Bush and his advisers correctly sensed that the rhetorical needs had not yet been met. The country and the world needed reassurance, but people also needed to derive inspiration and purpose from the terrible tragedy. Presidential adviser Karen P. Hughes reported that Bush told her, "This is a defining moment. We have an opportunity to restructure the world toward freedom, and we have to get it right."[15] Sensing that the occasion was also a political opportunity for Bush, a chance to establish himself firmly as the leader of a nation united, his advisers chose the magisterial venue of a joint session of Congress for a presidential speech. The preparation of the speech was a collective effort in which the president himself was heavily involved.[16] Although nominally addressed to the assembled senators and representatives, the prime-time televised address was also intended for the American people, foreign leaders, and the Taliban.[17]

The War Metaphor

The president's most significant rhetorical decision was made well before the speech: to describe the situation as war. This was an instinctive response, not the result of deliberate planning or calculation. Reportedly, "We are at war" was Bush's immediate reaction when told of the second attack on the World Trade Center. He told his Cabinet on September 12 that the attacks were "acts of war."[18] In his remarks at the National Cathedral, he said, "War has been waged against us by stealth and deceit and murder."[19] On September 15, he told senior advisers assembled at Camp David, "We're at war."[20] He made similar claims in the September 20 speech and has not wavered from that characterization since.

The president probably could not imagine any other conception of what was taking place. Yet although it may seem pedantic to do so, one should regard the term "war" as a metaphor, not a literal account.[21] What took place on September 11 had some of the characteristics of war: the United States was attacked and lives were lost. Yet other components of war were missing: the attack was not military, it did not come from another state, no country declared war on us, nor did we on any other nation. The congressional resolution authorizing response to the attacks did not label either the attacks or the response as war.

Moreover, the characterization of what took place could have been otherwise. One could regard the acts as crime—a crime of massive proportions, to be sure, and requiring an unprecedented response, but a response that would be seen as a police action with a goal of justice rather than victory.[22] Another possibility was to see the attacks as calling for a diplomatic response. This view would regard them as a high-tech version of the terrorist raids by the Barbary pirates during the 1790s, which John Adams correctly if inelegantly called a "half war." And Adams resisted the temptation to declare war against France in response. Still another option was to regard the attacks as sui generis, with terror located somewhere between crime and war, calling for punishment but emphasizing security and defense.

The point of suggesting that there might be a gap between what happened on September 11 and what counts as war, is not to dispute the president's definition of the situation but to recognize that it was a rhetorical choice. Understanding it that way directs us to focus on its implications and consequences, and there were many.[23] To begin with, the rhetoric of war assumes and celebrates national unity. No matter how we may disagree on other issues, in the face of war we all stand as one. The immediately visible signs of national unity were the display of flags everywhere and the swift and nearly unanimous passage of both the congressional resolution authorizing force and the Patriot Act. The widespread acceptance of the war metaphor with its emphasis on unity forestalls debate and criticism as luxuries that must await the return of more tranquil times. It makes a place only for the rhetoric of approval and support. In a critique of the use of the war metaphor, Susan Sontag noted its effectiveness in this regard. "Under the slogan United We Stand," she writes, "the call to reflectiveness was associated with dissent, dissent with lack of patriotism." She adds that to object to the terms of the conflict as one of good versus evil was to be "accused of condoning the attacks, or at least the legitimacy of the grievances behind the attacks."[24]

Second, the war metaphor justifies reprioritizing concerns. President Bush had told Cabinet members that, while they were still to pursue their previous agendas, the administration's success or failure ultimately would be determined by its response to terrorism.²⁵ Before September 11, the political landscape was dominated by controversies over education and stem-cell research, prescription drug costs and faith-based social services. Whether the Social Security trust fund would need to be raided to balance the operating budget was a hot topic. These concerns all seemingly disappeared in the wake of the terrorist attacks, as did the balanced budget itself, and few people seemed to mind. The new issue was homeland security. In the spring of 2002, the president belatedly accepted the recommendation of a bipartisan panel to reorganize the domestic-security agencies of the government into a new Cabinet-level department. Using the justification that we were at war, he insisted on the need for authority to bypass civil service protections for federal workers in the new department so that he would have maximum flexibility.²⁶ The House and Senate deadlocked on this specific issue and it became a major theme in the 2002 midterm elections. Meanwhile, the president proposed a budget projecting the need for deficit spending over the next several years, without suffering adverse political consequences. Members of his own party lobbied for even more tax cuts as a means of economic stimulus. The whole landscape of economic policy was reconfigured after the terrorist attacks. The recession that soon developed was attributed to the attacks and their aftermath, and it did not hurt the president's popularity.

Third, the war metaphor communicates resolve and focuses on a goal. It sends a clear message of determination to stay the course and to see the final surrender of the enemy. Limited wars may tax our patience, but so long as we are making progress toward the goal, we will persevere in the effort. The metaphor, Richard Kohn has written, "prepares the population for a long, costly, complex campaign that will subordinate American foreign and domestic policy to the struggle, necessitate changes in government organization, and result in some—perhaps substantial—casualties in the armed forces." Additionally, he notes, it informs allies and other governments of the seriousness of American resolve.²⁷

These considerations suggest that the war metaphor is a powerful rhetorical resource, as it has proved to be for President Bush. Nevertheless, it is not without potential difficulties. If the object to which it is applied falls short of the magnitude of military conflict, the metaphor can seem trite or trivial, as happened when war was declared on domestic problems ranging from poverty and drugs to energy shortages and street crime.²⁸ Obviously that was not a problem in this case; if attacks on American cities did not constitute war, it was hard to know what did. But there were other problems when the war metaphor was applied to terrorism. What, for example, counts as victory? By its nature, terrorism is an activity of stealth. Terrorist groups lack a clear center that, if eliminated, would mean victory. One could say that the war would be won when people felt more secure, but feelings of security and calm always could be disrupted by another unexpected attack. "The very word 'war' suggests military measures and, of course, victory," Stanley

Hoffmann has written, "rather than the difficult, slow, and partly clandestine operations that fighting terrorism entails."[29] Nor was it clear who the enemy was. Terrorists do not wear identifying uniforms; their mode of operation is to blend in
to a society and then to strike from within. And the attribution of "terrorist" is
laced with ideology. What one side defines as terrorists, the other may define as
oppressed fighters for freedom.

These difficulties may become serious over time and as a result of sober reflection, but the functions of the war metaphor in creating unity, limiting debate,
changing priorities, and mobilizing for action are immediate. They offered President Bush significant benefits and he took advantage of them.

The September 20 Speech

President Bush sustained the imagery of war in his speech of September 20. There
he defined the conflict as a war between freedom and fear. He organized the
speech as a series of answers to questions Americans were said to be asking, and
thereby put himself in the favorable position of both representing the concerns of
the citizenry and responding to those concerns with authoritative answers.[30] He
outlined the general strategy to be followed against the terrorist threat, issued
nonnegotiable demands and excluded the possibility of compromise, and predicted inevitable victory in the contest to follow.[31] These are all staples in the rhetoric of war. But the September 20 speech also reveals interesting nuances.

For example, President Bush stressed the unique character of the war. It was as
if, after placing the attacks in the genre of war, he wanted to distinguish this from
other wars so that the normal conventions of the genre need not constrain him.
"On September 11," he said, "enemies of freedom committed an act of war
against our country." This sentence contained three fundamental assumptions
stated as incontrovertible facts: that the terrorists were "enemies of freedom," that
the acts constituted acts of war, and that they were directed against our country
as a nation-state. These stipulations allowed President Bush to discuss the terrorist attacks as deliberate provocation by those who would start a war with the
United States. But he quickly added that this was not like other wars. Except for
Pearl Harbor, it was the first attack on American soil since 1865. It was not only
a surprise attack, but an attack on civilians in a great city. And the resulting conflict, he pointedly noted, would not be like the Gulf War of 1991—quick and
decisive—nor like the 1999 war in Kosovo, requiring no ground troops and leading to no American combat deaths. Far more than military actions would be encom-
passed by the war. As a result, it would be not "one battle, but a lengthy campaign
unlike any other we have ever seen. It may include dramatic strikes visible on TV
and covert operations, secret even in success." In short, President Bush is saying
first that we are at war, so we should subordinate other priorities, come together,
and act to repel this threat, and second that we cannot measure our success in

doing so by traditional standards since this war is exceptional. Juxtaposing these two themes, one sees in the president's speech an appeal for open-ended support of the administration's decisions about what to do and how to do it. The uniqueness of the war would become a warrant for the expansion of American (and presidential) power.

A second noteworthy feature of the September 20 speech is the portrayal of the enemy. In many wars, it has been thought desirable to personalize and then demonize the enemy, whether it be Hitler, Ho Chi Minh, or Saddam Hussein. Osama bin Laden only partially fills this role, because Bush's main focus is on loosely organized terrorist groups. He appears more concerned with definition by negation. First, he makes clear that Muslims are not the enemy; this is not a war of civilizations. Speaking "directly to Muslims throughout the world," he assured them, "We respect your faith. . . . Its teachings are good and peaceful. And those who commit evil in the name of Allah blaspheme the name of Allah. The terrorists are traitors to their own faith." Islam was not the enemy; nor were we at war with mainstream Muslims (or, by extension, Arabs).

Likewise, the enemy was not the people of Afghanistan. After illustrating the excesses of the Taliban, President Bush made clear that "the United States respects the people of Afghanistan. After all, we are currently its largest source of humanitarian aid." He would maintain this theme three weeks later. Even as he announced the start of military strikes in Afghanistan, he proclaimed the friendship of Americans for the Afghan people.[32]

The enemy, then, is different from what we normally would expect. It is not a people or a state, or even a ruling government necessarily, but what Bush described in one passage as "a collection of loosely affiliated terrorist organizations known as Al Qaeda" and in another as "a radical network of terrorists and every government that supports them." This latter is a crucial pairing, because if Al Qaeda is elusive, sovereign states are not. So, for example, while the Afghan people are not our enemy, the Taliban regime is, so long as it continues to harbor terrorists. Distinguishing regimes from people allows Bush both to regard the enemy as distant and furtive and to embody it in regimes such as those in Afghanistan and Iraq. At the same time, it makes the identification of any such regime as the enemy dependent on the seemingly empirical question of whether it supports terrorism.

President Bush explains why terrorists hate us, why they would make themselves our enemy, in a simple and straightforward way: "They hate our freedoms." They hate the fact that our government derives its authority from the people. They hate Christians and Jews and wish to expel them from much of Asia and Africa. And "they stand against us because we stand in their way." Although perhaps fitting for the occasion, this simplistic and self-serving account of terrorist motives was the weakest part of the speech. It in no way excuses terrorism to inquire why in much of the world there is antipathy to global capitalism or to some aspects of American culture. But the president's answer seals off the need for self-examination. Terrorists hate us because we are good and they are evil, he almost seems to say. On this reading the war becomes defined as a Manichean struggle. And if there were any remaining doubt of the evil of the enemy, it is dispelled by the president's linking terrorism with "all the murderous ideologies of the twentieth century—fascism, nazism, and totalitarianism" (obviously excluding communism since the support of several communist nations was sought for the antiterrorist coalition). In short, the enemy identified itself by its own actions. It could be furtive or it could be clearly visible, but its motivation was unmistakably evil.

Overcoming an amorphous enemy motivated by evil was an ambitious goal. Yet the formulation of the goal in the September 20 speech reveals an important nuance. Although still quite broad, it was less vast than might be suggested by the unmodified phrase, "war on terrorism." Probably realizing that the eradication of all terrorism everywhere was an impossible goal, Bush referred instead to defeating "every terrorist group of global reach." He never said that this formulation was a refinement or limitation of earlier statements. But it allowed him to bypass involvement in internal or small regional conflicts that did not threaten American interests, while still laying down the marker that the war will end only when every global terrorist group "has been found, stopped, and defeated." This statement certainly would encompass the destruction of the Al Qaeda network without returning to the cold war assumption that a threat anywhere was a threat everywhere.

If in one sense the president narrowed the conflict (by confining it to global terrorist organizations), in another he enlarged its scope. The war would be fought not just by the United States but by the whole civilized world. He had foreshadowed this move in remarks to his Cabinet, when he had said, "This enemy attacked not just our people, but all freedom-loving people everywhere in the world."[33] In the September 20 speech, although the principal focus was on the United States, President Bush mentioned that citizens of eighty other nations died in the terrorist attacks. And after outlining measures to be taken, he stated, "This is not, however, just America's fight. And what is at stake is not just America's freedom." This appeal served further to isolate the terrorists, defining them not just as enemies of the United States but as enemies of civilization. Such marginal figures did not deserve anyone's consideration or support. Additionally, Bush established the predicate for his attempt to build an antiterrorism coalition. He was not asking other nations to come to America's aid; rather, he was asking that all nations, out of mutual self-interest, form a coalition.

Moreover, he permitted no nation the luxury of evading this invitation. Nations that did not participate could be seen easily as harboring or supporting terrorists, and Bush made clear that any such nation would be regarded as a hostile power. The refusal to distinguish between terrorists and nations that harbored them was referred to sometimes as the "Bush Doctrine." This appeal, of course, was intended for nations who might have mixed motives or divided loyalties. When military operations against the Taliban were launched in early October, the president reiterated the theme, stating that "every nation has a choice to make. In this conflict there is no neutral ground."[34]

The attempt to force nations to choose between supporting the United States and supporting terrorists was itself a prominent feature of the speech. In one of the most memorable passages, Bush insisted, "Every nation in every region now has a choice to make. Either you are with us or you are with the terrorists." According to this formulation, there truly was no neutral ground. Since global terrorism was, by definition, a worldwide threat, no nation could claim to be uninvolved. On the other hand, the United States did not regard any government as our enemy a priori—certainly a departure from the normal circumstances of war. In the past, when we've entered a war we've known whom it has been against. But any nation could make itself our enemy by failing to take the needed steps to crack down on terrorism. Forcing this choice on other nations divided the world into friends and foes but left to others the decision about the category in which they belonged.

The features of the September 20 speech that have been identified so far speak to the justification for American military response. But unleashing an unchecked wave of militarism can be dangerous to democratic values. Other features of the September 20 speech, although they may have received less public notice, address this need and provide at least a measure of countervailing rhetoric. For example, the president did not altogether eschew the rhetoric of justice, even as he spoke of war. Toward the beginning of the speech he evoked the swiftness and certainty of frontier justice, saying, "Whether we bring our enemies to justice or justice to our enemies, justice will be done." This is an alternative to images of militarism, but only superficially so, since it suggests that America will be prosecutor, judge, and executioner all at once. At the end of the speech, however, the president tempered this image when he said, "Fellow citizens, we'll meet violence with patient justice" and appealed for the gifts of divine wisdom and guidance. Here was a suggestion, however subtle, that the rhetoric of war and the rhetoric of justice were not necessarily at odds.

War rhetoric typically includes calls for sacrifice, but here too the situation was atypical. If the goal of the terrorists was to undermine the American economy or life-style, then any sacrifice from normal routines could be taken as a sign that the terrorists had won. In this context, the patriotic thing to do was to carry on with one's life, to maintain consumer spending, and to uphold American values. This introduces a tension, for it is hard to mobilize national unity and invoke a war psychology for the purpose of exhorting people to go about business as usual. They may be more likely initially to support the war if it involves no sacrifice, but their support may be very thin.

The September 20 speech implicitly acknowledges this anomaly. Structurally, there is a section that seeks to answer the question Americans are said to be asking:

What is expected of us? It comes immediately after the announcement of steps to strengthen homeland security and after the promise of military and economic reprisal. But the six items President Bush mentioned really demand relatively little of any civilian: "live your lives and hug your children," be calm and uphold American values, give to charity, be patient with delays and inconveniences, participate in the economy, and pray "for the victims of terror and their families, for those in uniform and for our great country." For most people, these steps are thoroughly unobjectionable, yet they render it easy to caricature shopping at the mall or waiting in long lines at the airport as acts of great patriotism—and thereby to trivialize what the war on terrorism is all about.

President Bush's second request in this list is worthy of special mention. It is not uncommon for intolerance to be a byproduct of war. Not only did the president make clear that our quarrel was not with Muslims or with Islam, but he specifically urged Americans to uphold the values of tolerance and respect for difference. Indeed, he regarded yielding on these values as tantamount to granting victory to the terrorists. As he put it in the speech, "We're in a fight for our principles and our first responsibility is to live by them. No one should be singled out for unfair treatment or unkind words because of their ethnic background or religious faith." This is a theme that Bush has maintained consistently, as a counterweight to the ethnocentric nationalism that often characterizes wars.

In the short run, the relatively low level of sacrifice required has made it easy for the American people to rally behind their president. It is as if they are giving their endorsement to war by proxy, since it does not seem to cost them anything. They are acquiescing in presidentially directed war and, in going about their business, relegating themselves to a passive role. But Bush indicated that the war on terrorism would take a long time. As the memories of September 11 recede and life returns to something approaching normal, it may be harder to sustain support for the administration's military and economic moves against terrorism, and the tradeoffs against other goals that they will require, if the sense of war psychology is lost.

A final aspect of the September 20 speech that warrants note is the confident prediction of success. This too is a frequent feature of war rhetoric: however uncertain things might look at the moment, we are buoyed by the knowledge that our cause, being right, will prevail in the end. This note of optimism pervades the president's speech and probably has a good deal to do with its effectiveness in rallying the American people. At the very beginning, Bush paid tribute to the strength of the country's initial response: the courage of ordinary citizens, symbols of patriotism and solidarity, "the saying of prayers in English, Hebrew, and Arabic," the unusual display of congressional bipartisanship, and the messages of support and concern received from all over the world. These illustrations support the inference that the terrorists *already* have failed because they miscalculated. They aimed to weaken America but have strengthened it instead. By this standard, of course, the war is a success before it really begins.

This note of confidence is sustained throughout the speech. The terrorists will end "in history's unmarked grave of discarded lies." The president and Congress "will come together" on a host of legislative fronts to protect the nation. Reassuring those who might believe that we are facing a new age of terror and fear, the president acknowledged dangers but insisted that "this country will define our times, not be defined by them." He pledged that "our nation, this generation, will lift the dark threat of violence from our people and our future. We will rally the world to this cause by our efforts, by our courage." These notes of confidence were obviously intended to reassure a stunned and grieving nation. Then, in fairly obvious allusion to Winston Churchill, came the staccato phrases: "We will not tire. We will not falter and we will not fail." These were paralleled by Bush's personal pledges: "I will not forget the wound to our country and those who inflicted it. I will not yield. I will not rest. I will not relent."

The trump card in confident predictions of success is the claim that God is on our side, a recurrent theme in the rhetoric of war, and President Bush played this card as well. "Freedom and fear, justice and cruelty, have always been at war," he said. "And we know that God is not neutral between them." As a result, although the course this conflict will take is not yet known, "its outcome is certain." One might question how anyone could claim to know the will of God, but the significance of these statements is in their rhetorical function. Years ago, Murray Edelman suggested that "the most important task for leaders in crisis is clearly to convey that they are in control of things and know what to do."[35] Certainly the confident predictions of success help to sustain such an impression.

To summarize, then, President Bush's speech of September 20, 2001, embodies several decisions about how to respond rhetorically to terrorism: to regard it as war, but war of a different and possibly unique kind; to marginalize the enemy and define terrorism as opposed to world civilization; to force all nations to choose sides; to minimize the sacrifice required of ordinary citizens; and to forecast inevitable victory. Each of these decisions helped to establish a rhetorical response to terrorist attacks that resonated with the American people and their values.

By most accounts, Bush succeeded at his task in this speech. By a wide margin, people agreed with the judgment of *New York Times* columnist R. W. Apple Jr.: "Mr. Bush rose to the occasion, finding at times the eloquence that has eluded him in the past."[36] Of the respondents to a CNN/Gallup/*USA Today* poll, 87 percent rated the speech either excellent or good, and 78 percent felt that it clearly explained U.S. military goals.[37] Columnists echoed Apple's judgment. David Broder, for example, heard in Bush's speech the echoes of Abraham Lincoln, and Richard Cohen described the speech as Churchillian, noting that the "theater" of the occasion made Bush finally seem "presidential."[38]

Unintended Consequences

Like other actions, of course, rhetorical moves can have unintended consequences. The choice of the war metaphor was a terministic screen, and it is but a slight gloss on Kenneth Burke to say that we control our terms and then they control us.[39] The trajectory created by Bush's appeal, with its open-ended description of the enemy and its stark contrast between good and evil, likewise could lead to unsatisfactory results. Fitting as it was to the occasion, the speech and the rhetorical decisions it reflected could prove to be vulnerabilities in the long run. There is at least some evidence to suggest that this is the case.

The danger most often cited in the weeks after the speech was that the mindset of war would lead to a chilling effect on civil liberties. Racial profiling was acceptable in some quarters if the targets appeared to be from the Middle East. There have been cases of indefinite detention and reports of harsh treatment. And there have been repeated warnings, such as Paul Starr's comment that "the risk of using the term [war] is that it provides a rationale for restricting civil liberties and treating disagreement as disloyalty. . . . [T]he language of war in the struggle against terrorism is only the latest attempt to turn a national emergency into a political trump card."[40]

Although some of the provisions of the Patriot Act, some of the contingency plans for military tribunals, and some of the statements of Attorney General Ashcroft raise alarms, the danger of undermining individual freedoms—at least for U.S. citizens—does not at this writing appear to be clear and present. Nor have the new regulations been tested in court, and in general courts have been skeptical of government claims against civil liberties. Still, this is an issue on which eternal vigilance is vital. But the prospect for such vigilance is weakened if, as mentioned above, the public relegates itself to passivity. If the public opinion polls, congressional resolutions, and midterm election results are taken to constitute blanket endorsements of the administration, then the war on terrorism is protected from public scrutiny or political debate. The furtive nature of terrorism and the need for secrecy in response become the justifications for the administration's holding its cards very close to the vest. In return, the public is told that the sacrifices that normally characterize wartime will not be required, and indeed that it is a patriotic duty to go about one's normal routine. This is a combination that easily enables public disengagement and, if that happens, then the threat to civil liberties is greater.

A second possible unintended consequence is disregard for multilateral initiatives and a determination to "go it alone." The September 20 speech, while it encourages other nations to join in a coalition against terror, proclaims U.S. policies that are not contingent on anyone else's approval. To be sure, this was a concern about the Bush administration even before September 11. The United States refused to sign the Kyoto agreement on global warming and had indicated its intention to develop a missile defense system even if that required abrogating the antiballistic missile treaty with the Soviet Union. If anything, however, multilateral involvement has been enhanced since September 11. United Nations resolutions endorsed reprisal against the Taliban. And when the United States threatened unilateral action against Iraq in 2002, the response of the international community led the United States, despite statements by Vice President Cheney that the UN was ineffectual, to backpedal and seek a resolution from the Security Council demanding that Iraq disarm its weapons of mass destruction at the risk of war.

If these two possible consequences have not yet developed into actual problems, two others have. First, the very simplicity and comprehensiveness of President Bush's appeals allows for them to be universalized, stretched beyond their original context and invoked by others whose agendas the United States might not share. And in the face of such "copycat rhetoric," the United States may be immobilized by its own arguments from disagreeing, even if we otherwise wish to do so. The good-versus-evil formulation and the fact that "terrorism" is left undefined, help to make this possible. It is worth noting that some of the earliest endorsers of the United Nations resolution denouncing terrorism were nations with histories of repressing minorities—minorities who conveniently now could be classified as terrorists in order to justify their government's repression.[41] As *Chicago Tribune* correspondent Howard Witt put it, "Suddenly, nearly every country facing a domestic insurrection, a civil war or just an inconvenient opposition declared that it, too, was fighting terrorism and sought a place for itself on the right side of Washington's new world view."[42] Former national security adviser Zbigniew Brzezinski also warned of the risk that "foreign powers will seize upon the word 'terrorism' to promote their own agendas, as President Vladimir Putin of Russia, Prime Minister Ariel Sharon of Israel, Prime Minister Atal Bihari Vajpayee of India and President Jiang Zemin of China are doing."[43] In each case, these nations confronted enemies who might plausibly be labeled terrorists, and yet, as Stanley Hoffmann has written, "their circumstances were radically different from those under which Osama bin Laden deployed his rabid theological and anti-Western global network."[44] But the United States' ability to call attention to the differences or to disassociate itself from the leaders is quite limited.

The case of Israel and the Palestinians is particularly instructive. While the most militant of the Palestinians contend that they are struggling to overturn an illegal occupation or to recapture the land that was wrested from them in the 1948 war for independence, the Israeli government quite plausibly maintains that the violence that began in September 2000 is terror pure and simple. Prime Minister Sharon has made arguments very similar to those in President Bush's September 20 speech. What Bush had said about Osama bin Laden, Sharon said about Yasir Arafat. He was at the center of an infrastructure of terrorism. He must be isolated in order to dismantle this infrastructure, which is the goal of Israeli policy and a precondition for peace. President Bush has little choice but to endorse, or at least condone, Israel's action, as columnist David Sanger noted, if he is going "to retain a consistent and coherent stance against terrorism."[45] Bush repeatedly has emphasized Israel's right to defend itself against terror. In April 2002, he did call upon Israel to withdraw from Palestinian-controlled areas in the interest of peace, but that call was rebuffed with impunity. In June, he reverted to an endorsement of Sharon's position that progress toward peace and a Palestinian state would require that Yasir Arafat be replaced by a new Palestinian leadership truly committed to the campaign against terror. Now, Sharon's policy may be right, and endorsing it so strongly may be precisely the stance that Bush would choose to take under any circumstances, but that is doubtful. It dooms to irrelevance any efforts to establish a meaningful cease-fire, it is unlikely to stop Palestinian suicide bombers from attacking targets in Israel, and it encourages Arab doubts about whether the United States is an honest broker[46] or that it merits their support in a campaign to topple Saddam Hussein.

The conflict between India and Pakistan over the long-disputed territory of Kashmir proved particularly challenging for the Bush administration. India charged that Pakistani-trained terrorists were infiltrating the disputed region and threatened war unless this provocation ceased. The logic of antiterrorism would lead the Bush administration to side with India, but the United States was especially indebted to President Pervez Musharraf of Pakistan for supporting the effort to overthrow the Taliban in neighboring Afghanistan. The United States succeeded in defusing the crisis in June 2002, but the basic conflict remains—and with it the danger that either side might use the rationale of fighting terrorism to launch a preemptive nuclear strike.

The Bush administration is also placed in a difficult position when Russian president Vladimir Putin, also an ally in the campaign against the Taliban, insists that the war against international terrorism will not be complete unless it includes victory over the rebels in Chechnya. Drawing a distinction between the tactics of the Chechen rebels and Al Qaeda terrorists proved particularly difficult when the rebels commandeered a Moscow theater and held several hundred civilians hostage in October 2002.

The larger danger is that the Bush rhetorical stance, adopted in copycat fashion by other nations, could effectively deny the United States the option of prudent determination of what is in its own interest. Bush's Manichean struggle against terrorists of global reach neither contains gradations of threat nor makes room for extenuating circumstances. While wanting to avoid the cold war mindset by not having to become involved in local conflicts, the president risks bringing about the same result indirectly. If a threat to freedom anywhere is a threat to freedom everywhere, then we have no option to pick and choose the commitments that really matter. We must be willing, as President Kennedy said, to "pay any price, bear any burden." If we feel compelled to support or condone any nation that replicates our own argument against terrorism, we place ourselves largely at the mercy of other nations we ostensibly are seeking to aid.

Beyond the danger of inviting copycat rhetoric and being immobilized by it, the other serious unintended consequence of Bush's rhetorical moves is that they create a slippery slope for the United States itself. The seemingly reasonable position that terrorists should be stopped before they have an opportunity to strike could be used to justify a wide range of American actions for which warrants would otherwise be lacking. This is evident in the Bush administration's effort in the fall of 2002 to seek authorization for the use of force against Iraq.

Saddam Hussein had violated numerous United Nations resolutions adopted at the end of the Persian Gulf War to assure that Iraq would forswear efforts to develop weapons of mass destruction. United Nations inspectors were supposed to verify compliance, but they had not been permitted in Iraq since they had been withdrawn in late 1998 in advance of an American bombing raid. That the United Nations had grounds to enforce its resolutions was clear. Yet there was no evidence that things had changed so dramatically in 2002 or that there was a direct threat to the United States justifying a unilateral American response. Seemingly, deterrence had worked successfully for a dozen years; why was preemptive American action justified now?

For President Bush, the terrorist attacks of September 11 furnished the necessary warrant. Although he claimed that "some Al Qaeda leaders who fled Afghanistan went to Iraq" and that "Iraq has trained Al Qaeda members in bomb-making and poisons and deadly gases," there was no credible evidence linking Iraq to the September 11 attacks.[47] Yet the president, appealing for a congressional resolution authorizing the use of force, made a connection: "Some citizens wonder, after 11 years of living with this problem, why do we need to confront it now. And there's a reason. We have experienced the horrors of September 11." It was not that Iraq was involved in those attacks; it was that Iraq had the motivation and soon would have the capability to precipitate even deadlier threats. And Bush reminded his listeners that on September 11, "America felt its vulnerability even to threats that gather on the other side of the earth. We resolved then and we are resolved today to confront every threat from any source that could bring sudden terror and suffering to America."[48] Responding to concerns that an attack on Iraq would interfere with the war on terrorism (by alienating allies), he said that dealing with the Iraqi threat was necessary in order to win the war against terror.

The difficulty with this line of reasoning is that it could be extended beyond limit. Iran and North Korea, the other nations the president had declared to constitute an "axis of evil," could be equally threatening. Indeed, in October 2002, North Korea acknowledged that it was already engaged in a program to develop nuclear weapons. And beyond those nations, in theory any trouble spot could be depicted as a potential source of terrorist attacks. In the name of combating terrorism, preemptive attack could become an accepted element of U.S. policy and strategy. Interestingly, in justifying his policy against Iraq, Bush referred to President Kennedy's statement at the time of the Cuban missile crisis forty years earlier, that we no longer live in a world in which a nation faces maximum peril only from the

actual firing of weapons. Yet in considering how to respond to the placement of
Soviet missiles in Cuba, the Kennedy administration considered and rejected the
option of preemptive attack. Not only could it not guarantee the elimination of
all the missiles, but Attorney General Robert Kennedy forcefully argued that it
would erase the moral distinction between the contemporary United States and
the Japanese who launched the attack on Pearl Harbor.

It would be folly to suggest that President Bush's speech of September 20
could set these events—subservience to copycat rhetoric abroad and a slippery
slope at home—in motion in any direct causal way. Yet as Leland Griffin has pointedly argued, rhetoric has trajectories.[49] The speech, in responding to the immediate situation, also articulated a rhetorical vision congenial to such unintended
consequences as these. The implication is that leaders in moments of crisis need as
best they can to look down the road, exercising rhetorical leadership that not only
will meet the needs of the moment but that will wear well over time.

Reconsidering the Ethos *of Rhetoric*

What, finally, does the initial American response to terrorism suggest about the
ethos—the dwelling place—of rhetoric as a social practice? It bears out the claim
that, however much rhetoric may be disparaged during tranquil times, in moments
of crisis the American people seek it out and demand it of their President. Rhetorical leadership reassures, unites, and mobilizes. On September 20, 2001, President
George W. Bush rose to the occasion. He and his writers found the right words,
the right themes, the right voice. More than any military or diplomatic result—
for these have been somewhat equivocal—it is probably the president's rhetorical
success that has sustained the unusually high regard in which the country continues to hold him. So it seems that part of the answer is that rhetoric is a national
resource held in reserve, to be drawn upon when crisis conditions require it.

But there is a dark side to this account. What sort of rhetoric, after all, is it that
worked so well on September 20? Many theorists of rhetoric emphasize its contingent nature. Since Aristotle, we have regarded the uncertain as the subject matter of rhetorical deliberation. A strong rhetorical culture, on this view, is one that
recognizes that all discourses are partial, that they are put forward as ways to for-
mulate and test claims in the belief that speakers and listeners together are engaged
in the search for *phronesis,* for practical wisdom—and that it will emerge as the
outcome of deliberation rather than existing prior to it. Rhetoric is thus an invitation to participate in a process of reality construction.[50]

This view of rhetoric has very little in common with the dwelling place that
is implicit in President Bush's speech of September 20—or, for that matter, with
other Presidential responses to moments of crisis. As a thought experiment, one
might consider what the public reaction would have been had Bush said on September 20, "We forgive our enemies," or "We have suffered a great tragedy but

life must go on," or "We must decide together what to do about this threat; I call therefore for unfettered public discussion," or "We must show the world, by the power of our example, that fighting is not the way to resolve our differences," or "We must recognize that this is a calamity sent to us by God as punishment for our sins." Each of these responses would call forth a rhetoric different from that of September 20 and would suggest a very different dwelling place. It would be a place in which rhetoric humbles, is self-reflexive, and imbues one with the perspective of others. Each of these stances might have been adopted by other speakers or in other times or places. But given the contemporary American culture, it is simply not conceivable that George W. Bush or any other President could adopt a rhetoric along any of these lines. The options were not even imagined, and to have pursued them would have been suicidal. Crises do not invite deliberation; their urgency forestalls it. The rhetoric of war constructs an enemy unworthy of international deliberation and assumes a unity of purpose that does not require deliberation at home. Rather than setting forth claims and arguments, it constitutes a kind of argument by definition, setting forth partial discourses as if they were the complete picture and uncontestable.[51] This is the rhetoric not of the open hand but of the closed fist. In wartime it may be what we need, and it serves a positive social purpose, as it did for a troubled nation on September 20, 2001. But if it is the only acceptable dwelling place we can find for the social practice of rhetoric, then advocates of rhetorical culture should have real cause for concern.

Notes

1. For example, on the anniversary of the World Trade Center terrorist attack, the memorial program included no original speeches but recitations from the Declaration of Independence and speeches by Abraham Lincoln and Franklin D. Roosevelt. There was some criticism of the program planners for seemingly implying that no contemporary speaker could rise to the occasion.

2. James M. McPherson, *Abraham Lincoln and the Second American Revolution* (New York: Oxford Univ. Press, 1991), 112.

3. Fred I. Greenstein, *The Presidential Difference: Leadership Style from FDR to Clinton* (New York: Free Press, 2000), 5.

4. Erwin C. Hargrove, *The President as Leader: Appealing to the Better Angels of Our Nature* (Lawrence: Univ. Press of Kansas, 1998), vii–viii.

5. Jeffrey K. Tulis, *The Rhetorical Presidency* (Princeton, N.J.: Princeton Univ. Press, 1987).

6. Mary E. Stuckey, *The President as Interpreter-in-Chief* (Chatham, N.J.: Chatham House, 1991).

7. I discuss this idea more fully in David Zarefsky, "The Presidency Has Always Been a Place for Rhetorical Leadership," in *The Presidency and Rhetorical Leadership,* ed. Leroy G. Dorsey (College Station: Texas A&M University Press, 2002), 20–41.

8. For an example of the latter, see Mark Crispin Miller, *The Bush Dyslexicon: Observations on a National Disorder* (New York: W. W. Norton, 2001).

9. A summary of polls concerning George W. Bush during 2001 is available at the web site of the *National Journal* (November 13, 2002). I am indebted for this citation to Trevor Parry-Giles.

10. See D. T. Max, "The Making of the Speech," *New York Times Magazine,* October 7, 2001, 34. A similar view was advanced by Mary McGrory, "Leaders in the Breach," *Washington Post,* September 13, 2001, A2.

11. William Safire, "On Language: Words at War," *New York Times Magazine,* September 30, 2001, 26.

12. See Frank Bruni, "Bush, and His Presidency, Are Transformed," *New York Times,* September 22, 2001, B2.

13. Max, "Making," 34.

14. "'Islam is Peace' Says President," September 17, 2001, available at the web site of the *National Journal* (November 13, 2002).

15. Bruni, "Bush, and His Presidency," B2.

16. Max, "Making," 36.

17. Ibid., 34. These were the audiences identified by National Security Adviser Condoleeza Rice.

18. Katharine Q. Seelye and Elizabeth Bumiller, "Bush Labels Aerial Terrorist Attacks 'Acts of War,'" *New York Times,* September 13, 2001, A16.

19. "President's Remarks," *New York Times,* September 15, 2001, A6.

20. Elains Sciolino, "Bush Tells the Military to 'Get Ready'"; "Broader Spy Powers Gaining Support," *New York Times,* September 16, 2001, A1.

21. A similar point is made by Michael Walzer, "First, Define the Battlefield," *New York Times,* September 21, 2001, A27.

22. R. W. Apple Jr., "A Clear Message: 'I Will Not Relent,'" *New York Times,* September 21, 2001, A1, reports that many Europeans preferred the characterization of an international police action.

23. The functions of the war metaphor in this case are summarized by Richard H. Kohn, "A War Like No Other," *Organization of American Historians Newsletter* 29 (November 2001): 4.

24. Susan Sontag, "Real Battles and Empty Metaphors," *New York Times,* September 10, 2002, A31.

25. Bruni, "Bush, and His Presidency," A1.

26. Alison Mitchell, "The Perilous Search for Security at Home," *New York Times,* July 28, 2002, sec. 4, p. 4.

27. Kohn, "War Like No Other," 4.

28. I discuss domestic applications of the war metaphor in David Zarefsky, *President Johnson's War on Poverty: Rhetoric and History* (Tuscaloosa: Univ. of Alabama Press, 1986), passim.

29. Stanley Hoffmann, "America Alone in the World," *American Prospect* 13 (September 23, 2002): 20.

30. Trevor Parry-Giles and Shawn Parry-Giles, "Presidential Therapies and the Events of September 11: Mimesis, Methexis, and Nationalism in the Rhetorics of George W. Bush and *The West Wing*" (paper presented at the Eighth Biennial Public Address Conference, University of Georgia, October 5, 2002), 16.

31. "President Bush's Address on Terrorism Before a Joint Meeting of Congress," *New York Times,* September 21, 2001, B4. Subsequent quotations from the speech are taken from this text.

32. "Bush's Remarks on U.S. Military Strikes in Afghanistan," *New York Times,* October 8, 2001, B6.

33. Seelye and Bumiller, "Bush Labels," A16.

34. "Bush's Remarks on U.S. Military Strikes," B6.

35. See Murray Edelman, *The Symbolic Uses of Politics* (Urbana: Univ. of Illinois Press, 1964), and *Politics as Symbolic Action* (Chicago: Markham, 1971), for an elaboration of this view.

36. R. W. Apple Jr., "A Clear Message: I Will Not Relent," *New York Times,* September 22, 2001, A1.

37. These poll data may be found at the web site of the *National Journal* (November 13, 2002).

38. David S. Broder, "Echoes of Lincoln," *Washington Post,* September 23, 2001, B7; Richard Cohen, "Taking Command," *Washington Post,* September 22, 2001, A29. I am indebted for these citations to Trevor Parry-Giles.

39. On terministic screens, see Kenneth Burke, *Language as Symbolic Action* (Berkeley and Los Angeles: Univ. of California Press, 1966), 44–55.

40. Paul Starr, "9–11, One Year Later," *American Prospect* 13 (September 23, 2002): 2.

41. This argument is advanced, for example, by Serge Schmemann, "After Months of War, Long Fights Still to Wage," *New York Times,* May 26, 2002, sec. 4, p. 4.

42. Howard Witt, "Terror War Has U.S. in Dubious Alliances," *Chicago Tribune,* September 4, 2002, sec. 1, p. 1.

43. Zbigniew Brzezinski, "Confronting Anti-American Grievances," *New York Times,* September 1, 2002, sec. 4, p. 9.

44. Hoffmann, "America Alone," 20.

45. David E. Sanger, "Hard Choices for Bush," *New York Times,* April 1, 2002, A1.

46. See, for example, Neil MacFarquhar, "Egypt Assails the Lumping of U.S. War with Israel's," *New York Times,* May 1, 2002, A11.

47. "Transcript: Confronting Iraq Threat 'Is Crucial to Winning War on Terror,'" *New York Times,* October 8, 2002, A12. This is a transcript of a speech President Bush delivered in Cincinnati on October 7, 2002.

48. "Transcript: Confronting Iraq Threat," A12.

49. On the concept of rhetorical trajectories, see Leland M. Griffin, "When Dreams Collide: Rhetorical Trajectories in the Assassination of President Kennedy," *Quarterly Journal of Speech* 70 (May 1984): 111–31.

50. For a fuller exposition of this view of rhetorical culture, see Thomas B. Farrell, *Norms of Rhetorical Culture* (New Haven, Conn.: Yale Univ. Press, 1993).

51. I discuss this sort of discourse more fully in David Zarefsky, "Definitions," in *Argument in a Time of Change: Proceedings of the 10th NCA/AFA Summer Conference on Argumentation,* ed. James F. Klumpp (Annandale, Va.: National Communication Assn., 1998), 1–11.

The Rushmore Effect
Ethos *and National Collective Identity*

Carole Blair and Neil Michel

Isn't this whole thing a little—well, preposterous? Is the word "bizarre" too much here? We're talking about a 14-year project to hack four 60-foot heads out of a wilderness mountain 174 miles from everywhere.

Donald Dale Jackson

This project was initially motivated by a kind of incredulity, of the sort that asks, How in the world could this have happened? We have been unable to resist "irreverent musings" about Mount Rushmore (fig. 1), even without the encouragement offered by Donald Dale Jackson.[1] Like other U.S. residents, we ordinarily take for granted the faces blasted into the stone near Keystone, South Dakota, simply because of the figure's ubiquitous presence in our everyday lives. The predictable use of Rushmore as shorthand for patriotism or as a backdrop for political announcements is the least of it. From the memorable image of Cary Grant and Eva Marie Saint dangling from the presidential faces in Hitchcock's 1959 film *North by Northwest,* and the appropriations of Rushmore to advertise auto dealerships and department stores' Presidents' Day sales, to the memorial's recurrent satirization (e.g., by superimposing the face of Alfred E. Neuman or portraying the naked derrieres of the presidents on the lee side of the mountain), we are inundated by Mount Rushmore.

The omnipresence of Mount Rushmore's appropriation and reproduction garners for it an invisibility oddly wrought by its very familiarity. But when we look for it, it seems to be everywhere. Less frequently appropriated for political, commercial, or satirical ends are the two other U.S. "mountain carvings": Stone Mountain (Stone Mountain, Georgia) and Crazy Horse (Custer, South Dakota), and so our incredulous question might seem to have more resonance in relation to them.[2] But it remains for Rushmore as well: How in the world did a mountain in the Harney Range of the Black Hills of South Dakota end up as a giant commemorative monument? So, the initial question we seek to answer is how Rushmore came to be.

The story has been told often; historians, biographers, and site interpreters usually credit Rushmore to the visionary and courageous, if neurotic, sculptor Gutzon Borglum.[3] But they also acknowledge others in the telling, especially South Dakota State Historian Doane Robinson. In the early 1920s, Robinson had been thinking of new ways to increase tourism in the Black Hills in order to liberate the state's economic base from its "two-industry economy, its feast or famine mining booms dependent on markets thousands of miles away and its even more dependent farm and ranch community."[4] Borglum was a relatively prominent sculptor, and his fame had increased significantly because of the project he was working on—a Confederate memorial on Stone Mountain, in Georgia.[5] Invited by Robinson to South Dakota in 1924, Borglum agreed to a mountain sculpture in the Black Hills.[6] Although Robinson's original idea had been for a sculpture of "heroes of the old west," he agreed to Borglum's counterproposal to sculpt national figures.[7]

Mount Rushmore was "carved" during a fourteen-year period, extending from 1927 to 1941. The idea for the memorial evolved over time, but in the end, Borglum and his associates agreed on the four figures to be included—George Washington, Thomas Jefferson, Abraham Lincoln, and Theodore Roosevelt—along with a theme justifying their presence together on the mountain. Most Rushmore storytellers recount the herculean efforts of Senator Peter Norbeck, Congressman William Williamson, and businessman John A. Boland. These patient yet persistent South Dakotans kept the money flowing for the unlikely "sculptural" equipment to create the giant figures. And when funds were unavailable, they managed somehow to sustain their own and the sculptor's faith in the monument's completion.

The stories told about Rushmore almost always take account of the difficult economic conditions in the nation and the consequent struggles to raise funds, the occasionally negative or indifferent reaction of the citizenry, the varying effects of publicity stunts to enhance national interest (and financing), the often caustic relationships among the principal players involved in the project, the sometimes daunting institutional arrangements of the sculptor and the memorial association with the Department of Interior and Congress, the technical difficulties in carving a mountain, and so forth. But most accounts, including interpretation at the Rushmore site, tell the story of how these obstacles were encountered and overcome, to the great advantage of South Dakota and the nation. Rushmore was placed under the jurisdiction of the National Park Service on June 10, 1933, by executive order of President Franklin Roosevelt. Gutzon Borglum died in March 1941, before the memorial was finished. His son, Lincoln Borglum, who would also be named as the Park Service's first superintendent of Mount Rushmore National Memorial (1941–44), completed the finishing work on the mountain in October of that year.

The story of Mount Rushmore is more complicated than its usual telling, in at least two respects. First, while no one should dismiss the importance of the fiercely interesting, iconoclastic characters responsible for the Rushmore memorial, every culture and era has its quixotic artists and bit players who support their quests. Few, however, have made the extraordinary, arguably injudicious, decision to turn mountains into sculpture. So, while we will attend to the standard stories, complete with their engaging and ebullient characters, we hope to explore here also what may have been additional factors that made the Rushmore project seem not only possible but desirable.[8] Second, the Rushmore narratives typically end with the "completion" of the mountain carving in 1941.[9] But the story obviously does not end there; construction of the Rushmore memorial was not an end in itself. So we will focus attention on the related question of what happened after its completion, of what the Mount Rushmore memorial *did*. What effect did it have on South Dakota? What effect did it have on public commemoration? Given the evidence of official interpretation of the Memorial, what is the rhetorical response it seeks of its visitors? What are the contours of collective national identity offered by this implausible presence on the U.S. landscape? It is not only the questions we pose here that differentiate our account from most others about Rushmore. It differs in critical attitude as well. While most commentators take Rushmore to be an exemplary icon of the American patriotic landscape, we find it difficult to accept as a positive marker of national identity, virtue, or even commemoration.

Our focus in this chapter is on Mount Rushmore as a rhetorical phenomenon, that is, as a "partisan, meaningful, consequential" site.[10] More specifically, our concerns with Rushmore are animated by issues related to *ethos. Ethos* may not appear initially to be the most natural theoretical construct, given the questions we have posed. Our first question especially, about the historical conditions that produced Rushmore, at first may seem to oust the creativity or character of Gutzon Borglum, the rhetor/artist, from the motivational matrix of the memorial's rhetoric, thus rendering *ethos,* at least as traditionally conceived, irrelevant. As Kennedy claims, *ethos,* according to Aristotle, "means 'character,' [especially] 'moral character.'"[11] Craig R. Smith argues elsewhere in this book that the Aristotelian concept of *ethos* must be understood in terms of moral virtues and their relation to deliberate choice. Although our primary focus will not be upon Gutzon Borglum's register of virtues (or vices) nor the rhetorical choices he made in creating Mount Rushmore, a traditional understanding of *ethos* is still important, for Borglum's *narrated role* as rendered in historical accounts and in official interpretation remains significant to most views of Rushmore.

More important in dealing with Mount Rushmore, though, is a decidedly different understanding of *ethos.* Michael J. Hyde describes *ethos* as "the 'abode' or 'dwelling place' that founds our communal relationships with others and wherein a person's moral character is developed."[12] Hyde's description can bind what we take to be one of the most important assumptions of memory studies to both rhetoric and ethics. That assumption is that constructions of memory offer particular versions of collective identity to their adherents. Put differently, the way we understand the past at least implicitly underwrites our understandings of who we are or who we should be in the present and future. As Lefebvre argued, "Monumental space offered each member of a society an image of that membership, an image of his or her social visage. It thus constituted a collective mirror." He suggested that a monument "effected a 'consensus,' and this in the strongest sense of the term, rendering it practical and concrete."[13] We believe it is more convincing to suggest that monuments, as material constructions of memory, *seek* (rather than necessarily effect) a consensus.[14] But it is useful to think of Mount Rushmore, both figuratively and literally, as constituting a dwelling place of national character, a construction of the national *ethos*. This traditional idea of a commemorative monument is closely related also to the Isocratean notion of *ethos*. As Hyde argues in the introduction to this book, Isocrates advocated exposure to exemplary individuals and events as a way to cultivate moral character and civic responsibility.

Mount Rushmore is important, thus, because it nominates for us a particular "consensual" mirror of the American past and present.[15] It marks out a particular image of the national *ethos*. Its makers and interpreters have understood that clearly. As Lincoln Borglum remarked, "There on the mountain, the sculptor has spoken eloquently with his art, an eloquence that says simply, 'This is what it means to be an American!'"[16] The significance of the Rushmore message is predicated in statements like these about national identity, in the fact that approximately two million people each year travel to see the mountain carving,[17] and in its pervasive appropriation and reproduction in popular and political culture.

In the critical analysis that follows, we read other discourses together with the memorial in order to understand and assess it as a rhetorical phenomenon. As Assman suggests, "The topoi and narratives that appear in monuments need an institutionalized communication, without which their reuse cannot be organized. Therefore, we do not only inquire into the history, form and meaning of the monuments as artifacts, but also into the history of their use and reuse."[18] We take this "institutionalized communication" to consist of what Mechling and Mechling call the "home society" of a discourse, in which "[t]exts refer to each other, the ability to understand some texts depends upon experience with others, and so on."[19] We concentrate especially on interpretive and press accounts, both historical and contemporary, in "reading" Rushmore. Moreover, we situate it within a cultural discourse about other major building projects of the time, including but not limited to commemorative building. It is nearly impossible also, in a discussion of conditions and effects, to separate Rushmore from the other mountain carvings in the United States: Stone Mountain and Crazy Horse. Indeed, an account of the conditions that produced Mount Rushmore necessarily begins at Stone Mountain, Georgia.

What Made Rushmore Possible?

Stone Mountain

There is no doubt that the idea to enhance tourism by carving a mountain in the Black Hills of South Dakota came to Doane Robinson in part because of the publicity accorded to the Stone Mountain Confederate Memorial, already in progress in Georgia.[20] So the question of what made the Mount Rushmore memorial possible turns on the prior question of how the Stone Mountain project came to be. Stone Mountain is an isolated granite peak of about 825 feet, sixteen miles east of Atlanta. Generally acknowledged as the first public suggestion for a memorial there was a 1914 *Atlanta Constitution* editorial by William H. Terrell, a Confederate veteran and Atlanta resident. According to David B. Freeman, Terrell had been bothered for years "by the perception that the Southern perspective had been neglected in modern histories and that Northern states and the Grand Army of the Republic had spent millions of dollars on memorials to their heroes while the South had not."[21] Although many local monuments to the Confederacy populated towns throughout the region,[22] Terrell had something grander in mind, though interestingly, not a carving in the mountainside. He proposed "to carve niches into the vertical face of the mountain where might be placed great statues of leading Confederates. A museum in the form of a Greek temple could be erected on top of the mountain, which would be dedicated as a public park."[23]

Terrell's editorial and another several weeks later, by John Temple Graves, in *The Georgian,* caught the attention of C. Helen Plane, an organizer of both the Atlanta and Georgia state chapters of the United Daughters of the Confederacy (UDC).[24] It was she, with the support of other UDC members, who contacted Gutzon Borglum to consider the matter. The UDC members described to Borglum their hope for a relief carving of Robert E. Lee on the side of the Mountain. Borglum was interested in the UDC idea but reportedly suggested that they should plan for a much larger, more ambitious project, for the Mountain was too large for the sculpture they had in mind; he is reported to have said it would look like a postage stamp on a barn door.[25] He proposed that they consider a relief image of multiple Confederate leaders riding ahead of a whole army of marching soldiers. He told them the project would cost $2 million, and in an apparent act of exploiting sectional sensibilities, pointed out that that was a sum similar to the planned expenditures for the Lincoln Memorial in Washington, D.C.[26]

Borglum was commissioned in 1915 to complete his expanded version of the sculpture. His initial negotiations with the UDC and the newly formed Stone Mountain Confederate Memorial Association (SMCMA) occurred during a year of striking sectional and racial fervor, particularly in the South. Of the seventy lynchings in the United States in 1915, twenty-two occurred in Georgia.[27] D. W. Griffith's film *The Birth of a Nation* was released that year as well. Lavender suggests that whites "flocked to join the rejuvenated Ku Klux Klan" in the years following its release.[28] The Klan was reinvigorated in the autumn at Stone Mountain, promoted, as Boime argues, by "those still nursing resentments over Reconstruction and anxious about loss of status in the changing American social structure."[29] Among the participants in the first mountaintop ceremony was Samuel H. Venable, who owned Stone Mountain. But the enthusiasm for the Klan among the Stone Mountain participants was not limited to Venable. Borglum himself became an involved and high-ranking member. He even agreed to include a Klan altar in his plans for the memorial to acknowledge a request of Helen Plane, who wrote him in 1915: "'Birth of a Nation' will give us a percentage of Monday's matinee. . . . I feel it is due to the KKK which saved us from Negro domination and carpetbag rule, that it be immortalized on Stone Mountain. Why not represent a small group of them in their nightly uniform approaching in the distance?"[30] The Stone Mountain memorial would be massive, but in sentiment it would be not so very different from other Confederate memorials, which, as Breed suggests, "were erected as protests against Northern domination and to let locals know where things stood."[31]

Work on the Georgia memorial was slow and sporadic, partly due to the practical difficulty of the undertaking. Borglum and his site supervisor, Jesse Tucker, had to rig equipment so that they could work safely suspended from the top of the mountain, figure out a way to transfer scaled markings from the sculptural model to the mountain by means of a giant slide projector, and learn to use dynamite blasts and drills to remove stone in a controlled manner.[32] The project was stalled by Tucker's departure to fight in World War I. Because of the seemingly perpetual lack of funds for the project, work did not resume until 1923. Thereafter, Borglum would alternate work on the mountain and feuding with the SMCMA, usually over money. And in 1925, after having completed only the head of Robert E. Lee, Borglum was fired. His dismissal created quite a stir since he also destroyed all the plaster scale models for the project so that no other sculptor could appropriate his work.

The reasons for Borglum's dismissal probably were manifold. Some hold that it came about as a result of infighting among factions of the Ku Klux Klan with Borglum involved in the strife.[33] Whether the Klan conflict was the most proximate cause of Borglum's firing, there was considerable, often public, discord between Borglum and some members of the SMCMA.[34] Less often mentioned as a possible contributor to the anger of the SMCMA, though, was Borglum's publicized travel to South Dakota in 1924 to discuss the Rushmore project. Although it seems unlikely that the Georgians would be angry at Borglum for simply taking on a simultaneous project, he may have raised their ire by considering the project of a "Northern" or "Union" memorial. Rex Alan Smith accounts for the association members' hostility: "[Borglum] had even journeyed to South Dakota, they complained. . . . And why? To look into carving on a mountain there a memorial which, according to rumor, was to be to the *Union!*"[35]

Whatever the causes of the conflict, Borglum's days at Stone Mountain were over. The SMCMA made several inquiries of prominent sculptors to take over the work, but most refused. They finally came to an agreement with New York sculptor Augustus Lukeman to complete the memorial. Lukeman began the project with his own design and had Borglum's work blasted off the face of the mountain. But he was to make little more progress than Borglum had, again, presumably because of funding difficulties. The Stone Mountain project was closed down in 1928 and remained that way until 1962. Borglum's failure to produce on his promises for Stone Mountain created some difficulties for the planned Rushmore memorial. Among them was the simple fact that it looked like a risky investment to many possible financial contributors. Additionally, a number of public broadsides were launched by his opponents in Georgia, and they made certain to distribute the published attacks as widely as possible in South Dakota.[36]

Although the Stone Mountain debacle created some difficulties, it also helped to make Rushmore possible in at least three ways. First, despite having been discharged, Borglum had proven that he could carve a mountain. Boime appropriately calls Stone Mountain "a critical dress rehearsal for Borglum's Mount Rushmore" because it was "at Stone Mountain that the sculptor learned how to use dynamite and pneumatic drills to remove the stone and block out the design, as well as to think about ways in which to harness drillers to enable them to work safely and comfortably on the side of a mountain."[37] Second, the Stone Mountain humiliation most likely kept Borglum on the job at Rushmore. As Fite points out, "On many a trying occasion he might have quit at Mount Rushmore had not the specter of Stone Mountain haunted him. He frankly admitted that he wanted to vindicate himself elsewhere."[38] And of course, "a second Stone Mountain experience would undoubtedly have affected his reputation adversely."[39]

Third, despite the highly questionable objective of creating the "greatest monument in the world" to the memory of the Confederacy,[40] there appears to have been surprisingly little public opposition to the Stone Mountain project. The U.S. Mint's commemorative Stone Mountain coin, planned as part of a fundraising campaign for the memorial, was opposed by the Grand Army of the Republic (a Union veterans organization) on the grounds that it honored "treason," but the opposition failed to halt the production of the coin.[41] One explanation for the lack of more stringent opposition is the generally held view that public commemoration of the Civil War in the South was "part of a healthy process of sectional reconciliation."[42] Another is that Borglum had found a way of talking about the Stone Mountain memorial that would divert attention from the substantive message of the memorial's symbolism, a discourse that would prove useful with Rushmore as well. When it suited his purposes Borglum clearly exploited sectional anxieties and prejudices in talking to the memorials' sponsors.[43] Indeed, in correspondence with his supporters, he frequently referred to the two projects as "the Southern memorial" and "the Northern memorial." But Borglum spoke publicly about both Stone Mountain and Mount Rushmore in a decidedly different way, one that drew on themes that were familiar in popular discourses of the time and lent legitimacy to the mountain projects, thereby contributing to a profound change in public commemoration.

Shifting the Discourse of Commemoration

Any look at turn-of-the-century public commemorative art practices in the United States yields a glimpse of a clear dialectic between local and national commemoration, perhaps discussed most thoroughly in John Bodnar's, Grant Foster's, and Kirk Savage's fine works.[44] The Washington Monument finally had been completed in the 1880s. But local commemoration predominated until the early years of the twentieth century. Literally hundreds of local Civil War memorials were dedicated in villages and towns of the nation. While the South in particular mounted a serious effort to commemorate the Civil War, the monuments were, for the most part, small, underwhelming, and scattered. As Foster suggests, "At a distance, one looked pretty much like the next. . . . As time went on, more and more of the soldiers were mass-produced models purchased from monument companies. In 1915 North Carolina editor Clarence Poe claimed that most of the monuments did little to make 'anybody's heart beat faster' or give 'any child a vision of the spirit, heroism and pathos of our Civil War period.' Later, William Alexander Percy, who grew up among the monuments, damned them as 'pathetic' and unworthy of the men they honored."[45]

Around the turn of the century, the national government began to reappropriate the commemorative art scene, particularly in the nation's capital city. The 1893 Columbian Exhibition in Chicago and the ensuing City Beautiful movement were two of the more important influences on the development of the Senate Park Commission report, better known as the McMillan plan (1902), for Washington, D.C.'s development and beautification. Because the plan called for coordinated management of federal space, Congress created the U.S. Commission of Fine Arts to advise on matters of public art largely in Washington.

The effect was twofold. First, the Fine Arts Commission and the McMillan plans were harbingers of the nationalization of public commemoration that would take hold with the Perry Victory Memorial (Put-in-Bay, Ohio, 1912–13), and with planning for the Lincoln Memorial as well as the Grant Memorial. These tendencies would also produce the Tomb of the Unknown Soldier in Arlington National Cemetery.[46] Such centralization, indeed, nationalization of the commemorative impulse placed the new federal plans in competitive and critical juxtaposition with local commemoration. Local commemoration of war heroes, pioneers, and so forth would continue apace of course. But it was not unusual in the early years of the twentieth century to read commentary that suggested the federal government or other central authority needed to intervene in the domain of public artworks in the interests of purging the landscape of mass-produced, cheap, and aesthetically dreadful art. That description applied perhaps most coldly to the Southern civil war monuments. There would be no federal monuments to the South, of course, so unless a major project was undertaken cooperatively among the former Confederate states, they would be doomed to their small, cheap, local, and decidedly unfashionable monuments.

Second, the U.S. Fine Arts Commission and Macmillan board, like the City Beautiful movement, harbored a strong commitment to classical and Beaux-Arts tendencies, with strong leanings toward Greek columns, roman arches and domes, realistic equestrian statuary, European allegorical images, and a more than occasional obelisk. As Scott and Lee note, "Architectural advisors [to the Senate Park Commission] were Daniel Burnham of Chicago and Charles F. McKim of New York, the design leaders of the World's Columbian Exhibition.... The landscape architect was [Frederick Law] Olmstead, whose father had worked with Burnham and McKim in 1893. Augustus Saint-Gaudens, the chief sculptor at the Chicago fair, was later added to the commission.... Public buildings, they believed . . . should be varied in form but derived from classical prototypes."[47]

A common theme had been sounded since the nation's founding: the "problem" of establishing a uniquely American art.[48] As van Leeuwen points out, articles with nationalistic overtones, as for example, "'The Search for an American Style,' [in] *American Architect and Building News* . . . appeared with a certain regularity."[49] Artists in the early national period were almost all educated in Europe, and their works reflected the aesthetic of the French and Italian training they had received. The appropriation of classical architectural forms for most building projects, including major memorials, was explicit. Instead of understanding that derivation as a "problem," however, the Park Commission declared it a virtue.

Early-century commemorative artworks followed the directives of the Commission, in emulating classical and European styles. The only real departure from ancient Western and European prototypes was in their often massive scale. The Washington Monument's Egyptian form is unmistakable, and it was joined in the capital's monumental core by the Lincoln Memorial's emulation of the Parthenon and later by the Jefferson Memorial's apparent modeling of the Roman Pantheon.[50] Following the lead of the Washington Monument, which was the tallest structure in the world when it was built, many commemorative art pieces used visual scale to convey importance.[51] The Perry Victory and International Peace Memorial (Put-in-Bay, Ohio), commemorating the centennial of Perry's victory on the Great Lakes during the War of 1812, is a gigantic, Greek-inspired Ionic column, probably still the largest such column in the world, as it was when it was built. The Grant Memorial (Washington, D.C.), which follows the European equestrian statuary prototype, represented the largest cast sculptural group to be found anywhere in the United States. Its central equestrian figure of Grant was "said to be the second largest such bronze in the world" and, in fact, it still is.[52] Likewise, the Lincoln Memorial was touted as the "largest marble building ever constructed."[53]

Fig. 1. Mount Rushmore. Photograph by Neil Michel.

Fig. 2. Attractions on the "Road to Rushmore." Photograph by Neil Michel.

Fig. 3. Stone Mountain. Photograph by Neil Michel.

Fig. 4. The Crazy Horse Memorial. Photograph by Neil Michel.

Fig. 5. The visitor center at Mount Rushmore. Photograph by Neil Michel.

Fig. 6. Interactive exhibit in the museum area. Photograph by Neil Michel.

Fig. 7. Mount Rushmore. Photograph by Neil Michel.

Public discussions of the mountain carvings link up with the themes of these early twentieth-century discourses and building practices, but with some significant variations. Commonplace during and since the time of their construction have been commentaries on their immense scale, their contribution of a national art form for the United States, and their supposed links to wonders of the ancient world. It certainly is true that the mountain carvings did not emulate any classical genre; in fact, Borglum despised such an idea.[54] But while he eschewed classical forms, he used ancient structures as benchmarks of scale.

Borglum's own discourse was almost certainly accountable early on for the ways in which the mountain carvings would be articulated with public art and building projects. In a letter to one of his Southern supporters in 1915, he wrote that Stone Mountain "will make for the south a place of pilgrimage such as the Acropolis has been to Greece and pyramids such as for Egypt."[55] The media appropriated such discourse during the work on the Georgia monument. A *New York American* story titled "The World's Eighth Wonder" reported enthusiastically, "The great Sphinx at Gizah would sink out of sight behind Lee's head. The Colossi of Memnon at Thebes would barely reach to Lee's stirrup. The apex of the great Pyramid of Egypt would be short a hundred feet of reaching the hoofs of Lee's horse. A sixteen-story skyscraper would be overtopped by the central figure of the group. A horse's head measures fifty feet, the height of a five-story building."[56] Claims for mountain carving as a signature national art form would have been rather awkward in discussions of a memorial to the Confederacy. That theme would emerge only in the enthusiastic promotions for and receptions of the Rushmore project.

As with Stone Mountain, Borglum offered many of the words that would be repeated and circulated by media outlets. The three themes of scale, ancient prototypes, and an American national style emerged, indeed merged, in a 1931 publicity pamphlet for Mount Rushmore. There Borglum wrote of the great ancient civilizations of Greece, Rome, China, and Egypt, as well as ancient figures like Darius, Agrippa, Pericles, and Plutarch, as the context for his work.[57] He compared Rushmore to the Colossus of Rhodes, which, he suggested, would be "very little taller than the length of the face of Washington." And he concluded that "Colossal art has another value—human and soul stirring—that should be incorporated permanently in all National expression—consciously and deliberately in scale with its importance—in scale with the people whose life it expresses."[58] In what was perhaps his most brash assertion of the importance of scale, he claimed, "Once understood, life takes on a wholly new value for you have given a new standard of measurement for the material and the living, conscious universe; for the bigness as against the littleness of everything in it. I have said colossal was a matter of scale, relativity. And I have often hinted that we in America are developing in dimensions out of all proportion to the civilizations that inspired and freed us, but which long have cramped our style."[59]

Newspapers and magazines seemed only too happy to comment on the spectacle of the ongoing project, and in similar terms. Said Susman, "Sculptor Borglum has his own way of doing things. Generally they are done in a big way. The bigger the better." She continued: "If we compare this one [Washington] (remembering that there are four) of the national Black Hills faces in stone to other famous statues of the world, we find that the Colossus of Rhodes, one of the seven wonders of the ancient world, indeed seems a mere dwarf with its 105 feet, and the Great Sphinx of Gizah, with its head 30 feet in length, is only eight feet less than twice the size of Washington's nose."[60] Implying the nationalist theme as well, she referred to Rushmore as the "pyramids of America." Parmley called Rushmore "this greatest carving of the ages," also incorporating size comparisons to the Colossus of Rhodes, the Sphinx, and the Statue of Liberty.[61] The *Kansas City Star* reported that Borglum's "mission" was "giving America a national type of monument that will be as characteristic of this nation as the pyramids were of Egypt or the cathedrals of medieval Europe."[62] The *New York Times Magazine* crowed, "Never before has sculpture been undertaken on so great a scale,"[63] and the *Detroit News* dubbed Rushmore "the greatest sculpture ever conceived by man."[64] *Time* labeled Borglum appropriately "a specialist in immensity."[65]

This was unusual discourse to describe or promote a commemorative project not only because of its hubris but also because of its redistribution of the status of ancient structures. They were now to be benchmarks of size rather than the preferred stylistic models. But the ways in which Rushmore and its Georgia predecessor were described and lauded were familiar, in fact, nearly identical to the discourses about architectural and engineering projects of the time. The discourse of enormity almost certainly found its source in the culture of the corporation and giant public works projects. Pomeroy argues that "Rushmore was associated with other big projects of the '30s—Boulder Dam, TVA, and the Golden Gate Bridge—reinforcing ideas like Yankee ingenuity, impossible accomplishment, precision engineering, utilization of great power on a huge scale, new technology, man taming nature, and better living through science and industry."[66]

Skyscrapers, as Abramson suggests, "offered opportunities to design buildings larger than any others in history, firing creative imaginations, and creating strong personal identifications."[67] The Washington Monument lasted only a few years as the world's tallest structure before it was bested by the Eiffel Tower, in 1889. And it would be displaced as the nation's tallest structure in 1908, when the Singer Building was erected in New York City. As both Abramson and van Leeuwen point out, architects and patrons did not necessarily see themselves as in a contest for the tallest building, but "height competition made good news."[68] The skyscraper competition ended for a time with the Chrysler, RCA, and Empire State Buildings, in the early 1930s, the middle years of the Rushmore project.

The public works and corporate building projects also were described in the same kind of relationship to ancient works as the mountain carvings were. The

Brooklyn Bridge was hailed as "the eighth wonder of the world."[69] So was the Empire State Building. In fact, Theodore James Jr. claimed that this particular "eighth wonder" was "as high as all the original Seven Wonders piled on top of the other."[70] O. F. Semsch characterized the Singer Building as being "as distinctive a feature of the skyline of New York as the Egyptian pyramids are of the Valley of the River Nile."[71] As van Leeuwen observes, "Those involved with the creation of the American city were often thought to have been guided by the Wonders of the World."[72]

These new buildings and structures also were acclaimed as distinctively American. "Seldom," wrote Alfred Bossom in 1928, "has architecture so accurately portrayed the characteristics of a nation as does the skyscraper."[73] Louis Lozowick wrote in 1927, "The history of America is a history of gigantic engineering feats and colossal mechanical constructions."[74] Among the feats he enumerated were skyscrapers, grain elevators, steel mills, oil wells, and other very tall structures. Van Leeuwen concludes that "the skyscraper had achieved the status of a distinct architectural type, and had even been acknowledged as characteristic of American civilization."[75]

The idiom Borglum and the press had commandeered to describe Stone Mountain and Rushmore was already in use in the service of these marvels of engineering and architectural accomplishment. And the extension of the discourse could be made relatively easily, given that size already had been thematized as a feature of commemorative tribute, that classical models had been in vogue, and that the "Americanism" of commemorative works was considered a serious objective. Although Borglum also publicly assailed more traditional monuments on occasion, he never appears to have used that condemnation as the explicit motivation for a new kind of monument. He simply changed the discourse of commemorative sculpture to resemble that of corporate and public engineering projects.

Government Support and Public Reaction

Stone Mountain seemed to prove that mountain carving could be successful on a giant scale, and Rushmore's proponents' found a discourse for advocacy that dovetailed effectively with other popular themes of the era. But Rushmore still would not have materialized without financial support and ongoing public advocacy. Nearly everyone who has written about Mount Rushmore has taken note of the important contributions of Senator Peter Norbeck and Congressman William Williamson in working the Congress for public funding of the project. And most, too, have noted that Rushmore was in the news frequently, which helped to maintain public interest and to forestall most public opposition. Zinsser's personal memory of the project is telling:

> The carving of the four Presidents ran through my entire boyhood like an alternating current, stopping for long periods when the money ran out. I never quite

took it seriously; it was another one of those Depression-era oddities, like the Dionne quintuplets. Somewhere out West, starting in 1927, a sculptor whose very name said 'mad scientist'—Gutzon Borglum!—was blasting one of God's mountains and promising to bring forth four imminent heads. Even when the project was broke he was often in the news, badgering Congress for more money or hounding current occupants of the White House to turn up for dedication ceremonies that P. T. Barnum would have admired for their showmanship.[76]

If people were not quite swept up in Borglum's vision, they at least found it interesting, as Zinsser did. The Rushmore project never attracted the large private and corporate donors that Robinson, Borglum, and the others had hoped would contribute, but the largely positive reaction by the press was almost certainly an aid in securing government support and appropriation. The federal government would end up funding about 85 percent of the monument's approximately $1 million cost. The fact that most of that support materialized during the depths of the Depression suggests just how successful the Rushmore newsmakers and supportive congressmen were.

Early on, though, the stage was set for government support and public relations by a rather unlikely figure—President Calvin Coolidge. Coolidge made the Black Hills his summer retreat in 1927. Prior to his arrival that year, the Rushmore proponents had been working on a proposal to seek governmental funding, since so few and such small contributions had been made to the project. Coolidge's stay in South Dakota that summer proved to be just the opening necessary to secure both a federal appropriation and positive press. The president not only attended and spoke at a dedication ceremony and agreed to support federal matching funds but also lent his support for a component of the project that would keep Rushmore constantly in the news for the crucial early years of the enterprise.

Borglum had planned to carve on the mountain what he called "the entablature," a giant carving of a five-hundred-word history of the United States that would serve as a kind of "signature" or explanation for the presence of the presidential busts. While Coolidge was in South Dakota, Borglum secured his agreement to write the brief history that would be carved on Rushmore. The agreement, of course, made headlines. So did Coolidge's first two "chapters" of the history, for it came to light that Borglum had taken the liberty of editing the president. The flap that ensued was widely publicized, keeping Rushmore in the news for some time. After Coolidge withdrew from the agreement to complete the entablature history, the Hearst newspapers ran a national contest and offered a prize for the best short historical account and with the implication that the prize winning history would be carved on the mountain.[77] Obviously, the entablature never materialized. There was no room for it in the area of carveable stone on the mountain. And there was never enough money to do it or to accomplish Borglum's even grander alternative—a hall of records.[78] But the entablature saga had created considerable publicity for Rushmore, not to mention presidential support for it and its first appropriation.

Consideration of the entablature raises an additional issue related to public reaction, for reports about the contest and its planning represented the first opportunity for most people to learn about what the memorial was intended to represent. Since the entablature was envisioned as the explanatory vehicle for the memorial, it is important to attend to its intended content. Borglum specified nine events in U.S. history that were to be the sum and substance of the entablature's historical narrative: the Declaration of Independence, the framing of the Constitution, the Louisiana Purchase, the admission of Texas to the Union, the ceding of Florida to the United States, the Oregon boundary settlement, the acquisition of California, the Alaska purchase, and the building of the Panama Canal. As Hilburn and Walker note rather matter-of-factly, "The central theme of these historical events is the expansion of America through Manifest Destiny, the belief that America had a right and duty to expand across North America."[79] The imperialist theme of the entablature is unmistakable, but it was no less clear for the memorial itself. According to Borglum, in a 1931 speech on the Colliers Radio Hour, "Jefferson appears on Mount Rushmore because he drew the Declaration of Independence and completed the Louisiana Purchase; Washington, because as the great presiding officer, he guided in council, was great in battle, and made possible and successful the struggle that followed; Lincoln, because it was Lincoln . . . whose mind, heart and finally life, determined that we should continue as a common family of states and in union forever. Roosevelt is joined with the others, because he completed the dream of Columbus, opened the way to India, joined the waters of the great East and West."[80] Even Borglum's contract with the original group in charge of overseeing and funding the project betrayed the theme: "The association [Mount Harney Memorial Association] has been formed to obtain the necessary funds and to create upon Rushmore Mountain . . . a memorial to the continental expansion of the Republic of the United States of America substantially as hereinafter set forth."[81]

It seems difficult to imagine now, even allowing for the benefit of hindsight, that there was not substantial negative reaction to the memorial's theme as it emerged in the news about the entablature. It is especially astonishing when we take into consideration the irony of location. Here was a planned monument honoring "continental expansion," sited in a territory that, by treaty, still belonged to the Lakota, and that the local Native people considered consecrated ground. There was *some* comment. For example, an Iowa newspaper declared that the proposed entablature represented an "imperial history" and proposed eight different events that the inscribed history should include.[82] But such observations were remarkably few and scattered. And as Zinsser accurately notes, "On the separate issue of Indian integrity—the fact that the Black Hills are sacred to the Sioux—nobody seems to have been particularly bothered at the time."[83] Just as had been the case with Stone Mountain, public response to the memorial's symbolic content seemed largely quiescent. It is difficult to account for that, although the parallels with the discourse about Stone Mountain, detailed earlier, may offer an explanation. Although the publicity surrounding the entablature was extensive, there was always Borglum or the willing newspaper editor reminding the public about the fact that Rushmore would be the largest monument in the world, that it would represent the first truly American art form, and that it was the greater equivalent for the United States of the Egyptian pyramids or Sphinx, or Darius's Behistun relief, or the Lion of Lucerne.[84]

In fact, what little opposition was expressed seems to have focused not on the symbolic content, but on the wisdom of carving a mountain. Fite quotes Florence Davies, a Detroit art critic, as saying that the "mountain . . . is a kind of earth sculpture of its own and loses its intrinsic majesty when man uses it as a billboard."[85] Cora B. Johnson, editor of a Hot Springs, South Dakota newspaper, wrote, "I think I get your idea of the unique character of such a carving in such a place but the fact that it would be unique and on a stupendous scale would by no means justify it in my eyes. It would be something like the spirit college youths display in risking life, limb, and official punishment in order to plant their class emblem in a higher or more unexpected place than it has ever been carried before, or than any other class emblem is taken. We look tolerantly on their scrambling, knowing that they will learn in time to differentiate between physical altitude and real accomplishment. But we do not emulate them."[86] These statements were more acerbic than most; generally critics poked fun at the memorial project and speculated about having whole mountain ranges cut into human figures.[87] But nearly all focused on the already moot question of whether a mountain should be carved, and almost never on the issue of what it should represent.

There is little question that the Mount Rushmore artist and his supporters had a profound influence on the success and character of the memorial project. But there certainly were other conditions in place that made Rushmore possible. Would it have been possible absent government support, public acquiescence, the prior experience of Stone Mountain, or the prevailing attitudes and discourses about skyscrapers and earlier commemorative art? Obviously, it is impossible to answer the question, but it certainly seems unlikely. The question of what made Rushmore possible, though, should lead us to focus less on historical causation and more on what "Mount Rushmore" was and what it has become for those it is supposed to mirror. The cultural phenomenon we call "Mount Rushmore" is more than the carving on the mountain; the rhetoric of the memorial is constituted in historical and contemporary discourses and contexts as surely as it is by the four heads. If we turn our attention now to Rushmore's more contemporary instantiations and effects, the significance of its history comes back to perturb it and helps us understand the character of the social "mirror" the memorial holds up in order for us to see ourselves.

The Mount Rushmore Effect

Assessments of Rushmore—as an artwork, as a tourist attraction, as a tendered portrait of the U.S. "consensus"—are mixed, of course. One might expect a booklet advertising South Dakota attractions to call Mount Rushmore "one of the nation's most beloved memorials."[88] But fairly typical among other public pronouncements, is Fite's: "As a patriotic shrine, Mount Rushmore has no equal in the United States. Congressman William Lemke, a great admirer of Borglum, said, 'No man or woman can view this monument without becoming a better citizen for it.' In the presence of the carved likenesses of American leaders, 'one could be nothing else but conscious of the responsibilities and meaning of democracy,' declared another onlooker. A multitude of people have given similar testimonies."[89] Rex Alan Smith's appraisal is similar, if more fervent: "All things considered, Mount Rushmore National Memorial is not only America's greatest and most enduring monument, it is all of mankind's as well."[90] These judgments seem to beg the questions they try to answer. What is beloved about Mount Rushmore? What is its version of patriotism? What does it suggest about being a better citizen? What does the memorial suggest are the responsibilities and meaning of democracy? And what makes it a great monument? What exactly has Mount Rushmore wrought? What was its effect on the character of commemorative art? What does it say to its many visitors? What is considered its message? What is the nature of the consensual mirror it raises to the face of the collective? And how do the historical conditions that made it possible figure into the more contemporary matrix?

The South Dakota Effect

There is no question that Doane Robinson's plan to attract tourists worked, but better, or at least differently, than he ever might have imagined. His goal, and Norbeck's as well, was to draw people to the Black Hills with an "attraction" so they would enjoy the beautiful scenery of the Hills, prairies, and Badlands. What has occurred, of course, is that their "attraction" spurred the development and enlargement of other such tourist lures. Literally hundreds of attractions dot the "Road to Rushmore," and most of them advertise themselves and their locations in relation to it (fig. 2). For example, the family can visit the Black Hills Maze; Jackalope Village; Bear Country, USA; Black Hills Caverns; the Flintstones Bedrock City; the Flying Chuckwagon Cowboy Supper and Show; Reptile Gardens; Cosmos Mystery Area; Rushmore Waterslide Park; Sitting Bull Crystal Caverns; Big Thunder Gold Mine; Parade of Presidents Historic Wax Museum; and Beautiful Rushmore Cave. Or they can ride on the Rushmore Aerial Tramway, Rushmore Helicopters, the Black Hills Central Railroad, or Black Hills Balloons. If they are driving, a "must see" is Iron Mountain Road, one of Senator Peter Norbeck's lasting contributions to the area; at the end of each of the (completely unnecessary) tunnels, a view of Mount Rushmore is framed.[91] There are also, of course, plenty of t-shirt stands, Black Hills gold jewelry stores, tour guide services, camp grounds, restaurant and snack shops, hotels and motels, and souvenir shops.

The reach of Rushmore's influence in what Pomeroy calls this "parasitic growth" is extensive and direct.[92] One of the best examples, and certainly one of the most famous, is Wall Drug, well east of Rushmore but owing its contemporary existence almost exclusively to the memorial. Its story is told in tourist pamphlets and even on the menu in the coffee shop, where a cup of coffee is still 5 cents. Between 1931 and 1936, the young owner of Wall Drug, a recent pharmacy school graduate, struggled to make ends meet in a Depression-wracked town of 326. His wife came up with the idea of advertising free ice water on signs along the road—the major route to Rushmore. The idea brought in hundreds of thirsty tourists from the first day the signs were placed, many of the visitors on their way to see the progress of construction on Mount Rushmore. And it has become a giant tourist attraction in its own right, with a café that seats 520 as well as its individual shops and stands featuring pottery, prints and posters, camera and photo supplies, western clothing, post cards, fudge, jewelry, donuts, gifts, and books. There is a "jack-a-lope," a western art gallery, an apothecary shop and pharmacy museum, an eighty-foot dinosaur in an outdoor playground, and of course, the ice water stand.[93] Twenty thousand people now visit Wall Drug on a "good day" in the summer.

Granted, what some people call "contamination," others, both residents and willing visitors, welcome. The South Dakota Governor's Office of Economic Development heads its tourism web page with this statement: "Tourism is one of South Dakota's largest industries, generating approximately $1.28 billion worth of economic activity each year and employing 27,500 people. More than 2.5 million people visit Mount Rushmore, South Dakota's top attraction each year."[94] Not insignificant is the agency's web address: "sdgreatprofits.com," or its mention of Rushmore in relationship to the revenue produced each year in tourism. The numbers are important to the state. Tourism is the only rival to agriculture as South Dakota's top industry. To be fair, Rushmore fulfilled the original objective of economic enrichment through tourism. It did so only at the expense of some of the landscape the planners hoped to acquaint visitors with. But regardless of how one might react to the array of tourist attractions or the revenue they generate, to assess Mount Rushmore or any other national memorial on those grounds alone seems cynical and incomplete, even as an assessment of its declared purpose. It certainly has had other consequences as well.

The Commemorative Art Effect

The years after Rushmore brought a much different kind of commemoration. The classically inspired Beaux-Arts memorial had become a thing of the past in the United States. In fact, even by the early 1940s, the design for the Jefferson

Memorial encountered considerable opposition, particularly from modernists who considered it to be "hopelessly old fashioned."[95] Physical scale remained important, as seen in the Jefferson National Expansion Memorial (the Gateway Arch, St. Louis, Mo.) and the world's largest bronze sculpture, the Marine Corps Memorial (Arlington, Va.). But these memorials were exceptions in being built at all, for the period between the early 1940s and the early 1980s saw almost no new national efforts at public commemorative art.[96]

Commemoration took the form of functionalism almost exclusively during that approximately forty-year period. Events and individuals were marked for memory by public works and civil engineering projects: freeways, campus memorial unions, bridges, auditoriums, parks, libraries, swimming pools, highway rest areas, and other public facilities. The Kennedy Center for the Performing Arts in Washington, D.C., is a prominent example; like many other functional memorials, it was not intended or designed originally to serve a commemorative function. The national cultural center project was well underway when President Kennedy was assassinated, and because of Kennedy's strong support of the arts, an effort was quickly initiated to make the Center serve in his honor.[97] This "functional" commemoration continues still, but now it occurs alongside a revived commemorative art boom, initiated in the early 1980s.[98] More national-scope memorials have been proposed and built since 1982 than at any time during the nation's history, almost as if to serve as a compensatory aesthetic gesture to the functionalism of the midcentury.[99]

Why did the United States, particularly in the 1940s, turn almost exclusively to this "functional" form of public commemoration? There are a number of possible explanations.[100] Certainly contributing to the decline of *classically inspired* commemoration was its guilt by association with European fascism.[101] More generally, though, the Depression era support of the arts by government, in programs like the Federal Arts Project, sustained a fair amount of opposition, also probably contributing to the decline in commemorative artworks.[102] Perhaps the most relevant cultural sentiment was that American progress and technological achievements themselves were monuments to the nation and purely celebratory works were unnecessary, even wasteful.[103]

It is certain that this new functional commemorative practice was overdetermined. But we believe the Rushmore phenomenon at least reinforced, and probably even contributed, to the new direction of the 1940s. Importantly, this new kind of commemoration severed the bond between memory and art and replaced it with a connection between memory and engineering. Because the physical size of a structure remained important as a marker of monumentality, Mount Rushmore could maintain a certain status because of its immensity. It must have been difficult, though, for artists to imagine how to commemorate in its wake. Rushmore had raised the stakes of size, identifying it alone as the marker of an authentic American style of commemoration. Even in the concurrent public discourse about skyscrapers, there was a willingness to admit that there was some "practical limit."[104] But standard sculptural works had become simply that—standard. The only means to accomplish something approaching honorific monumentality were the tools of the engineer.[105] How could an artwork, after all, be considered seriously as a tribute to its subject, if not by blasting an even larger mountain sculpture?

Precisely that occurred, of course. The Stone Mountain memorial project was revived in 1962, promising to be larger than Mount Rushmore.[106] The state of Georgia acquired Stone Mountain and the surrounding property and engaged Walter Hancock as the new project sculptor. Dedicated finally in 1970, Stone Mountain now is the centerpiece of a state park (fig. 3), operated by, and resembling to some degree, a theme park. There are cable car, scenic railroad, and riverboat rides; nineteen buildings assembled and preserved as an "antebellum plantation"; an antique auto and music museum; a wildlife trail; carillon concerts; golf and tennis venues; and a popular evening laser show at the memorial site itself. The park has its own hotels, restaurants, and gift shops. Its major thoroughfares are named for the three figures sculpted on the mountain: Jefferson Davis, Robert E. Lee, and Stonewall Jackson. The development of the park, in some respects, resembles the development on the road to Rushmore—a mishmash of attractions. In 1998, theme park operator Silver Dollar City took over all of the park's "commercial aspects."[107] Not surprisingly, the park's web site names Stone Mountain as "the eighth wonder of the world" and identifies itself as home to "the world's largest relief carving on the world's largest mass of exposed granite."[108] Stone Mountain, thus, became both a condition and an effect of Mount Rushmore.

An even more direct effect of Mount Rushmore is the memorial to Crazy Horse, only a few miles away, near Custer, South Dakota (fig. 4). The case is interesting and significant enough to elaborate in some detail. In 1931, Henry Standing Bear, a Lakota chief, approached Gutzon Borglum with the proposal to add the image of Crazy Horse to Mount Rushmore.[109] Later, Korczak Ziolkowski, a Polish American sculptor who had worked briefly on the Rushmore project, agreed to a similar request from the chief.[110] The Crazy Horse Memorial, begun in 1948, is still years from completion. Ziolkowski died in 1982, but his sizable family has taken up the project. Crazy Horse's face was declared complete in 1998. According to the interpreters on site, all four of the presidential heads up the road would fit inside his forehead. The Crazy Horse Memorial is planned as a massive centerpiece of a large complex that will allegedly benefit the Lakota people, by providing them with a university and teaching hospital, recreational facilities, an airport, and museum.[111] There are few signs that this development will materialize anytime soon. Currently, there is only the in-progress mountain carving, a visitor center and museum complex, a tour of Ziolkowski's studio and home, a large restaurant, and an even more outsized gift shop. Crazy Horse is billed on the premises and the organization's web site as "the world's largest sculpture."[112]

The presence of the Crazy Horse project, of course, makes a clear statement about one of the serious ideological issues attaching to Rushmore. The irony of constructing in the Black Hills what amounts to a memorial to U.S. imperialism is intensified and further complicated with Crazy Horse. The Crazy Horse project was, at base, a reassertion of Native presence and possession in the Black Hills. According to the literature published by the Crazy Horse Memorial, Henry Standing Bear told Korzcak, "My fellow chiefs and I would like the white man to know the red man had great hero's too [sic]."[113] However, as Simon Schama observes, "Indian campaigns, from the 1930s onward, to have the face of Crazy Horse or Sitting Bull inscribed on Rushmore or another mountain in the Black Hills . . . have been tragically self-defeating. Emulating the white obsession with visible possession, with self-inscription, with cutting the mountain heights to the scale of the human head, would, in the most poignant way imaginable, be to accept the terms of the conqueror."[114] The problem can hardly be better expressed than in Ziolkowski's own arrogant statement, reported by Brooke without even a trace of the ironic: "I will give the few remaining Indians a little pride."[115]

Although the request for a mountain carving of Crazy Horse apparently originated within the Lakota tribal leadership, there is no real consensus about it in their community. The most succinct challenge is represented by Warner and Katada, who report that some Native American leaders "wonder why the inappropriate Mount Rushmore carvings should be answered with an inappropriate carving of Crazy Horse."[116] A more specific set of charges is detailed in a 1997 letter to the editor of the *Rapid City Journal*. The writer suggests that the project "seems to lack many Lakota fans." Citing objections ranging from the aesthetic to economic exploitation, the writer concludes that the mountain carving dishonors the "great chief [who] was martyred for the freedom of his people."[117] But the Ziolkowskis' response always is that it was the tribal elders, after all, who asked for a sculpture, and they continue with that work.

None of this even addresses the most basic problem of both projects—that they disfigured Native sacred ground, land that the Lakota retain claim to under the terms of the 1868 Fort Laramie Treaty.[118] In any case, both Stone Mountain and Crazy Horse are part of the Rushmore effect.[119] Both Stone Mountain and Crazy Horse repeat Rushmore's equation of scale and worthy commemoration. They represent the exceptional cases in the midst of a much more commonly practiced functional commemoration after Rushmore. And like Rushmore, they invite us, as we shall see, to overlook their problematic ideological contents.

The Mirror Effect: National Identity
Given the problems these memorials all pose in terms of their intended messages, one must wonder how they are interpreted on site, in "official" interpretive

publications, or in press accounts that rely on official materials for their information. All three are predicated in ideological positions, often confused and contradictory, that harbor the potential for serious contestation and did even at the time they were under construction. We are confronted by Stone Mountain, a memorial to leaders of the Confederacy and by Rushmore, honoring the concept of American imperialism. Crazy Horse, though intended to right the wrongs of Rushmore, simply repeats them. So, the question of interpretation is crucial. After all, such interpretation is often precisely what visitors use to make sense of their visits to public history sites.

Zinsser's sensitive narrative of his trip to Mount Rushmore poses two questions that are useful in organizing any discussion of the interpretation of the sites. "Obviously," he states, "one question to think about is: 'How was this thing done?' But the real question that Mount Rushmore puts to us is not 'How?' but 'Why?' Why are those four men up there? The longer I looked, the more I felt the question working on me. . . . I'm not sure I could have said exactly what unifying idea about America those four Presidents embody. . . . Assuming that there was such an idea, I was curious to know how it gets imparted to two million tourists a year."[120]

Zinsser's questions must spark surprise from anyone familiar with other public commemorative sites. The "why" question obviously is the most prominent one that official interpretation of any historic site typically seeks to answer. That is, interpretation of most such sites identifies why the content is what it is. Visitors to the Lincoln Memorial, for example, learn about Lincoln's accomplishments, just as they focus on Vietnam veterans at the Vietnam Veterans Memorial, or attend to the achievements of the U.S. Navy at Washington's Navy Memorial. Clear attempts are made to say why the commemorated person, group, or idea merits a lasting tribute. Although the "how" question is sometimes answered, for example, with a small display at the Lincoln Memorial about the "making of the memorial," it clearly is not the focus of interpretive talks, tours, or literature. Lincoln is.

Sometimes a third question, "who," is added to the mix, but that is fairly rare. Few visitors probably leave the Lincoln Memorial with any lasting memory of its architect, Henry Bacon, or the sculptor of the seated Lincoln, Daniel Chester French. How many visitors walk away from the Franklin D. Roosevelt Memorial, knowing (or caring) that it was designed by Lawrence Halprin? The usual point of interpretation, of course, remains the content of the memorial, why the commemorated subject has been singled out for remembrance. But the typicality of interpretation is shattered at Rushmore and at the other two mountain sculpture sites and in the literature that informs the public about them. We will describe Rushmore's interpretation most extensively in what follows, but we will supplement with Stone Mountain and Crazy Horse, for the differences are minimal and the parallels telling.

Interpretation of the mountain sculptures features principally the "how" question, with a secondary focus on "who." "Why" merits a tertiary status at most.

Emphasized most is how the mountains were turned into monuments. At Rushmore, the new Lincoln Borglum Museum features two principal environments: an anteroom with a view of the mountain and multiple storyboards and an interior museum display area (fig 5).[121] Both display areas are dominated by the materials and explanations of construction and preservation of the monument. Indeed, that focus is almost assured by an interactive exhibit in the museum area which allows the visitor to set off a simulated dynamite charge (fig 6). The constant sound of "explosions" and the loudly expressed delight from visitors draw other visitors to that location more than any other in the museum. The museum area's walls as well as the two flanking walls of the anteroom are lined with giant photo enlargements of men working on the mountain, usually suspended by cables over a prominent feature of a face.

Six boards front the anteroom view of the mountain, one about each of the presidents represented, one about the "unfinished dream" of Borglum to carve an entablature or to complete the hall of records, and one—picking up where Borglum left off—comparing Mount Rushmore in size to various others of the world's structures.[122] Down the middle of the visitor's path in the anteroom are four additional, three-sided display boards. One features popular culture appropriations of Rushmore, ranging from license plates and belt buckles to commemorative plates and videotaped advertising of Red Roof Inn, Colgate toothpaste, and McDonalds. Another, labeled "The Moods of Mt. Rushmore," focuses on lighting and video effects that render the mountain with different "looks." The other two are about preservation, one concentrating on the materials and technology now used to care for the sculpture, and the other on raising funds for the conservation effort.

There are five major displays in the inner museum area, the largest by far being the huge exhibit of equipment with the interactive, noisy "blasting" opportunity. Another, to which we will return, is called "The Meaning of Mount Rushmore." One is devoted to the local miners and laborers who worked on the mountain, another to the ancestry, character, and artistic career of Borglum. The "Times of Trial" exhibit features letters, newspaper articles, ledgers, and other documents from the fourteen-year period of the carving, along with photos of more recent visits by prominent figures. In many respects, it is another display about Borglum, because he is featured so prominently in the sequence as narrated by the museum objects.

The front storyboards and "The Meaning of Mount Rushmore" are the only two sections in the museum resembling an answer to the "why" question. Each of the anteroom boards carries a presidential portrait or other artistic rendering, but about half of the area of each board is a photo of the carved representation. Also included on each board are quotations from and achievements by each of the four presidents. The reasons Borglum long ago enumerated for the four to be included on Rushmore are contained within a list of other accomplishments. So, for example, the Roosevelt board names him as a conservationist, explains that he changed the relationship between the government and corporations, in addition to mentioning his responsibility for the construction of the Panama Canal. From the boards, taken as a composite, it would be nearly impossible to determine what unites the four presidents in a thematic suitable to being represented together on the mountain. The same is true of the larger "Meaning of Mount Rushmore" display. It does begin with the general statement that the memorial is dedicated to the "founding, growth, preservation, and development" of the country. But it offers no elaboration of how the memorial was intended to represent those historical moments. Instead, it narrates a rather fulsome history of the United States with a bit about each of the four presidents interspersed at the proper temporal juncture. Again, the reasons for the choices Borglum and his coworkers made are buried among a multitude of choices. There are no prominent representations of any other president, suppressing the likelihood of asking why these four, and not a substitution here or there.

What emerges in the interpretation of the museum, and in the film shown in the museum's twin theaters, is a strong focus on how the mountain was carved, followed by fond representations of Borglum, and virtually nothing about the meaning of the sculptural juxtaposition of Washington, Jefferson, Lincoln, and Roosevelt. Zinsser's "how" question is answered repeatedly. And the "who" of the construction—Borglum, the workers, and the geology experts who now conserve the memorial—is addressed also. But the question that Zinsser found so pressing at Rushmore is answered with the vaguest generality, by the "founding, growth, preservation, and development" framing phrase, never elaborated by reference to the presence of the four figures.[123]

The case is little different at Stone Mountain or Crazy Horse.[124] Unlike at most memorials, where the subject of commemoration is the central rhetorical theme of the monument, the mountain carvings themselves and their sculptors are the focal players. The signifier trumps the signified. The visitor centers at the sites are primarily dedicated to documenting the processes of constructing the carving, detailing the problems encountered and how all were solved by machines or other ingenious technical means, for example, giant image projectors, pneumatic drills, exact measurements, thermojet torches, precise dynamite blasting, and so forth. The correlative theme is scale, related, of course, to the technical problem solving necessary to such massive projects. So the visitor sees full-scale models of a man's finger or eye or the bridle of a horse; the equipment used for carving, along with detailed information about its development and use; film and docent narratives about "mistakes" or materials problems (fissures in the granite, for instance) and how those were resolved. The displays in the interpretive centers are self-congratulatory, pointing to how few workers were killed or injured during the construction process.[125] And these often include photos of men hanging over the side of the mountains working, along with charts or narratives juxtaposing the commemorative work with bridge or skyscraper projects in terms of their comparative safety records and mortality rates. Size comparisons to ancient works, like the Sphinx or the Colossus of Rhodes are standard fare.

Remarkably little is said about the Confederacy or the three Southern leaders whose images appear on Stone Mountain. And while Borglum cannot be the only focus of secondary attention (the "who" question) there, he and the other two subsequent sculptors as well as the workers are featured far more prominently than Jefferson Davis, Robert E. Lee, or Stonewall Jackson in the official interpretive program. The Crazy Horse site is slightly different in this regard. Although the historical figure of the Native American martyr is addressed a bit more prominently than are the sculptural subjects at the other two sites, he is still overshadowed by Ziolkowski. What focus there is on Crazy Horse seems to be almost defensive, as if to divert questions about why the project is controlled by a European American family and perhaps even why one sees so few Native Americans on the site, except as they represent entertainment or commerce—Native Americans are invited to perform occasional dances or other ceremonies at the visitor center, and there is a place set aside for them to market crafts. For a site presumably dedicated to the pride of Native Americans, though, there is a conspicuous lack of Native people in the Crazy Horse administration, staff, and visitor logs. In the end, it is still Ziolkowski who emerges in emphasis and interest at the site.

In sum, the technical equipment and explanations about how the mountain sculptures were created are given such presence by the interpretive vehicles at the sites (films, pamphlets, docents' stories, museum displays) that they dominate the scene rhetorically. The "heroes" in these commemorative places are not who we might predict them to be: Davis, Jackson, Lee, Washington, Jefferson, Lincoln, Roosevelt, or Crazy Horse. The "heroes"—those with vision, will, a sense of duty, and effort and success against all odds—are the mountain carvers themselves. Personal profiles of Gutzon Borglum and his successors at Stone Mountain, Borglum again at Mount Rushmore, and Korczak Ziolkowski at Crazy Horse eclipse the figures they carved. In fact, by the side of Borglum or Korczak (as he is referenced at Crazy Horse), there is little room for representations of the commemorated subjects to assume any rhetorical force. The mountain sculptures become visually prominent but virtually empty commemorative signifiers. Zinsser's "why" question recedes into unanswered (and usually unasked) oblivion. It is not that it is utterly impossible to find out the answers to "why," but that they are not emphasized or encouraged. Unless visitors probe or search rather assiduously, they are unlikely to find out much about the purposes or symbolic references they were intended to absorb.

In some respects, this brand of interpretation can hardly surprise us. The stories told by the memorials may simply be regarded by the official interpreters as too embarrassing to foreground at highly attended tourist attractions. As Pomeroy observes pointedly of Mount Rushmore, "It's important to invent alternative pasts for a culture that finds it hard to accept the real one. It's paradoxical that a Shrine of Democracy is placed in the center of land acquired through well documented rape—the most blatant example from 500 years of genocide and hemispheric conquest. Rushmore implies that the European has always been here. It obscures a shameful memory and eases racial guilt much the same way an individual represses thoughts reminding him of a painful experience."[126]

The case is a bit different, of course, at each. The National Park Service administrators are well aware of the "problems" of interpretation at Rushmore, and the personnel who have worked out the interpretive themes can hardly be blamed for making the best of a work that was wished upon their agency. Silver Dollar City expresses a commitment to preserving the heritage of Stone Mountain park, but it is clear that its focus is on the commercial venues in the park. At Crazy Horse, there is no acknowledgment at all, except if one detects a tone of defensiveness in the interpretation, that there might be any controversy involved in its creation. Whatever the motivations of the interpreters, however, all three memorials become the facts of their construction, a kind of zero-degree commemoration. This symbolic void is exacerbated, not compensated, by a set of sacralizing themes that have grown up in conjunction with the carvings and that are shored up by melodramatic performances at the sites.

Successful commemorative sites generally accrete some mythos of place and may even take on quasi-sacred significance for some. The hush and reverent distance visitors keep from the statue at the Lincoln Memorial, or the placing of mementos at the Vietnam Veterans Memorial, suggest that these places have taken on such status. The mountain carvings have assumed a mythos of their own, but with very particular valences and consequences. It is not just their often remarked presence in the "Paha Sapa, the mystic holy land of the once-mighty Sioux."[127] They borrow implied iconography from their cultural geography; the symbolism of mountains is powerful among various religious doctrines. As Schama points out, "Judaic, Christian, and Muslim traditions are full of mountain epiphanies and transfigurations."[128]

In line with his observation, general themes inspired by the three mountain memorials equate the mountains with ruins, mysterious keepers of ancient secrets with some connection to the cosmic or sacred (fig. 7). Often remarked is singer Cher's comment that she believed as a child that Rushmore had been carved by God.[129] Harlan suggests the same of Stone Mountain, that he and his brother knew nothing of Stone Mountain's history but that "the abandoned carvings on its north face were to us as timeless as ancient ruin."[130] Jim Popovich, the National Park Service's chief of interpretation at Mount Rushmore, told us that it is not uncommon for visitors to ask, "When was this discovered?"[131] And the mountain does bear the visual mark of a sacred ruin that would be "discovered," as Pomeroy argues: "It cannot be perceived directly, intimately as one deals with sculpture . . . but from distant, chosen places passively, always looking up, in the manner reserved for sacred, inviolable reverence." He adds that the "unfinished carving, awash with debris, easily affords a reading as a fragment, an artifact, a ruin."[132]

Boime's insightful observation about Borglum's South Dakota composition also links it to the sacred. Borglum, he notes, "borrowed a popular literary trope for his tourist showcase—taking the participants from various historical epochs and uniting them in a kind of Renaissance *Sacra Conversazione* (where various saints in profile and front view flank the Madonna and seem to converse with her) in the same space."[133] Zinsser suggests of the presidents' images, "Together they were gods, all-powerful."[134] Rex Alan Smith gives the imagery a different twist by emphasizing the spiritual timelessness of the memorial and, notably, using a biblical allusion as a temporal reference point: "Carved upon a cliff that has changed but little since mankind first appeared on earth and has worn down less than the thickness of a child's finger since Moses first led the Israelites out of Egypt, the faces will be there, looking down much as they do now, long after man has gone."[135]

The sacred themes are encouraged and have been since the beginning.[136] Borglum, in a rarely self-deferential statement, suggested his belief that "a nation's memorial should, like Washington, Jefferson, Lincoln, and Roosevelt, have a serenity, a nobility, a power that reflects the gods who inspired them and suggests the gods they have become."[137] References to the figures "emerging from" or being "released from" the stone, as if there by the hand of god, only to be excavated by human hands, were frequent and remain so. For example, in a 1941 essay, Hughes suggested that this "unparalleled accomplishment seems to have been not so much the carving of these vast heads upon the peaks as the beating away of the veiling, smothering stone and the releasing of the imprisoned statesmen so that they might look out upon the world and utter their lofty messages in a silence more pervasive and sonorous than any trumpet tone."[138]

Even prophetic tones are brought to bear. Rex Alan Smith reports that Borglum declared at the first Rushmore dedication in 1925, "The hand of Providence has decreed that this monument be built!"[139] And a *New York Times* article on the Crazy Horse Memorial reports, "On Sept. 6, 1877, the Indian rebel died after a soldier rammed a bayonet into his back during a meeting under a flag of truce at Fort Robinson, Neb. A few years after his death, a medicine man, Black Elk, told an interviewer that Crazy Horse had predicted to him: 'I will return to you in stone.'"[140] And the *National Geographic Traveler* suggests that some day "Crazy Horse will ride across the sky on a thundering horse, his hair flying free."[141] Much is made of the fact that Ziolkowski was born on the same date Crazy Horse was killed. "Some Indians read that as a sign Korczak was destined to return Crazy Horse in the stone," Crazy Horse spokesman DeWall asserts.[142]

Although these mystical and quasi-religious themes might afford the appearance of affective gravitas one might find at any serious memorial site, most are contrived and overtly absurd. Obviously, such readings fail to square with the most explicit interpretation at the sites, which emphasizes precisely the man- and machine-made character of the memorials. Nonetheless, such readings have been cultivated and encouraged, contradictory though they may be with others, by both on-site activity and interpretations for media sources. Both Rushmore and Stone Mountain have evening programs that surely contribute. Rushmore's is a worship services of sorts, complete with inspirational music, an interpretive program, and a dramatic lighting of the engraved figures. Stone Mountain's evening laser show introduces more levity, particularly given its lighting of the Memorial carving with sponsorship images for telephone and soft drink companies. The music, largely the work of popular contemporary southerners, represents a broader range too. But the theme reemerges when the laser lights "magically" bring the three Confederate leaders and their horses to life on the mountain, galloping into the sky brandishing their swords, while Dixie plays and visitors cheer.[143] Both the Stone Mountain and Rushmore sites have amphitheater areas for this kind of activity, where one may also sit and contemplate the seemingly holy figures at any time of the day. Although this sacralizing theater seems, and is, contrary to the self-referential interpretive efforts, at another level it complements those efforts by diverting visitors from alternative meanings that might otherwise arise at each site. Representations of the sacred at the mountain carvings simply act to solemnize the emptiness of the didactic interpretive programs each one offers.

This account of Mount Rushmore has identified a number of ways in which its history must be considered in a critical assessment of its rhetoric. The commercial motivation that initiated the project has returned huge profits to the South Dakota economy and has had obvious effects on the landscape. Stone Mountain, although two-thirds of a continent away, was a necessary condition *and* an unfortunate consequence of Rushmore's completion. Mount Rushmore was, in many respects, a product of the discourses and practices of public memory that preceded it. But it also contributed to major changes in mid-twentieth-century public commemoration, changes that would remain culturally entrenched for forty years. At the very least, it marked the transition from art to engineering as the principal means of producing public memory sites. And it exacerbated the already present tendency to confuse significance with size. In doing so, it promoted a paradoxical double effect: it sponsored the turn away from commemorative artworks at the same time that it encouraged even larger ones, in the form of Stone Mountain and Crazy Horse.

In sum, the "Rushmore effect," the rhetorical phenomenon of the Mount Rushmore memorial, is far more than the outsized figures on the mountain in South Dakota. It is a product of its history, its public interpretation, its appropriation and reproduction, even its satirization. To the extent it is considered a serious or important national memorial, it demands that we take account of its message(s) about our communal identity, character, and collective virtues. Put another way, if Mount Rushmore constitutes a dwelling place of national character, if it nominates a consensual mirror of the national *ethos,* it is imperative to assess the image it offers its audience.

Our analysis has foregrounded William Zinsser's "why" question, which places our interpretation at odds with official interpretation at the memorial site, most historical treatments, and virtually all of the tourist and popular press accounts of this national icon. So it seems fair to assess both of the mirrored images that have emerged here—the one that considers Rushmore's history and the one that we might label the culturally "preferred" or "official" interpretation. If we take Rushmore to be permeated by its history, its makers' objectives, its response to commemorative practices of the time, and its elicited response, the mirrored image is deplorable. It is an image of imperialist pride, an obsession with outlandish size, and an "aesthetic sensibility" that approves of accomplishing national commemoration by dynamiting scenic places. It implores us to be enthusiastic or at least acquiescent about any representation—even of an odious part of our national past —as long as it is immense.

We do not mean to suggest that we should be forgetful of elements of U.S. history that are shameful. But Rushmore does more than just remember; it advocates. It promotes an image of the national *ethos* that is anything but virtuous. If Lincoln Borglum was correct in suggesting that Mount Rushmore represents "what it means to be an American," the mirror it holds up for our contemplation offers a ghastly image. The same can be said of the other mountain carvings as well. Stone Mountain honors and enlarges the memory of warriors who fought to maintain a system of slavery in the South. And Crazy Horse, while honoring a true American martyr, can do so only in the rhetorical terms of the conqueror.

Obviously, these are not the images that emerge in the compelling interpretation in the press and at the memorial sites. Never encouraging or volunteering answers to the "why" question, this interpretation insists upon a focus on "how" and occasionally "who." No image of collective identity, of national *ethos,* appears in this mirror. The visual field of the mirror is blank because the only thing that matters is how a memorial is constructed, not what it says. Rex Alan Smith remarks that Rushmore pioneer Doane Robinson "would have been happy to settle for figures of, say Santa Claus and his elves had he thought they would serve his purpose better."[144] Indeed, given the almost exclusive focus on how each mountain was "carved," Santa Claus and the elves would have been perfectly acceptable stand-ins for the presidents, the Confederate leaders, or the Lakota chief. Perhaps the best evidence of that is the caricatures of Rushmore that permeate popular culture. While other national memorials are frequently appropriated to make a visual point, none is subjected to the kind of satire that Rushmore is. The insistent focus on how it was constructed, not what it represents, leaves open the possibility of adding almost any superimposed image or using the Rushmore figures to hail shoppers to a sale. Since there is no substantive message, only the facts of the memorial's construction, the message can be changed at will. It stands to reason that that is what has allowed also for the perpetual movements to carve another bust on the mountain, the most determined of which is one to add Ronald Reagan's visage to Rushmore.

There is an occasional move at the memorial sites and in tourist literature to answer the "who" question, to examine the character of those responsible for the mountain carvings. But it is a necessarily skewed message. One will not learn at Rushmore, or even at Stone Mountain, for example, that Gutzon Borglum was an enthusiastic member of the Ku Klux Klan, that he favored "a racially exclusionist immigration policy," or that he was an admirer of Mussolini.[145] Borglum and his associates are portrayed as zealous advocates of the memorial project and as admirable and impassioned patriots. Somewhat aside from the fulsomeness of the disclosure, though, is the more important (and obvious) point that the artists and financial supporters of public commemorative artworks are not the focal subject matter of memorials. At the mountain carving sites, though, the only human "heroes" that emerge are not the ones carved into the mountains, but the ones who did the carving. Traditional understandings of *ethos,* theorized in the context of persuasive speech, appropriately consider the character of the speaker. But in commemorative art, the artist is dematerialized. It becomes the burden of the commemorative work itself, not the artist, to render the image of collective virtue that will be assessed by its audience. Unfortunately, Mount Rushmore and the other U.S. mountain carvings offer their audiences more a register of vices than virtues. And they fail in offering anything like an admirable national *ethos* for contemplation, emulation, or moral character development.

Notes

1. Donald Dale Jackson, "Gutzon Borglum's Odd and Awesome Portraits in Granite," *Smithsonian,* August 1992, 64–75.

2. The term "mountain carving" is itself a source of incredulity, but it is the standard for referring to these gigantic works.

3. The standard sources on Mount Rushmore are Lincoln Borglum, *Mount Rushmore: The Story behind the Scenery,* rev. ed. (Las Vegas: KC Publications, 1977); Gilbert Fite, *Mount Rushmore* (Norman: University of Oklahoma Press, 1952); Howard Shaff and Audrey Karl Shaff, *Six Wars at a Time: The Life and Times of Gutzon Borglum, Sculptor of Mount Rushmore* (Sioux Falls, S.D.: Center for Western Studies, Augustana College, 1985); and Rex Alan Smith, *The Carving of Mount Rushmore* (New York: Abbeville Press, 1985). All of these fit the description about the way the story is told, although they vary in detail and emphasis. Recent and more critical accounts include Albert Boime, *The Unveiling of the National Icons: A Plea for Patriotic Iconoclasm in a Nationalist Era* (Cambridge: Cambridge University Press, 1998); Jesse Larner, *Mount Rushmore: An Icon Reconsidered* (New York: Nation Books, 2002); Jim Pomeroy, "Selections from Rushmore—Another Look," in *Critical Issues in Public Art: Content, Context, and Controversy,* ed. Harriett F. Senie and Sally Webster

(New York: HarperCollins, 1992), 44–56; and Simon Schama, *Landscape and Memory* (New York: Alfred A. Knopf, 1995). Visitors to Mount Rushmore, as well as those who read about it in popular press accounts, though, are much more likely to be exposed to the kind of story that renders Gutzon Borglum and his supporters as visionary and courageous heroes. As Larner suggests, children's books on Mount Rushmore follow that pattern as well (*Mount Rushmore,* 358–59).

4. Shaff and Shaff, *Six Wars,* 226. Also see Smith, *Carving,* 24.

5. Gutzon Borglum was productive and successful, although not widely considered to be of the caliber of other major sculptors of the time, such as Augustus Saint-Gaudens, Lorado Taft, or Daniel Chester French. But his work was popular. As Zinsser points out, "Borglum became one of America's most productive sculptors, creating, among other popular groups, the 12 apostles in the Cathedral of St. John the Divine in New York, the bronze equestrian statue of General Sheridan in New York, and two figures that are probably his best-loved works: the marble bust of Lincoln in the Rotunda of the Capitol and the seated Lincoln in Newark, sometimes known as 'the children's Lincoln' because children like to climb onto its lap." William Zinsser, *American Places: A Writer's Pilgrimage to 15 of This Country's Most Visited and Cherished Sites* (New York: HarperCollins, 1993), 11. For a more complete catalog of Borglum's works prior to Stone Mountain and Rushmore, see Robin Borglum Carter, *Gutzon Borglum: His Life and Work* (Austin, Tex.: Eakin Press, 1998).

6. Doane Robinson contacted prominent sculptor Lorado Taft initially, in 1923, but Taft declined Robinson's invitation because of ill health. See Fite, *Mount Rushmore,* 6.

7. When he wrote to Lorado Taft, Robinson named, among others, Lewis and Clark, Frémont, Redcloud, and Bill Cody. See Fite, *Mount Rushmore,* 6.

8. Because of this focus on additional historical conditions that made the Rushmore memorial possible, Tichi's work requires special note. She too explored some of those conditions, although in an entirely different domain. As she describes her project, "Mt. Rushmore . . . is defined historically only in part by the factual data of its key personnel, its financing, its construction in South Dakota, and so on. The greater understanding of its position in U.S. history requires analysis of the antecedent texts that make the very conception of such a project possible—texts from the late eighteenth century identifying mountains as male rulers, texts celebrating corporate heads as business leaders." Cecilia Tichi, *Embodiment of a Nation: Human Form in American Places* (Cambridge: Harvard University Press, 2001), 11.

9. Rushmore was never really "completed." An agreement was reached to end the project with finishing work on the four heads. Indeed, none of the mountain carvings in the United States has been completed in the sense of actualizing the planned designs.

10. Carole Blair, "Contemporary U.S. Memorial Sites as Exemplars of Rhetoric's Materiality," in *Rhetorical Bodies,* ed. Jack Selzer and Sharon Crowley (Madison: University of Wisconsin Press), 18. There is a growing body of work by rhetorical scholars devoted specifically to studies of memorial sites, including Bernard J. Armada, "'The Fierce Urgency of Now': Public Memory and Civic Transformation at the National Civil Rights Museum" (Ph.D. diss., Pennsylvania State University, 1999); Armada, "Memorial Agon: An Interpretive Tour of the National Civil Rights Museum," *Southern Communication Journal* 63 (1998): 235–43; Barbara Biesecker, "Remembering World War II: The Rhetoric and Politics of National Commemoration at the Turn of the 21st Century," *Quarterly*

Journal of Speech 88 (2002): 393–409; Blair, "Contemporary U.S. Memorial Sites"; Carole Blair, "Reflections on Criticism and Bodies: Parables from Public Places," *Western Journal of Communication* 65 (2001): 271–94; Carole Blair, Marsha S. Jeppeson, and Enrico Pucci Jr., "Public Memorializing in Postmodernity: The Vietnam Veterans Memorial as Prototype," *Quarterly Journal of Speech* 77 (1991): 263–88; Carole Blair and Neil Michel, "Commemorating in the Theme Park Zone: Reading the Astronauts Memorial," in *At the Intersection: Cultural Studies and Rhetorical Studies,* ed. Thomas Rosteck (New York: Guilford, 1999), 29–83; Carole Blair and Neil Michel, "Reproducing Civil Rights Tactics: The Rhetorical Performances of the Civil Rights Memorial," *Rhetoric Society Quarterly* 30 (2000): 31–55; A. Cheree Carlson and John E. Hocking, "Strategies of Redemption at the Vietnam Veterans' Memorial," *Western Journal of Speech Communication* 52 (1998): 203–15; Greg Dickinson, "Memories for Sale: Nostalgia and Construction of Identity in Old Pasadena," *Quarterly Journal of Speech* 83 (1997): 1–27; Peter Ehrenhaus, "Silence and Symbolic Expression," *Communication Monographs* 55 (1988): 41–57; Peter Ehrenhaus, "The Vietnam Veterans Memorial: An Invitation to Argument," *Journal of the American Forensic Association* 25 (1988): 54–64; Sonja K. Foss, "Ambiguity as Persuasion: The Vietnam Veterans Memorial," *Communication Quarterly* 34 (1986): 326–40; Victoria J. Gallagher, "Memory and Reconciliation in the Birmingham Civil Rights Institute," *Rhetoric and Public Affairs* 2 (1999): 303–20; Victoria A. Gallagher, "Remembering Together: Rhetorical Integration and the Case of the Martin Luther King, Jr. Memorial," *Southern Communication Journal* 60 (1995): 109–19; Harry W. Haines, "'What Kind of War?': An Analysis of the Vietnam Veterans Memorial," *Critical Studies in Mass Communication* 3 (1986): 1–20; Cheryl R. Jorgensen-Earp and Lori A. Lanzilotti, "Public Memory and Private Grief: The Construction of Shrines at the Sites of Public Tragedy," *Quarterly Journal of Speech* 84 (1998): 150–70; Richard Marback, "Detroit and the Closed Fist: Toward a Theory of Material Rhetoric," *Rhetoric Review* 17 (1998): 74–92; Marita Sturken, *Tangled Memories: The Vietnam War, the AIDS Epidemic, and the Politics of Remembering* (Berkeley and Los Angeles: University of California Press, 1997); and Nick Trujillo, "Interpreting November 22: A Critical Ethnography of an Assassination Site," *Quarterly Journal of Speech* 79 (1993): 447–66.

   11. Aristotle, *Aristotle on Rhetoric: A Theory of Civic Discourse,* ed. and trans. George A. Kennedy (New York: Oxford University Press, 1991), 37n. 40. Also see Thomas M. Conley, *Rhetoric in the European Tradition* (New York: Longman, 1990), 15.

   12. Michael J. Hyde, *The Call of Conscience: Heidegger, Levinas, Rhetoric and the Euthanasia Debate* (Columbia: University of South Carolina Press, 2001), 75.

   13. Henri Lefebvre, *The Production of Space,* trans. Donald Nicholson-Smith (Oxford: Blackwell, 1991), 220.

   14. We also have some discomfort with Lefebvre's use of the past tense. If the suggestion is that monuments once played this role successfully but do not any longer, we find an unjustified nostalgia in that rendering of the past. In any case, we believe our amendment, to suggest that monuments "nominate" a view for consensus solves both problems. Indeed, our amendment seems consonant with Lefebvre's own suggestion that a monument may be the outcome, in part, of "a particular way of *proposing* a meaning" (*Production,* 222; emphasis added). He is careful, however, to remind us that a monument or any material work "can be reduced neither to a language or discourse nor to the categories and concepts developed for the study of language" (ibid.).

15. There is something of a consensus on this point. See also, for example, Gerald A. Danzer, *Public Places: Exploring Their History* (Nashville, Tenn.: Association for State and Local History, 1987). "Monuments," he suggests, "tell us who we are, inform us where we came from, list the ideals we should honor, and suggest the goals toward which we should strive" (1).

16. Borglum, *Mount Rushmore,* 4. Recent renovation at the visitor center indicates the continued reinforcement of that message, with its walkway facing the mountain, lined with the flags of each U.S. state and territory and granite pillars engraved with the dates of admission of each to the union.

17. Visitation was 1,862,674 for fiscal year 2001. See U.S. National Park Service, "Park Facts," Mount Rushmore National Memorial, March 23, 2002, http://www.nps.gov/moru/pphtml/facgts.html. However, 2001 was an unusual tourism year because of post–September 11 travel fears and difficulties. The average annual visitation at Mount Rushmore for the baseline years of fiscal year 1992 to fiscal year 1996 was 2.65 million. See U.S. National Park Service, *Strategic Plan for Mount Rushmore National Memorial, October 1, 2000–September 30, 2005,* July 27, 2000, 10.

18. Jan Assman, *Das Kulturelle Gedachtnis: Schrift, Erinnerung und Politische Identität in Fruhen Hochkulturen* (Munich: Beck, 1992), 11; Jay Winter, "Remembrance and Redemption: A Social Interpretation of War Memorials," *Harvard Design Review* (Fall 1999): 71.

19. Elizabeth Walker Mechling and Jay Mechling, "The Campaign for Civil Defense and the Struggle to Naturalize the Bomb," in *Critical Questions: Invention, Creativity, and the Criticism of Discourse and Media,* ed. William Nothstine, Carole Blair, and Gary A. Copeland (New York: St. Martin's, 1994), 129, first published in *Western Journal of Speech Communication* 55 (1991): 105–33. Also see Brummett, who might describe what we have in mind for reading Rushmore as a "diffuse text." Such a construction, he argues, is "one with a perimeter that is not so clear, one that is mixed up with other signs." Barry Brummett, *Rhetoric in Popular Culture* (New York: St. Martin's, 1994), 80. Cultural studies scholars expand this notion, suggesting that we read texts in relationship to others, even if they do not seem to be in proximity to a target text. Grossberg suggests, "Articulation is not simply a matter of polysemy or decoding (notions which were already present in the founding texts of modern philosophy, including Spinoza's and Descartes') but the making, unmaking, and remaking of non-necessary relations and hence of contexts. Articulation assumes that relations (identities, effects, etc.) are real but not necessary. It describes the relation of a non-relation, and transforms cultural politics from a question of texts and audiences to one of contexts and effects." Lawrence Grossberg, "The Space of Culture, the Power of Space," in *The Post-Colonial Question: Common Skies, Divided Horizons,* ed. Iain Chambers and Lidia Curti (New York; Routledge, 1996), 169.

20. Fite claims that Robinson "had marveled with millions of Americans at the concept and imagination of Gutzon Borglum who had recently begun to carve a Confederate memorial on Stone Mountain" (*Mount Rushmore,* 5–6). Rex Alan Smith concurs, suggesting that Robinson had read newspaper accounts "about the tourists flocking to see the gigantic reliefs being carved into a Georgia mountain by a sculptor named Borglum" (*Carving,* 24).

21. David B. Freeman, *Carved in Stone: The History of Stone Mountain* (Macon, Ga.: Mercer University Press, 1997), 56.

22. According to Breed, "The United Daughters [of the Confederacy] once boasted that, through the group's efforts, 'the Southland has become a land of monuments.'" Allen G. Breed, "Confederate Markers Stir Passions," *New Orleans Times-Picayune,* February 20, 2000. Also see Gaines M. Foster, *Ghosts of the Confederacy: Defeat, the Lost Cause, and the Emergence of the New South, 1865–1913* (New York: Oxford University Press, 1987); and Kirk Savage, *Standing Soldiers, Kneeling Slaves: Race, War, and Monument in Nineteenth-Century America* (Princeton, N.J.: Princeton University Press, 1997).

23. Freeman, *Carved in Stone,* 55–56.

24. Ibid., 56.

25. Grace Elizabeth Hale, *Making Whiteness: The Culture of Segregation in the South, 1890–1940* (New York: Pantheon, 1998), 251.

26. Freeman, *Carved in Stone,* 60. Indeed, Congress had appropriated $2 million in 1911 in establishing the Lincoln Memorial Commission. See Pamela Scott and Antoinette J. Lee, *Buildings of the District of Columbia* (New York: Oxford University Press), 82. Plane must have had something of a similar or greater magnitude in mind, for she wrote, "Now the time has arrived for us to cease the erection of small and perishable local monuments . . . and concentrate our efforts on one which shall be a shrine for the South and of which all Americans may be justly proud." C. Helen Plane to *Philadelphia Public Ledger,* January 14, 1916, Helen Plane Papers, Special Collections Department, Robert W. Woodruff Library, Emory University, Atlanta, Ga. (hereafter cited as Plane Papers). However, as Thomas points out, the $2 million for the Lincoln Memorial was "an unprecedented sum for a federal monument," much less for a regional one. Christopher A. Thomas, *The Lincoln Memorial and American Life* (Princeton, N.J.: Princeton University Press 2002), 26.

27. Thomas, *Lincoln Memorial,* 128; and Kathy Sawyer, "A Lynching, a List and Re-opened Wounds," *Washington Post,* June 20, 2000. Of the 22, all but 1 were lynchings of African Americans. The single exception was a Jewish man. Fears reports, "During the half-century beginning in 1882, some 2,500 black men, women and children were lynched" and that Georgia ranked "second only to Mississippi at 423 lynchings." Darryl Fears, "Atlanta, Ready to Revisit an American Evil," *Washington Post,* January 28, 2002.

28. Catherine Lavender, "D. W. Griffith, *The Birth of a Nation* (1915)," http://www.library.sci.cuny.edu/dept/history/lavender/birth.html, June 11, 2001.

29. Boime, *Unveiling,* 142.

30. C. Helen Plane to Gutzon Borglum, December 17, 1915, Plane Papers.

31. Breed, "Confederate Markers."

32. See Gutzon Borglum, "Engineering Problems to Be Met in Mountain Sculpture," *Black Hills Engineer* 18 (November 1930): 308–34. Also see Boime, *Unveiling,* 146; Willard Neal, *Georgia's Stone Mountain,* pamphlet (n.p., n.d.), 3–4; and Fite, *Mount Rushmore,* 37.

33. The extent of Klan involvement in the memorial project is a matter of some dispute. Freeman insists that "the influence of the Klan over the memorial has been over-emphasized and exaggerated" (*Carved in Stone,* 79). But he acknowledges that Borglum and "some members of the executive committee and board of directors" of the SMCMA were also Klan participants. And even a Borglum family member suggests that considerable disruption was caused by "a split in local Ku Klux Klan leadership, and [that] Gutzon backed the wrong faction." Carter, *Gutzon Borglum,* 79. Certainly the most convincing case of Klan involvement is made by Larner, *Mount Rushmore,* 187–238. Also see Alex Heard,

"Mount Rushmore: The Real Story," *New Republic,* July 15,1991, 16–18; Boime, *Unveiling,* 141–46; Jackson, "Gutzon Borglum's Odd and Awesome Portraits," 72; and Shaff and Shaff, *Six Wars,* 195.

34. Borglum, even by admission of some of his most ardent admirers, was an obdurate character. Fite, *Mount Rushmore,* called him "unstable, inconsistent, unpredictable, and egotistical" (20), "temperamental and difficult," "erratic, impatient, and impractical," (137), as well as "aggravating" (159). Jackson, "Gutzon Borglum's Odd and Awesome Portraits," labels him "volcanic" (65) and "disputatious" (70). Smith, *Carving,* suggests that Borglum's associates always were "impressed by his capacity for affection, wrath, generosity, stinginess, nobility, pettiness, charm, and sheer obnoxiousness. Of modesty and humility, it was true, Borglum had a meager supply. Of pure mulish stubbornness, on the other hand, he had an abundance" (18). But it is difficult to conclude simply on the basis of his bellicose nature that Borglum was in the wrong in his conflicts with the SMCMA. In fact, as Freeman details, Borglum appears to have been justified in accusing the SMCMA of shortchanging both the memorial project and him; an audit in 1928 showed that the association had spent only 19 percent of its income on the carving (*Carved in Stone,* 118–20). Nonetheless, his public accusations certainly had an impact in the disaffection of the association's members.

35. Smith, *Carving,* 35. Freeman simply suggests that "it probably was not wise of Borglum to take a trip to South Dakota in September 1924, to discuss the carving of a national monument in the Black Hills" (*Carved in Stone,* 84). It is not clear whether his assessment is based upon Borglum's poor timing in relation to the political turmoil among the Georgia participants or to the fact that the Georgians were angry about the prospect of his taking on a *national* monument project in the North. A similar unclarity is present in Harlan's description: he attributes the Borglum firing directly to the SMCMA members having read about the Rushmore project in the newspapers. Louis B. Harlan, "Climbing Stone Mountain," in *American Places: Encounters with History,* ed. William E. Leuchtenburg (New York: Oxford University Press, 2000), 161. But he does not elaborate on what angered them about the idea. In a rather bizarre twist, Shaff suggests that some in the South later opposed the inclusion of Lincoln on Mount Rushmore: "After the bitter failure at Stone Mountain, Southerners were violently against 'their' artist honoring a man they thought of as a traitor, but the South had little influence on South Dakota thinking." Howard Shaff, "Mt. Rushmore," *Traveler Magazine,* South Dakota and NE Wyoming (n.p., 1997), 85.

36. Fite, *Mount Rushmore,* 41, 87.

37. Boime, *Unveiling,* 146. Also see Harlan, "Climbing Stone Mountain": "Gutzon Borglum once remarked that the chief lesson he took from Stone Mountain to Rushmore was that to achieve grandeur, he would have to double the scale" (167).

38. Fite, *Mount Rushmore,* 43.

39. Ibid., 146. At the time, as Bogart suggests, sculptors' "professional stature was linked to their activities as civic artists and to the production of public art." Michele H. Bogart, *Public Sculpture and the Civic Idea in New York City, 1890–1930* (Washington, D.C.: Smithsonian Institution Press, 1997), 9. Borglum had sufficient reputation to secure a number of civic works commissions over the years. Had he added a failure at Rushmore to that at Stone Mountain, however, it is unlikely that his career would have survived.

40. Gutzon Borglum to Miss Margaret Etheridge, August 29, 1915, Papers of Gutzon Borglum, Manuscript Division, Library of Congress (hereafter cited as Papers of Gutzon Borglum).

41. Freeman, *Carved in Stone,* 83.

42. Kirk Savage, "The Politics of Memory: Black Emancipation and the Civil War Monument," in *Commemorations: The Politics of National Identity,* ed. John Gillis (Princeton, N.J.: Princeton University Press, 1994), 132. Savage adds that "the local monuments that help recast the war in this light tell us in effect that neither side lost" ("Politics of Memory," 132). Also see Foster, *Ghosts,* 196. At the time, President Warren G. Harding endorsed the Stone Mountain Confederate memorial project on those grounds: "It will be one of the world's finest testimonies, one of history's most complete avowals, that unity and understanding may be brought even into the scene where faction, hatred, and hostility have once reigned supreme" (Hale, *Making Whiteness,* 252).

43. He suggested, for example, in a letter to the governor of North Carolina, that the Stone Mountain memorial would "compel a new world analysis of the Southern position." Gutzon Borglum to Angus McLean, July 15, 1925, Papers of Gutzon Borglum.

44. John Bodnar, *Remaking America: Public Memory, Commemoration, and Patriotism in the Twentieth Century* (Princeton, N.J.: Princeton University Press, 1992); Foster, *Ghosts;* and Savage, *Standing Soldiers.*

45. Foster, *Ghosts,* 129. Also see Bogart, *Public Sculpture,* 27; and Andrew M. Shanken, "Planning Memory: Living Memorials in the United States During World War II," *Art Bulletin* 84 (March 2002): 131, 136.

46. Kathy Ann Mabol, "Transitions in the American Memory of War: From the Civil War to World War I" (master's thesis, University of North Carolina, 2001).

47. Scott and Lee, *Buildings,* 77. Indeed, Bogart argues, it would be "by showing artistic continuity from the great classical civilizations" that the Columbian Exposition would "demonstrate the progress of American art" (*Public Sculpture,* 41).

48. Senie and Webster, *Critical Issues,* xii.

49. Thomas A. P. van Leeuwen, *The Skyward Trend of Thought: The Metaphysics of the American Skyscraper* (Cambridge, Mass.: MIT Press, 1988), 50n. 46. See also Bogart, *Public Sculpture,* 26.

50. Scott and Lee point out that, although the Pantheon is typically named as the principal influence, the Jefferson Memorial's "closest model" is William Kent's Ionic Temple of Ancient Virtue (1734) at Stowe (*Buildings,* 102).

51. Ibid., 100–102.

52. Federal Writers Project, *The WPA Guide to Washington, D.C.,* rev. ed. (New York: Pantheon, 1983), 202; and Christopher Weeks, *AIA Guide to the Architecture of Washington, D.C.* (Baltimore: Johns Hopkins University Press, 1994), 38.

53. Thomas, *Lincoln Memorial,* 101.

54. Fite, *Mount Rushmore,* 16.

55. Borglum to Etheridge.

56. World's Eighth Wonder—A Dream Coming True," *New York American,* August 5, 1923. It is important to note that this *New York American* article reported the plan, not the completed work, of Stone Mountain. Borglum had finished only the head of Lee by the time the article was printed.

57. Gutzon Borglum, "Colossal Sculpture: Its Value to Civilization," *Mount Rushmore National Memorial,* pamphlet (Mount Rushmore National Memorial Commission, 1931), 14–15, Papers of Gutzon Borglum.

58. Ibid., 16.

59. Gutzon Borglum, "Carving Mountains into Monuments," *New York Herald Tribune,* August 21, 1927.

60. Kate Susman, "Writing History with Drill and Dynamite a Mile above the Sea," *Chicago Sunday Times,* December 11, 1932.

61. J. W. Parmley, "A Letter from Parmley," *Mobridge (S.D.) Weekly Tribune,* December 30, 1926.

62. "The Story of an Empire," *Kansas City Star,* November 14, 1926.

63. "America's Story on a Mountain Cliff," *New York Times Magazine,* February 23, 1930.

64. "Drills Drum in Black Hills," *Detroit News,* June 3, 1927.

65. "By Borglum and Coolidge," *Time,* January 27, 1930.

66. Pomeroy, "Selections," 52.

67. Daniel M. Abramson, *Skyscraper Rivals: The AIG Building and the Architecture of Wall Street* (New York: Princeton Architectural Press, 2001), 181.

68. Ibid., 177.

69. Elizabeth L. Newhouse, ed., *The Builders: Marvels of Engineering* (Washington, D.C.: National Geographic Society, 1992), 63.

70. Van Leeuwen, *Skyward Trend,* 52.

71. O. F. Semsch, ed., *A History of the Singer Building Construction* (New York: Trow Press, 1908), 9.

72. Van Leeuwen, *Skyward Trend,* 52.

73. Abramson, *Skyscraper Rivals,* 179.

74. Ibid., 177–78.

75. Van Leeuwen, *Skyward Trend,* 118.

76. Zinsser, *American Places,* 6–7.

77. For a more complete rendition of this portion of Rushmore's history, see Fite, *Mount Rushmore,* 100–106.

78. The hall of records actually was completed in 1998. As Higbee notes, "Sealed inside the chamber are records of American history and of Rushmore's creation." Paul Higbee, *Mount Rushmore's Hall of Records* (Keystone, S.D.: Mount Rushmore Historical Assn., 1999), 1. What amounts to a time capsule certainly is far less grand than Borglum's plan: "He talked about the Declaration of Independence text cut into granite in three languages, a bronze and lapis blue mosaic entrance, 25 busts of storied Americans, and messages to posterity from great citizens" (Higbee, *Mount Rushmore's Hall,* 6).

79. Dorothy K. Hilburn and Steven L. Walker, *Mount Rushmore: Monument to America's Democracy* (Scottsdale, Ariz.: Camelback/Canyonlands Venture, 1997), 39.

80. Gutzon Borglum, speech, *Collier's Radio Hour,* New York, January 18, 1931; Carter, *Gutzon Borglum,* 85–86.

81. Contract between Mount Harney Memorial Association and Gutzon Borglum (duplicate), March 1927, Papers of Gutzon Borglum.

82. Editorial, *Dubuque Telegraph Herald,* February 19, 1930.

83. Zinsser, *American Places,* 13.

84. Fite, *Mount Rushmore,* 34–36. The Behistun relief, located between the modern Hamadan, Iran, and Baghdad, Iraq, is cut into the side of a cliff. It details Darius's military exploits. *The Lion of Lucerne,* by Albert Bertel Thorvalsen (1819), honors the Swiss Guard who fought in the French Revolution.

85. Fite, *Mount Rushmore,* 109.

86. Cora B. Johnson to Doane Robinson, December 6, 1924, display, Lincoln Borglum Museum, Mount Rushmore National Memorial Collection.

87. Fite, *Mount Rushmore,* 110.

88. "Mount Rushmore," *Traveler Magazine,* South Dakota and NE Wyoming (n.p., 1997), 144.

89. Fite, *Mount Rushmore,* 237.

90. Smith, *Carving,* 13.

91. Ibid., 326.

92. Pomeroy, "Selections," 50.

93. *Welcome to Wall Drug and the Badlands!* pamphlet and map, n.d.

94. "South Dakota Tourism," Governor's Office for Economic Development web page, http://www.sdgreatprofits.com/SD_Profile/sdtourism, March 29, 2002.

95. Scott and Lee, *Buildings,* 85. Also see Sue A. Kohler, *The Commission of Fine Arts: A Brief History, 1910–1990* (Washington, D.C.: U.S. Commission of Fine Arts, 1990), 68–73.

96. See Shanken, "Planning Memory," 132. Even the Jefferson National Expansion Memorial, one of the seeming exceptions, really is not exceptional, for while it was built in the 1960s, it had been in the planning stages for decades.

97. Ralph E. Becker, *Miracle on the Potomac: The Kennedy Center from the Beginning* (Silver Spring, Md.: Bartleby Press, 1990), 37–72.

98. Gillis claims that the Vietnam Veterans Memorial is "generally agreed to represent a turning point in the history of public memory, a decisive departure." John Gillis, *Commemorations,* 13. That seems an overstatement, but we would be willing to venture that the Vietnam Veterans Memorial represented a decisive turning point in public commemorative building in the United States.

99. These include the Civil Rights Memorial (Montgomery, Ala.), the AIDS Memorial Quilt (mobile; variable display locations), the U.S. Law Enforcement Officers Memorial (Washington, D.C.), the Astronauts Memorial (Cape Canaveral, Fla.), the Witch Trials Tercentenary Memorial (Salem, Mass.), the Women in the Military Services for America Memorial (Arlington National Cemetery, Va.), the Freedom Forum Journalists Memorial (Arlington, Va.), the May 4 Memorial at Kent State University (Kent, Ohio), the Korean War Veterans Memorial (Washington, D.C.), the Franklin Delano Roosevelt Memorial (Washington, D.C.), the U.S. Navy Memorial (Washington, D.C.), the memorial to those killed in the 1995 Murrah Building bombing (Oklahoma City, Okla.), and a memorial honoring Japanese Americans interned during World War II (Washington, D.C.). In process are a new World War II memorial in Washington, D.C., a U.S. Air Force memorial in Arlington, Virginia, an "Indian memorial" for the Little Bighorn National Historic Site, and a memorial in Washington, D.C., to honor Martin Luther King Jr. Hundreds more national-scope memorials have been proposed, and others remain suspended in the

rather complex processes of political and aesthetic approval agencies. Most, but not all, of the memorials above are maintained on federal property and/or are designated officially as "national." Those that are not, however, have been rendered prominent for citizens of the nation in other ways, typically by media coverage. They do not include the thousands of less visible, local memorials that have also been undertaken since the early 1980s.

Although not without its detractors, Maya Lin's simple design for the Vietnam Veterans Memorial was quite successful, and the memorials that followed were frequently modeled to reenact its success. Although these new commemorative artworks differ considerably among themselves in design and circumstance, it is relatively clear that they were all enabled in some way by the presence of the Vietnam Veterans Memorial.

100. Andrew Shankin's fine work, "Planning Memory," addresses this question in far more depth than is possible here. Also see Bogart, *Public Sculpture,* 284–303. Both Bogart and Shankin document the most important reasons for this new trend. Neither mentions the mountain carvings. We are in agreement with their assessment of conditions that produced the functional memorials, but we would simply add the mountain carving phenomenon as another of the conditions.

101. Edwin Heathcote, *Monument Builders: Modern Architecture and Death* (West Sussex, U.K.: Academy Editions, 1999), 62.

102. As Pomeroy points out, the "Federal Art, Writers', Theatre, and Music projects and the documentary photography of the Farm Security Administration were under frequent attack by conservative factions" ("Selections," 54). Also see Bruce I. Bustard, *A New Deal for the Arts* (Washington, D.C.: National Archives and Records Administration and the University of Washington Press, 1997); and Richard D. McKinzie, *The New Deal for Artists* (Princeton, N.J.: Princeton University Press, 1973).

103. Shanken, "Planning Memory," 136. Also see Christiane C. Collins and George R. Collins, "Monumentality: A Critical Matter in Modern Architecture," *Harvard Architectural Review* 4 (1984): 28; Blair, Jeppeson, and Pucci, "Public Memorializing," 264–66; Steven Connor, *Postmodern Culture: An Introduction to Theories of the Contemporary* (Oxford: Basil Blackwell, 1989), 66–71; William J. R. Curtis, *Modern Architecture Since 1900,* 2d ed. (Englewood Cliffs, N.J.: Prentice-Hall, 1987), 174–85 and 306–16; David Harvey, *The Condition of Postmodernity* (Oxford: Basil Blackwell, 1989), 66–112; and Darryl Hattenhauer, "The Rhetoric of Architecture: A Semiotic Approach," *Communication Quarterly* 32 (1984): 71–77.

104. Abramson, *Skyscraper Rivals,* 175. As Abramson notes, with the completion of the Empire State Building, the headline of the *New York Times,* for May 2, 1931, read "Rivalry for Height Is Seen as Ended. . . . Practical Limit Reached."

105. Fite cites some commentators who clearly feared that "[e]very village . . . will be looking for some defenseless hill out of which some tombstone chiseler may be hired to make a statue" (*Mount Rushmore,* 110).

106. For a general history of the project during this time, see Freeman, *Carved in Stone,* 140ff. He suggests that the motivation for the resuscitated project was the South's "massive resistance to racial integration. In 1958, capitalizing on this impulse, [the] Georgia legislature funded the completion of the project for use as a tourist attraction" (2–3). Also see Minna Morse, "The Changing Face of Stone Mountain," *Smithsonian,* January 1999, 61. Harlan suggests that "Stone Mountain's monumental failure must have haunted many

southerners during the decades of depression and war, particularly those around Atlanta who still dreamed the ancient dream of southern triumphalism" ("Climbing Stone Mountain," 166).

107. "Stone Mountain Park," http://www.stonemountainpark.com/general/index. html, March 23, 2002.

108. ibid.

109. Henry Standing Bear to Gutzon Borglum, 4 December 1931, Papers of Gutzon Borglum.

110. We assume it was a similar request, and certainly that is the inference that the Crazy Horse Memorial Foundation wishes to be drawn. However, the letter from Standing Bear displayed in the museum at the Crazy Horse complex says only this: "A number of my fellow chiefs and I are interested in finding some sculptor who can carve a head of an Indian chief who was killed many years ago." Henry Standing Bear to Korczak Ziolkowski, November 7, 1939, Indian Museum of North America, Crazy Horse, S.D. There is no mention of a mountain sculpture. If that was what Henry Standing Bear had in mind, that must have emerged in personal conversations with the sculptor. In all fairness, the available historical record does not indicate that the Lakota chiefs asked for a mountain carving, but it may have been what they envisioned, since Standing Bear had already made the request of Borglum to include Crazy Horse on Rushmore.

111. Rob DeWall, *Carving a Dream,* 8th rev. ed. (Crazy Horse, S.D.: Korczak's Heritage, 1999), 36–37.

112. "Visiting Crazy Horse," Crazy Horse Memorial, S.D., http://www.crazyhorse.org/ visiting

113. *Indian Museum of North America: Crazy Horse Memorial* (Crazy Horse, S.D.: Korczak's Heritage, 1996), 2.

114. Schama, *Landscape,* 399.

115. James Brooke, "Crazy Horse Is Riding Again in the Hills of South Dakota," *New York Times,* June 29, 1997.

116. Gary A. Warner and Michael Kitada, "Face Off: Mount Rushmore and Crazy Horse Share Space and Controversy in the Black Hills of South Dakota," *Sacramento Bee,* August 1, 1999.

117. Rosalie Glenn, "Monument Dishonors," *Rapid City (S.D.) Journal,* June 15, 1997.

118. Boime, *Unveiling,* 161.

119. Another potential outcome is the recent plan by the Chicago-based Alexander the Great Foundation and Greek American sculptor Tassos Papadopoulos to carve a 240-foot-high cliff sculpture of Alexander in northern Greece. The *New York Times* is quick to point out that it would be "four times the size of the presidents of Mount Rushmore." See Anthee Carassava, "Plan for Alexander Statue Too Great for Many Greeks," *New York Times,* August 28, 2002. Never mind that the Greek Culture Ministry is opposed and has even threatened to "forcefully block" attempts to work on the cliff. Again, as reported by the *Times,* "James Rigas, president of the United Hellenic American Congress, which supports the project, said the planners were not seeking to cause political mischief. 'This project is all about Greece expanding its vistas,' he said, 'being more flexible in its outlook as a modernizing Western state and boosting tourism, its primary source of income.'"

120. Zinsser, *American Places,* 8.

121. Our description of the interpretation on site is based upon multiple visits to all three of the memorials since 1994, but dependent most on extended observations at the three locations during the spring of 2001.

122. The standard comparisons to the Sphinx, pyramids, and Colossus of Rhodes are all still there. Added to the list now are more contemporary structures: the Washington Monument, Gateway Arch, and Statue of Liberty.

123. On occasion, one finds a different interpretive strategy—that of simply reconstructing what the monument is about and why the presidents were chosen. For example, a Reader's Digest's illustrated book has this to say about Borglum's plan: "As subjects he chose . . . the four presidents he felt symbolized great themes in American history. George Washington represented independence, liberty, and the dignity of the presidency. Thomas Jefferson recalled the principle of self-government. Abraham Lincoln symbolized the permanence of the Union; and Theodore Roosevelt, economic freedom and the importance of the West." Reader's Digest, *America's Historic Places: An Illustrated Guide to Our Country's Past* (Pleasantville, N.Y.: Reader's Digest, 1988), 226.

124. In fact, the "how" and "who" questions are articulated as the only obvious ones about Stone Mountain by Bari Rosenthal Love, "The South Looms Large at Georgia's Stone Mountain," *Southern Living,* June 1984, 97.

125. This too seems to be a result of the mountain carvings' articulation with major public works and civil engineering projects of the late nineteenth and early twentieth centuries. It is still standard in discussions of projects like the Panama Canal, the Brooklyn and Golden Gate Bridges, the Empire State Building, and so forth, to mention the number of workers who were killed during their construction. See Newhouse, *Builders,* 37, 62, 67, 135.

126. Pomeroy, "Selections," 53.

127. Shaff and Shaff, *Six Wars,* 1.

128. Schama, *Landscape,* 410.

129. Senie and Webster, *Critical Issues,* 3.

130. Harlan, "Climbing Stone Mountain," 158.

131. Jim Popovich, interview by authors, Mount Rushmore National Memorial, June 9, 2001.

132. Pomeroy, "Selections," 51.

133. Boime, *Unveiling,* 140.

134. Zinsser, *American Places,* 7.

135. Smith, *Carving,* 13.

136. Indeed, Glass reports on a number of incidents that provoked fears of "profaning" or "desecrating" Rushmore, terms typically reserved for the destruction or defacement of sacred places. Matthew Glass, "'Alexanders All': Symbols of Conquest and Resistance at Mount Rushmore," in *American Sacred Space,* ed. David Chidester and Edward T. Linenthal (Bloomington: Indiana University Press, 1995), 164–65.

137. Russ Finley, "The Making of Rushmore," *Mount Rushmore Magazine* (San Francisco: American Park Network, 1997), 25.

138. Rupert Hughes, "The Mighty Works of Borglum," in *Mount Rushmore National Memorial,* pamphlet (Mount Rushmore National Memorial Commission, August 1941), 5, Papers of Gutzon Borglum.

139. Smith, *Carving,* 111.

140. Brooke, "Crazy Horse."

141. Jerry Camarillo Dunn Jr., "Big, Bad, and Beautiful," *National Geographic Traveler,* May/June 1996, 58.

142. Robb DeWall, "Thunder in the Sky," in *Korczak: Storyteller in Stone,* 5th rev. ed., ed. Robb DeWall (Crazy Horse, S.D.: Korczak's Heritage, 1997), 29.

143. That this component of the program draws the most audience response is based on our own observations, but Love concurs ("South Looms," 101).

144. Smith, *Carving,* 129.

145. Jackson, "Gutzon Borglum's Odd and Awesome Portraits," 70. Jackson names Borglum overtly as a "racist" and "anti-Semitic" (70–72). For reference to Borglum's views of Mussolini, see Boime, *Unveiling,* 157.

Expertise and Agency
Transformations of Ethos *in Human-Computer Interaction*

CAROLYN R. MILLER

In a recent book, historian Paul Edwards examines computers "as machines and as metaphors in the politics and culture" of the cold war.[1] In his account, the development of computer technology had a lot to do with making cold war ideology what it was, and that ideology in turn became embedded in computers in a mutually reinforcing process. Edwards discusses the development of operations research at the RAND Corporation, the rise of cybernetics, Robert MacNamara's implementation of the Planning-Programming-Budgeting System (PPBS) at the Pentagon, the Air Force's Semi-Automatic Ground Environment (SAGE) computerized air defense system, and President Reagan's Strategic Defense Initiative, among other things. He also explores the ways these political and technological developments affected social consciousness through popular fictions such as the *Star Wars* trilogy, *The Terminator, Blade Runner,* and other films.

The cold war computer culture, according to Edwards, produced two related discourses, which he calls closed-world discourse and cyborg discourse. By "closed-world discourse," he means "the language, technologies, and practices that together supported the visions of centrally controlled, automated global power at the heart of American Cold War politics" (7). Its central metaphor is containment (6, 8), and its paradigm instantiation is C^{3}I (command, control, communications, and information), an approach to military functioning adapted to the nuclear era that both centralized and automated strategic and tactical decision making (131). "Cyborg discourse" developed from, complements, and supports closed-world discourse, providing a mode of subjectivity for the information age (3). It focuses on "the psychological, metaphorical and philosophical aspects of computer use, rather than on their political, social, and material dimension" (21). Its central metaphor is the computer as mind, and it encourages integration between the human and the machine. Supported by theories of information processing and cognitive science, cyborg discourse constructed "the subjects who inhabited the electronic battlefields of global cold war" (172). Closed-world discourse and cyborg discourse are linked; they "collaborate" as the politics and psychology of a cultural moment (26–27).

Edwards understands "discourse" as "a way of knowledge, a background of assumptions and agreements about how reality is to be interpreted and expressed, supported by paradigmatic metaphors, techniques and technologies and potentially embodied in social institutions" (34). Drawing on Foucault, he says that discourse produces both power and knowledge in the form of "individual and institutional behavior, facts, logic, and the authority that reinforces it" (40). Looked at another way, a discourse is a rhetoric—or rather it *has* a rhetoric. The "heterogeneous ensemble" (40) that constitutes a discourse in Edwards's sense provides premises and values, produces facts and relationships, shapes audiences and exigences, enables identifications and dissociations. A discourse thus conceived delineates a rhetorical community and consequently an *ethos*—a *sensus communis* and a *locus communis*—a place where interlocutors abide, about which they contest, and from which they draw appeals. Those who dwell within a rhetorical community acquire their character as rhetorical participants from it, as it educates and socializes them. The community does this at least in part by supplying the Aristotelian components of *ethos*—the judgment (*phronesis*), values (*arete*), and feelings (*eunoia*) that make a rhetor persuasive to other members of the community.

Like "community," *ethos* has both normative and descriptive uses, which are closely entangled. Raymond Williams once noted that community is almost never used unfavorably;[2] similarly, *ethos* is used most often as a normative term, denoting those positive qualities that warrant assent to contingent claims in situations of uncertainty: good sense, good values, goodwill.[3] But Aristotle showed that *ethos* has descriptive utility as well. Because the city-states in ancient Greece had different customs and constitutions, he advised that "we should be acquainted with the kinds of character distinctive of each form of constitution; for the character distinctive of each is necessarily most persuasive to each."[4] His discussion of this point invokes two closely related Greek words, *êthos* (initial eta) and *ethos* (initial episilon), the former designating personal or moral character, as well as what the latter signifies, custom or habit.[5] *Êthos* seems to be the older word, originally meaning an accustomed place, haunt, or abode; the sense of variation by location would thus seem more fundamental than any normative virtue. If we take seriously the descriptive value of the concept, we may find that an exploration of rhetorical *ethos* can help us discern aspects of our community and our communal character that we might not otherwise notice.

Edwards's characterization of the computer culture of the cold war is suggestive for a study of the *ethos* of technology during this time, as well as for understanding the rhetorical climate of the *post*–cold war period. In particular, his descriptions of closed-world discourse and cyborg discourse alert us to the possibility that there are two modes by which computer technology can influence contemporary rhetorical character—two modes of human-computer interaction. In this essay, I will explore these two modes as the rhetoric of machine control and the rhetoric of computational subjectivity, using the specific examples of expert systems and intelligent agents, two technologies in which the role of *ethos* is foregrounded. Both expert systems and intelligent agents blur the boundaries between human and machine, creating "hybrids" (in Latour's term) or "cyborgs" (in Haraway's).[6] Such human-computer hybrids transfer to the computer some aspects of human character and require some adaptation by a human interactant, creating a "system," or dwelling place, where both must abide. The question whether *ethos* belongs to the computational system or to the humans who design, use, and value it becomes a strategic ambiguity.

The cases of expert systems and intelligent agents, I argue, illuminate two major strategies for human-computer interaction and thereby reveal two dimensions of the dwelling place we have built for ourselves with our technologies. I also suggest that these two cases illustrate a fundamental instability in the concept of *ethos* itself, as in the first case it allies itself strongly with logos and in the second with pathos. This instability can be seen historically in the differences between Aristotelian and Roman rhetorics. Aristotle treats *ethos* as a distinct rationalized appeal, which Jakob Wisse has characterized as an *ethos* of reliability or trustworthiness. In Cicero and Quintilian, on the other hand, *ethos* is "thoroughly intertwined" with pathos, in James Baumlin's phrase, producing what Wisse calls an *ethos* of sympathy.[7] Attention to the configurations and affiliations of *ethos* and its sister appeals can help reveal the complex nature of the community in which these appeals have their effects. Moreover, the normative dimensions of *ethos* thus conceived can alert us to aspects of our communal character that warrant our vigilance. An *ethos* may metonymize a community that is oppressive, restrictive, secretive, deceptive; its virtues may be ones we would not choose to emulate, even though in many situations we may find ourselves persuaded by them.

The Ethos *of Expert Systems*

According to those who work with them, expert systems are a type of artificial intelligence (AI) designed to "emulate" or "mimic" the abilities of human experts; they "address problems normally thought to require human specialists for their solution."[8] Edward Feigenbaum, developer of the first computer system of this type and an outspoken promoter of them in the 1980s, defined an expert system as "a computer program that has built into it the knowledge and capability that will allow it to operate at the expert's level."[9] The feature that distinguishes expert systems from other forms of computer-based "intelligence" is their dependence on a database of knowledge specific to the domain in which they operate.[10] In addition, expert systems are usually designed to "learn" (that is, accommodate new information into their databases), to provide accounts of their reasoning (usually by referring to a specific part of the knowledge base), and to provide reasonable responses even when knowledge is uncertain or incomplete. Whatever their success in achieving these aims, the development and use of expert systems represent a significant willingness to delegate expertise to machines. The expert system acquires the authority and credibility of a human expert and adds the virtues of the machine: speed, consistency, precision, tirelessness. It thereby acquires a particular character, or *ethos,* and presupposes a community in which its expertise will be valued.

Expert systems are part of the general methodizing of decision making over the course of the nineteenth and twentieth centuries described in Theodore Porter's *Trust in Numbers.* Porter details the pursuit of objectivity in public decision making through a variety of quantification techniques applied to economics, engineering, accountancy, medicine, and other realms. Objectivity was sought as what Porter calls a "strategy of impersonality" to protect decision makers from suspicion of bias or fallibility; such protection became important as decision makers were responsible for increasingly complex technical problems and responsible to increasingly large and diverse constituencies. In such conditions, Porter argues, trust in institutions and expert judgment declines; methodization substitutes an impersonal expertise for personal and institutional credibility and thus reduces the need for them.[11] Methodized objectivity can thus be seen as a rhetorical strategy, one that operates specifically to produce an *ethos* that will enhance the credibility of claims in this rhetorical environment. It does this by rebalancing the components of *ethos,* trading off an increasingly remote goodwill and increasingly unavailable common values for a strengthening of "good sense" through methodization or mechanization.

Let me describe one expert system in some detail. In 1985, engineers at IBM's San José manufacturing facility began developing a computer program that could help technicians interpret results of tests conducted on computer disk drives as they rolled off the assembly line. The disk drives had more than five hundred parts, and these final tests simulated the operating conditions and actions of an end-user. With the help of two of the best technicians in the test area, the engineers reduced some thirty pounds of engineering documentation to computer code that could interpret failure data, provide repair or solution strategies, and explain its solutions by providing citations to the engineering documentation. The system, named DEFT (Diagnostic Expert for Final Test), was introduced to other test technicians as a new tool that could help them do their jobs faster and better, and indeed, DEFT was reported to solve 98 percent of problems with 100 percent accuracy and to diagnose failures five to twenty times faster than the technicians could, in less than a minute. In addition, it cut the time required to train a test technician from fifteen to four months and dramatically reduced the amount of waste (perfectly good parts being erroneously replaced and discarded) from 38 to 3 percent. DEFT cost about $100,000 to develop and was valued in 1990 at

$10 million annually (including its extension into other manufacturing and testing areas).[12]

Other expert systems also had significant successes. The first commercially successful one was XCON, introduced in 1980 at DEC to help engineers configure the new VAX computers for specific customer requirements; it reduced the time to configure orders by a factor of 15 and improved the accuracy of orders from 70 percent for human experts to 98 percent.[13] By 1986, XCON was providing annual savings of $40 million in testing and manufacturing costs.[14] In the late 1980s, a number of expert systems were featured as success stories in the business press. In 1988, an article in *Harvard Business Review* described the American Express Authorizer's Assistant, which helps with phone authorization of credit purchases; Westinghouse Electric's Process Diagnostic System, which monitors steam turbine performance; and N L Baroid's MUDMAN, which analyzes twenty parameters of oil well drilling fluids to help adjust the drilling process to specific conditions. These systems and others are described as saving their companies money and improving the performance of technical specialists.[15] Similarly, the April 1987 issue of *High Technology* featured some of these same systems as well as others used in financial planning, homeowners' insurance, aircraft manufacturing (at Northrop), electrical relay configuration (at Westinghouse), and robot diagnosis and repair (at Ford).[16] A 1996 survey of expert systems in business covering 1983 to 1990 found records of 440 systems "in actual use" in areas such as production and operations management (at 47 percent, the largest area), finance (17 percent), information systems, human resources, marketing, and strategic management. The reported productivity increases due to these systems ranged from 20 to 480 percent. A classification by function showed that 25 percent of the systems primarily performed interpretation, 21 percent planning, and 14 percent design, the three largest categories.[17]

Reports in the 1980s encouraged managers to believe that major efficiencies and improvements could be made with the help of expert systems and that the rather steep development costs and lengthy development times would be well worth it: "[E]xpert systems have already allowed novices to perform expertlike tasks. . . . The next wave . . . may be even more powerful and valuable"; "expert systems [are] a key to future competitiveness"; "Expert systems . . . will make expertise more generally available throughout the industry . . . and could significantly help to solve the skills shortage."[18] Feigenbaum wrote several books for the mass market, explaining expert systems and documenting their successes; in one typical statement he says, "Recalling the great machines for assisting human muscles . . . we can think of the expert systems of today and tomorrow as power tools for the knowledge worker, tools to assist minds, not muscles."[19]

To appreciate how expertise is conceptualized—and automated—in expert systems, it helps to know something about how they work.[20] Generally, an expert system has three major components: the knowledge base for the domain of expertise, an "inference engine" that operates on (or "reasons" with) that knowledge, and a user interface. The knowledge base is usually represented in the form of rules, or if . . . then statements, although other methods are also used. DEFT, for example, had a knowledge base of about two hundred rules articulating the relationships between failure symptoms and causes or diagnoses; these rules apply only to the specific tests conducted on a specific disk drive.[21] The inference engine commonly uses forward chaining (reasoning from facts and conditions to implications or conclusions) or backward chaining (reasoning from a goal or conclusion back through the conditions that make it possible), or both. The user interface allows querying about a problem to be answered, acquiring new knowledge, reporting conclusions, and explaining them by reference to the facts and rules invoked. Expertise, then, is operationalized as the effective combination of two components, knowledge and inference, and it is put to work and made available to others through the interface.

Expert systems were a departure from the earliest AI efforts by Allan Newell and Herbert A. Simon, who had focused on general strategies, or heuristics, that could apply to a range of specific problems, heuristics such as search, generate and test (or trial and error), reason backward from a goal, and the like. But it soon became apparent that intelligent problem solving on issues of any real complexity (including chess) could not be achieved through general heuristics, no matter how powerful. In 1977, this realization was called a "shift in paradigm": "The fundamental problem of understanding intelligence is not the identification of a few powerful techniques but the question of how to represent large amounts of knowledge in a fashion that permits their effective use and interaction. . . . [T]he problem solver (whether man or machine) must know explicitly how to use its knowledge—with general techniques supplemented by domain-specific pragmatic know-how. Thus, we see AI as having shifted from a *power-based* strategy for achieving intelligence to a *knowledge-based* strategy."[22]

As early as 1971, Feigenbaum had argued that there was a tradeoff between generality and power, that expert levels of problem solving required specialization, not generality, and that there was not much transfer of expertise between specialty areas.[23] Feigenbaum was involved in the first project to use the knowledge strategy, begun in 1965 at Stanford with chemists Joshua Lederberg and Carl Djerassi. They produced a program called DENDRAL that infers molecular structure from mass spectrometer data. The program was widely accepted by chemists, contributing to refereed journal publications.[24] DENDRAL was "almost the antithesis" of the General Problem Solver, according to McCorduck's early history of the field,[25] and Feigenbaum became an outspoken advocate for this new strategy: "DENDRAL was an early herald of AI's shift to the knowledge-based paradigm. It demonstrated the point of the primacy of domain-specific knowledge in achieving expert levels of performance."[26] He claimed, "Our agents must be knowledge-rich, even if they are methods-poor," and, in rejecting the "power strategy," he asserted that "in the knowledge is the power" ("Art of Artificial Intelligence," 1016, 1018).

The term "expert system" did not come into use until about 1980;[27] before that, such systems were referred to as knowledge-based systems. Feigenbaum created the expression "knowledge engineering" in 1977 to name the process by which the knowledge database is acquired and created.[28] The knowledge engineer, says Feigenbaum, must "take the knowledge, the experience, the hard-earned intuitions of experts and put them in computer software."[29] This process, which turned out to be a major part of the work involved in creating an expert system, involves asking questions, observing the expert at work on a problem, presenting the expert with an incomplete prototype system and finding out what is wrong with it.[30] The knowledge engineer's work is complicated when more than one expert is consulted, since experts do not often agree,[31] but expert systems that combine the knowledge of more than one expert are acknowledged to have an advantage over any single expert.[32]

To the computer scientists and engineers who jumped on the expert systems bandwagon in the 1980s, knowledge was a commodity—that was what created a practical market for their efforts—but it was also a resource that could be mastered, shaped, and improved by computer modeling. Feigenbaum's maxim, "In the knowledge is the power," emanates from the closed world that Edwards describes. The closed-world approach to expert systems emphasizes not only the social and economic advantages to be gained but also, according to the 1982 *Handbook of Artificial Intelligence,* the role of computers and computer scientists in mastering "fundamental questions concerning the nature of knowledge, both in terms of formal representational systems and as an essentially social phenomenon."[33] The assumptions of the closed world constitute the *ethos* of the culture of cold war technology—that expert knowledge produces progress, that mechanization improves expertise, that expertise implies authority, that expert authority convinces the rational. The effort to automate expertise is one of the extreme expressions of this cultural moment.

This effort is also an excellent illustration of how logos and *ethos* are related in closed-world discourse. The technological community has a longstanding preference for logos over *ethos*. A scientist or engineer is supposed to support a claim with factual observations and sound reasoning, abjuring appeals to emotion or personal character. However, one of the primary conclusions of recent work in the rhetoric of science and technology is that this rhetorical style of impersonality, in which facts "speak for themselves," is itself an appeal that universalizes results originating in particularity: the scientist must seem fungible, so that her results could have been—and might be—achieved by anyone.[34] This appeal is an *ethos* that denies the importance of *ethos*.[35] The technical *ethos* must be informed but impartial, authoritative but self-effacing. One of the major strategies for achieving this delicate balance is the transformation of *ethos* into logos. Thus, qualities that might in other situations be central to an ethotic appeal—affiliation, prior success, masterful expertise—in technical discourse are treated as factual evidence or even as inartistic proofs, attributes of the technical situation rather than of an advocate in a rhetorical situation.[36]

Expert systems implement this transformation by commodifying expertise as a programmable combination of knowledge and reasoning, detaching both from the experience and judgment of human experts and making them impersonal, portable, reproducible. Someone who consults a human expert to solve a problem will accept the solution—will believe it—based at least in part on how well the expert understands the problem, on what kinds of reasons the solution is grounded in, on how the expert displays authority. The user of an expert system, on the other hand, is provided few of these signs of human expertise. Moreover, even if its solution is the same as one from a human expert, the expert system offers a computed product rather than a judgment; all its resources—knowledge, understanding, authority—are equally based in computation, and all must thus be understood as logos. Expertise from an expert system presents itself not as the property of a rhetorical agent but as the algorithmic product of knowledge-base times inference.

Another strategy for producing the technical *ethos* is the suppression of the relational components of *ethos,* Aristotelian *arete* and *eunoia.* At the same time, the third component of *ethos, phronesis,* or "good sense," is transformed into a narrower and more technical form of knowledge, diminishing the practical, or relational, dimensions of knowledge itself. An *ethos* of pure expertise addresses its audience only in terms of knowledge and not in terms of values or interests. In its reliance on the authority of knowledge, technical discourse approximates what Aristotle called dialectic, which took place not in the public forum but in the more restricted company of the wise. Dialectic reasons syllogistically from generally accepted opinions that "seem right to all people or most people or the wise—and in the latter case all the wise or most of them or those best known and generally accepted."[37] The intellectual quality needed by the dialectician or the wise person is not *phronesis, arete,* or *eunoia,* but *sophia* (wisdom), and it is needed not in order to persuade others, but simply in order to know the premises and conclusions. And if we think of dialectic as an ideal communicative situation, in which there is agreement on ends and values and a perfectly knowledgeable and rational audience, then expertise is the only quality of character needed to prevail. In dialectic, as Eugene Garver notes, logos drives out *ethos.*[38] We can conclude that in Aristotelian rhetoric, *ethos stands in for expertise,* because rhetoric occurs in situations where either complete knowledge is not available or the audience is not adequately knowledgeable or competent: pathos and *ethos, arete* and *eunoia* make up for the lack of knowledge. But scholarship in the rhetoric of science has also challenged the distinction between dialectic and rhetoric, showing that the idealized conditions of dialectic never hold in actual discourse. Thus, we have to reverse the Aristotelian presumptions and take the relational complexities of rhetoric rather than the idealizations of dialectic as the grounds for theorizing. Under these conditions we must conclude, conversely, that in a technical discourse, a discourse that banks on logos, *expertise stands in for ethos,* because technical discourse cannot acknowledge the contingencies of the audience and the uncertainties of the situation.

As noted earlier, Jakob Wisse describes Aristotle's conception of *ethos* as "rational," since it is focused not on the arousing of emotions in the audience but on their need for a speaker to be reliable and trustworthy.[39] Wisse points to the *Rhetoric* 2.1.5–7 as "unambiguous" in indicating that Aristotle takes "telling the truth" as central to *ethos* (32), since his reasoning is that a speaker who lacks *phronesis, arete,* or *eunoia* may not tell the truth. But Wisse also notes that this passage is the only place where Aristotle mentions the element of *phronesis,* which is central to the rational concept of *ethos* (54),[40] and that Aristotle's use of *ethos* in this way, to include intellectual in addition to moral qualities, seems to be an exception in his work (although this broader use was common in other authors) (31). If my analysis here is correct, it may be that Aristotle's interest in dialectic shaped his discussion of *ethos,* providing a special role for expertise and giving specific prominence to the intellectual qualities of the speaker.

Closed-world technical discourse, aspiring to be a dialectic for the modern world, presents a contemporary model for the "rational" conception of *ethos,* and the case of expert systems represents the perfection of such technical discourse, bringing its features into sharp relief. Rational *ethos* finds a close rhetorical ally in logos: it focuses our attention on the "knowledge-base" that authorizes claims. Closed-world discourse offers an *ethos* that is both diminished and disguised. It is diminished from its full Aristotelian form to expertise alone and then disguised as logos. Zeno's image of the closed fist, though meant for dialectic, is a fitting image for the character of this rhetoric and for the kind of relationships we can expect to find in the closed world.

The Ethos of Intelligent Agents

Like many technological developments, expert systems created enthusiastic expectations that turned out not to be wholly justified. Early predictions were that the market for expert systems would reach $4 billion by 1990, but it reached only one-tenth of that value by then.[41] In 1993, a panel of twenty-five industry experts judged the AI market (primarily expert systems) to be flat or declining, and their predictions for 1996 and 1999 were similar.[42] A 1995 survey exploring how the first wave of commercial expert systems built in the mid-1980s had fared over time showed that only one-third were being actively used and maintained and that about half of them had been abandoned between 1987 and 1992. The major reasons offered for abandoning these systems were not technical but managerial and organizational; that is, the systems performed as expected, but they became unnecessary because of changes in operations or strategy, they were not accepted by users, or they were not kept up to date.[43]

But there were also technical reasons for what in the late 1980s turned into a sudden collapse in the expert systems industry. In his history of AI, Daniel Crevier points out that the initial wave of expert systems used expensive, dedicated hardware platforms and the specialized programming language LISP. By the late 1980s, mass-produced and therefore low-cost desk-top microprocessors were becoming common; these were networkable, unlike the LISP machines, and required less specialized programming skills. Crevier describes a recovery starting in the early 1990s, as expert systems were adapted to the microcomputer environment, but notes that many companies were reluctant to use the terms "AI" or "expert system" because of "psychological scars" from the earlier disasters.[44] Expert systems were embedded covertly into more conventional business and industrial systems, adding functionality without the hype or the labels. Similarly, Janet Vaux has suggested that in an attempt to salvage knowledge "as a marketable commodity," expert systems were "rebranded" as Knowledge-Based Systems (KBS) in deliberate avoidance of the terms "AI" and "expert systems" that had become associated with failure.[45]

While there were both technical and market reasons for the decline of expert systems, there were also rhetorical reasons. It seems that the automation of expertise was not a sustainably persuasive idea. The fate of expert systems was caught up in a general shift in the rhetorical environment for expertise in the last decades of the twentieth century, a shift that undermined closed-world discourse and its *ethos* of expertise. The poverty of that *ethos* is not a sufficient explanation for its diminishing success, because it had been quite successful in the immediate postwar period. Roger Cooke, for example, calls that period one of "almost unlimited faith in expert opinion" and notes that by the late 1960s there were more than eleven thousand think tanks advising the U.S. government. But he notes that the percentage of Americans with "great confidence" in the leaders of a variety of institutions (medicine, education, religion, industry, and others) declined sharply between the mid-1960s and the early 1970s, pointing to the war in Vietnam as a significant factor.[46] Other factors were the environmental and consumer movements, including the dramatic reversal of public opinion about nuclear power between 1965 and 1975 and the congressional decision in 1971 to cancel support for the SST, the Boeing Corporation's heavily subsidized supersonic passenger plane.[47] Further, as Richard Gaskins notes, a series of court decisions shifted legal presumption away from the discretionary expertise of government agencies. He concludes that the traditional (and conservative) presumption in favor of existing institutions posited by Richard Whately was replaced in the late twentieth century by "the increasingly radical presumption of institutional failure."[48] Insofar as expertise is an attribute of established institutions, this change in presumption works against its rhetorical appeal.

If the closed world did not end with the end of the cold war, it has certainly been transformed. The politics and rhetoric of centralized, expert control no longer have the scope and assurance they once did. Trends that began in the 1960s, including the loss of confidence in elites, the suspicion of institutions, and the diversification of markets and information, combined with continuing advances in technology, have created a world at once more complex and less certain than the immediate postwar world. In an image that captures this transformation well, Anthony Giddens has described the contemporary world as "like being aboard a careering juggernaut ... rather than being in a carefully controlled and well-driven motor car."[49] One result has been a widely remarked loss of trust—in institutions, technology, and expertise. If, as Niklas Luhmann emphasizes, trust both reduces perceived complexity and increases our tolerance for uncertainty, then conditions of increased complexity and uncertainty make trust increasingly necessary.[50]

Trust has become a subject of interest in many disciplines recently, including political theory, philosophy, sociology, and psychology. Definitions of trust invoke reliance on another's goodwill, judgments about motivation and competence, confidence in the reliability, knowledge, probity, or love of another.[51] Rhetoricians will recognize trust as a function of *ethos* and will hear echoes of Aristotle's discussion of *ethos* in these definitions. We trust those in whom we sense goodwill, appropriate moral qualities, and knowledge that can be applied to our problems. In his discussion of Aristotle's rhetorical treatise as an "art of character," Garver argues that *ethos* and trust "are identical."[52] In fact, he says, it is trust that allows reasoning to persuade: "reasoning persuades *because* it is evidence of character and so gives grounds for trust" (162; emphasis added). This relationship is precisely the Aristotelian *ethos* of reliability.[53] The corollary is that argument fails to persuade when it is "too strong," that is, when it relies disproportionately on logos (178). Because rhetoric is situated and addressed, it needs *ethos* (and pathos) in addition to logos (182); we might therefore have predicted that an *ethos* that allies itself too closely to logos, like the *ethos* of expert systems, will fail to persuade. An *ethos* without *arete* and *eunoia* provides no basis for agreement on values or for belief in the good intentions of a rhetorical agent. Thus, the ethotic strategies of expert systems cannot have had much purchase, except to the extent that they reflected the prevailing cultural values of the closed-world cold war era, including specifically the characteristic deference to expertise. But as the closed world began to change, the *ethos* of expert systems became increasingly ineffective. And in fact, with the decline of expert systems and the change in rhetorical environment sketched above came a shift of strategy in the rhetoric of computation—including an identifiable shift in ethotic strategy. The new *ethos* for computational systems, which I associate with cyborg discourse, focuses on the establishment of trust.

Expert systems have been largely succeeded by a class of AI programs called "intelligent agents."[54] Such agents interact with their environments. In order to do so, they must be able to perceive the environment and to initiate action in it; they must be both reactive and to some degree autonomous.[55] Although hardware robots exhibit a kind of agency, the term "intelligent agent" is usually applied to software robots, often called "softbots" and sometimes just "bots." Examples of such agents include some computer viruses, many Internet search and indexing tools, and newer systems for air traffic control, manufacturing control, and financial transaction management. Such agents go beyond the capabilities of expert systems not only in being at least semiautonomous but also in being able to make choices among conflicting goals.[56] In addition to the database of "expertise" encapsulated in expert systems, they require a restricted but interactive "common sense" of the kind that Newell and Simon were after.

Agency was presumed early on even for expert systems. In 1977, Feigenbaum insisted on the need for the expert system to explain its decisions, "else the question arises of who is in control of the agent's activity."[57] The explanation facility is also justified by the need to make the expert system's responses acceptable, that is, credible to its users,[58] and credibility, in turn, is an attribute of rhetorical agents. Moreover, an expert system may be designed to enact its own agency with the first-person pronoun in its output. One well-known system called MYCIN, for example, was programmed to deliver recommended drug therapies like this: "My preferred therapy recommendation is as follows: Give the following in combination: 1) ETHAMBUTAL, Dose: 1.28 g (13.0 100-mg tablets) q24h PO for 60 days.... Although I suspect that fungus may be a possible pathogen, in the absence of definitive evidence, I will not recommend antifungal therapy at this time. Please obtain samples for fungal, TB, and viral cultures."[59] Many expert systems had names and thus could be referred to as agents; a few were even named after the expert whose knowledge they represent, such as "Mike-in-the-Box" at Du Pont, which monitored a touchy distillation column twenty-four hours a day, exceeding the capacities of the only engineer who had ever done the job successfully. Crevier describes "Aldo on a Disk," an expert system designed to replace Aldo Cimino, an employee of Campbell Soup who was the company expert on large bacteria-killing cookers.[60]

Intelligent agents carry these trends further. Two examples will illustrate the ways that agency can be instantiated in these software systems. An early software agent with a significant reputation and literature is Julia, a softbot that inhabits a multi-user domain (MUD), interacting with players and providing them information about the labyrinthine virtual structure of the MUD and about other players. "She" interacts with other players conversationally:

You say, "julia, what can you do?"
Julia says, "I relay messages, Lenny."

You say, "do you have a message for me, julia?"
Julia says, "I have no messages for you."
. . .
You say, "julia, how many messages are you carrying?"
Julia says, "I am holding 114 messages for 98 players, Lenny."[61]

"Lenny" in the example above is Leonard Foner, who has written a detailed case study of Julia. He points out many skills Julia has that are not surprising for a piece of software: she can perform computations on request, provide information about her own code, and carry current information about the ever-changing structure of the MUD. But Foner also notes several less typical features that are important to Julia's ability to interact with other players: Julia can describe herself ("I'm 5'1" tall, weigh 123 lbs, with close-cropped frizzy blond hair and dark brown eyes") (11), express emotion ("Julia is offended by Lenny's suggestion") (13), and fend off passes:

Space-Ace says, "So why won't you kiss me, Julia?"
Julia says, "Sorry, I'm not into geeks, Space-Ace." (14)

Julia was created in the late 1980s and is implemented as typed conversation, a relatively primitive form of interaction. More recent agents use animated visual representations. An example is Herman the Bug, a pedagogical agent designed to provide motivation and customized feedback within interactive learning environments. Herman is described by his creators as "a talkative, quirky, somewhat churlish insect with a propensity to fly about the screen . . . as it provides students with problem-solving advice. Its behaviors include 30 animated segments, 160 audio clips, and several songs." The animations range from twenty seconds to two minutes long and are accompanied by a musical score "assembled from a large library of runtime-mixable, soundtrack elements." Herman's communicative behaviors include demonstrations with spoken explanations, abstract advice without demonstrations, and task-specific suggestions. In a study of Herman's effect on student learning and attitude, middle-school children learned significant amounts of material presented and reacted favorably to the helpfulness and entertainment value of the agent.[62]

How do computational agents work?[63] Compared with expert systems, this question is harder to answer because no single architecture has been adopted. But an interactive system must have both sensors and actuators to receive information about the environment and to take action within that environment. An autonomous system must have some representation of goals or plans. Some agents are designed with a hierarchical, top-down structure, including a central planner with defined goals that collects data from the sensors and sends commands to actuators to bring the system closer to its goals. Others are designed with a bottom-up structure, with no central reasoner but with smaller distributed competence modules that are each connected to relevant sensors and actuators. Beyond these operational features, an intelligent agent must have "social ability" and "adaptivity"; these are more sophisticated levels of organization for the sensors and actuators at the system's interface with the environment. Social ability requires "some kind of agent-communication language," of course, and adaptivity permits the system to learn and adapt to new situations. Although an agent such as a search engine needs only minimal social ability at the interface, and an agent such as a virus interacts only with other forms of software, agents like Julia and Herman require much more elaborate interfaces, often involving linguistic parsers, models of common-sense knowledge, and ways of relating such knowledge to specific domains of operation.

The rhetorical approach of these agents is quite different from "the knowledge strategy" of the expert systems era. Neither Julia nor Herman is presented overtly or primarily as a source of information or expertise, and both work because users have *relationships* with them. As a consequence, the interface is critical, perhaps more critical than any other component, and certainly more than it was for expert systems. Foner argues that Julia's success is instructive about what features a successful agent needs to have; these include autonomy, anthropomorphism, personalizability (Julia remembers user preferences), interactive discourse, cooperation, and trust (35–36).[64] The creators of Herman the Bug hypothesize a "persona effect" for agents, which they credit for the strong positive effect on students' perception of their experience in the interactive learning environment: the persona effect is demonstrated by "students' perception of the agent's concern for them, the high degree of credibility they ascribed to it, and their perception of its utility and entertainment value."[65] More generally, computer scientists increasingly recognize that interactive computational agents engage users in social relationships in which anthropomorphic "personality" has an effect: "It is clear that agents that understand social relationships, maintain histories with users, have some knowledge of human emotion, are beginning to understand human speech, can speak themselves, and have control over media channels to deliver morphing faces, music, and theater-quality sound—all responsively and in real time—have tremendous inherent attachment-forming capabilities."[66] Another researcher notes that such systems invite us to take an intentional stance in which we base explanations of and predictions about their actions on our imposition of representations and intentions. In this approach, we seek empathy, defined as a "measure of representational comparability between two systems," that of the user and that of the agent. Other discussions emphasize credibility and trust as the crucial features of interactive systems.[67]

In order to function as agents, computational systems must be interactive and therefore must be social; and in order to engage as social interactants, they must offer an *ethos* that promises empathy and invites trust. Such an *ethos* highlights *arete* and *eunoia,* and, though it cannot abandon *phronesis,* certainly leaves it out of the spotlight. Such an *ethos* is allied with pathos, not with logos, and can be under-stood as a Ciceronian *ethos* of sympathy rather than an Aristotelian *ethos* of ration-ality. Although in *De Oratore* Cicero does not use a term equivalent to *ethos,* like Aristotle, he divides the art of speaking into three efforts on which persuasion "wholly" relies: "the proof of our allegations, the winning of our hearers' favour, and the rousing of their feelings to whatever impulse our case may require."[68] The second effort, winning favor, is elaborated in a later passage: "[I]t is a very impor-tant contribution to winning a case that ... the minds of the audience are, as much as possible, won over to feel sympathy toward the orator as well as towards the person the orator is speaking for" (2.182).[69] Here sympathy is from the Latin *benevolentia* (literally, goodwill), and winning over is from the verb *conciliare.* As Wisse summarizes it, Ciceronian *ethos* has not only content (the presentation of favorable aspects of character) but also effect (a sympathetic response from the audience) (240). In this way, as many commentators have noted, Ciceronian *ethos* is allied with pathos; in fact, beginning at least as early as Quintilian, many have conceived both *ethos* and pathos as concerned with emotion, the "gentle" emo-tions and violent emotions, respectively.[70] The connection between *ethos* and pathos occurs through *eunoia,* which, as Aristotle discusses it, is a disposition with-in the character of the rhetor, but which, as Cicero applies it, has affective conse-quences.

Clearly, both disposition and effect are necessary for *ethos* to have any rhetori-cal force: character matters only if it matters to an audience, if it changes their uptake of the rest of the discourse. Rhetorical goodwill must be recognized and acknowledged; trustworthiness must be complemented by trust. As Wisse points out, Cicero's framework for *ethos* may not be as conceptually neat as Aristotle's, but it may be more practically useful, since it makes a distinction that Aristotle does not: "the qualities required in a speech to win sympathy are very different from those necessary for arousing violent emotions" (247). Thus, *ethos* needs its association with pathos, more in some situations than in others, just as it needs its association with logos, in order that goodwill not be dismissed as foolish and trust-worthiness as naïve.

Intelligent agents, then, have adopted an *ethos* of sympathy, an *ethos* strongly allied with pathos, and it is for this reason that we can understand their rhetoric as a form of "cyborg discourse." In Edwards's discussion, cyborg discourse is part of the same enterprise that closed-world discourse represents, but it addresses us as individual subjectivities rather than as members of the public; it offers inter-action, identification, assimilation. By now, cyborg discourse has accommodated us to such forms of human-machine integration as "wearable computing," bio-engineering, and virtual reality, concepts that just twenty years ago seemed far more weird than they do today. Intelligent agents instantiate the cyborg metaphor of computer as mind and work hard to make it literal,[71] but they succeed only to the extent that they are "user-friendly." They fit Edwards's description of the two cyborg-model robots in the first *Star Wars* film, perhaps better than the robots do themselves: they are "embodied subjectivities that [are] friendly, familiar, unthreatening, and personal" (336).

Cyborg discourse, I am claiming, presents a contemporary model for the Ciceronian *ethos* of sympathy.[72] An *ethos* of sympathy emphasizes the Aristotelian component of *eunoia,* finding its rhetorical ally in pathos; it focuses our attention on the interest that a rhetor has in us, in the audience's feelings, needs, sensitivities, and interests. An *ethos* of sympathy is always looking for a response, and Zeno's image of rhetoric as an open hand represents its character well. However, as Cicero reminds us through the figure of Antonius, the effort to create a desired response in an audience requires strategy and technique and, although Antonius himself swears he has never attempted "to arouse either indignation or compassion, either ill-will or hatred" in an audience "without being really stirred" himself, his very raising of the issue acknowledges that deception is possible (2.189). The *ethos* of sympathy, which appears to be about the audience, may in fact be about the rhetor. But because it continually deflects attention away from the agent and back to the audience, the *ethos* of sympathy makes it difficult for us to know the rhetor.

The Closed World as Dwelling Place

Although expert systems may have been replaced by other technologies, the closed world is still with us. For Edwards, cyborg discourse is not a way out of the closed world but a strategy for accommodating us to it. He notes that the "politics of disembodied, pervasive Others mirrored the politics of the cold war itself—a grand struggle between Us and Them. Embodied AI came to stand for another way of dwelling in the closed world, one that accepted its terms but sought actively to construct new and coherent subject positions within it, . . . a kind of liberal détente in human-cyborg relations" (340). The closed world remains powerful, capable of appropriating or absorbing alternatives, such as the "green world," an open, human-centered, natural yet magical and spiritual community, which Edwards finds represented in older literary traditions and in some contemporary science fictions, as well as in some marginal social movements such as animism, feminist witchcraft, deep ecology, and the like (13, 350). Yet he sees some hope for escape from the determinisms of the closed world in the "recombinant" possibilities of the cyborg: "reconstructions of traditional relationships among rationality, intelligence, emotion, gender, and embodiment" (350) may "cross and recross the neon landscapes of cyberspace" and "find a habitation, if not a home, inside the closed world" (351).

In the two cases of expert systems and intelligent agents, and possibly in the larger patterns that Edwards describes, we can see the swinging of a pendulum, from an overemphasis on expertise to an overemphasis on interaction, from a logos-centric to a pathos-centric *ethos.* Cyborg discourse works to ameliorate the crisis of trust that closed-world discourse both created and foundered on, yet it can offer no assurance that trust is not misplaced. The *ethos* of rational reliability and the *ethos* of sympathy are not only rhetorical strategies but also rhetorical modes of being, each with its limitations. Each in its own way attempts to create a version of the closed world in which we might dwell by modeling a character who belongs there—a set of judgments, a way of feeling, a mode of interaction. The closed-world discourse of expert systems creates an asymmetric yet ordered and systematic space where some are experts with knowledge and authority and some must be suppliants to expertise, where the only mode of relationship is through knowledge. The cyborg discourse of intelligent agents creates an apparently symmetrical and friendly space where feeling and response are sought, but where they must be offered blindly, to an agent who is never disclosed, who remains unknown, unrevealed.

The rhetorical criticism of both these spaces is an ethical criticism: both the logos-centered *ethos* of expert systems and the pathos-centered *ethos* of intelligent agents need to be balanced with *arete*, with the specifically *ethical* component of *ethos*. Moral virtue, the goal-setting locus of intentionality that ultimately defines the identity of a character or a community, is largely absent from both the *ethos* of expert systems and the *ethos* of intelligent agents. Perhaps virtue cannot be captured in computational systems, though the effort will surely be made. If rhetoric is an art—that is, a considered, productive effort to make and remake our ourselves and our world—then *arete* itself may be, as Aristotle thought, an artful product, and artificial intelligence may one day produce artificial virtue. Such a virtue may well be yet another version of ourselves, or it may show us some new recombinant possibilities. Either way, rhetorical criticism of such an *ethos* will be essential.

Notes

1. Paul N. Edwards, *The Closed World: Computers and the Politics of Discourse in Cold War America* (Cambridge, Mass.: MIT Press, 1996), 1. Subsequent references to this work will be cited in the text.

2. Raymond Williams, *Keywords: A Vocabulary of Culture and Society* (New York: Oxford, 1976), 66.

3. See also the useful review of the notion of community by political scientist Robert Plant, who also makes the point that community is "inherently normative" in "Community: Concept, Conception, and Ideology," *Politics and Society* 8, no. 1 (1978): 80.

4. Aristotle, *On Rhetoric: A Theory of Civic Discourse,* ed. and trans. George A. Kennedy (New York: Oxford University Press, 1991), 1.8.6. Subsequent citations will be to this translation unless otherwise noted.

5. See also the discussion of "Ethos" in James Jasinski, *Sourcebook on Rhetoric: Key Concepts in Contemporary Rhetorical Studies,* ed. Herbert W. Simons, *Rhetoric and Society* (Thousand Oaks, Calif.: Sage Publications, 2001), 230.

6. Bruno Latour, *We Have Never Been Modern,* trans. Catherine Porter (Cambridge: Harvard University Press, 1993); Donna Haraway, "A Manifesto for Cyborgs: Science, Technology, and Socialist Feminism in the 1980s," *Socialist Review* 15, no. 2 (1985): 65–107.

7. James S. Baumlin, "Ethos," in *Encyclopedia of Rhetoric,* ed. Thomas O. Sloane (New York: Oxford University Press, 2001), 269; Jakob Wisse, *Ethos and Pathos from Aristotle to Cicero* (Amsterdam: Adolf M. Hakkert, 1989).

8. Joseph Giarratano and Gary Riley, *Expert Systems: Principles and Programming,* 3d ed. (Boston: PWS, 1998), 2; Dorothy Leonard-Barton and John J. Sviokla, "Putting Expert Systems to Work," *Harvard Business Review* 88, no. 2 (1988): 91; Richard O. Duda and Edward H. Shortliffe, "Expert Systems Research," *Science* 220, no. 4594 (1983): 261.

9. Edward A. Feigenbaum and Pamela McCorduck, *The Fifth Generation: Artificial Intelligence and Japan's Computer Challenge to the World* (Reading, Mass.: Addison-Wesley, 1983), 63–64.

10. The field of artificial intelligence includes multiple subfields, not only expert systems but also speech recognition, robotics, vision and pattern recognition, as well as general reasoning and logic programs; see Giarratano and Riley, *Expert Systems,* 2.

11. Theodore M. Porter, *Trust in Numbers: The Pursuit of Objectivity in Science and Public Life* (Princeton, N.J.: Princeton University Press, 1995), xi, 214.

12. Roland J. Braun, "Turning Computers into Experts," *Quality Progress* 23 (1990): 71–75; Edward Feigenbaum, Pamela McCorduck, and H. Penny Nii, *The Rise of the Expert Company: How Visionary Companies Are Using Artificial Intelligence to Achieve Higher Productivity and Profits* (New York: Times Books, 1988).

13. Giarratano and Riley, *Expert Systems,* 16.

14. Daniel Crevier, *AI: The Tumultuous History of the Search for Artificial Intelligence* (New York: Basic Books, 1993), 198.

15. Leonard-Barton and Sviokla, "Putting Expert Systems to Work."

16. Dwight B. Davis, "Artificial Intelligence Goes to Work," *High Technology* 7, no. 4 (1987): 16–27.

17. Sean B. Eom, "A Survey of Operational Expert Systems in Business (1980–1993)," *Interfaces* 26, no. 5 (1996): 55. There are similar classifications in Feigenbaum and McCorduck, *Fifth Generation;* Raj Reddy, "Foundations and Grand Challenges of Artificial Intelligence," *AI Magazine* 9, no. 4 (1988): 9–21; K. P. Valavanis, A. I. Kokkinaki, and S. G. Tzafestas, "Knowledge-Based (Expert) Systems in Engineering Applications: A Survey," *Journal of Intelligent and Robotic Systems* 10 (1994): 113–45. The 1998 (third) edition of Giarratano and Riley's major textbook classifies "hundreds" of systems according to the major kinds of tasks they do: configuration, diagnosis, instruction, interpretation of data, monitoring, planning, prediction, prescribing remedies, and process control. Other systems exist but have not been reported on because of the military or proprietary secrets in their knowledge base.

18. Leonard-Barton and Sviokla, "Putting Expert Systems to Work," 98; John Burgess, "The Electronic Experts; Software Systems Enter Area Heretofore the Preserve of Humans: Decision-Making," *Washington Post,* October 1, 1989, H1; Kate Taphouse, "Using Computers in Business and Industry; Radical New Solutions—How Knowledge-Based Systems Provide Expert Skills," *Financial Times,* November 24, 1989, x.

19. Feigenbaum, McCorduck, and Nii, *Rise of the Expert Company,* 6.

20. My account here relies on several sources: Braun, "Turning Computers into Experts"; Duda and Shortliffe, "Expert Systems Research"; Feigenbaum and McCorduck, *Fifth Generation;* Giarratano and Riley, *Expert Systems;* Valavanis, Kokkinaki, and Tzafestas, "Knowledge-Based (Expert) Systems."

21. Here's an example of a rule from the knowledge base of DEFT: "IF the testcase failure is not CFTSA(E) and there are multiple failures and multiple devices are failing and the failures are on A1 controller and multiple parts are failing THEN the cause of the failure is A1M2 DHPLO (VFO) card with 60% probability or A1X2 DDC/DXB card with 20% probability or A1N2 SERDES/CLOCK card with 20% probability" (Feigenbaum, McCorduck, and Nii, *Rise of the Expert Company,* 69, paragraphing changed).

22. Ira Goldstein and Seymour Papert, "Artificial Intelligence, Language, and the Study of Knowledge," *Cognitive Science* 1, no. 1 (1977): 85–86.

23. E. A. Feigenbaum, B. G. Buchanan, and J. Lederberg, "On Generality and Problem Solving: A Case Study Using the DENDRAL Program," *Machine Intelligence* 6 (1971): 165–90.

24. Duda and Shortliffe, "Expert Systems Research," 264.

25. McCorduck, *Machines Who Think,* 284.

26. Edward A. Feigenbaum, "The Art of Artificial Intelligence: I. Themes and Case Studies of Knowledge Engineering" (paper presented at the Fifth International Joint Conference on Artificial Intelligence, Cambridge, Mass., 1977), 1020.

27. The titles of papers listed under "expert systems" in the *Index to Artificial Intelligence Research, 1954–1984* do not include the term itself until 1981, although papers going back to 1970 are listed under that subject term (Scientific Datalink, *Index to Artificial Intelligence Research, 1954–1984,* 4 vols. [New York: Scientific Datalink, 1985]). Similarly, the earliest subject-term entries in Lexis-Nexis are in 1981, in Periodicals Abstract Research (ProQuest) 1980, in Web of Science 1982, and in INSPEC (WebSPIRS) 1980. All of these databases cover material before 1980. The first two journals in this subfield of artificial intelligence both began publishing in 1984, *Expert Systems* (Oxford) and *Knowledge Engineering Review* (Cambridge).

28. Feigenbaum, "Art of Artificial Intelligence," 1017.

29. Feigenbaum, McCorduck, and Nii, *Rise of the Expert Company,* 7. In "The Art of Artificial Intelligence," Feigenbaum suggests that the job of the knowledge engineer is to "transfer" from the expert to the program "rules of good judgment" (1016).

30. Feigenbaum describes this process in some detail in Feigenbaum and McCorduck, *Fifth Generation,* 80–84; Feigenbaum, McCorduck, and Nii, *Rise of the Expert Company,* 43–47.

31. Davis, "Amplifying Expertise," 25; Duda and Shortliffe, "Expert Systems Research," 264.

32. Feigenbaum, "Art of Artificial Intelligence," 1028; Giarratano and Riley, *Expert Systems,* 5.

33. Avron Barr and Edward A. Feigenbaum, eds., *The Handbook of Artificial Intelligence,* 4 vols. (Los Altos, Calif.: William Kaufmann, 1982), 2:79.

34. Alan G. Gross, *The Rhetoric of Science* (Cambridge: Harvard University Press, 1990); Evelyn Fox Keller, "The Paradox of Scientific Subjectivity," in *Rethinking Objectivity,* ed. Allan Megill (Durham, N.C.: Duke University Press, 1994); Bruno Latour and Steve Woolgar, *Laboratory Life: The Social Construction of Scientific Facts* (Beverly Hills, Calif.: Sage, 1979).

35. S. Michael Halloran has made a similar point about media emphasis on personality and feelings as opposed to character and public issues; this is, he says, "an ethos that denies the importance of ethos" ("Aristotle's Concept of Ethos, or If Not His, Somebody Else's," *Rhetoric Review* 1 [1982]: 63).

36. I have described this same transformation in "The Presumptions of Expertise: Ethos in Risk Analysis," in *Configurations* 11 (2003): 163–202. The analysis in the next few paragraphs draws on my argument there.

37. Aristotle, *Topica,* trans. E. S. Forster, Loeb Classical Library (Cambridge: Harvard University Press, 1960), 1.1.18.

38. Eugene Garver, *Aristotle's Rhetoric: An Art of Character* (Chicago: University of Chicago Press, 1994), 183.

39. Wisse, *Ethos and Pathos,* 33, 246.

40. He does mention the importance of trustworthiness in two other places, 1.2.4 and 1.9.1.

41. T. Grandon Gill, "Early Expert Systems: Where Are They Now?" *MIS Quarterly* 19, no. 1 (1995): 51.

42. Kevin Coleman, "The AI Marketplace in the Year 2000," *AI Expert* 8, no. 1 (1993): 35–36.

43. Gill, "Early Expert Systems," 68, 64–66.

44. Crevier, *AI,* 209–10, 212.

45. Janet Vaux, "From Expert Systems to Knowledge-Based Companies: How the AI Industry Negotiated a Market for Knowledge," *Social Epistemology* 15, no. 3 (2001): 239, 241.

46. Roger M. Cooke, *Experts in Uncertainty: Opinion and Subjective Probability in Science* (New York: Oxford University Press, 1991), 4–5.

47. Randall L. Bytwerk, "The SST Controversy: A Case Study in the Rhetoric of Technology," *Central States Speech Journal* 30 (1979): 187–98.

48. Richard H. Gaskins, *Burdens of Proof in Modern Discourse* (New Haven, Conn.: Yale University Press, 1992), 46.

49. Anthony Giddens, *The Consequences of Modernity* (Stanford, Calif.: Stanford University Press, 1990), 53.

50. Niklas Luhmann, *Trust and Power* (Chichester: John Wiley & Sons, 1979), 7–15.

51. These definitions are from philosopher Annette Baier, *Moral Prejudices: Essays on Ethics* (Cambridge: Harvard University Press, 1994), 99; philosopher Trudy Govier, *Social Trust and Human Communities* (Montreal: McGill Queen's University Press, 1997), 4; and social theorist Giddens, *Consequences,* 34.

52. Garver, *Aristotle's Rhetoric,* 181.

53. The *ethos* of reliability requires what Luhmann calls confidence, which presumes that expectations will not be disappointed, rather than trust, which admits that they may be ("Familiarity, Confidence, Trust: Problems and Alternatives," in *Trust: Making and Breaking Cooperative Relations,* ed. Diego Gambetta [Oxford: Basil Blackwell, 1988], 94–107). The distinction between confidence and trust reflects that between the *ethos* of reliability and the *ethos* of sympathy.

54. The term "intelligent agent" starts to appear in the mid-1980s, usually in quotation marks or accompanied by an explanation. The first occurrence in the INSPEC database is 1984, in Lexis-Nexis Business/Industry News in 1982, in InfoTrac One File in 1986,

and in Web of Science in 1991. Neither "agent" nor "intelligent agent" appears in the *Index to Artificial Intelligence Research, 1954–1984.*

55. Albertas Caplinskas, "AI Paradigms," *Journal of Intelligent Manufacturing* 9 (1998): 495; James A. Hendler, "Intelligent Agents: Where AI Meets Information Technology," *IEEE Expert* 11, no. 6 (1996): 21.

56. Hendler, "Intelligent Agents," 22.

57. Feigenbaum, "Art of Artificial Intelligence," 1027–28. Of course, an explanation does not *resolve* the question of control; rather, it places the question on the table, highlighting the fact there are *two* agents involved in the decision, the system and the human who will presumable enact or approve the decision.

58. Bruce G. Buchanan, "Expert Systems: Working Systems and the Research Literature," *Expert Systems* 3, no. 1 (1986): 32; Duda and Shortliffe, "Expert Systems Research," 263; Feigenbaum and McCorduck, *Fifth Generation,* 64.

59. Duda and Shortliffe, "Expert Systems Research," 263, paragraphing omitted.

60. Feigenbaum, McCorduck, and Nii, *Rise of the Expert Company,* 147; Crevier, *AI,* 198. Feigenbaum gives other examples of eponymous expert systems, including "Geoff's Book" at an Australian construction company and "God-in-the-Works" at a Japanese steel company (158, 164). All of these are cases involving an apparently one-of-a-kind expert whose skills were in greater demand than could be humanly met.

61. Leonard Foner, *What's an Agent, Anyway? A Sociological Case Study,* PDF file, Agents Group, MIT Media Lab, May 1993 (cited October 27, 1999), available from http://foner.www.media.mit.edu/people/foner/agents.html, 9. Subsequent references to this work will be cited in the text. For a more complete discussion of the issues that Julia raises for rhetorical *ethos,* see my "Writing in a Culture of Simulation: *Ethos* Online," in *Towards a Rhetoric of Everyday Life: New Directions on Writing, Text, and Discourse,* eds. Martin Nystrand and John Duffy (Madison: University of Wisconsin Press, 2003). Julia is also discussed in Andrew Leonard, *Bots: The Origin of New Species* (San Francisco: HardWired, 1997); Janet H. Murray, *Hamlet on the Holodeck: The Future of Narrative in Cyberspace* (Cambridge, Mass.: MIT Press, 1999); and Sherry Turkle, *Life on the Screen: Identity in the Age of the Internet* (New York: Touchstone, 1997).

62. James C. Lester, Sharolyn A. Converse, Susan E. Kahler, S. Todd Barlow, Brian A. Stone and Ravimder S. Bhogal, "The Persona Effect: Affective Impact of Animated Pedagogical Agents" (paper presented at the CHI '97: Human Factors in Computing Systems, Atlanta, Ga., 1997), 360–61.

63. My sketch here is based on Caplinskas, "AI Paradigms."

64. Other researchers list similar desirable features for agents: autonomy, temporal continuity, personality, communication ability, adaptability, commonsense knowledge ad reasoning, ability to learn from experience; see Caplinskas, "AI Paradigms"; Oren Etzioni and Daniel S. Weld, "Intelligent Agents on the Internet: Fact, Fiction, and Forecast," *IEEE Expert* 10, no. 4 (1995): 44–49.

65. Lester et al., "Persona Effect," 364.

66. Clark Elliott and Jacek Brzezinski, "Autonomous Agents as Synthetic Characters," *AI Magazine* 19, no. 2 (1998): 15.

67. Empathy is discussed in Ken Haase, "Do Agents Need Understanding?" *IEEE Expert* 12, no. 4 (1997): 5; trust in Rino Falcone, Munindar Singh, and Yao-Hua Tan, eds.,

Trust in Cyber-societies: Integrating the Human and Artificial Perspectives, vol. 2246 of *Lecture Notes in Artificial Intelligence* (Berlin: Springer, 2001); Michael Lewis, "Designing for Human-Agent Interaction," *AI Magazine* 19, no. 2 (1998): 67–78; Shawn Tseng and B. J. Fogg, "Credibility and Computing Technology," *Communications of the ACM* 42, no. 5 (1999): 39–44; For a research program at Stanford called the CASA paradigm ("Computers Are Social Actors"), see Clifford Nass, Youngme Moon, B. J. Fogg, Byron Reeves, and D. Christopher Dryer, "Can Computer Personalities Be Human Personalities?" *International Journal of Human-Computer Studies* 43 (1995): 223–39. The major computer science organization, the Association for Computing Machinery, includes a group focusing on "captology" (from the phrase "Computers as Persuasive Technologies"); see B. J. Fogg, "Persuasive Technologies," *Communications of the ACM* 42, no. 5 (1999): 27–29.

68. *De Oratore,* trans. H. Rackham, 2 vols., *Loeb Classical Library* (Cambridge: Harvard University Press, 1942), 2:115. Subsequent references will be to this translation unless otherwise noted.

69. This translation is by Wisse, *Ethos and Pathos,* 229.

70. See Baumlin's overview of this issue in Baumlin, "Ethos."

71. According to Edwards, cyborg discourse stems from the metaphor of computer as mind, encouraging integration between human and machine. However, my analysis here complicates this picture because, like *ethos,* "mind" can have multiple components. In my view, the closed-world discourse of expert systems is closer to a simple model of computer as purely rational mind, and cyborg discourse involves other components of character that we often do not think of as primarily "mental," that is, the moral and the emotional.

72. There are certainly other examples, of which the rhetoric of advertising is the most obvious.

Contributors

CAROLE BLAIR is professor of communication studies at the University of North Carolina, Chapel Hill. She is the coeditor and cotranslator of *Friedrich Nietzsche on Rhetoric and Language,* and the coeditor of *Critical Questions: Invention, Creativity, and the Criticism of Discourse and Media.* Her numerous scholarly essays appear in such journals as the *Quarterly Journal of Speech* and *Philosophy and Rhetoric,* as well as in edited volumes.

MICHAEL J. HYDE is the University Distinguished Professor of Communication Ethics at Wake Forest University and a fellow of the W. K. Kellogg Foundation. He is the editor of *Communication Philosophy and the Technological Age,* coeditor of *Rhetoric and Hermeneutics in our Time,* and author of the award-winning *The Call of Conscience: Heidegger and Levinas, Rhetoric and the Euthanasia Debate* and *The Life-Giving Gift of Acknowledgment: A Philosophical and Rhetorical Inquiry* (forthcoming). His many scholarly essays appear in such journals as the *Quarterly Journal of Speech, Philosophy and Rhetoric, Journal of Applied Communication,* and *Journal of Medical Humanities,* as well as in edited volumes. He is the producer of the documentary film *Negotiating Death: A Rhetorical Perspective on Euthanasia.*

WALTER JOST is professor in the Department of English at the University of Virginia. He is the author of *Rhetorical Thought in John Henry Newman, Rhetorical Investigations: Studies in Ordinary Language Criticism* and the coeditor of several books on rhetorical theory.

ROBERT WADE KENNY is associate professor of rhetoric at the University of Dayton. His scholarly essays appear in such journals as the *Quarterly Journal of Speech, Sociological Theory,* and *Health Communication.* He is also a writer of fiction whose stories appear in a number of anthologies.

MARTIN J. MEDHURST is Distinguished Professor of Rhetoric and Communication at Baylor University. He is the author or editor of nine books, including *Presidential Speechwriting: From the New Deal to the Reagan Revolution and Beyond, Critical Reflections on the Cold War: Linking Rhetoric and History,* and *Beyond the Rhetorical Presidency.* He is the recipient of the NCA Golden Anniversary Monograph Award and twice has won the Marie Hochmuth Nichols Award for Outstanding Scholarship in Public Address.

NEIL MICHEL is a partner at Axiom, a commercial art studio in Davis, California. He received a master's degree in rhetoric from the University of California, Davis in 1993. Michel's photography is published widely in books, brochures, newspapers, and magazines, including the *New York Times,* the *San Francisco Chronicle,* the *Chronicle of Higher Education, Science Magazine,* the *Journal of the American Medical Association,* and *Landscape Architecture.* Michel's current research blends rhetoric, cultural studies, and photography in examining the history and evolution of American memorial architecture.

CAROLYN R. MILLER is Alumni Distinguished Professor of English and codirector of the Center for Information Society Studies at North Carolina State University. She has published essays on rhetorical theory and the rhetoric of science and technology in *Argumentation,* the *Quarterly Journal of Speech, Rhetorica, Rhetoric Society Quarterly,* and other journals, as well as in many edited volumes. She is a past president of the Rhetoric Society of America.

JOHN POULAKOS is associate professor in the Department of Communication at the University of Pittsburgh. He is author of the award-winning *Sophistical Rhetoric in Classical Greece* and coauthor of *Classical Rhetorical Theory.* His many scholarly essays on rhetorical theory, the history of rhetoric, and the relationship between philosophy and rhetoric appear in such journals as the *Quarterly Journal of Speech* and *Philosophy and Rhetoric.* He is currently writing on the relationship between rhetoric and aesthetics.

CRAIG R. SMITH is professor of communication studies at California State University, Long Beach, where he directs the Center for First Amendment Studies. He has written fifty scholarly articles and thirteen books, including *The Quest for Charisma: Christianity and Persuasion.*

BARBARA WARNICK is professor of communication at the University of Washington. She is the author of *The Sixth Canon: Belletristic Rhetorical Theory and Its French Antecedents, Critical Literacy in a Digital Era: Technology, Rhetoric, and the Public Interest,* and coauthor of *Critical Thinking and Communication: The Use of Reason in Argument, 4th ed.* Her many scholarly essays appear in such journals as the *Quarterly Journal of Speech, Argumentation, Critical Studies in Media Communication,* and *Rhetoric Review,* as well as in edited volumes.

ERIC KING WATTS is associate professor of communication at Wake Forest University. His research interests include explorations of the Harlem Renaissance, the Black Arts movement, W. E. B. Du Bois, and hip hop culture. His scholarly essays appear in such journals as the *Quarterly Journal of Speech, Rhetoric and Public Affairs* and *Critical Studies in Media Communication,* as well as in edited volumes. He is a recipient of the New Investigator Award granted by the Rhetorical and Communication Theory Division of the National Communication Association.

DAVID ZAREFSKY is Owen L. Coon Professor of Argumentation and Debate and professor of communication studies at Northwestern University, where he is the former Dean of the School of Speech. He is author of the award-winning books *Lincoln, Douglas, and Slavery: In the Crucible of Public Debate* and *President Johnson's War on Poverty: Rhetoric and History,* among other works. His scholarly essays appear in such journals as the *Quarterly Journal of Speech, Rhetoric and Public Affairs* and *Argumentation and Advocacy.* He is a former president of the National Communication Association and has been named a Distinguished Scholar by that organization.

MARGARET D. ZULICK is associate professor of communication at Wake Forest University. Her research interests include rhetoric of the Hebrew Bible. Her scholarly essays appear in such journals as the *Quarterly Journal of Speech, Rhetorica,* and *Argumentation.*

Index